T0312117

The Power Brokers

The Power Brokers

The Struggle to Shape and Control the Electric Power Industry

Jeremiah D. Lambert

The MIT Press
Cambridge, Massachusetts
London, England

First MIT Press paperback edition, 2016

© 2015 Massachusetts Institute of Technology

This book was set in Stone Serif by Toppan Best-set Premedia Limited.

Library of Congress Cataloging-in-Publication Data

Lambert, Jeremiah D., 1934–
   The power brokers: the struggle to shape and control the electric power industry / Jeremiah D. Lambert.
      pages cm
   Includes bibliographical references and index.
   ISBN 978-0-262-52978-5 (paperback)
   ISBN 978-0-262-02950-6 (hardcover: alk. paper) 1. Electric utilities–United States–History. I. Title.
   HD9685.U5L253 2015
   333.793′20973–dc23

                                                              2015008766

Contents

Acknowledgments

This book has been a labor of love, fraught with detours and occasional anguish. My wife, Sanda Lambert, has been an unfailing pillar of support, encouragement, and literary judgment throughout, notwithstanding the book's inevitable encroachments on family time. Without her, the book would not have reached print.

My assistant, Cynthia King, helped with many of the book's endless clerical details, ever cheerful and reliable.

Also deserving of mention is my friend and law school classmate of years ago, Larry Hewes, who encouraged me to write the book and made time to provide a useful sounding board for its broad themes.

Jeremiah D. Lambert

Introduction

From its inception to the present day the investor-owned electric power industry in the United States has confronted, and sought to manage and profit from, government regulation. Service to the public invited government oversight. Samuel Insull and much later Ken Lay and Jim Rogers, among others, were all acutely aware of the "perils of political capitalism"[1]—the state's intrusive power to reorder markets and set the terms of business engagement, famously described by James Madison as "sudden changes and legislative interferences, in cases affecting personal rights, [that] become jobs in the hands of enterprising and influential speculators, and snares to the more-industrious and less informed part of the community. ..."[2] This book charts the continuing government effort to shape and control an essential industry and the strategic countervailing responses it evoked.

The initial response to government control was not a plea for laissez-faire economics. For Insull, plunged into the disorderly and chaotic infant electricity marketplace of late nineteenth-century Chicago, the imperative was instead consolidation and monopoly control, gained by acquiring vulnerable local competitors. "The best service at the lowest possible price," he said, "can only be obtained ... by exclusive control of a given territory being placed in the hands of one undertaking."[3] Above all, Insull feared rapacious and corrupt municipal politicians, who determined rates and dispensed utility franchises. Insull wanted to deal with a single benign state agency, not hundreds of problematic city councils, and called for state regulation of privately owned utility monopolies. Regulation, he understood, meant protection from competitors, state sanction for his monopoly enterprise, and a reliable return on invested capital enabling him to finance more centralized generating plants and transmission lines. In fact, as he had foreseen, state commissions embedded exclusive utility franchises and did not regulate interstate wholesale transactions. Insull took advantage and built a nationwide utility holding company empire in a regulatory vacuum, driven by advanced technology, ever-lower electricity rates, new methods of finance, and personal ego. He overreached, made powerful enemies, and suffered a historic downfall but remains the arch-creator of the nation's electric utility industry.

The New Deal attacked Insull's signature utility holding company and others by legislative fiat but, even more important, used government monopolies to compete with and rein in investor-owned utility monopolies. TVA became the government's instrument in the competitive struggle that ensued. David Lilienthal, first a director and later chairman of TVA, was indispensable to TVA's survival and eventual success. A whip-smart, well-connected lawyer, Lilienthal needed a market for TVA's hydroelectric power and, like Insull, wanted to drive down electric rates to increase consumption and sell power to farmers and small users. He saw the private power industry's resistance to rate reductions as a bar to electrification of the Tennessee Valley. As TVA engaged Wendell Willkie's Commonwealth & Southern in an epic struggle for market control, Lilienthal pulled every political lever at his command, up to and including President Roosevelt, to pry business from Willkie's firm and establish TVA as a viable competitor. Lilienthal's political connections were essential. At every stage of its early development, TVA's very existence as an autonomous government enterprise was under siege from the investor-owned utility industry, jealous members of Congress, a domineering secretary of the interior, and a rogue chairman. Lilienthal managed to outflank and deflect them all but ultimately presided over an institution that resembled more and more the vertically integrated private utilities it was designed to displace.

TVA was not the only arrow in President Roosevelt's public power quiver. Bonneville Power Administration (BPA), he thought, would serve the same purpose for the Pacific Northwest, unlocking the low-cost power potential of the Columbia River. But there was a major structural difference. Unlike TVA, which Republican opponents in Congress did not wish to recreate elsewhere, BPA was not a freestanding government utility. It served instead as a marketing agency for hydroelectric power from dams built by the Corps of Engineers and remained under the thumb of the secretary of the interior. Although it built a network of transmission lines and sold cheap power to preference customers in competition with private utilities, BPA could not generate its own power.

In the 1970s, BPA foresaw a power shortage and embarked on an ill-considered thermal expansion program. BPA needed a surrogate to own and construct the nuclear generating plants it planned and used an association of municipal utilities, Washington Public Power Supply System (WPPSS), for that purpose. Two dysfunctional command-and-control government bureaucracies, one federal and the other local, then interacted to mount a disastrous multiproject construction program, financed by WPPSS municipal bonds sold to small investors in much the same way as Insull had sold holding company securities to clerks, foremen, and company employees many years before. Under Don Hodel BPA ignored warnings that the expected power shortage was a mirage and, prodded by its overseer in Washington, D.C., pushed forward relentlessly. The program went spectacularly awry. As costs mounted, all but one of the planned nuclear plants had to be abandoned and scrapped, and WPPSS defaulted on the bonds it had issued, imposing huge losses on bondholders and ratepayers. Top-down monopoly control, whether exercised by private or government ownership, revealed common flaws of political capitalism: the arrogance of overweening managerial ambition and, in BPA's case, an absence of grass-roots and competitive constraints.

Insull's industry paradigm—vertically integrated and legally sanctioned utility monopolies operating large-scale remote power stations and long transmission lines—proved remarkably resistant to change. By the 1980s market-oriented scholars in academia seriously questioned the prevailing model, characterized by inefficiency, high administered prices, and failed nuclear projects. While transmission and distribution remained natural monopolies, generation of power was seen as ripe for competition. Paul Joskow, then an MIT economist, envisioned a restructured electric utility industry in which customers could bid for electricity from competitive suppliers and have it transported at fair rates over transmission lines free from monopoly control. An independent operator would run the lines and make a competitive real-time and day-ahead power market at marginal cost. Joskow's 1983 book, *Markets for Power*, anticipated by more than a decade the changes that actually reshaped much of the nation's utility industry, first in California and then federally. But Joskow was a student of institutional complexity, not simply a theoretician, and foresaw many of the practical difficulties restructuring would entail. Making his blueprint work, he cautioned, would require an exercise of industry smarts, sound oversight, and political will, none of which was in evidence as the badly designed and easily manipulated California market imploded. After that extraordinary failure, a competitive market for electric power seemed a cruel oxymoron but nonetheless gained traction at the utility group PJM and elsewhere as an alternative to historic command-and-control price regulation.

Ken Lay, like Insull, was an empire builder, driven by extreme ambition and ego. He consolidated prosaic gas pipeline companies and repurposed the resulting enterprise, Enron, as a new-age company that challenged the business model of traditional, vertically integrated electric utilities. Lay became an ardent proponent of deregulating gas and electricity markets. He saw the restructured industry model, envisaged by Joskow, as an open door to trading profit. Mandatory open access of gas pipelines and transmission lines created the competitive opportunity—buying and selling natural gas and electricity—that Lay exploited through Internet-based trading, enabling Enron to capture a sizable fraction of the national energy-trading market. All the while he remained intently focused on restrictive regulation and the indispensable need for political patronage to overcome it. As Enron grew so did his involvement in politics. A prolific Republican Party contributor, he used influence with well-placed political allies to extract favorable rulings from FERC, the SEC, and the CFTC. "We believe in markets," he said, but judged by its behavior in California and elsewhere, Enron really believed in market rigging and manipulation. Lay preached the gospel of free enterprise but perfected rent seeking on a massive scale. Enron's collapse and Lay's criminal trial leave little room for retrospective redemption.

A thought leader and profound critic of the established utility industry, Amory Lovins early on announced his opposition to Insull's centralized monopoly legacy, "run by a faraway bureaucratized technical elite" and prone to "malfunctions, mistakes, and deliberate disruptions."[4] In a game-changing article in *Foreign Affairs* in 1976, Lovins proposed a radical reset of a bedrock industry, arguing for "soft technologies" of conservation, efficiency, renewable power, and distributed generation long before those concepts were seriously entertained.[5] A passionate advocate for nonnuclear renewable power, whose declining cost he said would enable it to reduce the primacy of fossil fuels, Lovins also foresaw the onset of coal-driven climate change years before it became a mainstream concern, predicting a market-based solution based on smart grid efficiency, improved technology, and cost-competitiveness rather than a government-imposed carbon tax or global treaty. This placed him at odds with other students of climate change and energy executives such as Jim Rogers of Duke Energy.

An adept business strategist, Rogers advanced by personal charisma and an ability to see beyond the insular confines of a hidebound industry. At the pinnacle of his career, following a succession of corporate acquisitions, he found himself in charge of Duke Energy, the nation's largest electric utility. Rogers's ascent owed much to his acute understanding of the regulatory process, environmental concerns, and the implications for his coal-burning utility. With the expectation that by midcentury "virtually every power plant in this country will be retired and replaced,"[6] Rogers sought a transitional political accommodation to protect his company and its customers from what he called stroke-of-the-pen regulation, bargained intensely for an outcome acceptable to the industry, but still played a critical role in support of federal CO_2 cap-and-trade legislation (that ultimately fell victim to partisan politics). Like Madison, Rogers feared "sudden changes and legislative interferences."[7] He sought to anticipate and moderate change but believed nonetheless Congress would ultimately have to act by altering the economics of coal-fired electricity. To protect his company's assets and his own career, he tried to manage interferences at least cost but still moved his company and the utility industry toward an uncertain, decarbonized future shaped by government action.

A common economic thread linking these diverse protagonists is the cost of electricity. Insull and Lilienthal saw low-cost power as indispensable to creating and expanding a consumer market and, in Lilienthal's case, competing with private utilities. Hodel at BPA used cheap hydropower as a means of blunting the expense of a politically driven, high-cost thermal power program. Disillusioned with conventional utility cost regulation, Joskow contemplated industry restructuring as a means of introducing competition and reducing the cost of power. Lay used the promise of cost-saving in deregulated markets as a lure, enabling Enron to control and extract extraordinary profit from those markets. Lovins saw advanced technology, demand response, renewables, and distributed power as the key to a low-cost energy future. As a utility executive, Rogers focused intently on the cost of coal-fired power and the need to avoid cap-and-trade rate shock. In each instance, the economic driver of cost required political engagement between the private sector and government overseers, often expressed as a struggle over market share.

As this book reveals, the electric power industry has proved attractive to smart, hyper-ambitious players as a platform for control over people, institutions, and markets. Marked by technical complexity and economies of scale, the industry has typically treated regulatory change, or its prospect, as an opportunity to preserve or secure a dominant position. Introduction of competition to a monopoly industry over the last twenty years has invited market manipulation by companies bent on gaming the system and has not yet significantly enhanced consumer welfare. Creating rules to govern an innovation-based and restructured electricity market has proved a difficult experiment in integrating regulation and competition.

1 Samuel Insull: Architect and Prime Mover of the Electric Utility Business in the United States

Dynamics of Growth and Consolidation

Samuel Insull, born poor in Victorian England, was a prime mover of the electric power industry in the United States. He had little formal education or patronage but burned with extraordinary ambition. Starting as an indispensable assistant to Thomas Edison, the great inventor, he launched a career that lasted more than fifty years and defined the power industry's economics, structure, and governance. An apostle of growth and consumption in an era of rapid industrialization, he set out to replace old technology with new, establish a territorial monopoly, and make his profit from sheer volume.[1] His influence peaked in the 1920s; survived bankruptcy, the ruin of his reputation, and criminal prosecution during the Depression; and continued long after his death to determine how the utility business is organized and operated.

Insull feared political interference in business matters. Early on, to foil the schemes of Chicago's aldermen and municipal competition, he said utilities were natural monopolies that should be regulated by state commissions. Insull's proposal eventually gained traction and became a plank of Progressive Era reform. State commissions, established early in the twentieth century, displaced the control once exercised by cities and towns but lacked rigor and had no jurisdiction at all over Insull's signature vehicle, the interstate holding company. Without effective government oversight, he was able to build a highly leveraged corporate pyramid that took advantage of porous laws and laissez-faire politics. Its collapse in the Depression led to New Deal legislation designed to undo what Insull had so carefully constructed.

Insull wanted to capture markets through monopoly enterprise and relentless price reductions. He linked money, electricity, mass consumption, and stock ownership in a complex system, housed in a holding company pyramid that brought electric utilities in thirty-two states under his financial control and captured almost ten percent of the nation's power supply market.[2] For thirty-five years he was among the most influential and dynamic executives on the American business scene.[3]

Reduced to its essentials, Insull's business plan was to prevent "duplication of investment ... by concentrating production under one organization."[4] Above all, he feared being replaced or constrained by competitors, bankers, or regulators. His drive to create a monopoly under his control succeeded brilliantly for decades, but his byzantine holding company edifice collapsed in scandal in the early years of the Depression, wounding shareholders and creditors alike. He became a pariah and economic villain of the old order, dying shortly after Roosevelt's New Deal dismantled the empire he had created, but remained a principal architect of the nation's utility industry long after he was gone and, to many, forgotten.

Early Years

Insull might have been the subject of a Dickens novel or a Horatio Alger story. He went to work at age fourteen, the child of a lower middle-class family of religious dissenters and temperance workers down on its luck. As a young man, he embraced the Victorian virtues of hard work, self-discipline, honesty, thrift, pluck, diligence, and determination.[5] In his first job for a firm of auctioneers, Insull learned shorthand, taught himself bookkeeping, and read books on political economy, history, and literature. "And most important, because time was more than money—it was his very life— he learned to systematize and render efficient whatever he dealt with."[6] Insull's career soon unfolded in a series of fortuitous events. "The Insull story and the Alger formula agree precisely," wrote the *New York Times* years later. "Lowly beginning, painstaking devotion to humble tasks, promotion, fidelity to the boss, and success."[7]

Insull became head bookkeeper to Edison's London representative, soon learned every detail of Edison's affairs, and within a few years was invited to work as Edison's personal secretary in the United States. This was Insull's main chance. "I knew that the making or marring of my career must

happen within the first few weeks of my connection with Mr. Edison,"
Insull recalled, "during which time I would either succeed or fail in getting
his confidence."[8] Insull and Edison were a study in opposites—Insull, small,
preternaturally bright, a born organizer with a cockney accent; Edison a
large, untidy man with nocturnal work habits, impatient of routine and
business detail.

Insull arrived in New York and started work in March 1881. He was
barely twenty-one years old. His arrival was well timed. Edison had recently
perfected the incandescent light, and New York financiers had funded his
Electric Light Company to license his inventions and underwrite ongoing laboratory work. Only months before Insull came to his door, Edison
had also organized the Edison Electric Illuminating Company of New York
to construct a central electricity generating station at Pearl Street in New
York's financial district. As a field demonstration of Edison's incandescent
light and the viability of the central station concept, the Pearl Street station would produce electricity in bulk and distribute it in competition with
companies offering arc lighting and gas lighting, the prevailing technologies at the time.[9]

Assigned a vacant desk in Edison's office, Insull became his factotum and
"looked after all kinds of affairs, from buying his clothes to financing his
business."[10] Insull soon assumed duties as he saw fit and organized Edison's
office without attempting to organize Edison's own idiosyncratic work
habits.[11] Edison appointed him secretary of the Edison Machine Works
(electricity generating equipment), Edison Electric Tube Company (underground distribution equipment), and Edison Lamp Company (lamps).
Insull became Edison's chief financial advisor, held his power of attorney,
and signed his checks.[12] Insull's "mind was much older than his years would
indicate," recalled Alfred Tate, an Edison confidant. "He possessed unusual
intuitive judgment in the affairs of business which compensated largely
for his lack of experience. ... His devotion to business almost constituted a
religion. He permitted nothing to interfere with his duties."[13] At the same
time it did not go unnoticed that Insull also "loved power and glorified in
the exercise of authority."[14]

Edison was (as Insull was to become) a fierce proponent of central
station electric systems to capture the economies of scale necessary to
support an asset-heavy infrastructural business. Edison electric equipment, he argued, should be built for and sold to central stations rather

than to each individual building owner generating electricity on an ad hoc basis.[15] Edison's views were at odds with conventional wisdom since most electricity was then produced by isolated stations, each with its own generating equipment. The Pearl Street station was proof of Edison's central station concept and the first to power incandescent lights. Other central stations in 1882, when Pearl Street went online, provided power for outdoor arc lighting, but only incandescent stations served residential customers.[16] To Edison's displeasure, "The isolated plant proved to be as easy to sell as the central station was difficult."[17] Edison's financial backers demanded he promote isolated stations as a ready source of revenue. Edison's response was characteristic. He formed the Thomas A. Edison Construction Department, with Insull in charge, to establish the central station as the industry model.

In marketing the central station system as a source of power for incandescent lighting, Edison distinguished between cities under ten thousand in population and larger cities that had gas lighting, the principal incumbent competitor to the incandescent lamp. He offered two kinds of franchises. A central station in a smaller town would pay cash for its equipment and receive a license to use it in that location only. A central station in a larger city served by gas would receive a license enabling it to sell isolated plants and resell Edison equipment and lamps, and in return Electric Light would acquire twenty-five percent of the central station's equity and five percent of its capitalization in cash. This arrangement gave Electric Light a stake in large-city central station firms and a captive market for patented Edison products.[18] It also recognized the undeniable commercial importance of isolated plants.

In his new job Insull became the principal traveling salesman for the Edison system. His mission was to visit every town that wanted a new power plant and help local sponsors raise seed money. "The scheme," he said, "is to raise from fifty thousand to a quarter of a million dollars, according to the size of the town or city, and form a local Edison electric illuminating company."[19]

Insull soon found it necessary to work around pervasive municipal corruption. Electric utility systems could not be built without using the city streets. A municipal franchise was therefore indispensable and attractive to private investors. City fathers knew a municipality could extract a quid pro quo for awarding utility operating rights.[20] If there was a competing gas company, the city "council had usually been bought beforehand, and promoting an electric company involved outwitting both politicians and competitors."[21] A common approach was for the municipality to sell a short-term franchise to the highest bidder; another was to demand low rates for street lighting.[22] A city or town could also own and operate a power station itself, either exclusively or in competition with private systems. Insull learned, early on, that city governments could be a mortal threat to the nascent utility business, experience that framed his views about natural monopoly and state regulation.

Insull saw the infant central station electric utility business would require a central platform. In 1885 he organized the Association of Edison Illuminating Companies (AEIC), a trade association including his close friends and executives of small Edison central stations and Edison manufacturing companies. AEIC's nominal purpose was to improve the management of licensee central stations and enhance the business of the Edison manufacturing companies as equipment vendors to those stations, but it soon became the nerve center of an emerging industry[23] and determined its technology, operations, and market scope.[24] AEIC was the counterpart of the National Electric Light Association (NELA), formed in the same year by manufacturers of arc lighting systems that competed aggressively for market share with incandescent lighting.

Together AEIC and NELA leveraged the influence of Insull and his coterie and defined the structure and governance of the electric utility industry. From its inception AEIC bore the stamp of four Edison executives (Insull, John Lieb, Charles Edgar, and Louis Ferguson) who had worked at the Electric Light Company's Goerck Street plant in Manhattan. The "Insull circle," as it came to be called, promoted privately owned central station service as a natural monopoly and a "growth dynamic" strategy based on load building, diversification, territorial expansion, and rate reductions.[25] AEIC, and later NELA, shaped industry development for the next forty years.[26]

In 1886, Insull moved Edison's manufacturing business from cramped quarters in New York to an abandoned factory upstate. On completing the move, Insull asked his boss for instructions. Edison simply told him to "run the whole thing. ... Do it big, Sammy. Make it either a big success or a big failure."[27] Insull found himself in charge of Edison's manufacturing and sales divisions—a formidable responsibility for a man not yet thirty—but, in Insull's words, "the greatest opportunity that [Edison] could possibly have given me."[28] In two years Insull quadrupled sales and increased annual return on investment to 30 percent while, characteristically, using "every nickel of profit to increase the size of the plant."[29] In six years under Insull's aegis the Schenectady plant grew from 200 to 6,000 workers.[30]

But expansion was not without problems. Despite Insull's best efforts, the business remained undercapitalized. It also faced increasing competition. Insull struggled to fund Edison Light with hand-to-mouth short-term loans, acquiring in the process a lifelong distaste for New York bankers. Edison's central stations continued their commitment to direct current (DC) transmission, while new entrants used alternating current (AC) technology developed by Westinghouse—the first major electricity development in a decade that Edison had not sponsored.

Edison's DC transmission system consisted of generating plants feeding heavy distribution conductors to customer loads (lighting and motors). The system operated at the same voltage level throughout. Thus, 100-volt lamps at the customer's location would be connected to a generator supplying 110 volts, to allow for some voltage drop in the wires between the generator and load. However, the typical voltage drop caused by the resistance of the system conductors was so high that generating plants had to be located very close to the load they served. The DC system was constrained. It could not use higher voltages absent an efficient low-cost technology that would allow reduction of high transmission voltage to low utilization voltage.

The AC system interposed a transformer between the high-voltage distribution system and customer loads. The transformer allowed power to be transmitted at much higher voltages, stepped down at the point of distribution. As a result, fewer, larger generating plants could serve the load in a given area. The same distribution network could serve large loads, such as industrial motors or converters for electric railway power, and smaller loads, primarily incandescent lighting.

DC transmission, subject to intolerable line losses, limited service to a one-mile radius from a generating station. AC could be transmitted at high voltages over relatively long distances with far less loss of energy and greatly expanded the reach of each central station's commercial service area. AC's technical superiority threatened Edison's dominance in the field.[31] Even in the face of such obstacles, however, Insull's extraordinary success in promoting Edison's business had outrun its capital base. As Edison recalled,

"Our orders were far in excess of our capital to handle the business, and both Mr. Insull and I were afraid we might get into trouble for lack of money."[32]

Edison turned to Henry Villard, a Bavarian-born promoter with financial connections in Germany, who had served as a director of Edison Electric Illuminating Company for almost a decade. After an absence of several years, Villard returned to the United States with a mandate from Deutsche Bank to negotiate with Drexel Morgan to invest German money in American enterprises, including those in the electric power industry.[33] With different shareholder constituencies and largely uncoordinated operations, the Edison companies were a prime target for reorganization. Armed with foreign capital, Villard proposed to consolidate the companies under a new corporate rubric, Edison General Electric Company, folding in Edison Electric Light Company, Edison Lamp Company, Edison Machine Company, and a lead cable maker owned by Siemens, a German company.[34]

J. P. Morgan set the terms, and Edison General Electric Company was formed in 1889 with a par value capitalization of $12 million. Four Edison men (including Edison and Insull) joined the five appointed by Villard on the new company's board. Drexel Morgan placed its shares with private investors, more than half going to Deutsche Bank. Edison received shares in the new company valued at $1.75 million. Insull's equity participation was far less, but at $75,000 still significant, and he was appointed vice president in charge of manufacturing and sales. Villard was president, but Insull ran the show.[35]

True to form, Insull followed an aggressive growth strategy, retaining all earnings, selling stock in the consolidated enterprise, and borrowing to the hilt. His business plan was to amortize fixed costs over many units, lower prices, and maximize sales. "Toward the end of 1891," Insull writes in his *Memoirs*, "a consolidation of the Edison General Electric Company and the Thomson-Houston Electric Company was under negotiation."[36] The Thomson-Houston Electric Company had achieved a dominant position in arc lighting and streetcar equipment (having acquired rights to the inventions of Charles F. Brush and Charles Van Depoele) and AC and incandescent lighting equipment (by infringing on patents held by Westinghouse and Edison). Villard, under severe financial pressure at a critical moment in the negotiations, sold his Edison G.E. stock to J. P. Morgan and others and lost his footing in the transaction.[37]

Without notice to Villard or Edison G.E., Morgan, then in a controlling position, set the merger terms by valuing Thomson-Houston at $18 million and Edison G.E. at $15 million. Morgan also favored Thomson-Houston nominees on the board of the combined company. Villard was told that his "courteous resignation would be courteously received."[38] This left Charles Coffin of Thomson-Houston as the chief executive officer. Edison, who had covertly opposed the consolidation, was not consulted. "And so it was that J. Pierpont Morgan, whose house had been the first in New York to be wired for electricity by Edison but a decade earlier, now erased Edison's name out of corporate existence without even the courtesy of a telegram or phone call to the great inventor."[39]

The merged company, General Electric, was incorporated in April 1892 with a capitalization of $50 million. Insull accepted the number three position as second vice president in charge of manufacturing and sales at a salary of $36,000 per year but continued only long enough to integrate Edison G.E.'s 6,000 workers in the new enterprise.[40] Insull had no desire to work as Coffin's subordinate and believed, in any event, that the central station industry, and not manufacturing, was the wave of the future.[41]

As it happened, Chicago Edison Company, a small central station licensee, needed a new president, and two of its board members asked Insull for recommendations. Insull saw Chicago Edison as a platform for his personal ambitions, proposed himself for the position, but asked the board to authorize construction of a large new generating plant financed by an issuance of common stock, all of which he would purchase. When the board agreed, a deal was cut. At a farewell dinner given for him at Delmonico's by Edison, Coffin, and other business colleagues—including "most of my intimate friends and intimate enemies"—Insull cheekily predicted that Chicago Edison would probably equal or exceed the investment in the then vastly larger General Electric.[42] On July 1, 1892 he took office as Chicago Edison's president at a salary of $12,000 per year, one-third of what he had been making at General Electric.[43] "I was ... not looking to the amount of my remuneration," Insull recalled. "I was looking to the opportunity that was offered me to develop the central station business in Chicago."[44] Although taking his leave of New York, Insull never forgot his debt to Edison. "He was my hero when I was a boy," he wrote in his *Memoirs* much later, "and after fifty-five years engaged in various businesses of which his inventions were the fundamental basis, my admiration for him and his accomplishments [was] greater than ever."[45]

Chicago

Insull called it a "frontier town."[46] Chicago was a raw city on the cusp of radical industrial transformation where transportation, industry, and electric power interacted and developed without plan or design.[47] Theodore Dreiser famously described the young, thrusting city as a "giant magnet, drawing to itself, from all quarters, the hopeful and the hopeless—those who had their fortunes yet to make and those whose fortunes and affairs had reached a disastrous climax elsewhere."[48] In the two decades following 1890, the formative years of the electric utility industry, Chicago's population grew by 600,000, the largest increase in its history.

The city was a "cauldron of every imaginable industry,"[49] served by many small, inefficient power stations. The city inspector's report of 1892 listed eighteen central stations and almost 500 self-contained systems powering 273,600 incandescent lights and 16,415 arc lamps. Although foundries, machine shops, and electric traction companies offered market opportunities to central station utilities seeking customers beyond home lighting,[50] business conditions were chaotic. The electric utility business was an ever-changing patchwork of "franchise holders, shoestring utility companies, and 'isolated' plant operators"[51] subject to a city government run by venal, pliable politicians. Many small utilities struggled to survive. All remained vulnerable to municipal corruption.

Insull had honed his skills during twelve years as Edison's principal lieutenant. He arrived in Chicago with a battle plan and firm grasp of the technology and arcane economics of the utility industry. To avoid ruinous competition he wanted a monopoly. Central station power was capital intensive; its success depended on economies of scale. Insull's first order of business was to consolidate the many small central stations then operating in Chicago, a task requiring boldness, financial acumen, and a knack for commercial predation. To grow the business, he would need high volume and a visionary belief in the power industry's mass market potential.[52] The trick would be to expand his residential customer base by selling electricity at lower and lower prices. In fact, the average rate for Insull's residential customers declined from 20 cents a kilowatt-hour in the early 1890s to 2.5 cents twenty years later.[53]

Unshakably confident in his grasp of the market, Insull was willing to bet the company that his high-volume, low-cost strategy would succeed. He set in motion a plan to acquire Chicago Arc Light and Power Company, its biggest rival, and "smaller plants operating not only in the center of town, but also ... in the ... suburbs of the then city."[54] When it closed on the Chicago Arc Light acquisition in 1893, Insull's company had in a single stroke neutralized its largest competitor and become the dominant central station in Chicago. "La Salle Street was astonished by this," one journalist observed. "It had predicted Insull's absorption, but the sparrow had eaten the cat."[55]

Insull's plan depended on controlling the supply of patented electrical equipment in Chicago.[56] To do this, he systematically obtained exclusive legal rights to use every major kind of domestic equipment and asked General Electric, a major supplier, not to sell patented products to anyone in Cook County except Chicago Edison.[57] His goal was to gain "exclusive Central Station rights ... in Cook County."[58] Insull knew such rights would block competitors from doing business on his home turf.

Hammered by the financial panic of 1893 and virtually unable to buy needed equipment, even lightbulbs, six small central stations in Chicago soon sold out to Chicago Edison.[59] In just a few years Insull had established Chicago Edison's monopoly grip on the central city. He was to enlarge it many times over through progressively lower rates, profit extracted from mass production, and ruthless managerial efficiency.

The second prong of Insull's plan presupposed a major power upgrade and construction of a state-of-the-art generating plant. Insull had his chief engineer design such a station at Harrison Street, near the Chicago River. The station used efficient triple compound steam engines and massive condensing generators that had first powered the spectacular incandescent light display at the 1893 World's Fair in Chicago. Insull opportunistically purchased the engines and generators from General Electric.[60] The new station produced power at half the historic unit fuel cost, became the largest plant in the world at the time,[61] and enabled his company to dominate the Chicago market. To serve Chicago Edison's expanded system, Insull used the recently invented rotary converter to change DC into polyphase AC and reverse the process as well. The rotary converter coupled AC and

DC systems—the first step in realizing a universal electric supply system capable of supplying incandescent lamps, arc lights, DC motors, single-phase AC motors, polyphase motors, and energy for thermoelectric applications from a common transmission line. All Chicago could now be served from a single generating plant without a costly investment in wholly new technology.[62]

Insull now had both the means of large-scale power production and the opportunity as a prime mover to reach a huge potential market. In 1892 Chicago was a city of more than a million with fewer than 5,000 users of electric lights. Optimists predicted the market would grow to 25,000 customers. Insull intended to serve a million.[63] To do this, however, he would need a new and different economic regime. The first order of business was to price the product correctly. "No one in the central station business at that time really understood the fundamental economics," Insull recalled. "Operators ... had a hazy idea that energy sold for light would be used mainly at night on the average for only a few hours each day, and that sold for power would be used mainly in the day time for a longer average period."[64]

Edison's original charge for electricity was so much per lamp per hour (including the price of the lamp) with consumption measured by a chemical meter. Central stations charged a flat rate based on metered consumption or a flat rate per month determined by building size or the number of lights installed.[65] Insull realized this formula failed to capture central station supply economics. His residential customers used large amounts of electricity in the morning and evening but relatively little in between. He needed a better meter.

Unlike other products, electricity cannot be stored or inventoried but must be produced, delivered, and consumed instantly in real time. A central station must be large enough to supply peak demand even if it continues for only a short time and then subsides, leaving plant capacity underutilized during the balance of the day. The central station's generators, boilers, cables, conduits, and wires must be paid for even when not fully used to serve maximum load.[66] "The investment necessary to take care of that maximum load," Insull wrote, "has to be carried the whole year."[67] The lower a station's average percentage use, or load factor, the more idle capacity exists and the more difficult it is to earn a profit. Edison's primitive rate scheme left Insull and other central station operators unable to solve this problem.

Insull at first adopted a sliding scale of quantity discounts for large and off-peak customers and told his salesmen to offer whatever price was required to get the business.[68] In a signature transaction, he convinced the owners of the Great Northern Hotel to give central electricity a try at a price far below Chicago Edison's published rates. By offering similar long-term private contracts to others at rock-bottom rates, Insull captured big customers and quadrupled his company's annual sales.[69] Such private contracts, at first an effective sales tool, came to be regarded as a form of price discrimination. Preferential treatment of large customers could not remain secret and offended smaller customers paying higher, posted rates. Legislative inquiries raised the specter of forcible imposition of rate systems. Insull needed a consistent and defensible system of charging for electric power.[70]

While in England on vacation in 1894, Insull encountered Arthur Wright, the manager of Brighton's municipal electricity plant and inventor of the demand meter. Wright's meter measured every customer's use of electricity in two parts: "one part to see how much equipment the customer necessitated, and one part to see how much he used the equipment. The charge for the service was a combination of the two."[71] Seizing on Wright's brilliant insight, Insull made the further crucial determination that profits depended not on load but on what came to be called the load factor—that is, the percentage of time a plant was in active use. Further refined, load factor economics shaped utility ratemaking throughout the world.[72] "The nearer you can bring your average to the maximum load," Insull observed, "the closer you approximate the most economical condition of production, and the lower you can afford to sell your current."[73]

The Wright system prevailed over several alternative systems after heated debate at meetings of AEIC and NELA, trade associations dominated by Insull and his circle. Insull had a financial stake in Wright's meter, whose design served his core purpose of acquiring new customers and growing revenues, even if achieved with a less balanced load. In heated competition with gas lighting, not-for-profit electric systems, and isolated electric plants, Insull wanted to capture new customers and rising revenues to preempt the market; efficiency was secondary.[74] "The object of any system is to get business," said Insull's chief engineer. "What you are running your plant for is to increase its revenue."[75] The Wright system confirmed Insull's policy of enlisting as many customers as possible, disfavoring isolated plants as uneconomic, and adopting monopoly as the surest means of driving down costs and rates.[76] Endorsement of the Wright system was therefore not just a minor technical matter. It was instead a key factor in Insull's "growth dynamic" strategy. It allowed his utilities to set prices based on value of service rather than cost and "led to a century of hegemony by vertically integrated companies, generating, transmitting, and distributing huge amounts of power over very long distances, and protected by a complex regulatory apparatus."[77]

Urban Politics, Natural Monopoly, and State Regulation

Chicago, like many other American cities, witnessed an ongoing political struggle to resolve a vexing question: whether and under what circumstances to let a private company handle a public service or, in the alternative, have the city do the job itself. Transportation, gas, and, eventually, electric power companies were drawn into a municipal spiderweb.

In the late nineteenth century more than a dozen elevated and street railway companies served Chicago, the former regulated by the state and the latter by the city. State law prohibited municipal franchises for more than twenty years, and bribes were the expected price for renewal or amendment.[78] The balance of power in the Chicago city council lay with a bipartisan group of aldermen called the Gray Wolves, who ruled as feudal barons and extracted a regular schedule of bribes—a "low-browed, dull-witted, base-minded gang of plug-uglies with no outstanding characteristics beyond an unquenchable lust for money."[79]

Their principal victim was Charles Tyson Yerkes, a financier with a checkered past who controlled two of the three major streetcar lines and eight smaller electric suburban railways. Yerkes had assembled his traction empire based on graft and became vulnerable to further exactions when one or another of his properties required a franchise extension. His ability to issue bonds to finance his companies "was inseparable from franchise security, simply because no one was anxious to buy thirty-year bonds from a company which might cease to exist in less than a decade."[80] Yerkes conceived a solution by submitting his business to state control.

In 1897 Yerkes had one of his kept politicians, State Senator John Humphrey, introduce bills extending all streetcar and elevated franchises for fifty years, removing control from corrupt city councils, placing it with a three-person state regulatory commission, and requiring franchisees to pay compensation based on a percentage of gross revenues. Yerkes had proposed nothing less than a model for eventual Progressive Era utility regulation but, perversely, bribed state legislators to ensure its passage, provoking a scandal that enabled reformers to kill the bills and gain control of the Chicago city council in 1898. Yerkes left Chicago soon thereafter but managed, in retreat, to secure passage of the Allen Law, which authorized city councils to grant franchises for up to fifty years, although it existed on the statute books only briefly.[81]

Within a week after passage of the Allen Law in 1898 the Gray Wolves told Insull how much it would cost him to prevent enfranchisement of a competitor to Chicago Edison. The scheme replicated their recent grant of a franchise to Ogden Gas Company, created for the sole purpose of inducing Peoples Gas Light and Coke Company, the existing gas monopoly, to buy its stock (for more than $7 million). Insull refused to play a similar game. The Gray Wolves then granted a fifty-year franchise to a dummy corporation, Commonwealth Electric Company, transforming it into an active competitor.

Having acquired exclusive local rights to buy and use electrical equipment of every American manufacturer, however, Insull was unmoved. "Commonwealth could hold its franchise for eternity but could never light a single bulb."[82] After several months, Insull was able to buy Commonwealth and its valuable franchise for $50,000, an unbelievable bargain. The Allen Law was then conveniently repealed, leaving Insull the only electric utility operator in the state with a franchise of more than twenty years—the key to long-term financing of his capital-intensive, highly leveraged electric utility business.[83] Under an operating agreement devised by Insull's counsel, Chicago Edison would stay confined to the Loop and use DC transmission while Commonwealth's AC wires would serve the rest of Chicago.[84] Insull was to rely on the Commonwealth franchise as the foundation of an integrated utility serving the greater metropolitan Chicago area and, ultimately, a vast multistate holding company.

By granting franchises to competing gas and electric companies Chicago had for a time been able to control rates and impose a measure of municipal control, but competition, while fierce at first, proved short-lived. Following initial price wars, the city's gas companies were absorbed into a single firm. The electric utility business followed a similar pattern.[85] At the same time state and federal courts made it clear that, without an enabling act from the Illinois legislature, the Chicago city council had no power to dictate utility rates unilaterally and that municipal rate ordinances were therefore unenforceable.[86] In fact, municipal authorities had no control over Chicago Edison's accounts, and it paid no compensation to the city.[87]

Given reform takeover of the Chicago city council following the Yerkes scandal, however, this was small comfort to Insull, who feared unpredictable municipal oversight or even municipal ownership of utilities as the next step. Insull's concern was not ill-founded. By the turn of the twentieth century municipalization of public services was a hotly debated issue, championed by progressives, including Chicago Mayor Carter Harrison. Municipally owned electric plants constituted almost one-quarter of all such facilities,[88] and home rule—if not outright ownership— had many advocates.[89] Among these were the influential founders of the American Economic Association, who rejected laissez-faire economics and urged government ownership of electric utilities and other natural monopolies.[90]

In June 1898, at the annual meeting of NELA, the industry trade association, Insull made a famous speech proposing regulation of the electric utility industry by state commissions, armed with full power to fix rates and standards of service. At the time this was a radical proposal, unlikely to be supported by the industry rank and file. But Insull loathed the disorderly utility market and municipal meddling, and his proposal addressed both evils. "Acute competition necessarily frightens the investor," he said, "and compels corporations to pay a very high price for capital. … The best service at the lowest possible price can only be obtained … by exclusive control of a given territory being placed in the hands of one undertaking."[91]

In lieu of public ownership, Insull proposed that a single operator be granted an exclusive franchise to provide electricity at prices fixed by state commissions based on "cost plus a reasonable profit."[92] The benefit of protection against competition would appear first in the market for capital, and only collaterally in the market for electricity: "The more certain this protection is made," he said, "the lower the rate of interest and the lower the total cost of operation will be, and, consequently the lower the price of the service to public and private users."[93] Insull believed state regulation would reduce the risk of investing in electric utilities, make utility bonds and stocks more attractive, increase the availability of capital, and lower its price.[94] He was proved right on all counts.

Insull's natural monopoly concept—startling on its face but dictated by canny political instinct—differed only in emphasis from the proposal Yerkes had recently put before the Illinois legislature. It enjoyed wide acceptance in the Progressive Era and became embedded in state utility regulation, but it eventually lost support among economists and industry analysts, who attacked its central premise of economic efficiency.[95] The novel and correlative idea of state regulation found little support at the NELA convention. Yet Insull had planted the seed that would flourish a decade later as part of Progressive regulatory reform. As the push for municipal ownership of utilities gained strength, he used the electric utility industry's fear of takeover to mobilize support for state regulation. NELA persuaded the National Civil Federation (NCF), a broad-based public interest organization, to take up the issue, and Insull joined its study committee alongside future Supreme Court Justice Louis Brandeis and United Mine Workers president John Mitchell.

In 1907 the NCF issued an influential three-volume report, largely financed by investor-owned utility and traction firms and their executives, board members, and suppliers.[96] The report adopted Insull's core rationale that "public utilities, whether in public or private hands, are best conducted under a system of legalized and regulated monopoly."[97] It recommended guaranteed returns based on capital valuation, long-term franchise duration, natural monopoly, and equal value of all stocks, principles that decisively shaped future industry development.[98] NELA meanwhile proselytized for state regulation, contending state commissions should have the power to "control franchises, protect users against unreasonable or discriminatory rates, enforce a uniform system of accounting, and make public all pertinent information about the affairs of the regulated companies."[99]

Momentum in favor of state regulation gathered just as the municipal-ownership movement began to stall. John Commons, an economist who had worked on the NCF report, recast its main recommendation in the form of a law establishing state commission regulation of utilities. Commons's draft was adopted in 1907 with little change by Wisconsin and New York and followed within a decade by twenty-five other states.[100] Insull's vision was now reality. Technocratic state commissions, far removed from sordid municipal politics, would regulate utilities. To get an exclusive franchise, a utility would submit its rates and services to government oversight.

The trade-off seemed symmetrical on its face. In practice it was seriously flawed.

As adopted, state regulation imposed on a utility an obligation to serve all customers in its service area without discrimination. To fulfill its obligation, the utility had to raise capital and build plants capable of supplying all electricity demanded at a "just and reasonable" price covering its operating costs plus a fair return on capital invested. In exchange, the utility earned a valuable concession. It was treated as a natural monopoly, protected from competitors within its service area, and clothed with the power of eminent domain. This regulatory compact arguably secured for the public economies of scale and prevented the utility from cutting production below or raising prices above competitive levels. In the influential utility ratemaking case *Smyth v. Ames*,[101] the U.S. Supreme Court concluded that "what the company is entitled to ask is a fair return upon the value of that which it *employs* for the public convenience"[102]—that is, assets it uses currently to provide service to customers. The fair-return-on-fair-value test, although appealing as a judicial formulation, was problematic in practice since it required a regulator to determine the "fair value" of a utility enterprise, a task that proved complex and imprecise. Experienced utility counsel were more than a match for their counterparts at state commissions in interpreting and applying the law.

State regulation changed the field of play in favor of Insull and other operators. By raising rates and profits it rewarded urban, capital-rich investor-owned utilities. In the five years after its formation, the Wisconsin Utility Commission approved fifty of fifty-two rate increases sought by utilities, while denying rate reductions to public firms by a similar margin.[103] State regulation also reduced the borrowing costs of a capital-intensive and highly leveraged industry.[104]

In 1914, long after its counterparts in Wisconsin and New York, the Illinois Public Utility Commission began operations, only to encounter a renewed home rule movement dedicated to its replacement. Prodded by reform-minded politicians, the Illinois House of Representatives appointed a committee to study home rule, a cause expediently joined by the mayor of Chicago, William Hale Thompson. As wartime inflation drove utilities to seek rate increases from the new commission, home rule gathered supporters, including Midwest Progressive Senators La Follette, Borah, and Wheeler. In 1920 the legislature abolished the Illinois Public Utility Commission but replaced it later in the session with a successor, the Illinois Commerce Commission, invested "with all the powers to regulate utilities that the original commission had held."[105]

Insull's campaign for state regulation reflected a hardheaded, pragmatic grasp of politics, industry economics, and the threat posed by municipalization. State regulation rewarded "a 'growth dynamic' strategy"and firms with the greatest access to investment capital.[106] It also required utility regulators to promote the public interest while ensuring that regulated firms earned returns sufficient to attract capital—an implicit conflict that fueled a race toward regulatory laxity.[107] "Equal value" of stocks accorded previous investments full value even if watered, while "guaranteed returns" assured investors that questionable investments would still be profitable. "In the long run," said Insull, "regulation means protection."[108] In exchange for control over utilities' rates and terms, state utility commissions recognized exclusive service territories and precluded cities from imposing onerous regulations, a bargain that benefited investor-owned utilities, their stockholders, and their bankers.[109] Limiting the market to a single provider, it was thought, would "realize economies of scale"—that is, the public would get less expensive service from one regulated utility than it would if multiple utilities engaged in price competition.[110] As a result, the system of municipal franchises for private gas and electric utilities largely disappeared.[111] The new regulatory compact fostered nationwide emergence of vertically integrated utilities that generated their own power, moved it over high-voltage transmission lines, and delivered it to retail customers within franchised service areas using their own local distribution networks.[112] This was Insull's legacy and still largely describes today's industry.

Growth and Mass Production

Insull's acquisition of Commonwealth Electric Company ignited a period of feverish growth, driven by new technology, new sources of business, and Insull's relentless drive to achieve economies of scale by "massing of energy production."[113] To get a large daytime load, Insull pursued Chicago's transit companies, which were burdened by the high cost of self-generation and consumed three times more electric power than Chicago Edison's existing light and power customers.[114] In the next five years Chicago Edison captured nearly thirty percent of transit company power business and financed an ambitious expansion program.[115] The key to growth was Insull's formula of "transit contracts, large generators, low rates, and load management."[116] Of these, low rates were the indispensable element. Insull once explained it thus: "If you will bring your price down to a point where you can compel the manufacturer to shut down his private plant because he will save money by doing so; if you can compel the street railway to shut down its generating plant; if you can compel the city waterworks, whether privately or public owned, to shut down its power plant because of the price you quote—then you will begin to realize the possibilities of this business, and these possibilities may exceed your wildest dreams."[117]

Insull had seized on a fundamental truth about the electricity market. He knew reducing rates would accelerate increased demand for the product. He also knew advanced technology (e.g., the steam turbine), shrewd salesmanship, and mass production would enable him to cut costs, lower rates, and therefore capture market share. It was not necessary, as many of his successors thought, to await a spontaneous increase in demand. In a capital-intensive industry that sold a standard product, cost was paramount. Electricity also had knock-on effects. It changed the working methods of many industries, including coal mines, oil wells, machine shops, aluminum plants, and manufacturers: "Electricity made possible a redesign of the work process; it increased productivity both quantitatively and qualitatively ... [and] overturned the old industrial system. ... [A] twentieth-century capitalist using electrical machinery could make enormous increases in efficiency without making a corresponding large capital investment."[118] Insull's business plan captured a portion of that productivity gain.

Insull did not live by price alone. He was also a relentless merchandiser of power to diverse urban customers. He needed more daytime electricity business to shrink the gulf between average and peak load on his system. Traction companies were not the only source of that business. To reach other daytime customers Insull had Chicago Edison form a "business getting" department, launch an advertising campaign, and publish *Electric City*, a glossy magazine distributed by downtown drugstores in exchange for free wiring and discounted rates. A principal target of opportunity was found in Chicago's central business district where hotels, large department stores, and office buildings self-generated power for lighting, steam heat, elevators, electric appliances, and new AC motors, recently perfected by inventor Nikola Tesla. All represented new demand Insull could wean from isolated power sources through concessional electricity prices, particularly in off-peak hours, undercutting the cost of freestanding plants and opening new central station markets in electrochemicals, electroplating, arc welding, and other industrial processes. Chicago Edison also supplied electricity to the city's elevated transit system. Shortly after the turn of the century one-third of its electric output served power applications.[119]

Expansion strained the capacity of existing generators and wires to the limit.[120] To support further growth Insull needed a quantum increase in power output, driven by new generating and transmission technology. The Harrison Street station's reciprocating steam engines were simply not up to the task. Insull turned his attention to a recent invention, the steam turbine, then under development by his old firm, General Electric.[121] Insull placed an order for a five-megawatt steam turbine, far larger than any then on the drawing board. It was a calculated bet on new technology, doubled down on an unproven turbine manufacturer and made against the advice of his own engineers.[122]

On taking delivery in 1903, Insull housed the new turbine at a station on the north bank of the Chicago River at Fisk Street. It marked the beginning of a radical increase in generating capacity. The Fisk Street station eventually housed fourteen turbines, each retrofitted and upgraded to twelve megawatts, all, in Insull's words, "with the same building, the same number of boilers, the same stack capacity, practically the same amount of money invested."[123] Steam turbines cut production costs by half and revolutionized the power business. Turbines eliminated the need for belts and gears, spun ten times faster than reciprocating units, were one-tenth the weight, occupied one-tenth the space, and required far less fuel per unit of output.[124] Fabricated from the latest metal alloys, they were also capable of operating consistently twenty-four hours a day. Turbine technology was transformative. It allowed Insull to realize his dream of "mass-producing" low-cost energy and extended his reach far beyond downtown Chicago. Turbine technology increased company profits despite rate cuts. Lower rates also stimulated demand that led to significant economies of scale. Insull's gospel of consumption, based on falling rates and increased output, appeared to be an iron law of economics.[125] The steam turbine, in Insull's view, "had a greater influence on the development of our business during the last decade than any other one thing."[126] It also changed Chicago, which was on its way to becoming the most energy-intensive place in the world.[127]

Steam turbines coincided with changes in transmission technology. Following its triumph at the 1893 World's Fair in Chicago, AC had begun to displace DC, which could not travel long distances without repeated voltage support. AC overcame the one-mile limitation on transmission of DC power and, after voltage step-up, could flow many miles without significant line loss or degradation. AC power illuminated lights, just as DC did, and powered the AC polyphase motors that had recently come into common use. Insull developed Commonwealth Electric as an AC company, closely integrated with Chicago Edison but operating outside the central business district. He also adopted the latest developments in transmission technology, having installed a network of high-voltage compound transmission lines and substations to serve his companies' growing market.[128] "The combination of high-efficiency steam turbines, high-tension transmission lines, and many substations," Insull wrote, "forced ... the abandonment of small generating stations and the massing of production on a very large scale."[129] Remote large-scale central generating plants, connected to an intricate distribution system and operated by load dispatchers to balance supply and demand, became the industry norm.

In 1907 Chicago Edison merged with Commonwealth Electric, its wholly owned affiliate, to form Commonwealth Edison Company. Far from a simple corporate transaction, the merger faced formidable political headwinds. In 1905 the Illinois legislature empowered Chicago to fix rates, through contract ordinances, for all utility service and passed another law authorizing the city to convert its street lighting plant into an electric system in competition with Insull's companies. That same year Chicago's new reform mayor, Edward F. Dunne, promised immediate municipal ownership of all transportation companies with the clear implication that electric companies were next.[130] The proposed merger hung in the balance.

Insull conceded the city's authority to regulate the price of utility services. He also announced a rate cut, hoping to get the city's blessing on Chicago Edison's rate structure, which discriminated among customer classes by quantity of energy consumed. After a three-month study, despite suspicions of rate inequity, the city accepted the existing rates, a decision that "exposed many of the inherent difficulties facing the government in its attempt to regulate utility enterprises in the public interest."[131] Insull's rate cuts succeeded in deflecting political opposition. In 1907 Mayor Dunne was succeeded by a no-reform Republican, and the city council approved the merger.

Commonwealth Edison was sixty times larger than the company Insull had joined fifteen years before. Insull now had a creditworthy vehicle that dominated the local market and had ready access to public finance. "The Commonwealth Edison Company," wrote the *Electrical World and Engineer* soon after its formation, "has among its customers establishments run by some of the largest isolated plants in the city."[132] Switching those customers to central station service was proof of Insull's vision and Commonwealth Edison's standing.

Insull lost no time in shaping the Fisk Street, the Harrison Street, and the new Quarry Street stations into an integrated system capable of serving diverse light and power markets. The system marshaled massive generating capacity connected to high-voltage transmission lines and an underground low-voltage distribution system that spread throughout the growing metropolis.[133] Two-thirds of the electricity produced powered transportation, which offered loads large enough to support major economies of scale and resulting rate reductions.[134] Commonwealth Edison would now show the world what could be accomplished by "massing production and distribution of electrical energy, and reducing its cost as a result, giving cheap electricity to the smallest consumer and the largest corporation."[135]

Regional Outreach

Insull's restless ambition was not satisfied with dominance of the Chicago market. "As a result," he wrote, "I began to look for opportunities to purchase and combine the various small country central stations around Chicago."[136] Insull wanted to reach out for new territory, new customers, and new organizational structures. Several years before forming Commonwealth Edison, he had invested personally in two small utilities in Highland Park and Evanston, suburbs of Chicago, and later transferred his interests to a newly created Chicago Edison affiliate, North Shore Electric Company. Insull's country home in Libertyville, another Chicago suburb, was virtually without electricity. So he ran a line to his home from Lake Bluff, already served by North Shore. The experiment engaged his curiosity. Just as customers in the city drew power from a single source, he speculated, why not lay transmission lines to link isolated towns and realize the same economy?

1881

Figure 1.1
Likeness of Samuel Insull as a young man, circa 1881, from booklet titled *To Commemorate the 50th Anniversary of the Arrival in America of Mr. Samuel Insull*. Samuel Insull Collection. Courtesy of Loyola University Chicago Archives & Special Collections.

A century ago, with few exceptions, the countryside was largely untouched by electricity. Farmers used kerosene lamps; suburban villages were gas lit; electrical conveniences were virtually unknown. Most central station operators dismissed operations beyond the city limits as uneconomic. Insull's plan to electrify the hinterlands outside Chicago formed the basis for holding company expansion in the following years and brought electric power to outlying communities decades before the New Deal's rural electrification programs.

Ever methodical, in 1909 Insull undertook a survey of the region and launched the "Lake County experiment," embracing twenty-two towns,

Figure 1.2
Likeness of Samuel Insull, circa 1931, from booklet titled *To Commemorate the 50th Anniversary of the Arrival in America of Mr. Samuel Insull*. Samuel Insull Collection. Courtesy of Loyola University Chicago Archives & Special Collections.

each with a population of no more than three hundred, twelve without power and ten with dusk-to-midnight service only. Rural electrification was the least promising aspect of the central station business. Few utility companies were willing to invest in rural distribution grids.[137] Against the advice of the Chicago financial community, he acquired ten part-time local plants—dismissed by his critics as "junk piles"—then built a network of transmission lines connecting the towns and a number of outlying farms.[138]

Insull centralized production in a single remote station, then converted the small plants into substations connected to long high-voltage

Figure 1.3
Northwest Station boiler room. Samuel Insull Collection. Courtesy of Loyola University Chicago Archives & Special Collections.

transmission lines. Towns previously too small to serve themselves now had access to low-cost power.[139] "We came to the conclusion," he said, "that the economical way to produce and distribute energy was to mass its production at a given point, convey [it] by means of high-tension transmission lines to whatever subcenters of distribution we thought desirable, and then to distribute at possibly lower pressure from those substations."[140] This became the electric power industry's paradigmatic structural feature.

The experiment worked. The efficiency of large-scale generating units more than offset the cost of new transmission lines (and their associated towers, insulators, circuit breakers, switches, and transformers) and attracted additional customers to the system. In two years Insull was able to cut rates, reduce costs, double the load factor, and realize a profit,[141] vindicating the central station economic doctrine he had long preached. North Shore eventually served over 90,000 customers in forty-three communities

Figure 1.4
Turbine room—Fisk Street Station. Samuel Insull Collection. Courtesy of Loyola
University Chicago Archives & Special Collections.

spread across 1,250 square miles. By 1910 Insull's Lake County experiment
had created the nation's first working model of rural electrification.[142]

Using the same formula, Insull extended his system to villages southwest of Chicago and to Cicero, Berwyn, and Oak Park west of the city. In
1911 he consolidated these holdings and North Shore into a new company,
Public Service Company of Northern Illinois, which served a regional network interconnected with Commonwealth that extended from Milwaukee
on the north to the eastern banks of the Mississippi on the west, and from
Michigan City and South Bend, Indiana, on the east and southeast to the
Illinois coal fields south of Chicago. "Insull secured sovereignty over [these]
regions," wrote a recent commentator, "by tethering them to a 138-kilovolt
transmission line."[143] Still acquisitive, Public Service then purchased other
local power companies and, within four years, while cutting rates in half,
came to serve 150 new towns and 65,000 new electric customers.[144] It now

Figure 1.5
Samuel Insull, circa late 1920s. Samuel Insull Collection. Courtesy of Loyola University Chicago Archives & Special Collections.

Figure 1.6
Samuel Insull as he is walked down hall at federal office building in Chicago on May
8, 1934, by U.S. Marshalls. (AP Photo.)

embraced utilities providing electric, gas, water, and interurban railway
services, whose diversity in demand enabled Insull to cut electric rates
further.[145]

In 1913 over half the population of Illinois remained without service.[146]
Extending electric power to benighted small towns in the countryside drew
them into the twentieth century and improved sanitation, sewerage, and
communication.[147] "It was an effort," Insull said, "to bring service to all
classes of people residing in communities of vastly different conditions ...
at the lowest possible cost."[148] Regional integration of patchwork electric
grids spread the benefits of electricity beyond city limits. Insull's efforts
to power the countryside preceded the New Deal's rural electrification
programs by more than two decades and distinguished him from many
others in the investor-owned utility industry, who were indifferent to rural
markets.

Origins of the Holding Company

At the turn of the century, state legislatures and courts made a crucial
change in the law, abandoning a long-held rule that considered it improper

for one corporation to use the power of stock ownership to control the affairs of another. Under the changed law, a holding company could sell its own stock and use the proceeds to acquire stock in and gain control over multiple operating subsidiaries to coordinate their operations. A holding company could also use the stock of its operating subsidiaries as collateral for loans and further investment. As reconceived, the law gave a holding company the right to ensure a subsidiary acted not simply to make a profit for itself but also to enhance the holding company's profit.

Businessmen saw an opportunity to shift and combine the profit streams of constituent companies, manipulate assets within a corporate group, impose fees and charges, and deflect or avoid liabilities. A holding company could also provide technical expertise, management services, and financial leverage, in the process imposing costs on "any local company to any limit they wish."[149] As managerial practice evolved, many holding companies set up affiliated service companies with extraordinarily broad powers to run their operating subsidiaries. Neither utility holding companies nor their service affiliates were regulated; nor were their true costs transparent to state regulators. Yet service companies charged well for their services, and the costs of those services, borne by local utilities, were recoverable from customers in their rates.

Entrepreneurs and businessmen took notice of a commercially fertile prospect. Following New Jersey's statutory grant of corporate power to own stock, well over a thousand companies, with authorized capital of over $2 billion, organized in the state during the first seven months of 1899.[150] The lesson was not lost on utility owners, who needed to rationalize a fragmented and undercapitalized industry. State regulation, long sought by Insull, de-risked the industry by ensuring that utilities would recover their costs and earn an adequate profit. Financing became easier as a result, and the holding company, as a consolidating device, enabled this process. By upstreaming profits from its constituent operating companies and using their securities as collateral, the holding company gave investor-owned utilities entrée to public debt and equity markets.

In 1912 Insull formed Middle West Utilities Company as a holding company to buy Public Service of Northern Illinois and a group of local electric, gas, and streetcar companies then operated in Indiana by Insull's younger brother, Martin (who became vice president of Middle West under Insull's presidency). To finance the acquisition and provide operating capital,

Middle West issued common and preferred stock in a series of complex transactions. Its immediate challenge was to rationalize the operations of many small generation plants and transmission lines stretched over hundreds of miles. Insull also intended to use Middle West to serve hinterland areas still without electricity, repeating on a larger scale his Lake County experiment.

Shortly after its organization, Middle West acquired Central Illinois Public Service Company, which operated a streetcar line, an interurban line, and several small central stations. Over the next dozen years Central Illinois brought electric power to nearly five hundred communities and enlarged its customer base exponentially. "Insull and his lieutenants appeared to be everywhere at once," noted an industry observer, "selling kilowatt-hours in Chicago and Chillicothe, expanding to Maine and Missouri, extending transmission lines across the Midwest, and peddling ice in downstate hamlets."[151] In a few short years Middle West's ramshackle empire extended Insull's reach from Chicago and its immediate suburbs to a good part of the continental United States. Its operating subsidiaries served over 130,000 electric and 40,000 gas customers in four hundred towns in thirteen states.[152] In the process Insull replaced existing municipal or privately owned electric plants with substations linked by high-tension transmission lines to efficient, large-scale central stations.[153] Together Commonwealth Edison and Middle West ultimately gave Insull ten percent of the nation's $2.5 billion electricity market and marked him as "the most prominent figure in the public utility field."[154]

Lessons Learned

The First World War proved to be a turning point for Insull's utility holding company empire. Illinois created a State Council of Defense, which Governor Lowden asked Insull to chair. Lowden's choice was hardly surprising. In addition to his extraordinary business success, Insull had actively supported U.S. intervention during President Wilson's long interlude of neutrality and was well known to Sir Edward Grey, the British minister of foreign affairs, Lloyd George (then chancellor of the exchequer), and Joseph Tumulty, Wilson's private secretary, among other influential people. Insull agreed to devote his time and organizational genius to the new job.

"From that day," he wrote, "until the Illinois State Council of Defense was liquidated, I gave very little time indeed to my business."[155] Insull transformed the council from a thinly disguised vigilante committee into a dynamic instrument in aid of the war effort and populated its board with prominent businessmen, politicians, and labor leaders. He recruited state-wide volunteers and launched a campaign to mobilize public opinion. "In a world without radio, sound films, television, or any other instantaneous mass media," writes his biographer, "Insull and his organization infused the people of Illinois with a zeal that many thought excessive; he produced a band of militant enthusiasts whose momentum never allowed patriotic fervor a moment's rest."[156]

The council enrolled a small army of ministers, fraternal orders, labor organizations, nationalistic societies, mayors, and civil and commercial groups; established speakers' bureaus and neighborhood committees; and arranged thousands of public meetings. Most important, the council was a premier fundraising organization. With only $50,000 as seed money, it raised $24 million for war relief and, using high-pressure techniques, sold over $1 billion of Liberty Bonds in only eighteen months. It was said that if Insull had been running the war, he would have run it at a profit. His council leadership established him "as a miracle worker with a Midas touch" and gave him the selling tools he later used to finance unprecedented postwar utility expansion largely free of New York bankers, for whom there was no love lost.

To blunt political opposition and turn hostile voters into utility stake-holders, at war's end he converted the council's propaganda machinery to peacetime use, changing its name from the Committee on Public Information to the Committee on Public Utility Information. Drawing on his experience in selling Liberty Bonds to the public, Insull envisioned a program of customer ownership that would in the next decade revolutionize corporate finance.

Commonwealth Edison turned to its own employees to sell stock to friends, family, and customers. Middle West did likewise when its operating subsidiaries experienced a huge increase in demand requiring capital on an equal scale—financial support Insull for a time had to provide out of his own pocket or by intercorporate borrowing.[157] During the postwar boom, he relied on financial self-help to raise equity capital, align company and customer interests, and generate political goodwill.[158] "What I am deliberately after," he said, "is public ownership ... that will result in a vast army of stockholders ... to stand guard over their own property."[159] Customer ownership was to prove more than a financial device. It also enabled Insull to disarm critics and mobilize public opinion on behalf of utility interests.

Halsey, Stuart & Co., Insull's underwriter of choice, built a mass retail market for his companies' corporate bonds, sold in $1,000 denominations to an inexhaustible number of willing small investors. Halsey, Stuart soon increased bond underwriting levels spectacularly, selling almost $200 million worth in a single year.[160] In short order, the number of Insull company security holders in Illinois alone increased tenfold.[161]

Insull's companies, like their holding company counterparts, attracted small investors who believed utility securities were a safe haven, virtually without risk. By 1926 the market for utility bonds and debentures approached a billion dollars a year, and Halsey, Stuart had by far the greatest share of the business.[162] By raising funds from many small bondholders and shareholders, Insull was able to break the stranglehold of New York bankers on public financings. "Mr. Insull wouldn't let bankers tell him how to run his business," said Charles Stuart, "and when it touched his affairs he told them how to run theirs. He pushed bankers around. He said the only way to deal with them was to get so you could call them on the phone and make them come to your office to do business." [163]

Using a "maze of intercorporate relationships,"[164] Insull also fundamentally changed the way big companies were run by separating ownership and control. When the number of owners multiplies, wrote Berle and Means in their landmark study, "control may be held by the directors or titular managers who can employ the proxy machinery to become a self-perpetuating body, even though as a group they own but a small fraction of the stock outstanding."[165] To Insull's army of small investors, separation of ownership and control was of little consequence. He was widely regarded as a financial wizard, and the financial prospects of his holding companies, however overleveraged, seemed limitless.

The 1920s saw a surge in consumer demand for electric service and appliances (irons, vacuum cleaners, toasters, coffee percolators, and washing machines), promoted by Insull's aggressive salesmen. In a decade Commonwealth Edison's customers more than doubled their per capita consumption of electricity. Insull's "engineering methods of selling" became an orchestrated campaign that included constant mass media advertising, special incentives, installment plans, and door-to-door solicitation. As residential electrification neared completion, Chicago did indeed became the most energy-intensive city in the world.[166] Insull successfully linked finance with mass consumption and production. "His innovations democratized electricity, spreading it into broad areas of American life until it became as much a staple as the automobile."[167]

Holding Company Principles Applied

As the 1920s dawned, it was clear the utility industry had outgrown its local origins. Steady improvements in technology enabled integrated grids to reach well beyond the service area of a single utility, just as powerful steam turbines increased output and productivity. "The discoveries in long-distance transmission," wrote Herbert Hoover in his *Memoirs*, "had now opened a new vista in the production and use of electrical power which had not yet been much availed of."[168] But wider markets, while inviting, presented risks. An operating utility, with its rates and terms of service set by a single state commission, confronted conflicts with the law of neighboring states if it did business beyond its home base. An operating utility might also fail to convince hard-nosed bankers to underwrite problematic multistate expansion plans.

The industry's delay in developing larger systems initially led to two abortive government policy proposals. The Superpower plan of 1921, sponsored by the U.S. Geological Survey and promoted by Herbert Hoover (then secretary of commerce), proposed to convert the Boston-Washington corridor into a single integrated system. It promised huge cost reductions but failed to convince existing utilities that benefits to each justified their loss of individual control. The Giant Power study of 1925, initiated by Governor Gifford Pinchot, proposed radical reorganization of Pennsylvania's power industry, including common-carrier transmission, but did not survive strong opposition from local utilities.[169]

In the event, top-down, command-and-control government intervention proved unnecessary. Insull's vehicle of choice, the utility holding company, addressed both regulatory and financing concerns. "Up to the fatal year 1929," said James C. Bonbright, a preeminent industry analyst, "public utility executives and financiers were able to make a strong case for their assertion that the rapid and remarkable development of the country's electrical industry was due in large measure to the domination of that industry by a group of financially strong and well-managed holding companies."[170]

Insull's Middle West Utilities represented a hierarchy of power. On the eve of the First World War it operated in thirteen Midwest and New England states. By 1924 Middle West had doubled in size and sales, and its system covered "virtually a third of the states of the Union, reaching from New England across the Middle West into the valley of the Platte and from Canada's door on the North to the meeting place of new and old civilizations at the Mexico border."[171] High-voltage transmission lines interconnected almost a thousand service areas. Middle West had become an organizational ziggurat with five direct subsidiaries and twenty second-tier subsidiaries. Further subsidiaries cascaded down thereafter to third, fourth, fifth, and sixth levels. Control was centralized at the top, allowing Insull to run a large pyramid of companies with a small equity stake.[172] "We are now getting well into the third stage of public-utility development," he said, "which is marked by still further concentration in production and still wider distribution."[173]

As Middle West's success proved, the holding company offered critical advantages. Insull characterized it as "more properly an investment company, even more accurately perhaps, a development company," whose "primary purpose is to expand and energize the facilities and resources and activities of the local or subsidiary companies that are under its wing, and to broaden the opportunity for safe investment."[174] By issuing its own (typically preferred or nonvoting) stock, a holding company could finance the acquisition of equity interests in and obtain control over multiple operating companies, each of which in turn could control still other operating companies, with the result that a relatively small investment at the apex of the corporate pyramid could, through leverage, coordinate and dictate the activities of a structured constellation of related businesses. With an equity investment of less than $30 million, Insull controlled assets worth over half a billion dollars.[175] Profits flowed upward through service contracts, intercorporate dividends, watered stock, accounting adjustments, and margins realized from reorganization and promotional activities. In return, the holding company offered subsidiary companies technological, business, and administrative services.[176]

Operating companies sold electricity at retail and recovered the often inflated cost of these services from ratepayers within a single state. The holding company did wholesale electricity business in interstate commerce. It was not answerable to state regulators, nor were its costs subject to review.[177] The regulatory gap was embedded in federal law. In a famous Supreme Court case, *Public Utilities Commission v. Attleboro Steam & Electric Co.*,[178] the plaintiff, a Rhode Island utility, sold power to a Massachusetts utility. The Public Utilities Commission of Rhode Island found the contract rate unreasonably low and issued an order increasing it. On review, the court said nothing would prevent Massachusetts from reducing the rate in retaliation and found "the paramount interest in the interstate business carried on between the two companies is not local to either State, but is essentially national in character." Only Congress had the power to regulate interstate wholesale electricity business. State regulation ended with the operating company. Until Congress passed the Federal Power Act[179] years later, Insull's utility holding company empire and others like it were free to expand, acquire, consolidate, pyramid, and deal at will. "In the laissez-faire milieu thus created, utility holding companies flourished, and behind the Attleboro shield abuses became flagrant."[180] Excessive leverage generated huge profits during boom years but resulted in fragile financial structures unable to withstand reversal of fortune after the crash.[181]

State commissions, adopted with such promise in the flush of Progressive Era reform, failed to provide, as expected, "scientific regulation by administrators armed with authority to determine facts and issue rules and orders."[182] Instead, as one industry commentator noted: "Regulation is in a state of flux. It has seemingly taken on an entirely new aspect of late, perhaps an aspect which seems altogether unexpected and unwarranted to those who were its early protagonists. Originally a 'people's' or a 'consumer's' movement, today regulation has become by force of circumstance the champion of the rights of utilities."[183]

Political Backlash

By 1925 the Insull companies served over 1,800 communities in 16 states, totals that would increase to over 5,000 communities in 32 states within the next five years and account for more than ten percent of the nation's electric output.[184] For more than a decade, within an ever-expanding holding company envelope, the companies had consistently made interest and dividend payments to a legion of small investors and produced cheap electric power for customers in the city and countryside alike. But operating success was not proof against political opposition. The industry's explosive growth and increasing concentration attracted formidable enemies. In 1925 Senator Walsh of Montana sponsored a resolution directing the Federal Trade Commission to "investigate ... and to report to the Senate the manner in which the General Electric Company has acquired and maintained such monopoly or exercises such control in restraint of trade or commerce and in violation of law."[185] The resulting study of the U.S. electric industry, although inconclusive, was a straw in the wind.[186]

In 1926 Insull contributed $160,000 to the political campaign of Frank Smith, chairman of the Illinois Commerce Commission, who defeated the incumbent, Senator William McKinley, in a bitterly contested Republican senatorial primary in Illinois. Spurred by Insull's huge donation to his rival, McKinley spent over half a million dollars seeking reelection. Ignoring a blatant conflict of interest, Insull explained that Smith, as chairman of the Illinois Commerce Commission, had "never granted any of my companies anything they were not strictly entitled to."[187] Smith won the election, but the facts were stark. The state's dominant utility operator had financed the campaign of the state's top utility regulator. No explanation could quell the bad publicity. Insull's ill-fated contribution, driven by his long-standing hatred for McKinley, triggered a chain of adverse political events.[188]

Following the Illinois primary and a similar money-drenched primary in Pennsylvania, the Senate began an investigation of corrupt practices in senatorial elections. At hearings during the summer of 1926 Insull was a star witness, and "hardly a day passed without some newspaper or another, from Maine to California, attacking political corruption in general and Insull in particular."[189] When the committee resumed its investigation early in 1927, Insull refused to reveal his local contributions and was cited for contempt of Congress (only avoiding prosecution by later testimony). Spurred by Senator Norris of Nebraska, the Senate ultimately refused to seat Smith.[190]

Senator Norris's concerns were broader than electoral politics. He was also a dedicated foe of investor-owed utilities, a "gigantic trust that has fastened its fangs upon the people of the United States from the Atlantic to the Pacific and from the Great Lakes to the Gulf."[191] Norris was, unsurprisingly, an advocate of public power at two federal hydroelectric sites, Muscle Shoals and Boulder Canyon. The Smith affair gave him an opening. He claimed the power trust was corrupting the nation's elections. "God only knows," said Norris, "how many Senatorial campaigns Mr. Insull has financed."[192] In 1928, as retribution, Norris got Congress to pass a bill, later vetoed by President Coolidge, putting the United States in the electric power business at Muscle Shoals.

At the same time, unsatisfied with the earlier report of the Federal Trade Commission, the Senate authorized the commission once again to investigate the electric utility industry. The investigation took seven years to complete and foreshadowed the politics of the next decade. Its purpose, said Senator Walsh, "is to protect two classes of our citizens: First, the 17,000,000 of householders who pay for electric lighting; and, second, the great body of our people who are now putting their savings into the securities of these corporations."[193]

The FTC investigation called the holding company the "keystone and culmination of the financial structure of the utilities organization"[194] and focused on a handful of huge articulated pyramids—Electric Bond and Share, the Byllesby Group, Stone & Webster, Cities Service, the North American Company, and, of course, the Insull Group with its "two top companies at the head, their subsidiaries and sub-subsidiaries, and sub-sub-sub-subsidiaries down to the seventh degree."[195] The investigation conceded the existence of some holding company virtues but was primarily a catalog of corporate abuses. "The highly pyramided holding company group," it said, "represents the holding company system at its worst. It is bad in that it allows one or two individuals, or a small coterie of capitalists, to control arbitrarily enormous amounts of investments supplied by many people."[196]

The "trade secrets of extortion" included watered stock, overcapitalization, excessive service charges, and extreme concentration of profits and control.[197] For Insull and the industry at large the investigation was an ongoing public relations bloodbath. It allowed hostile politicians such as Norris, Walsh, and Pinchot, who hated the so-called power trust, to expose venality, corporate self-dealing, and monopoly enterprise. Industry lobbyists (including the Illinois Public Information Committee and its counterparts) and trade associations worked overtime to control the damage, but public opinion was turning against Insull and other holding company

chieftains. For a time, however, the raging bull market of the late 1920s
masked the problems unearthed by the FTC in its plodding investigation.

Restless Expansion; Pyramiding and the Crash

Insull was not content to dominate the Midwest. As early as 1913 he had
acquired Twin State Gas & Electric with operations in Maine, New Hampshire, New York, and Vermont. Over a decade later he was provoked to look
eastward again. In 1927, Insull's bête noire, J. P. Morgan, formed a super-
holding company, the United Corporation, with a capitalization twenty
times that of U.S. Steel, to control Columbia Gas and Electric Corporation,
Consolidated Gas Company, Niagara Hudson Power Corporation, Public
Service Corporation of New Jersey, United Gas Improvement Company,
and Commonwealth and Southern. Morgan was hungry for a slice of the
lucrative utility securities business, used the United Corporation as a stalk-
ing horse for that purpose, and realized his objective by underwriting over
half a billion dollars' worth of utility bonds in one year.[198] Insull despised
the Morgan bankers and endorsed a fateful territorial decision made by
his brother Martin, an executive at Middle West Utilities, to acquire two
dangerously pyramided holding company systems with operations in the
Northeast, far from its home base. Insull's footprint now extended to every
Eastern state but Rhode Island. Daringly, he had established a major presence under Morgan's very nose—an act of hubris that proved to be, in the
words of one observer, "as successful as Napoleon's invasion of Russia." [199]

For the moment, however, Insull commanded a formidable corporate
empire. Commonwealth Edison Company, the great electric power company, and Peoples Gas Light and Coke Company provided Chicago with
electricity and gas. Public Service Company of Northern Illinois served the
Chicago suburbs. Middle West Utilities was the holding company for Insull
properties outside Indiana and Chicago, whose operating companies served
5,000 communities in thirty-two states over 45,000 miles of transmission
lines. Midland United Company, another holding company, had operating subsidiaries in Indiana, Ohio, Michigan, and Illinois. Special-purpose
subsidiaries included Peabody Coal Company, Super Power Company of
Illinois, and the Chicago District Generating Company. Radiating outward
and downward were prosperous operating companies, such as Central and
Southwest Utilities Company. Insull's companies had 600,000 stockholders

and almost as many bondholders, served more than four million customers, and produced a significant percentage of the electricity and gas consumed in the United States.[200]

Insull had built this business monolith with uncommon managerial skill, political cunning, and willingness to assume calculated risk. Invincibly confident in his generalship, he had overcome obstacles that turned back lesser men. Until the Depression, his corporate career was an unbroken record of success. As chief executive, he kept close control over a sprawling, complex enterprise, having learned early in his career, at the hands of J. P. Morgan and Charles Coffin of General Electric, never to allow others to determine his fate. He installed a cadre of trusted associates as company officers and then was able to operate by consensus. "I did not attempt to run all of the various corporations in detail," he wrote. "They all had very able men as executive officers, who had mainly grown up from the ranks and whose judgment was based on experience they had obtained as a result."[201] But there was never the slightest doubt who had the final word. For many years unchallenged in his leadership and widely respected, even feared, in the business world, Insull grew imperious and overconfident, character flaws reflected in his rash political contribution to the Smith campaign and decision to do business in Morgan's backyard. For all his talk of consensus, there were no restraining voices within his company domain.

Nor was Insull restrained by threats from dissident shareholders. "I never had any concern as to holding the control of any of the companies I operated," he said, "so long as the securities issued were distributed over a wide ownership and mainly locally in Chicago."[202] In 1928, for the first time, however, Insull had good reason to be concerned. Cyrus Eaton, a financier and stock market speculator, began quietly purchasing through nominees large blocks of stock in Insull's four flagship companies, including Commonwealth Edison and Middle West Utilities. By mid-1928 Insull learned Eaton's holdings were several times larger than his own.

Eaton posed a formidable threat. A partner in a Cleveland investment banking firm and twenty-year veteran of the utility business, he had already acquired control of two holding companies formerly dominated by Mellon interests. In the summer of 1928 Insull and Eaton, quite by chance, met while returning from Europe on the same ocean liner. Eaton said nothing about his stock purchases just as his agents were increasing his stake in Commonwealth Edison by 80,000 shares. To Insull, who knew about this purchase, Eaton's silence was eloquent. Insull feared a raid that would oust him from his perch atop his corporate pyramid. "I came to the conclusion," he said, "that the best thing for me to do would be to form an investment company to hold the securities of the four companies in question owned by my family and myself, and to acquire additional stock by purchase in the market."[203]

In December 1928 Insull formed Insull Utility Investments, Inc. (IUI) "to perpetuate the existing management of the Insull group of public utilities."[204] Insull, his family, and his close business associates transferred shares representing working control of the four top-tier holding companies to IUI in exchange for its common and preferred stock and an option to purchase a large additional block of shares. IUI common was priced at $15 per share. On its first day of trading in January 1929, it opened at $25, and by midsummer it had soared to $150. In the same period Commonwealth Edison and Middle West Utilities stock also made spectacular gains, supported by insider purchases. Insull's personal fortune, recently valued at only $5 million, now had a book value of $150 million. In October 1929, to cement his control of IUI and capitalize on the bull market, Insull formed a second investment trust, Corporation Securities Company (CSC), controlled by three voting trustees (himself, his son Samuel Insull Jr., and Harold Stuart of Halsey, Stuart).[205]

In October and November 1929 CSC took in almost $50 million from sale of its shares to the public through Utility Securities Company, formed for the sole purpose of disposing of Insull company securities with a mandate to go after "small investors, clerks, elevator men, conductors, [and] janitors," who were assured that CSC "is putting investments into bedrock American securities, particularly the electric-power industry."[206] Following complex borrowings and sales, IUI and CSC were connected by cross-ownership. IUI owned 28.8 percent of CSC, while CSC held 19.7 percent of IUI. Together they controlled Middle West Utilities (111 subsidiaries); People's Gas, Light and Coke Company (8 subsidiaries); Commonwealth Edison (6 subsidiaries); Public Service Company of Northern Illinois (1 subsidiary); and, through these four holding companies, Midland United Company (30 subsidiaries). The entire complex had assets valued at more than $2.5 billion.[207]

The crash of October 1929 had little immediate impact on Insull. "The stock market," he said, "hasn't made the slightest difference to our policies."[208] During the following year, he relieved employees who had purchased stock on margin by supplying collateral from his personal portfolio; financed the city of Chicago's rescue from municipal bankruptcy; and, in a contrarian demonstration of business confidence, caused his companies to commit almost $200 million to ambitious capital projects, including an $80 million Texas-to-Chicago gas pipeline.[209]

After the crash, however, stock floatations were no longer possible, and Insull's companies had to rely on debt financing. In 1930 IUI issued $60 million in debentures, CSC $30 million in serial gold notes, and Middle West $50 million in five-year serial gold notes. Hard times had not damaged Insull's credit, and buyers lined up to subscribe for the bonds, marketed by Halsey, Stuart, Insull's Chicago investment banker. In a widely publicized speech at the Chicago Stock Exchange in May 1930, Insull, buoyed by easy bond sales made without intervention of the New York banks, urged a war of financial liberation against Wall Street.[210] It was ill-advised bravado for one whose empire was now encumbered with debt. "These New York fellows were jealous of their prerogatives," said Charles Stuart (Harold Stuart's brother), "and if you wanted to get along you had to be deferential to them and keep your opinions to yourself. Mr. Insull wouldn't, and that made bad blood between them. Real bad blood."[211]

Insull meanwhile remained preoccupied with Cyrus Eaton, whose aggressive acquisition of stock in Insull's companies had prompted the pyramiding strategy. In 1930 Insull foolishly declined Eaton's offer to consolidate his holdings with Insull's under the latter's exclusive management. Years later, Eaton recalled, "I came to Chicago to discuss my holdings in the operating companies with Insull. I wanted to assure him that our large investments in these companies would not affect his control. I told him that Continental Shares [Eaton's investment trust] was organized as an investment company, not for quick turnover, and that we acquired his stocks as they offered the best opportunity in the utilities field."[212]

Eaton's assurances fell on deaf ears. Insull feared Eaton would dump his holdings on the open market. Importuned by Donald McLennan, an insurance salesman and "ardent aspirant after Cyrus Eaton's insurance account," Insull was finally persuaded to buy 160,000 shares of Commonwealth Edison, Peoples Gas, and Public Service from Eaton for $56 million at an average price of $350 per share, $40 above market. Most of the purchase price represented borrowed funds ($48 million from IUI and CSC, which had increased their floating indebtedness by that amount and in the process had borrowed close to $20 million from New York banks tied to the house of Morgan, and the balance in shares of IUI and CSC). The New York banks took as collateral the very voting stock in IUI and CSC on which Insull relied to control his empire. These banks now had the whip hand. By driving down the price of the pledged stock, they could demand additional shares as collateral and, if security were not forthcoming, remove Insull from office. Behind the New York banks lurked J. P. Morgan & Co., whose traders on the New York Stock Exchange were well versed in the art of market manipulation through short selling, tape advertising, wash and matched sales, planted rumors, and other methods of the bear raid.[213]

For the first six months of 1931, however, the earnings of the operating companies continued to grow, and the market value of their securities held by IUI and CSC increased by almost $90 million, erased previous losses, and approached book value.[214] Insull was for a time able to support the price of IUI and CSC stock by carefully timed wash sales on the open market but drew the line at selling his own stock short as New York drove prices down. "We've got a responsibility to our stockholders," he explained to Fred Scheel, his principal securities salesman. "We can't let them down."[215] But the choice was not Insull's to make. In September 1931, England went off the gold standard, and the U.S. stock market fell by almost one-third. The stocks of IUI, CSC, Commonwealth Edison, and Middle West Utilities lost $150 million and in the following weeks suffered further sharp declines. CSC common stock finally traded at $2.25 per share. As the market fell, IUI and CSC had to put up additional securities as collateral. "By mid-December the well had run dry; every nickel of the combined portfolios of the two investment trusts was in the hands of bank creditors."[216] The New York money men were now in control.

The new year brought further bad news. IUI, CSC, and Middle West suspended dividends. The New York banks "began to be very much concerned"; and, as Insull recalled in his *Memoirs*, "it looked as if my influence had practically ceased owing to the financial troubles" of these companies.[217] Instead of simply assuming outright control, the bankers appointed an up-and-coming accountant, Arthur Andersen, as their representative with "absolute jurisdiction [over] all disbursements."[218] Andersen's firm, Arthur Andersen & Co., also installed a new accounting system, using straight-line depreciation. "By a stroke of the pen Middle West became insolvent;

and when the system was extended backward, Middle West became retroactively insolvent, never having earned any money and thus but a worthless pile of paper that had been kept alive only by continuous impairment of capital, disguised by improper bookkeeping."[219] Andersen also uncovered questionable intercorporate loans, tainting Insull's once formidable hometown reputation. In April 1932 the New York banks, under Morgan's direction, refused to renew a $10 million note of Middle West Utilities, sending it, CSC, and IUI into receivership.[220] Because of his "vast knowledge of [its] corporate structure,"[221] Insull was one of three receivers of Middle West but served less than two months before being asked to resign.

Amid the collapse of Insull's holding companies, his principal operating companies—Commonwealth Edison, Peoples Gas, and Public Service— remained solvent and would continue so during the long years of the Depression.[222] Unfortunately for Insull, the companies had $60 million in notes falling due in July. Outside directors, under pressure from the New York banks, demanded Insull's resignation, contending the notes could not be refinanced with Insull still in charge. "It was quite apparent to me ...," Insull wrote, "that the banking forces that had compelled me to accept the receivership of the Middle West Utilities Company and that had forced upon me the system of control of the three large operating companies had ceased to find me of use to them and had decided that the time had come to throw me overboard."[223] Stanley Field, nephew of Marshall Field, who had financed Insull's entry into Chicago Edison forty years before, asked Insull to step down. He resigned on June 6, 1932, exiting chairmanships and presidencies of over sixty corporations.[224] At the time of his resignation, the public owned over $2.6 billion of common and preferred stock, bonds, and guaranteed obligations issued by his companies. Losses to investors occurred in forty-one Insull companies, some sustained immediately and others several years later. It was not until 1946, when reorganization had been completed and all claims adjusted, that total loss to the public holders of Insull securities could be finally determined at more than $600 million.[225]

New Deal; Trial; Acquittal

Campaigning for the presidency in 1932, Franklin Roosevelt attacked the evils unearthed in the FTC investigation and confirmed by collapse of Insull's holding company empire. Roosevelt ardently supported public power and numbered among his campaign managers and speechwriters Donald Richberg and Harold Ickes, each a progressive and long-standing Insull enemy bearing grudges from political wars in Chicago.[226] Roosevelt viewed Insull as the architect of the utility industry's concerted effort to defeat municipal ownership and, even more sinister, as the organizer of a power trust that was a menace to the whole country.[227] "We have allowed many utility companies," he said in a famous campaign speech in Portland, Oregon, "to capitalize themselves without regard to actual investment made in property, to pyramid capital through holding companies, and, without restraint of law, to sell billions of dollars of securities which the public have been falsely led into believing were properly supervised by the government itself." Roosevelt singled out the "great Insull monstrosity," citing arbitrary asset write-ups, inflation of vast capital accounts, milking of sound subsidiaries, and terrific overcharges—"private manipulation [that] had outsmarted the slow-moving power of government." The power industry, he said, "has grown into interstate business of vast proportions and requires the strict regulation and control of the Federal Government."[228]

Roosevelt was not alone in making political capital out of Insull's collapse. In Chicago John Swanson, the state's attorney for Cook County, mounted a widely publicized investigation, soon followed by announcement of a Department of Justice investigation. On September 30, 1932, Swanson published the names of members of an IUI stock-selling syndicate, including the mayor of Chicago, state and federal judges, lieutenant governors of Illinois (past and present), and Woodrow Wilson's former private secretary. A few days later the Cook County grand jury indicted Insull and his brother for embezzlement and grand larceny. Insull had meanwhile left the country, landing first in Paris and then, following his indictment, in Greece, which did not yet have an extradition treaty with the United States. As the *Literary Digest* reported, he was living in "voluntary exile, while investigators study the extradition laws and hunt for evidences of criminality in his transactions." In November 1932, one month after Insull's arrival in the country, the U.S. Senate ratified an extradition treaty with Greece. In June 1933 Insull was the subject of a federal indictment alleging use of the mails to defraud; several months later Insull, his brother, and his son were charged with criminally fraudulent conveyances to defeat claims under the National Bankruptcy Act. In March 1934 the Greek government, under mounting pressure from the United States, ordered Insull to leave the country.[229]

Insull chartered a small Greek steamship, the SS *Maiotis*, and cruised the eastern Mediterranean for several weeks, pondering his next move. While he was at sea, at the urgent request of the State Department, Congress passed a bill authorizing removal of U.S. citizens from any country where it exercised extraterritorial rights. A week later, when the *Maiotis* landed at Istanbul, the U.S. ambassador, under orders from the State Department, demanded that the Turkish government arrest Insull. Although Turkey had not yet ratified its extradition treaty with the United States, the Turkish police abducted Insull from his boat, detained him in Istanbul for several days, and after a hearing lasting less than twenty minutes delivered him to an official of the U.S. Embassy, who accompanied him on the long trip back to Chicago. "I looked upon the court proceedings as mere camouflage," wrote Insull. "I had been kidnapped by the Turkish government for the purpose of handing me over to the United States authorities."[230] After three days in the Cook County jail, Insull posted bond for the state and federal charges and issued a public statement that revealed the defense he would use at trial. "I made mistakes," he said, "but they were honest mistakes. They were errors in judgment and not dishonest manipulations."[231]

The first criminal trial, involving federal mail fraud charges against Insull, his son, Harold L. Stuart of Halsey, Stuart, and fourteen codefendants associated with Insull in managing CSC, opened on October 2, 1934. Reading from a fifty-page, twenty-five-count indictment, the district attorney called the case a "simple conspiracy to swindle, cheat, and defraud the public" and promised to prove that "each defendant had some part to play in this gigantic scheme whereby thousands of people were induced to invest millions of dollars in the stock of the company by means of false representation."[232]

The case was anything but simple. Government evidence rested on the testimony of 200 witnesses and 2,500 documentary exhibits collected in huge specially built bookcases along the walls of the courtroom—the paper trail supporting the government's claim that investors lost $100 million in nationwide stock sales to raise new money for Insull's financial pyramid. Among the small businessmen and unemployed workers listening in the jury box, none was an Insull investor.[233]

The government case rested largely in the hands of Leslie Salter, special assistant to the attorney general of the United States and a rising star who had cut his teeth prosecuting prohibition violators in New York. Salter's mind was said to be "as sharp as a rapier and as devastating as an ax."[234] In numbing detail, Salter recounted a complex chain of events set in motion by Insull's decision to reorganize Middle West Utilities, advance the price of its stock, and transfer a controlling block of shares to CSC in 1929, which, he told the jury, thereafter sold shares of its common and preferred stock nationwide to unsuspecting small investors at rigged prices as the value of the stock in its portfolio depreciated sharply. In simplest terms, the promoters of CSC stood accused of "selling the public shares in an enormous dead horse."[235]

Insull's counsel, Floyd Thompson, defended Insull—still honored as a hometown boy made good—by putting his entire life on trial. When Insull took the stand as a witness in his own defense, he recounted the remarkable history of his Chicago years, a tale of entrepreneurial pluck and technological progress that transformed an entire region. A former state's attorney, representing one of the codefendants, said of Insull: "This old man, now on the rim of his dying day, with the courage of a lion, fought for the only thing he had left—his honor and his good name."[236] As Insull and the other defendants relived for the jury careers of undeniable business accomplishment, "the tragic stories told by a score of victims … receded into the background."[237] On November 24, 1934, after deliberating for no more than two hours, the jury acquitted all defendants of all charges.[238] The prosecution had no better luck in later state and federal trials. In March 1935 Insull and his brother were acquitted in Illinois state court of embezzling from Middle West. Several months later a federal court granted a directed verdict of not guilty in favor of Insull and Harold Stuart, who had been accused of making illegal asset transfers in contemplation of bankruptcy.[239] Although his reputation was irreversibly tarnished, Insull had salvaged a legal reckoning of innocence from the wreckage.

Insull's miraculous legal escape did not deflect the course of receivership and bankruptcy proceedings affecting Middle West Utilities, reorganized into Middle West Corporation, the "groggy skeleton of a Midwest power empire which still included 44 active subsidiaries giving electricity, gas, ice to 2,100 communities in 15 Midwest states and Ontario."[240] Middle West's creditors and stockholders fought over the corporate remains for more than three years in federal court in Chicago. The banks, with secured loans, got the lion's share; 600,000 shareholders received pennies on the dollar.[241] Insull's operating companies were a different matter. None went into receivership or bankruptcy, and security holders lost less than 1 percent of their investment.[242] The total loss to the public holders of Insull securities, although difficult to quantify, was less than 25 percent.[243]

Legislative Response

"Notwithstanding the great calamity that overtook me ...," Insull wrote in his *Memoirs*, "I feel that what I have been able to contribute to the permanent success of the electric light and power industry ... has helped to create an amount of wealth that far exceeds the losses in connection with the financial debacle of some of my institutions."[244] Others did not agree. In the legislative debates that preceded the Securities Act of 1933, Representative Chapman of Kentucky observed that "such a remedial measure would have saved $25,000,000,000 to the American people. ... If it had been on the statute books, it would have been the salvation of thousands of people who today shudder at the mention of Insull's name."[245] As President Roosevelt took office in 1933, it was clear the political and economic tides had turned. The laissez-faire policies of the previous decade had given way to New Deal regulatory reform, propelled in part by collapse of the Insull empire.

In July 1934 Roosevelt convened a National Power Policy Committee, chaired by Insull's old political enemy, Harold Ickes, now secretary of the interior, to address electric power supply. The committee's report, released early in 1935, noted that thirteen holding companies controlled three-quarters of the privately owned electric utility industry and that the three largest groups—United Corporation, Electric Bond & Share, and the Insull Group—controlled 40 percent by themselves. Calling this concentration of economic power "a private form of socialism inimical to the functioning of democratic institutions," the report recommended "the practical elimination ... of the holding company where it serves no demonstrably useful and necessary purpose."[246] Congressional hearings also made the case for holding company regulation.[247]

The resulting legislation, the Public Utility Holding Company Act of 1935, also known as the Wheeler-Rayburn Act, aimed at regulating an industry that had operated largely without restraint and became a centerpiece of the Second New Deal. It required all interstate public holding companies to register with the Securities and Exchange Commission; prohibited intercompany loans; and regulated dividends, securities issuances, asset sales, as well as service, sales, and construction contracts. Most importantly, as originally framed, the Wheeler-Rayburn Act contained a "death sentence" clause, stating that the utility industry must, within five years, voluntarily terminate utility holding companies that had no useful function and authorizing the SEC thereafter to dissolve every holding company lacking an economic reason for its existence. The public utility lobby rose in fierce opposition.[248] "Utility executives regarded the Wheeler-Rayburn bill as a declaration of war," wrote historian Michael Parrish. "Armed with a war chest of millions of dollars, their public relations firms bombarded Congress and the public with pamphlets, letters, and advertisements designed to discredit the legislation."[249]

Unmoved by the industry's campaign, Roosevelt said that except "where it is absolutely necessary to the continued functioning of a geographically integrated operating utility system, the holding companies must go."[250] There followed months of testimony before the Rayburn Committee, orchestrated by Wendell Willkie, president of Commonwealth and Southern Corporation. The "death sentence" clause remained a sticking point. A legislative impasse, fueled by intense utility lobbying efforts, continued until Senator Hugo Black of Alabama compelled utility executives to appear before a special committee on lobbying and subpoenaed their records to expose fraudulent efforts to influence Congress. Black's investigation saved the day, and the Wheeler-Rayburn bill, slightly modified, passed into law as the Public Utility Holding Company Act of 1935.[251]

The pivotal provision of the act, Section 11(b)(1), required the SEC to limit each utility holding company "to a single integrated public utility system."[252] Another section sought to simplify holding company structures and limit use of preferred stock to dilute voting rights.[253] Holding companies had to divest thousands of gas and electric operating companies as a result.[254] Between 1938 and 1955, when the SEC's divestment work was complete, over 200 holding companies controlling more than 900 electric and gas utilities and over 1,000 nonutility companies were reduced to 25 holding companies with under 200 electric and gas subsidiaries and 150 nonutility subsidiaries.[255] "The public utility holding company as a device of financial legerdemain," wrote one industry observer, "was to pass from the scene."[256]

While devoting intense attention to holding companies, Congress also passed the Federal Power Act of 1935, extending regulation to "transmission of electric energy in interstate commerce and to the sale of electric energy at wholesale in interstate commerce."[257] Within six months of passage of the act, as a condition of conducting interstate business, all jurisdictional companies had to get an order from the Federal Power Commission,[258] which was empowered to set "just and reasonable" rates by determining the "fair value" of a utility's property, setting the proper depreciation rate, and prescribing a system of accounts.[259] Thus did Congress close the regulatory gap that had permitted holding companies like Insull's to operate virtually free of government oversight.

Coda

Insull created the organizational and technical foundations of the nation's electric utility industry, still largely in place despite decades of intervening change. He was an indefatigable proponent of centralized electric supply, an astute analyst of utility economics, a pioneer in the mass production of power, a first mover in interregional integration of the nation's electric power supply, and a devout believer in the gospel of consumption that set in motion "a self-perpetuating cycle of rising use and declining rates that eventually enveloped an urban society in a ubiquitous world of energy."[260]

Insull had an unquenchable thirst for expansion and financial adventure, driven by a singular need to assert control in the face of endemic political, economic, and business pressures. For many years he was able to neutralize politicians and outflank business rivals. "One of his most deep-rooted traits was that he was absolutely unable, save on an abstract and purely intellectual level, to imagine the possibility of his own failure."[261] The holding company became the institutional expression of Insull's impulse to control but proved a trap when a corporate raider threatened Insull's personal security and led him into the bankers' den. Those who remember Insull, it is said, remember the scandalous endgame much more than his genius, his revolutionary innovations, or his acquittal.[262] It is fairer to say that those who can, in the fullness of time, look beyond Insull's demise will find him to be an extraordinary, if flawed, embodiment of technocratic business genius, very much in the American grain.

2 David Lilienthal and the Era of Public Power

Origins

The imminent collapse of Insull's holding company empire in April 1932 galvanized Roosevelt's presidential campaign. On learning the sensational news that Insull's utility business was headed for bankruptcy, Roosevelt, en route by train to deliver a Jefferson Day speech in St. Paul, Minnesota, summoned Raymond Moley, his principal speechwriter, to board the train in Detroit. Between Detroit and St. Paul, Moley redrafted the speech. As revised, it attacked holding company overreach and threatened distribution of power from government-owned hydroelectric stations "if ... private initiative and private capital" were unwilling to do so "for a reasonable and fair return."[1] Moley's additions framed a key issue of the 1932 election. Roosevelt was mounting an all-out attack on the privately owned electric utility industry, with the prospect of direct government intervention in the electricity marketplace as a potent threat to recalcitrant and still entrenched holding companies.

In September in Portland, Oregon, Roosevelt again addressed the power problem, calling for government regulation of holding companies and, conditionally, public ownership of power facilities. "Where a community ... is not satisfied with the service rendered or the rates charged by the private utility," he said, "it has the undeniable right ... to set up ... its own governmentally owned and operated service." He characterized this right as "a birch rod in the cupboard"[2] and saw water power as an inviting case for public ownership of generation and distribution.[3] Four great government hydroelectric power projects—the St. Lawrence River, Muscle Shoals on the Tennessee River in Alabama, Boulder Dam, and the Columbia River—could each serve, Roosevelt said, as "a national yardstick to prevent extortion against the public and to encourage the wider use of ... electric power."[4] Roosevelt's Portland speech reflected his long-standing interest in public power as a means of forcing industry change. Government competition with private-sector monopoly, he thought, would drive down rates and make electric power available to underserved communities.

Roosevelt's yardstick metaphor was not new. In 1929, while governor of New York, he had published an article urging state development of water power at those same sites "as a yardstick with which to measure the cost of producing and transmitting electricity."[5] Weeks later, in his annual speech to the New York legislature, he proposed a state power agency that would finance and retain ownership of "any system of statewide transmission of electricity made necessary by the new power development."[6] Where the state power agency relied on private companies to distribute power, they would do so at rates fixed by contract with the power agency, not the ineffective Public Service Commission.[7]

The New York Power Authority, formed in 1930 to realize Roosevelt's goal by building its own transmission lines, if necessary, to deliver power from hydroelectric facilities on the St. Lawrence River, could not overcome the fierce resistance of private utilities, Republican legislators, and the Hoover administration. When Roosevelt's term as governor expired, Niagara-Hudson (the dominant local utility) remained firmly in control. Roosevelt drew on his frustrating defeat at the hands of the New York investor-owned utility business and its protectors to relaunch his public power program at the national level. The best guide to his thinking, before the 1932 campaign, can be found in the policies of those he appointed to the New York Power Authority, including Morris L. Cooke and Leland Olds, bitter opponents of private utility interests. Cooke served as first head of the Rural Electrification Administration and Olds as chair of the Federal Power Commission during the New Deal years.[8]

Of the four sites mentioned in Roosevelt's Portland speech, the nitrate plants and Wilson Dam at Muscle Shoals, Alabama—relics of World War I military preparedness—were ground zero in the struggle for public power. "Politically," wrote the *New York Times*, "Muscle Shoals long ago became a symbol ... [of the] extreme progressives. ... Their end is not the best utilization of a war heritage, but government ownership of electric utilities generally. In their hands, Muscle Shoals is only a fulcrum, the 'Power Trust' a lever."[9] Although the *Times'* insight was penetrating, the history of Muscle

Shoals also revealed a legacy of many failed attempts to turn its power and fertilizer potential to public use. Muscle Shoals had consistently frustrated the plans of Senator George W. Norris of Nebraska, its principal sponsor, and other Progressives.

Public development of Muscle Shoals' water power was a persistent but ever-receding mirage. It first surfaced in 1916 as a defense measure when the government wanted hydroelectric power at Wilson Dam for wartime nitrate manufacture.[10] The war ended before completion of the intended nitrate plants or Wilson Dam, stranding a government investment of more than $75 million.[11] Between 1918 and 1933 disposition of Muscle Shoals commanded more attention in committees and on the floor of Congress than any other single issue.[12] Encouraged by successive Republican administrations, private interests—including Henry Ford, American Cyanamid, and Alabama Power Company—made repeated attempts to acquire Muscle Shoals and its vast hydroelectric power potential. None of the offers came near to making the government whole. Each was thwarted by Senator Norris, a passionate champion of multipurpose river valley development for whom private ownership was anathema.

Equally, Norris's many proposals for public ownership of Muscle Shoals found no success in the laissez-faire postwar years. One was vetoed by President Coolidge, another by President Hoover; but the last, following Roosevelt's overwhelming victory in the 1932 election, became the core of signature New Deal legislation, the Tennessee Valley Authority Act.[13] TVA was the consummation of Norris's long and dogged pursuit of public power and his guardianship of Muscle Shoals against the predatory plans of schemers such as Henry Ford. In January 1933, on a preinauguration visit to Muscle Shoals, Norris and the president-elect watched the currents of the Tennessee River swirl through the floodgates of Wilson Dam. Over the roar of the spillways Roosevelt shouted to Norris how huge an operation it was and how much energy was being wasted. "This should be a happy day for you, George," said Roosevelt. "It is, Mr. President," Norris replied. "I see my dreams come true."[14]

Norris's dreams embraced coordinated development of the entire Tennessee River system, flowing 1,200 miles from the Appalachians to the Ohio River, touching seven states, and covering a watershed of 40,000 square miles, now home to devastated forests, dirt-poor subsistence farmers, and worn-out farms almost universally without electric power. Roosevelt's dreams, shaped by the great forester and conservationist, Gifford Pinchot, envisioned public development of the valley's hydropower and a union of agriculture, forestry, and flood prevention to create "a machine-driven Arcadia in the countryside."[15] Roosevelt's soaring rhetoric about regional development, however inspirational, had little effect on passage of the Tennessee Valley Authority Act, which was a broader version of Norris's ultimate Muscle Shoals bill.[16]

In his postinauguration message to Congress, Roosevelt urged "national planning for a complete river watershed involving many States and the future lives and welfare of millions."[17] On March 9, 1933, the first day of the first session of the Seventy-Third Congress, Norris introduced a joint resolution calling for development of the Tennessee Valley. Among other things, Norris's bill contemplated that the Authority would construct, lease, and buy transmission lines without regard to existing lines, a measure opposed by private utility interests.[18]

The fight over Norris's bill had nothing to do with planning; it centered, instead, on the prospect that the federal government would enter the power business in competition with investor-owned utilities. The president of Georgia Power told the House committee: "I do not think we need additional lines, and no power is needed to serve that territory generally." Also opposed was Wendell L. Willkie, president of Commonwealth and Southern, the dominant utility holding company in the valley, who warned that "if this bill passes, this $400,000,000 worth of securities [stocks and bonds of his company] will be eventually destroyed."[19] Willkie's dire prediction could not dislodge the bill's authorization of transmission lines, which, as provided in the final version, the Tennessee Valley Authority could construct, lease, or buy as its needs dictated.[20] On May 18, 1933, Roosevelt signed into law the Tennessee Valley Authority Act.[21] After twelve years as a voice in the wilderness, Senator Norris had at last triumphed.

The act envisaged development on a grand scale, encompassing conservation, flood control, navigation, fertilizer production and distribution, agriculture, power, and the first conscious national effort at regional planning. The preamble of the act, a statement of objectives, omits any mention of hydroelectric power, discreetly subsumed under "other purposes." To realize its broad goals, the act established TVA as a government corporation with a national charter but regional autonomy, owned by the United States as sole stockholder and run by three directors with exceedingly broad discretionary powers, appointed by the president with senatorial approval for overlapping nine-year terms. They were to administer TVA free of civil service laws and unconnected with regular federal departments. The corporation—clothed with the power of government but possessed of the flexibility and initiative of a private enterprise—was empowered to sell surplus electric power, giving preference to municipal and consumers' cooperative power systems over private utilities. It could also prescribe the retail rates at which its power would be sold to the consumer by intermediate public or private agencies. To establish a yardstick against which to measure private utility rates, the corporation was required to allocate joint costs.

Although it embodied features long sought by Progressives, TVA was at its inception an unstructured, multipurpose government program awaiting further expression of Roosevelt's intentions, notably hard to divine given the president's famous elliptical style. A few days before the original TVA bill was sent to Congress, Senator Norris asked the president, "What are you going to say when they ask you the political philosophy behind TVA?" Roosevelt replied, "I'll tell them it's neither fish nor fowl, but whatever it is, it will taste awfully good to the people of Tennessee Valley."[22]

The Arriviste

Arthur Morgan, chosen by Roosevelt as a director and first chair of TVA, was a brilliant, experienced civil engineer, former college president, and technical manager, famous for building flood control dams and creating a unique conservancy district in Ohio. He was also a moralistic social visionary, who saw TVA as a "project for bringing industrial and social order out of the haphazard growth that had characterized the national life."[23] Inspired by Edward Bellamy,[24] the late nineteenth-century utopian socialist, he disdained the "accumulation of small modifications in existing customs" in favor of designing "a radically new way of life."[25] Flood control, dam building, finances, and conservation were Morgan's nominal province at TVA. But he was also the standard bearer for ardent reformers, such as Rexford Tugwell, who told him TVA was a "deliberate turning toward the future, a commitment to an ideal" whose "success can depopulate cities, destroy a thousand entrenched privileges, invalidate a whole tradition of single-hearted self-interest."[26] Morgan's holistic philosophy was to clash with that of the man he picked to run TVA's power portfolio.

In May 1933 David E. Lilienthal, then a thirty-three-year-old commissioner of the Wisconsin Public Service Commission, had become a rumored

choice for the power directorship at TVA. From a modest background Lilienthal had risen to prominence by sheer force of ambition and intelligence.
The oldest son of Jewish immigrants, he had grown up in small-town Indiana; attended DePauw University, where he earned a Phi Beta Kappa key
and notice as a light heavyweight boxer; and then moved on to Harvard
Law School, graduating in 1923. In a candid self-appraisal, confided years
later to his journal, Lilienthal described himself as "resourceful; ingenious,
particularly in discussion and in strategy development ... impatient and
critical ... not a natural mixer ... carried along so far by an intense and
absorbing desire for achievement."[27] Like Sam Insull, Lilienthal was driven
by ambition and desperately eager to seize the main chance.

Acting on a recommendation from Justice Brandeis and with the support
of the president, Morgan sent an aide to Madison to evaluate Lilienthal,
who was found to be "quickminded and vigorous" but harboring "overweening personal ambitions." Undiscouraged by the report, Morgan met
with Lilienthal in Chicago, evidently liked what he saw, offered him the
power slot at TVA, and wired his approval to Washington. Lilienthal's nomination was announced on June 3, 1933, and confirmed later that month.[28]
It was a portentous appointment, strongly endorsed by Lilienthal's mentor,
Harvard Law School Professor Felix Frankfurter, who wrote the president:
"Not often does one get such a combination of training, courage, understanding, and youthful ardor."[29]

A dedicated advocate of public power, Lilienthal had good reason to dis-
trust the investor-owned utility business. Only ten years out of Harvard
Law School, he had successfully cultivated the patronage of powerful players in the Progressive movement including A. A. Berle, Donald Richberg,
Felix Frankfurter, Louis Brandeis, and Robert La Follette, who valued his
hard work, grasp of public utility law,[30] commitment to public power, and
tough-minded advocacy. With a strong recommendation from Frankfurter,
Lilienthal joined Donald Richberg's labor law firm in Chicago, then left a
few years later to concentrate on public utility law[31] and became a prolific
pamphleteer. Between 1923 and 1931 Lilienthal published more than thirty
works, including a dozen law review articles and ten pieces in journals such
as *The Nation*.[32]

Now widely known in liberal circles, he made his next career move
when Robert La Follette Jr. became governor of Wisconsin in 1930 on a Progressive platform, including, as a central plank, "public utility regulation

... unhampered by restrictions of monopoly and unretarded by exorbitant power and light rates."[33] In 1931 La Follette appointed Lilienthal to a two-year term on the state Railroad Commission with a mandate to develop a new utility law. Within days the state legislature debated a bill granting broad powers to the Railroad Commission, now renamed the Public Service Commission, to regulate relationships between local utilities and out-of-state holding companies (as suggested by Lilienthal in an article published in the *Columbia Law Review*). Governor La Follette signed the bill on June 6, 1931.

Not more than a week later the newly robust PSC under Lilienthal's leadership ordered a comprehensive investigation of Wisconsin Power & Light (an Insull system operating company), one of over 400 cases opened that year. The PSC later imposed widespread utility rate reduction assessments, including a bright-line rate reduction case against Wisconsin Telephone Company on the novel theory that it should not charge more "than the services rendered by it are reasonably worth"[34]—that is, invoking value of service as a substitute for reasonable return on the fair value of property used and useful, the traditional rate base standard. In his short tenure on the PSC, Lilienthal attracted praise, notoriety, and bitter opposition. One observer thought his accomplishments were "offset by the friction and animosity he created in the relations between the utilities and the Commission."[35] When La Follette failed to get his party's nomination in 1932, Lilienthal's future on the PSC was seriously at risk. Wisconsin Telephone Company had mounted a campaign to deny him reconfirmation; other utility enemies lay in wait. The TVA appointment afforded a convenient exit and placed Lilienthal on the national stage.

The first meeting of the three-person TVA board took place on June 16, 1933, before Lilienthal's confirmation, at the Willard Hotel in Washington. In addition to A. E. Morgan and Lilienthal, the board included Harcourt Morgan (no relation to A. E. Morgan), former president of the University of Tennessee and an advocate of farming interests. As Lilienthal later recalled, the meeting was a portent of the managerial schism that was to plague TVA for the better part of a decade:

Dr. Arthur Morgan had on his lap a great stack of letters and perhaps memoranda, but mostly correspondence directed to him. ... Most of these letters inquired about employment opportunities, or key specific matters, one completely unrelated to the other. After several hours of this, of going through this stack of disparate and unrelated subjects ... I caught Dr. Harcourt Morgan's eye and by common consent we got up. ... We went over to one of the great tall windows at the Willard Hotel and had what was probably a decisive conversation of very few words but with a great deal of meaning. ... Harcourt Morgan was completely caught off base with this way of beginning a big enterprise, without ... any proposals for organization, without any ideas about staffing or where we go from here, or where we have our offices, or who our general manager should be, as I was. ... Harcourt Morgan ... said in effect, "What do you make of this fellow? We can't go on like this."[36]

Among the correspondence received by A. E. Morgan was a letter from Wendell Willkie, president of Commonwealth & Southern, a billion-dollar multistate public utility holding company with major operating subsidiaries in the Tennessee Valley. "It occurs to me," Willkie wrote, "that your new undertaking presents to both of us problems of mutual interest, the proper solution of which, for the good of all concerned, will require our early and continued cooperative efforts."[37] Willkie's congressional testimony seeking to limit the competitive impact of TVA's power program was fresh in Lilienthal's mind, and he had no desire to engage in conciliatory negotiations with an arch enemy. "It is the worst kind of strategy," he wrote in a memo to the board, "to base one's policy ... upon a premise contrary to all past experience."[38] A. E. Morgan wished to cooperate with private utilities and seemed well disposed to a compromise. As Lilienthal recorded dryly in his journal, Willkie's letter signaled a profound difference of opinion between Lilienthal and A. E. Morgan "as to what attitude the board should take toward the private utilities" and "will require a good deal of working out."[39] That difference of opinion, for a time exploited by Willkie, was never worked out, and as events unfolded, A. E. Morgan found himself increasingly isolated from both his fellow directors.

A Strategy Unfolds

A. E. Morgan urged a cooperative power policy. He was prepared to divide markets with Commonwealth & Southern to avoid building duplicate power lines. He assured Willkie TVA would "endeavor to work out some harmonious arrangement." Lilienthal was passionately opposed to territorial restrictions and feared that A. E. Morgan, cleverly manipulated by Willkie, would compromise TVA's program at the very outset. The roiling dispute could not be contained within the executive offices of

TVA. A. E. Morgan and Lilienthal met with the president on August 19, 1933. Roosevelt, characteristically, declined to take sides and told the parties to work out a policy they could both live with.[40] The president was, at bottom, far from a radical on the power question. Although favoring municipally owned local systems and public development of hydropower, he believed the utility industry should remain a private enterprise.[41] For the moment he remained agnostic about the best approach to Commonwealth & Southern.

TVA needed a market for the power produced at Wilson Dam and the power to be generated by the Norris Dam near Knoxville. To create a market TVA had to determine the cost of producing power, the rates to be charged, and the practical application of the yardstick. As a first step, just days after Morgan's and Lilienthal's meeting with the president, TVA announced a power policy, largely authored by Lilienthal. The policy asserted, as a core principle, that the business of generating and distributing electric power is a public business and that the interest of the public in the widest possible use of power is superior to any private interest. It further stated that the right of the community to own and operate its own electric plant is undeniable and may take the form of acquiring an existing plant or setting up a competing plant, notwithstanding the adverse economic effect on a privately owned utility. Except for a temporary period pending completion of the Norris Dam, TVA reserved the right to extend its operations into wider areas as the public interest required. Finally, the policy promised TVA would supply a yardstick cost comparison as an incentive to both public and private managers.[42] In one stroke Lilienthal appeared to have undercut A. E. Morgan while declaring war on Commonwealth & Southern. The policy, he wrote, "represents an attempt to regulate public utilities not by quasi-judicial commissions, but by competition. The [Tennessee Valley Authority Act] definitely puts the Federal Government into the business of rendering electric service."[43]

Lilienthal lost no time in acting on TVA's policy declaration. In the first of two press releases, he announced a TVA retail electricity price for the "typical general consumer" of 2 cents per kilowatt-hour at a time when the national average was 5.5 cents and customers of Commonwealth & Southern operating utilities were paying between 4.6 and 5.8 cents. The second press release stated: "All costs of service are included, and ... provision has been made for ... taxes and interest ... to make fair comparison with privately operated utilities for 'yardstick purposes.'"[44] Lilienthal gave concrete expression to President Roosevelt's long-standing expectation that cheap electricity would benefit "the people ... as a whole and particularly [its] domestic and rural customers."[45]

Lilienthal's aggressive pricing strategy was a high-stakes bet—not unlike one taken by Sam Insull in an earlier era—that lower rates would call forth a surge of demand. "Increase in use is essential to bring down unit costs," he wrote at the time. "And yet to increase the use, the rates to the consumers must be decreased."[46] To spread the message Lilienthal made speeches at local Rotary Clubs in Knoxville, Chattanooga, Nashville, and Memphis, promising a major increase in power use throughout the region and drastic rate reductions.[47] Commonwealth & Southern, like other private utilities, reversed Lilienthal's business logic: it was willing to cut power rates only after an increase in demand had reduced costs and dismissed low TVA rates as unfair competition made possible by federal subsidies.[48]

Although disinclined to negotiate with Willkie, Lilienthal knew some sort of settlement with Commonwealth & Southern was unavoidable. Alabama Power Corporation, a Commonwealth & Southern operating company, was buying electricity produced by Wilson Dam under a War Department contract that expired on January 1, 1934. Unless the contract was extended, TVA would lose a critical source of income and had only just begun to identify other customers, mostly small municipalities. Notwithstanding its bold policy declaration, TVA needed to cut a deal. On October 4, 1933, Lilienthal and Willkie met in the gloomy precincts of the Cosmos Club in Washington. As Lilienthal later recalled, Willkie opened with a sweeping offer: "I will take all your power off your hands, and that will give you about one-half million dollars' revenue and make you independent of Congress." Cleverly aimed at TVA's fiscal vulnerability, Willkie's proposal "didn't evoke any enthusiasm on my part," Lilienthal remembered.[49]

Willkie knew that TVA had authorized a transmission line from Wilson to Norris (a new town under construction) and that a growing number of cities were interested in TVA power. As Lilienthal later recorded in his *Journal*, "[Willkie] was determined to prevent ... the building of transmission lines by the TVA. ... If he could be successful in having power sold at the switchboard, it would be sold only to his companies. ... Accordingly, his next proposal after I explained the need for a market was to offer to sell the three properties near Muscle Shoals in the towns of Florence, Sheffield, and Tuscumbia, where the franchises had expired and which would not require transmission of any substantial amount."[50] Willkie was engaged in a risky poker game. "However," Lilienthal recalled, "there was never any time when there was the least danger that I would avoid a fight by accepting a proposal that would ... have put an end to TVA before it was really started."[51]

Before his next meeting with Willkie, Lilienthal's negotiating leverage improved. TVA had entered into its first power contract with the city of Tupelo, Mississippi, including provisions allowing it to control Tupelo's retail rates. Lilienthal made it plain to Willkie that "we were under contractual obligations to get power to Tupelo by February, 1934, and we would get it there over his lines or we would build a line."[52] Tupelo owned a public distribution system and could negotiate immediately with TVA. It could also serve as a yardstick area, allowing TVA's power program to go forward without Willkie's participation. Willkie feared TVA would build a transmission line from Muscle Shoals to Norris Dam through the heart of Commonwealth & Southern's market. The Tupelo agreement therefore posed a real threat.[53]

On December 12, 1933, shortly before the contract expiration deadline, Lilienthal and Willkie met. The singular bone of contention was the territory TVA would receive as a yardstick. Lilienthal proposed that TVA be granted properties in certain counties in Alabama, Mississippi, and Tennessee and the transmission lines to reach them. Willkie refused to go beyond his offer to sell three distribution systems in northern Alabama. Encouraged by presidential support, Lilienthal demanded that Commonwealth & Southern "sell us their properties in certain counties in Alabama and Mississippi." He said that "we would buy everything in those counties, including the distribution systems in Mississippi, and get legislation in some way to provide for the purchase in Alabama. This was contingent upon my seeing the President, which I did that afternoon."[54]

Willkie knew he risked losing part of his market because several towns, using low-cost loans and grants from the Public Works Administration, had already decided to build their own distribution systems to deliver TVA power. On January 4, 1934, he and Lilienthal entered into a formal contract memorializing their hard-fought agreement. Commonwealth & Southern continued its option to purchase wholesale power from Wilson Dam, agreed to sell TVA specific systems in northeastern Mississippi, granted options on properties in northern Alabama and eastern Tennessee, and agreed to make a domestic rate reduction. Most important, Commonwealth & Southern agreed it would not sell electricity within the ceded area, and TVA reciprocally agreed—notwithstanding Lilienthal's stated objection to territorial limitations—that it would not further penetrate the private companies' markets. The contract was to continue for five years or until the Norris Dam began producing power, whichever came first.[55]

Willkie had assumed the Norris Dam could not be completed for another six years (by which time, he thought, electoral politics might well have reversed TVA's aggressive power policy). In fact the dam was finished in half that time. Its rapid completion accelerated TVA's construction, through the heart of Commonwealth & Southern's Tennessee market, of the long transmission line that would tie the Wilson and Norris Dams together, making a power system out of two otherwise isolated dams and providing transmission entry into markets served by Tennessee Electric Power Company (TEPCO), a Commonwealth & Southern operating company. Matters were not working out as Willkie had planned. Commonwealth & Southern could not, as he had hoped, confine TVA's power output to a small direct market area while purchasing its surplus power for resale.

Willkie therefore found reasons to revisit the January 4 contract. Alabama Power Company refused to sell its distribution systems to municipalities except for cash at a time when raising cash was nearly impossible. Lilienthal complained to Willkie and threatened to have the Public Works Administration finance new distribution systems. TVA tried to resolve the problem by buying the distribution systems at a lower negotiated price and reselling them to the municipalities. When TVA made a tender for the properties, however, Chemical Bank & Trust Company refused to relinquish its lien without an appraisal or indemnity—a clear violation of the January 4 contract in which Willkie had promised to "secure any necessary waiver of liens or encumbrances." Finally, in June, Willkie made clear TEPCO would not sell its properties near the Norris Dam as provided in the January 4 contract. Willkie insisted TVA should instead use its power of condemnation, a course of action Lilienthal regarded as a trap, prone to litigation and delay.[56] Willkie had proved to be a formidable adversary, prepared at every step to protect his corporate interests against government competition.

Nonetheless TVA "signaled imminent death by reduced electricity rates for Commonwealth & Southern's Tennessee, Mississippi and Alabama operations."[57] In a public statement issued on November 20, 1934, Willkie took the offensive, arguing TVA had an unfair retail price advantage over his company through Public Works Administration grants, an unrealistically low book value for Wilson Dam, and concessional tax rates. If private utility companies received as much government subsidy as TVA, he argued, they could charge lower rates than those of TVA. Others in the private sector agreed. Testifying before Congress in 1935, the executive secretary of the National Coal Association said, "We are willing to be put out of business if it can be done in a plain straightforward business-like manner, but we do object to our government putting us out of business."[58]

Addressing the Rotary Club of Birmingham weeks later, Lilienthal charged Wall Street with "a desire to retain control of the country and to continue the sending of a stream of money from other sections of the country to its vaults."[59] Vivid rhetoric could not conceal the fact that TVA's market area comprised only a few towns in Mississippi and small parts of Alabama unaffected by failure of the January 4 contract—too small a territory in which to establish a viable yardstick.[60]

War in the Courts

Investor-owned utilities viewed TVA with fear and loathing, hoped to strangle the infant in its crib, and took to the courts with a vengeance. Litigation came, surprisingly, in the form of a derivative suit. In September 1934 George Ashwander and thirteen other preferred stockholders of Alabama Power Company sued to enjoin performance of the January 4 contract.[61] The suit mounted a broad constitutional challenge to the TVA program, alleging it would open "every essential industry and service to direct and permanent government competition."[62] Lilienthal mobilized a muscular response. He built a strong in-house legal department to fight the suit, engaged nationally known litigators, and insisted on TVA's right to represent itself in the courts rather than rely on the Department of Justice.[63] Nonetheless *Ashwander* scored a damaging blow.

A federal district court ruled that TVA, acting as a proprietary utility, was unconstitutionally engaged in the general business of producing and selling electric power as its primary function in illegal competition with Alabama

Power Company. The court granted the injunction, annulled the January 4 contract, and also enjoined the Public Works Administration from making loans to municipalities for use of electricity generated by TVA. Lilienthal's aggressive power policy, now thwarted by judicial decree, had yielded little after two years. Following the injunction, power revenues plummeted.[64] TVA's very existence was at risk, and it lodged an immediate appeal. Willkie's role in orchestrating the suit was unclear. In a telegram to Presidential Secretary Steve Early, he vehemently denied any connection with the case: "I say to you that any such statement made to you by anybody is an absolute and unqualified falsehood and readily demonstrable as such."[65] Willkie nonetheless served on the board of directors of the Edison Electric Institute, which had contributed $150,000 to finance the litigation.[66]

TVA's business was in disarray; its future hung on the outcome of the *Ashwander* suit. In July 1935, a federal court of appeals overturned the district court's injunction, setting the stage for review by the Supreme Court,[67] then heavily influenced by four conservative justices.[68] Lilienthal feared the worst. In an 8–1 opinion, to his vast relief, the court upheld TVA's right to make and enforce the January 4 contract. Chief Justice Hughes invoked the war power, commerce power, and power to dispose of and make rules and regulations respecting property belonging to the United States as authority for TVA's sale of surplus electrical energy under the January 4 contract. But he expressly limited his opinion, noting that

The question here is simply as to the acquisition of the transmission lines as a facility for the disposal of that energy. ... As we have said, these transmission lines lead directly from the dam, which has been lawfully constructed, and the question of the constitutional right of the Government to acquire or operate local or urban distribution systems is not involved. We express no opinion as to the validity of such an effort, as to the status of any other dam or power development in the Tennessee Valley, whether connected with or apart from the Wilson Dam, or as to the validity of the Tennessee Valley Authority Act.[69]

Lilienthal was ecstatic. "I had completely resigned myself to a bad decision," he wrote in his journal, "only holding out that we would have some crumb of comfort in that unlike AAA and NRA we would not be swept completely out to sea, bag and baggage. To have a decision by an undivided [sic] Court, sustaining every one of our contentions and giving us a clear road ahead is just too much—too much to comprehend in such a short time."[70]

But Lilienthal wisely tempered his enthusiasm: "[W]e must be very careful not to be, at least publicly, exultant and not to ride the horse too hard. You can win a lawsuit and lose a war just as you can lose a lawsuit and win the war, and our problem ahead is by no means solved simply because we had the first beaten down so unexpectedly and completely."[71] Neither the utility companies nor the administration in Washington was satisfied with the narrow ruling. The utilities responded by filing new suits testing TVA's constitutionality,[72] and President Roosevelt, after his landslide victory in the 1936 election, urged Congress to authorize reorganization of the Supreme Court, enabling him to nominate additional justices.[73]

Ashwander preserved TVA's right to sell surplus electric power but did nothing to resolve its potential oversupply problem. With each new dam TVA's generating capacity increased. "From 1936 on," wrote Rexford Tugwell and Edward Banfield, "the TVA should have been called the Tennessee Valley Power Production and Flood Control Corporation."[74] TVA could not await the outcome of constitutional litigation before building out its system to reach new customers. Lilienthal became a tireless advocate for public power, speaking often to groups in the Tennessee Valley. "We kept talking about how money is drained out of the community by these remote-control power setups," he wrote his boyhood friend, Newton Arvin, "and as the figures for community-owned distribution agencies ... came in, those figures ... came alive."[75] Lilienthal matched his rhetoric with institutional muscle. To shape an effective marketing program, he appointed a three-member New Contracts Committee, chaired by Joseph Swidler, his trusted in-house counsel.

Swidler focused his attention initially on small municipal systems in Mississippi, Alabama, and Tennessee. TVA also built a transmission line from Wilson Dam to western Tennessee. The loads were small, but the program was gaining momentum. Low rates and unlimited supplies encouraged demand and relieved cities of the need to build and finance new generation units as volume grew. Soon no municipal generating plants were left in the TVA market area. By 1936 TVA was selling power to seventeen municipalities and fifteen cooperatives in four states.[76] Many localities had purchased or built their own distributing systems with funding from the Public Works Administration, whose loans and grants had withstood a legal challenge from Alabama Power Corporation.[77]

Meanwhile Lilienthal and Willkie remained locked in conflict over transfer of Alabama Power Company and TEPCO properties and territorial restrictions. With the Norris Dam soon to come online, both sides were looking for a solution outside the four corners of the January 4 contract. In 1936 such a solution emerged. Alexander Sachs, an investment banker at Lehman Brothers, proposed to the president that TVA and the Commonwealth & Southern operating companies combine their power by selling it to a newly created pool organization, which would then distribute it at uniform rates to local buyers. By coordinating distribution, pooling would serve consumers and align the interests of TVA and the operating companies. Since the pool would buy power from the cheapest production sources first, TVA could continue its yardstick function. Pooling would also open large markets, lower the cost of transmitted power, avoid the need for private companies to build expensive new generating plants, and permit the companies to refinance their bonded indebtedness. Roosevelt was immediately receptive to Sachs's pooling proposal but failed to grasp the sharp differences of opinion about it within his administration.[78]

In March 1936, at the president's suggestion, Sachs met with Lilienthal to describe his proposal. Lilienthal was skeptical. He feared pooling, however plausible, would dilute TVA's control and divert the public's attention. "I will tell you frankly," he said to Sachs, "we are [a] good deal disturbed about any division of responsibility."[79] Lilienthal nonetheless suggested pooling to Willkie as an alternative to his demand that TVA and Commonwealth & Southern divide the region into exclusive service areas, adding the proviso that any community served by a private company could buy out that company's distribution facilities and purchase power from the pooled system. Willkie was not convinced, anticipating buyouts made possible by cheap Public Works Administration loans and grants.[80] He was also mindful of the growing public schism between Lilienthal and A. E. Morgan, TVA's chair, and was prepared to litigate or negotiate, as circumstances required.

In May 1936 nineteen public utility companies (including five Commonwealth & Southern operating subsidiaries) selling power wholesale in direct competition with TVA sued to enjoin execution of its power program except for the Wilson Dam activities upheld in *Ashwander*.[81] The suit sought to stop the sale of electricity generated by the three TVA dams already built (including the Wilson Dam), restrict development of four dams under construction and a fifth authorized but not yet begun, and prevent TVA from receiving congressional funds for four more dams. TVA maintained the dams were designed primarily for flood control, improvement of navigation, and national defense. Company attorneys argued they were designed to generate and sell electric power and drive their private competitors out of the utility business. "The present status," Willkie wrote Roosevelt at the time, "is practically one of open warfare and, as long as that status continues, the utilities in that district naturally feel they are fighting for their lives and are obliged to defend themselves by every legitimate means."[82]

Once described as having the "strength and smaller weaknesses of the American zealot,"[83] Morgan viewed the bitter struggle between Lilienthal and Willkie with extreme distaste. He saw his dream of TVA as the agent of rational social change subverted by Lilienthal's ruthless pursuit of cheap power. As Lilienthal's term as director was about to expire in May 1936, Morgan proposed to Roosevelt a reorganization of TVA's structure, placing operating authority in a general manager, nominated by the chair, and requiring unanimous board approval for the adoption of policies. He also lobbied the president, Norris, and Ickes against Lilienthal's reappointment, threatening to resign if he did not prevail. Lilienthal fought back, enlisting Norris's powerful support.[84]

Lilienthal met with the president as he pondered the tricky politics posed by bureaucratic warfare within TVA. "If I don't reappoint you," he told Lilienthal, "it will be heralded all over the country as a power company victory, and if [Morgan] resigns ... it will be bad for the project and the whole idea of planning."[85] Morgan had put a gun to the president's head. "I'll have A.E. in tomorrow afternoon," Roosevelt mused, "and although he is many years my elder, I'll talk to him like a Dutch uncle; I'll tell him that I am going to send your name in, and that he must be ready to take responsibility for delaying and perhaps disrupting not only TVA but the whole future."[86] True to his opaque administrative style, Roosevelt had dealt with Morgan and Lilienthal separately, encouraging each to believe the president agreed with him. A divided board allowed Roosevelt the luxury of continued indecision about TVA's ultimate objectives.

Lilienthal was ultimately confirmed, A. E. Morgan did not resign, and disagreement within TVA hardened. Lilienthal feared capitulation to the power companies; Morgan thought the emphasis on power would overtake TVA's humanitarian mission. The chairman found himself on the defensive. Several 2–1 board decisions confirmed the depth of the internal conflict. In May, over A. E. Morgan's vigorous protest, the board majority created the position of general manager and appointed Morgan's former personal assistant to the post. Morgan was so incensed he refused to sign the board minutes.

The Fontana Dam project similarly divided the board. The dam site, located on one of the three main tributaries of the Tennessee River system, was a major potential source of hydroelectric power, its planned reservoir the fourth largest east of the Mississippi River. Alcoa, the big aluminum manufacturer, had for years been accumulating parcels of land in anticipation it would someday build the dam.[87] Since TVA had now assumed control, Morgan was eager to construct the dam and start negotiations. Any transaction with Alcoa would involve a large share of TVA's total output and critically affect the economics of its power program. Alcoa wanted an extremely low power price and a thirty-year contract term. Lilienthal thought Morgan incapable of protecting TVA's interests and was desperate to avoid a bad bargain on a major piece of business.[88] On June 2, 1936, he and H. A. Morgan convened a board meeting when the chair was out of town and voted to discontinue negotiations with Alcoa. "If there had ever been hope that the board could work together," wrote Joseph Swidler in his *Memoirs*, "the split on the Fontana negotiations closed the door."[89]

In August 1936 Lilienthal forced through a further 2–1 board resolution prohibiting any future agreement by TVA to stay out of Commonwealth & Southern's territory. Frustrated by loss of face and leverage, Morgan appealed the decision to the president, who once again confronted a difficult political impasse in an election year. He responded by convening a high-level conference to consider the power-pool proposal.[90]

The thrust of the conference was conciliatory; its theme was cooperation between TVA and private utility companies. Attendees included the TVA board, Alexander Sachs, the chairman and vice-chairman of the Federal Power Commission, the head of the Rural Electrification Administration, and several utility executives, including Wendell Willkie, who saw the pooling concept as a means of preventing TVA from building its own transmission lines. "If we go into this thing," Willkie said, "we have to know that the pooled power won't be sold to cities and that we would not lose our best markets."[91] Lilienthal at first equivocated, viewing the pooling proposal as facially reasonable but fearing TVA would lose the initiative. Morgan had no doubt. He saw pooling as an opportunity to settle the power imbroglio and establish a national policy. He circulated a supporting memorandum, prepared with the assistance of the former chief engineer of Insull's Middle West Utilities, that appeared little different from an advocacy brief for Commonwealth & Southern. Lilienthal was outraged as was Senator Norris, who wrote the president Morgan had defected to the enemy.[92] "No good can come," he said publicly, "from pooling interests with enemies of the TVA program."[93]

The conference did not resolve the conflict between TVA and Commonwealth & Southern. Lilienthal and Willkie wrangled over the fairness of the yardstick and Willkie's claim that TVA was stealing his customers. Under strong pressure, the antagonists agreed to a three-month extension of the January 4 contract but left unresolved the extent to which, if at all, TVA was barred from Commonwealth & Southern's territory and the question of continued Public Works Administration allotments. Meanwhile, the TEPCO plaintiffs won a sweeping injunction forbidding TVA to make any new contracts for six months and paralyzing its expansion program. Lilienthal regarded the injunction as a "breach of faith" and urged immediate suspension of negotiations until it was dissolved. Roosevelt agreed, and the pool talks came to an end, never to be resurrected.

Months later, on remand from the Sixth Circuit Court of Appeals, a three-judge federal district court dismissed the injunction in a decision far broader than *Ashwander*, which had merely upheld the right of TVA to buy transmission lines from private companies and sell surplus power generated by the Wilson Dam. The district court swept away the legal obstacles to a full-fledged public utility program. It also dismissed Willkie's contention of unfair competition. "In view of the inevitable effect of the low rate of the TVA within this area and the economic necessity forced upon the complainants of lowering their rates to meet the competitive rates of the authority," said the court, "we conclude that the record presents evidence of substantial future damage to these complainants. Such damage constitutes *damnum absque injuria* (loss without injury)."[94] The Supreme Court later affirmed on the ground the complainants had no right to be free from competition and therefore had no standing to maintain the lawsuit.[95] The *TEPCO* decision was dispositive, ending five years of uncertainty and constitutional challenge.

Figure 2.1
Lilienthal speaking from courthouse steps, Corinth, Mississippi, 1934. David E. Lilienthal Papers, Public Policy Papers, Department of Rare Books and Special Collections, Princeton University Library.

Figure 2.2
Original TVA board of directors in session in 1935. From left: Dr. H. A. Morgan, Lilienthal, and Chairman A. E. Morgan. David E. Lilienthal Papers, Public Policy Papers, Department of Rare Books and Special Collections, Princeton University Library.

Boardroom Dissension

Since his appointment in 1933, Lilienthal had been embroiled in controversy. He thrived on contention and became adept at crisis management. "I'm a fighter," he recalled years later. "I enjoyed the controversy. I happen to think that conflict is about the only thing that really produces creativity."[96] Lilienthal brought formidable talents to bear in his fight on behalf of TVA and, not least, his reputation and career: first-class rhetorical skills, enabling him to persuade and co-opt; networking ability that gave him access to powerful people, up to and including the president; a trained lawyer's capacity for organization and bureaucratic finesse; and, finally, an unshakable conviction in the necessity of public power and the central importance of cheap electricity. He was to need all of these and more in the continuing internecine battle with A. E. Morgan that became a protracted and increasingly messy civil war.[97]

Figure 2.3
Lilienthal and Wendell L. Willkie on August 15, 1939, the date when TVA purchased
properties of private utilities represented by Willkie after six years of negotiation between the two men. David E. Lilienthal Papers, Public Policy Papers, Department of
Rare Books and Special Collections, Princeton University Library.

In January 1937, shortly before Roosevelt abandoned the pooling concept, Morgan captured the front page of the *New York Times* with a white
paper that argued for "agreement between TVA and the public utilities,"
insisting that finding "common ground with the utilities" through "rea-
sonableness, fair play and open dealing" was necessary to avoid "bitter class
controversies." In a thinly veiled attack on Lilienthal, he warned about
"people who are ruled by a Napoleonic complex which leads them to use
any method at hand, including intrigue, arbitrary force and appeal to class
hatred."[98] Lilienthal complained to the president Morgan had impaired
morale, caused resignations at TVA, and betrayed an "utter lack of administration." The election behind him, Roosevelt saw no need yet to take sides.
Instead he appointed a committee headed by Secretary of the Interior Harold Ickes to suggest a broad national power policy.[99]

Morgan continued his public attacks. A September 1937 article in *Atlantic Monthly* took direct aim at Lilienthal, whose "bitter hatred" had led to
a "war without quarter against the private companies."[100] H. A. Morgan

Figure 2.4
President and Mrs. Roosevelt, Governor Hill McAlister, and Lilienthal at the Norris Dam dedication, 1936. David E. Lilienthal Papers, Public Policy Papers, Department of Rare Books and Special Collections, Princeton University Library.

protested the chairman's remarks to the president as contrary to TVA's interest on the eve of trial in the TEPCO case. Roosevelt wrote a sharp letter to A. E. Morgan, insisting he substantiate his charges or retract them. Morgan did not respond. Instead he turned over TVA affairs to Vice-Chairman H. A. Morgan, disappeared until November, but returned unchastened. Making a surprise appearance as a witness in a claim proceeding against TVA in December, he impugned the integrity of his codirectors, contending an "effort was underway to defraud the government." Outraged, Lilienthal and H. A. Morgan accused the chair of "making statements with 'false and malicious inference.'"[101] The impact of the ongoing high-level feud on morale within TVA was palpable.

Early in 1938 the feud erupted in a public brawl. In a letter to a Texas congressman, Morgan assailed his fellow directors for a "practice of evasion, intrigue, and sharp strategy" and called for a congressional investigation,

Figure 2.5
Lilienthal speaking at ceremonies marking the initial operation of the Douglas Dam in March 1943. David E. Lilienthal Papers, Public Policy Papers, Department of Rare Books and Special Collections, Princeton University Library.

a demand soon echoed by conservative Senator Styles Bridges and columnist Dorothy Thompson, who feared Morgan would be "railroaded out of office." Lilienthal and H. A. Morgan called the chairman's policy one of "rule or ruin."[102] It was clear Roosevelt's tactic of deferral and equivocation could no longer contain the bitter intramural dispute. Lilienthal met with Roosevelt in early March. "What in hell are we going to do about Arthur Morgan?," the president asked. "He's out again." Lilienthal offered to resign "if you feel my presence on the board is embarrassing you and this project." Roosevelt replied, "Don't be silly. The only embarrassment is the embarrassment of having a befuddled old man on our hands."[103]

The president's solution, as he described it to Lilienthal a few days later, was to summon the directors to a meeting at his office at which he would ask the questions and be the judge. "I pointed out that by calling on both

Figure 2.6
Lilienthal speaking to a large group of construction workers at the Douglas Dam in
October 1942. David E. Lilienthal Papers, Public Policy Papers, Department of Rare
Books and Special Collections, Princeton University Library.

sides to produce facts," Lilienthal wrote, "he would avoid any charge of
prejudging the case."[104] A grueling six-hour meeting took place in the
president's office on March 11. It proved a disaster for the chairman, who
greeted the president's repeated requests for evidence by denying he was "a
participant in this alleged process of fact finding." Ever patient, the president reconvened the meeting a week later to give the chairman a chance to
answer simple factual questions, failing which it was clear he would have
no choice but to resign or be removed from office. At an adjourned meeting on March 21 the chairman declined to "participate further in these
proceedings." Exasperated and offended, Roosevelt removed A. E. Morgan
from the TVA board for "contumacious behavior."[105] Morgan was quick to
accuse his colleagues of "conspiracy, secretiveness, and bureaucratic manipulation" and called for a "fair and open hearing."[106]

Figure 2.7
Lilienthal looking over the Muscle Shoals plant, 1944. David E. Lilienthal Papers,
Public Policy Papers, Department of Rare Books and Special Collections, Princeton
University Library.

An investigation, spurred by Republican members eager to undermine TVA, soon followed. On April 4, 1938, a Congressional Joint Committee on the Investigation of the Tennessee Valley Authority was formed to review a litany of alleged charges, including wasting public funds, coercion of rural customers, and interference in labor disputes. Hearings ran from May until December 1938, consumed seventy days, produced 6,000 pages of testimony, and resulted in a majority report of 259 pages. The Joint Committee called more than one hundred witnesses, including Wendell Willkie, who testified, predictably, that "T.V.A. should go out of the power business and confine itself to its functions of flood control, navigation, and soil conservation."[107]

The burden of preparing for the investigation brought virtually all other TVA management business to a halt. Morgan made an endless stream of accusations but failed, as he had in questioning by the president, to provide supporting facts. Lilienthal defended himself in crisp lawyerlike fashion, showing the controversy to be "a case of difference of opinion on policy rather than dishonesty."[108] In the end the majority report vindicated TVA's programs and administration. It devoted close analysis to TVA's allocation of investment and costs, finding the "yardstick" in the operating records and results of the municipalities and cooperatives that distributed TVA's power and charged its low retail rates. The report concluded those rates were unsubsidized and in line with charges by private industry. Finally, it dismissed Morgan's claims of Lilienthal's dishonesty, referencing the chairman's "unfortunate propensity for attributing moral delinquency to anyone who differed with him."[109]

Settlement with Willkie

Boardroom warfare may have eroded TVA's image and the morale of its staff, but it did not prevent TVA from engineering the Tennessee River Valley. By 1938, thanks in good measure to A. E. Morgan and an excellent technical staff, twenty-one major TVA dams were under construction or about to begin. In 1933 fewer than a quarter million valley residents, most living in towns or cities, had electric service; five years later over two million enjoyed the benefits of TVA electricity, carried by one hundred ten municipal systems and fifty rural cooperatives. Per capita electricity use in the valley was twice the national average, and the price of power one-half the national average, proving Lilienthal's claim that low rates would greatly stimulate usage.[110] As the TVA construction program developed to encompass the entire Tennessee River, including several dams and transmission lines in TEPCO territory, Lilienthal knew TVA would not be able to establish a large integrated service area unless it acquired TEPCO's properties.[111] TVA needed a market for its rapidly growing power supply; TEPCO needed a settlement that would preserve its investors' capital from ruinous government competition financed by the Public Works Administration.[112] Setting the terms of a deal proved difficult.

Even before the Supreme Court ruled in the *TEPCO* case in 1938, Willkie had offered to sell TEPCO's entire system to TVA. Lilienthal was willing to purchase parts of the Alabama and Mississippi Power Company properties at a price based on historic cost less depreciation. Willkie's price for these properties assumed "going concern" value, a metric not susceptible of easy determination. Willkie also insisted on a territorial agreement to prevent TVA from encroaching on properties Commonwealth & Southern retained. Given Lilienthal's steadfast resistance to such limitations, Willkie's requirement appeared to be a major stumbling block (but one that would presumably become moot once TVA had acquired a market for all its power after purchasing TEPCO's assets).[113] Willkie also faced the loss of distribution properties in Chattanooga, a major hub, which had begun to build its own competitive system with Public Works Administration funding, and he had no choice but to deal. At a meeting in Washington the adversaries reluctantly agreed to start work on negotiating a purchase price. After three months they remained far apart. Willkie wanted $106 million; Lilienthal proposed $56.9 million.[114] To accept Lilienthal's offer, Willkie said, "would violate my obligation as a trustee."[115]

The gap appeared unbridgeable, and negotiations came to a standstill. In August 1938, however, the unexpected happened. Lilienthal fell ill with undulant fever, was *hors de combat* for months, and had to designate two trusted lieutenants, Joseph Swidler and Julius "Cap" Krug, to carry on. "We were pleased with the assignment," Swidler recalled in his *Memoirs*, "and to be candid, with the freedom that went with it in light of Lilienthal's desire not to be troubled during the painful stages of his malady."[116] In their dealings Willkie and Lilienthal had been tense and distrustful; the new negotiating team was smoothly polite but effective. In February 1939 the parties reached agreement on a figure of $78.6 million. TVA would buy TEPCO's generating plants and transmission lines; the municipalities would buy its distribution systems; and negotiations would continue for the purchase by TVA of other Commonwealth & Southern properties in Mississippi and Alabama. TEPCO's bondholders and preferred stockholders would be made whole, and common stockholders would receive $7 million—the first recognition by the government of equity or common stock value in utility systems.[117]

Agreement on price did not end negotiations. To fund the transaction TVA had to issue bonds and was advised that bond issuance would require new legislation. The TEPCO acquisition was therefore subject to approval by Congress, where TVA's enemies in the House saw an opportunity to impose territorial limitations, forbid competition with private companies, and withhold the benefit of a federal government guarantee—restrictions "in no small measure ... attributable to the cumulative efforts of Wendell Willkie."[118] On March 15 Lilienthal, by now recovered, met with the president to discuss legislative strategy. "The form of proposed legislation and the magnitude of the financing had been cleared ... with the Director of the Budget, the Treasury, Senator Barkley, and Senator Norris," Lilienthal recalled. "The plan was to try to pass it in the Senate and then attach it, if possible, to some House bill. ... This procedure [the president] approved, saying when that time came he would call in Speaker Bankhead, Majority Leader Rayburn ... and urge them to help it along."[119]

Weeks of bickering followed, with neither the House nor the Senate willing to yield. Finally, under pressure from Senator Norris and the president, TVA's opponents relented. The bill passed both houses and was signed by the president on July 26. It authorized a bond issue of $61.5 million, dropped all restrictions, but required congressional authorization before TVA could expand its area of operations (now, in view of the acquisition, only a nominal limitation).[120]

With financing secured, Lilienthal and Willkie were at last ready to close their deal. The adversaries met on August 15—amid a crowd of two hundred fifty people—on the sixth floor of First National Bank in New York's financial district. Lilienthal described the epochal moment in his *Memoirs*. He wrote:

Before the formalities began, Willkie and I ... went down to one of the offices where three newsreels had set up their cameras. They wanted us very badly to say something about TVA, but I insisted that we confine it strictly to my passing a check and Willkie's accepting it; otherwise we would have been in a debate, especially since both Willkie and I are pretty careful not to let the other fellow get in one word without answering it! So that was decided, and Willkie agreed. I held the check for $44,728,300 in my hand, and handing it to Willkie, said, "I hand you a check for TVA's part of the total price of $78,425,000, which you are being paid for your Tennessee properties." He ... looked at the check quizzically ... saying, "Dave, this is a lot of money for a couple of Indiana boys to be handling," and then handed me the "deeds" (actually just a stack of papers that happened to be lying around). Then we rose, shook hands, and broke up.[121]

The exchange marked the surrender of the last privately owned utility in the Tennessee Valley. For the first time the federal government, acting through TVA, had assumed responsibility for meeting the power requirements of a major region. Yet Lilienthal, uncharacteristically, seemed ill at ease and sullen.[122] "When the actual transfers began, around ten o'clock," he recalled, "I had a strange sensation. ... The entire last six years seemed to flash past as on a quickly moving film, too fast to see."[123]

Lilienthal had stopped at nothing to preserve TVA against entrenched private utility interests, political enemies, and the sharp arrows of a renegade chairman. He made cheap power the focus of TVA's policy; after a long struggle acquired exclusive markets in Tennessee and parts of Alabama and Mississippi; and successfully promoted, with the indispensable help of the Public Works Administration, TVA's own network of affiliated municipal and cooperative power distributors. Yet private utilities remained potent adversaries. They harassed TVA with propaganda, litigation, and investigation, questioning its costs, rates, finances, taxes, and accounting, and fought to block municipal competition wherever possible.[124] Willkie personified this opposition. He took the case of private utilities to the public, arguing for private ownership and claiming he had been forced to sell low by a subsidized government competitor. Willkie hoped TEPCO would "arouse the American people against government invasion of their business."[125] To press the point he took full-page signed advertisements in major newspapers. His fight against TVA drew national attention and made him a public figure. Willkie became a dark-horse Republican presidential possibility for 1940.[126]

The Enemy Within

Lilienthal was not able to savor his TEPCO triumph at leisure. He soon confronted a mortal threat to TVA's very existence, mounted by Harold Ickes, secretary of the interior, who wanted personal control over all federal power operations. An accomplished turf warrior, Ickes ran the Public Works Administration during Roosevelt's first term when he fought notorious bureaucratic battles with Harry Hopkins's Works Progress Administration, now part of New Deal lore. Ickes was a problematic figure who combined undeniable administrative talent with jarring character flaws.[127] In a review of *The Secret Diaries of Harold L. Ickes*, Richard Rovere famously wrote: "He was, by the testimony of these pages, selfish, vindictive, suspicious, servile, and disloyal. Lust for power ruled him. He loved no one and admired only those who regularly bathed him in flattery or conferred on him some portion of their authority. ... He was corrupt on the inside and pure as the driven snow on the outside."[128]

In 1938, concerned about the adequacy of the nation's power supply in wartime, Roosevelt created the National Defense Power Committee (NDPC), chaired by Assistant Secretary of War Louis Johnson but including Ickes as a member. The role of investor-owned utilities became a contested issue. Construction of new high-capacity transmission lines, Johnson contended, must be left to private industry. Ickes, an outspoken public power proponent, feared utilities would demand a quid pro quo for their cooperation, perhaps undermining the municipal ownership movement. He insisted the NDPC work only with utility officials cleared by the SEC. Separately, Senator Norris warned the president against "private companies ... [making] the development with government aid." Sensing an opportunity, Ickes challenged Johnson's command of the defense power program and boldly advanced his own plan to have the president appoint him "power czar" with exclusive jurisdiction over matters now run by separate government agencies. The utility industry, he argued, might use the war emergency to undermine the president's power program. After years of fighting the likes of Sam Insull, Ickes could not believe utility executives would ever cooperate with the government.[129]

In October 1939 Ickes persuaded the president to reestablish the National Power Policy Committee (which Ickes headed before its suspension several years before) and rename it the National Power Policy and

Defense Committee. Ickes then became chair with a mandate to pursue "immediate concrete action necessary to meet power needs as estimated by the National Defense Power Committee." Ickes's ploy was a naked grab for power, a zero-sum game played at the expense of Lilienthal and the heads of other independent agencies with a stake in the power business.[130] It drew substance from the Reorganization Act of 1939, which authorized the president to issue executive orders placing independent agencies under the control of mainline government departments.[131] Lilienthal had received a legal opinion from TVA's chief counsel that TVA could be reorganized out of existence, either carved up with parts returning to several departments or totally subsumed under one department. Lilienthal knew full well TVA must continue as a decentralized agency, with the special privileges inherent in its form, or it would vanish.[132] In the spring of 1939 Ickes added TVA to the list of programs he wanted for Interior.[133] Lilienthal, who thrived on conflict, mobilized for action.

Instinctively, he reached out to Senator Norris, pillar of the public power movement and legislative father of TVA, who wrote the president, objecting to Ickes's proposed takeover. The TVA board followed with its own letter, arguing that without independence "the experiment will be ended" and invoking "grass roots" to defend "TVA's program of cooperation with local agencies." Norris met with Ickes and his formidable legislative shock troops, Tom Corcoran and Ben Cohen. Norris rejected out of hand their well-tooled arguments for folding TVA into Interior. "I made it damn clear," Norris told Lilienthal, "that I would never consent."[134] As Lilienthal recorded in his journal, Norris said he knew "all about the TVA Act ... because, by God, he wrote it ... and ... it was the very essence of the Act that the TVA board should be independent." Norris's opposition appeared to resonate with the president, who assured him the "Ickes-Corcoran-Cohen proposal 'was on ice' ... [and] was going to stay in the refrigerator."[135] But the matter was far from over.

On October 23 Lilienthal and Ickes had a fateful interview. "He was sitting in his elegant, huge office," Lilienthal recalled, "surrounded by all the panoply of high office, but, as usual, in an ordinary straight office chair and in his vest, open, his shirt frilled around the top of his generous waistline, and no belt. There is no pose about all this—he is genuinely and not deliberately picturesque."[136] Ickes laid the controversial proposal at Roosevelt's door: "The President said he planned to put all the power agencies in one place, and that would be here [at Interior]. ... I take orders from the President, and I have never disputed any of his orders. And then I find that you go to Senator Norris and get him all worked up and putting heat on your own Chief. ... You are just being selfish, Lilienthal."[137] Lilienthal declined to respond in kind but defended TVA's autonomy. Ickes was not persuaded. "All I would do, if this transfer took place," he said, "would be to abolish your board and appoint you Administrator; I don't believe in boards."[138]

With broad discretionary authority, TVA's three-member board was the bedrock of its independence but not its guarantor. Ickes's prehensile approach to TVA posed a serious threat, given the president's unpredictable views on consolidation of control. Lilienthal searched for a compelling rationale to capture public support for TVA's independence. He found it in TVA's intimate connection with local interests. "Electricity is the people's business," he wrote in 1939. "The business of supplying electricity must be run by the servants of the community. ... Electricity must become an instrument of democracy."[139] Lilienthal called this process decentralization, where the greatest possible number of decisions is made in the field. "For six years now," he observed, "the TVA has been making a conscious effort to push its administration farther down into the grass roots."[140]

TVA was, in short, a national agency with power to act locally. Consolidation under Ickes's thumb would sever its connection with the communities it served. In November 1939 Lilienthal marshaled these concepts in a "Grass Roots" speech in Knoxville before an audience of TVA employees and social scientists, sending more than one hundred copies around the country and to the Bureau of the Budget, where it became required reading. The speech was a notable success and launched grassroots as a recurrent theme in many later outreach efforts. However far removed from reality on the ground, Lilienthal's formulation became an effective talking point against encroachment from Washington. It also projected a utopian vision of grassroots democracy and bureaucratic efficiency.[141]

Lilienthal needed all the arguments at his disposal; the fight with Ickes, which lay dormant for a while, was far from over. Lilienthal's journal entry for July 19, 1941, provides a vivid description: "TVA is in a crisis of utmost gravity. It has been brewing for some months, actually, but reached a climax ... on last Thursday morning. It was then I learned definitely for the first time that Ickes' plan to absorb all power agencies into the Interior, under the guise of defense necessity, had reached a stage where it was likely to be put into effect momentarily."[142] Roosevelt, Lilienthal had learned, was about to sign an executive order authorizing Ickes in the president's name to "supervise and direct the plans and programs" of the "constituent agencies" (including TVA, Federal Power Commission, and Rural Electrification Administration). "It was," Lilienthal recalled, "one of the most brazen documents I have ever seen in my life."[143]

Lilienthal worked frantically to avert disaster, enlisting as allies Senator Norris, Leland Olds (Federal Power Commission), Cap Krug (Office of Production Management), John Lord O'Brien (OPM chief counsel), Senator Bone of Washington, Adolph Berle (assistant secretary of state), and Bernard Baruch. Norris dismissed pro-consolidation arguments advanced by representatives from Ickes's Power Division and later told the president he "didn't want to see Ickes have anything to do with power." At the same time Ickes fatally damaged his cause during a difficult meeting with the president by threatening to resign if he did not get his way. Ickes's intemperate behavior was reason enough for Roosevelt not to expand his power base, and he withdrew support for Interior's takeover. By mid-August the crisis was over. Lilienthal wrote in his journal: "The Ickes bushwhacking seems pretty well turned back."[144] Despite Roosevelt's indecision and equivocation, Lilienthal and Norris had narrowly repelled Ickes's assault on TVA.

A Pillar of National Defense

The coming of the Second World War decisively changed the political environment and TVA itself. The defense industry required a massive increase in power output for war production. TVA already had a national defense mandate—a legacy of the *Ashwander* decision that based constitutionality of the agency's electricity marketing program in part on the war power. As a national security institution TVA would enlarge its role far beyond the contours of its authorizing statute. Preparation for war trumped political orthodoxy, and many of TVA's historic antagonists became its allies. Ever alert to public opinion, Lilienthal launched an "education" campaign to highlight the critical importance of TVA's role as power supplier. Speeches and nationwide radio broadcasts followed. "We have been hammering away at national defense ...," he wrote, "not as a justification or answer to the critics of TVA ..., but as a definitive statement of a program that has a theme running through it."[145]

Aluminum production on the Tennessee River and the atomic energy project at Oakridge required electricity in vast quantities. TVA's initial problem of creating demand became one of creating supply. As war approached, TVA embarked on an emergency construction program. Fortunately, it knew how to build dams with its own labor force, purchase land, and relocate populations. In August 1940 TVA started work on the Cherokee Dam, completing it in just sixteen months, two days before Pearl Harbor.[146] In August 1941 Alcoa turned over the Fontana Dam site to TVA. The turnover placed all five Alcoa dams on the Little Tennessee River under TVA's integrated operation and allowed it to begin construction of the long-deferred Fontana Dam on January 1, 1942. TVA supplied power to Alcoa's new aluminum plant and rolling mill.[147] The agreement with Alcoa, Lilienthal observed, put "TVA virtually into partnership with a huge private concern. ... So far as I know, there is nothing like that anywhere in America."[148]

Defense preparedness did not end political opposition. The fight for congressional authorization of the Douglas Dam in 1941 "became a mythic event in the institutionalized memory of TVA."[149] The agency proposed to build the dam within twenty-five miles of the nearly finished Cherokee Dam on the French Broad River, largest tributary of the Tennessee. The dam would flood thousands of acres of fertile bottomland, and local canning companies (Stokely and Swann)—purporting to speak on behalf of poor farmers—lobbied hard against the proposal. TVA received the president's blessing but ran afoul of Kenneth McKellar, the powerful and irascible senior senator from Tennessee, who believed TVA had ignored his patronage requests and therefore opposed the Douglas Dam site.[150]

Lilienthal framed the issue starkly: "whether the TVA's decisions will be straightforward administrative decisions ... or whether we will turn the decisions over to individual members of Congress."[151] McKellar's opposition was vicious and directed personally at Lilienthal. "Senator McKellar has declared war," Lilienthal recalled, "and asserted that I will not do because ... I have refused to allow anyone to determine what our recommendations should be about the building of dams. He has taken this as a direct assault upon his Senatorial prerogative and has replied in the way that so often occurs in Congress, namely, a violent, unmitigated attack on the administrator who offends. ... He has declared that there will be no more appropriations for TVA and no more dams unless we accede to his insistence that the Douglas Dam recommendations be withdrawn."[152] Lilienthal saw the dispute with McKellar as a matter of fundamental principle. "If we yield ...," he wrote, "then immediately we will be prey to every big and little politician in the Valley, and every transaction, every purchase of land or equipment, will sooner or later start down the same route."[153]

McKellar was intransigent. For a time he resisted the combined pleas of the president, the vice president, and OPM officials. In solidarity with a powerful colleague, members of the House and Senate Appropriations Committees refused to act. Finally, in January 1942, confronted with accusations he was sabotaging the war effort, McKellar gave way, Congress approved the Douglas Dam bill, and Roosevelt signed it into law. TVA completed the Douglas Dam in record time just over a year later but, irreversibly, incurred McKellar's undying enmity.

For the remaining war years McKellar attacked TVA as an institution and Lilienthal personally. He introduced legislation requiring congressional approval for TVA's operating expenses, repealing its authority to use power revenues to run its power system, and transferring TVA condemnation cases from court-appointed commissions to local citizen panels.[154] His personal bias knew no bounds. He used Senate Appropriations Committee hearings to bully and discredit Lilienthal while his henchmen in Chattanooga spread the message, "We all love TVA, but Lilienthal must go." The assault was ugly. "To make it stick," Lilienthal wrote in his journal, "they appeal to anything: not excepting, of course, prejudice because I am a Jew. If they could only 'get' something on me that would stand up, would they go to town, and I would be stamped on!"[155]

Lilienthal was not quiescent in the face of McKellar's scorched-earth tactics. His instinctive response, as it had been to other efforts to undermine TVA, was public outreach. He fought back in the Tennessee Valley, denouncing "political management" in Chattanooga, preaching the "gospel of no politics in an important governmental enterprise" in Tupelo and Columbus, and encouraging local civic clubs to sponsor "Save TVA from Politics" advertisements in local papers.[156] Grassroots activism worked. "The members of Congress from Tennessee," he noted, "who went into hiding before rather than brave the storm of McKellar's lash, have heard from home, and almost all of them have committed themselves publicly to Douglas. It will be *the* political issue in the state for some time to come even if nothing further happens."[157] McKellar's anti-TVA legislative agenda drew a similar response. "Since the Senate committee's report was filed with

[McKellar's] proposals in it, there has been a really amazing response from the grass roots. ... Particularly, was their violent opposition expressed to the idea that these amendments would put TVA into politics."[158]

TVA was seeking to protect itself politically by claiming nonpolitical status. When the mayor of Tupelo urged his constituents to "wire your Senators and Congressman to keep TVA out of politics," the irony of his plea was not lost on Lilienthal. "Here again," he wrote, "is the unusual picture of a politician urging the people to bring pressure on other politicians to lay off a public, that is, a politically created, institution."[159] The rationale for preserving TVA's nonpolitical status was its managerial efficiency and business effectiveness, but the downside of that status was, potentially, erosion of TVA's public accountability, which could only be ensured through the political process itself. Protecting TVA from political interference thus had long-range antidemocratic implications even as Lilienthal struggled to free the agency from McKellar's machinations.[160]

Since his appointment in 1933, Lilienthal had consistently fought off threats to TVA's autonomy and freedom of action, whether posed by private utility interests seeking constitutional disqualification, predatory federal administrators eager to end TVA's freestanding corporate existence, investigating congressmen bent on uncovering scandal, or hostile senators wishing to gain control over its spending, funding, and business decisions. In each instance, Lilienthal took aggressive defensive measures, using his access to the president and skilled public advocacy to ensure TVA's survival as an autonomous government enterprise. "TVA has never, not once, lost a battle," he wrote. "Appropriation battles every year, recently several a year; legislation; the investigation—it is quite a list. That kind of luck can't possibly continue indefinitely—I ought to get out now, so far as my own standing is concerned, before this incredible record is broken."[161]

The Nation's Largest Utility

In September 1941 Roosevelt appointed Lilienthal chair of TVA, a change endorsed by H. A. Morgan, the incumbent chairman, who was then seventy-four. The appointment was a formality. "I have been doing most of the work of a chairman for years," Lilienthal noted at the time, "acting as spokesman in public and with other government agencies ... and generally regarded as the key member of the board. ... So I thought the mere formal shift of title would not be so important. ... [But] strangely, I feel a heavy, solemn, and at times scary sense of responsibility that I didn't feel before. Curious, but very true."[162] Lilienthal's installation as chair came on the cusp of TVA's vast wartime expansion.

In 1940 and 1941 Congress voted supplemental appropriations for TVA to finance the rapid growth of its power output, both hydroelectric and steam-fired, to meet burgeoning wartime demand at Oak Ridge Laboratory, Alcoa, and other defense installations. By mid-1942, TVA's generating capacity had increased by one-third in less than a year, and it had over 40,000 employees. Fertilizer plants at Muscle Shoals were converted to production of phosphorus and other chemicals for war. As the war ended, TVA operated twenty-six dams, sixteen of them built by itself, and its electricity output reached twelve billion kilowatt-hours. It also built and ran steam plants to provide firm power during low-water periods. TVA was producing more electric power than any other single, integrated system in the nation, had acquired monopoly control over a wide market, and had become indispensable to the war effort. Its focus had shifted, inevitably, from reversing the decline of a benighted region to meeting its huge new power demand, now integrated with the national economy. "[It] has become in fact," Lilienthal wrote, "the inner citadel of the nation's war production."[163]

Revisiting the Blueprint

TVA's wartime success could not mask Lilienthal's unease that the agency had strayed from its original mission. "I have been troubled for some time," he wrote, "that something isn't quite right with the administration of our power program. ... We are in considerable danger of running the electricity program as if it were a private utility, a good, well-organized, efficient private utility, but a utility nevertheless."[164] TVA had in a short time embraced the features of the very organization it had set out to challenge. Convergence grew in the postwar period as TVA exhausted available sources of water power and built new, independent steam plants, financed by congressional appropriations, able to compete with private suppliers free of territorial limitations.[165] Although a militant proponent of TVA's low-cost power function, Lilienthal was nevertheless reluctant to abandon its broader purposes. "We are not," he said, "an ordinary utility."[166] Yet it was true that, by the late 1930s, TVA had largely given up on regional planning while the yardstick concept, so central to its negotiations with private utilities, had fallen out of favor, given the agency's multipurpose aims and the tax advantages enjoyed by municipalities and cooperatives distributing its power at retail.[167] Bureaucratic growth limited policy options and creativity while cheap power production conferred ever more control over natural resources and human habitats. Idealistic critics such as Rexford Tugwell complained that TVA had sacrificed its birthright as an agent of fundamental change.[168]

Lilienthal addressed these issues in *TVA: Democracy on the March*, an enormously successful book, published in 1944, that did more than all his prolific press releases, interviews, magazine articles, and other publications to burnish his public image as *primus inter pares* in the pantheon of TVA founders. The book sold thousands of hardback copies and tens of thousands more in a paperback edition. It was distributed to U.S. soldiers and translated into ten foreign languages.[169] In the book Lilienthal articulated favorite themes. "Valley development ...," he said, "could become a reality if and only if the people of a region did much of the planning, and participated in most of the decisions."[170] Decentralization was a corollary idea. "Every important decision need not be made in Washington," he argued. "Genuine decentralization means ... an emigration of talent to the grass roots."[171] TVA did not represent command-and-control socialism, he said, precisely because it was committed to letting local actors and management make choices.

The grassroots concept, endlessly repeated in public rhetoric, deflected ambitious federal wire-pullers who wanted to limit TVA's regional, autonomous character.[172] Lilienthal's book presented TVA not as a massive power producer but instead as a transformative, multipurpose democratic social experiment. In doing so, paradoxically, he adopted an idea advanced by A. E. Morgan—a holistic concept transcending power development and embracing conservation of people as well as water, soil, forests, and grass. It was nothing less than the all-encompassing program that had led the president to undertake TVA in the first place.[173] In the face of mounting contrary evidence, Lilienthal's book evoked a utopian world of small-holders and artisans. Critical appraisal was not long in coming.

In 1949 Philip Selznick, a young UCLA sociologist, examined the reality underlying *TVA: Democracy on the March* in his classic, groundbreaking book, *TVA and the Grass Roots*.[174] Selznick argued that TVA's reliance on grassroots participation was simply a politically driven rationale to justify

managerial discretion and the legitimacy of its program. Actual authority, Selznick contended, remained firmly in the hands of the administer-
ing agency. He also noted the deliberate surrender of TVA's agricultural
assistance programs to land-grant colleges and the American Farm Bureau
Federation, powerful conservative interests serving the large farmer constituency and hostile to poor white and black tenant farmers. Under pressure from the American Farm Bureau, he noted, TVA did not recognize the
Farm Security Administration or the Soil Conservation Service, New Deal
agencies chiefly concerned with low-income farmers. To ensure support
for public ownership of land for flood control and power production, TVA
found it expedient instead to cede the American Farm Bureau and state
universities a controlling influence over distribution of chemical fertilizer
and related farming techniques. By acquiescing, TVA enlisted powerful allies
that helped protect it from private utilities, political patronage machines,
and other enemies, but the trade-off tarnished its idealistic principles.[175] It
also anticipated TVA's future institutional pattern that, in later decades, saw
reckless expansion into nuclear power, indifference to thermal and sulfur
dioxide pollution, and unwise pursuit of the environmentally challenged
Tellico Dam project.[176]

When Selznick's critique appeared, Lilienthal was long gone from TVA,
having moved on to chair the Atomic Energy Commission and wage other
battles. Such was the influence of Lilienthal's book that its signature issues,
grassroots democracy and decentralization, continued to have broad appeal
notwithstanding the retrospective criticism of Selznick and other academ-
ics. Whatever the contrary facts on the ground, Lilienthal's passionate
belief in TVA's mission attracted a wide audience. "I am sure," he wrote,
"the country is ready for the fresh, vigorous *reality* of the TVA idea, the way
it deals with the familiar, its emphasis upon bringing all kinds of people
and interests together, its lack of dogma, the militant attitude about politics."[177] As New Deal programs faded postwar and TVA became more like a
conventional utility, Lilienthal's assessment proved optimistic.

Proof of Concept

Production and distribution of cheap, plentiful electric power framed Lilienthal's driving purpose at TVA. By pricing electricity at cost and passing
low prices through to retail customers, Lilienthal spurred consumption and

created a yardstick for rate comparisons with private utilities. As he anticipated (and Insull had shown earlier), rock-bottom residential rates called
forth quantum increases in household electricity use and caused investor-
owned utilities to lower their rates to remain competitive. Lilienthal won
his bold gamble, based more on intuitive hunch than hard empirical data.
Private utilities could not ignore the resulting elasticity of demand for electricity. "Ever cheaper power became a secular religion which ... fused the
TVA organization into a coherent whole."[178] During the New Deal period,
TVA charged rates that were from 20 to 35 percent less than those of private
investor-owned utilities. While regulation by state commissions did little to
restrain utility rates, government competition was a powerful lever. TVA's
competitive threat to private utilities' monopoly pricing power—a key element in Lilienthal's struggles with Commonwealth & Southern—achieved
its objective. The private sector reduced prices, became more competitive,
and still provided investors normal returns. Roosevelt's "birch rod," as
wielded by Lilienthal, worked.[179]

Low-cost power did not wholly define Lilienthal's agenda. He saw TVA as
the first federal agency to be solely responsible for development of an entire
river system from land purchase to dam construction to power transmission
and sale—functions that might otherwise have been assigned to separate
bureaucracies. He vigilantly defended TVA's unique autonomous regional
mandate against assaults by an array of enemies, jealous of its largely self-
sustaining nature, operational discretion, political influence, and managerial freedom. Lilienthal (like Insull) focused obsessively on control and was
quick to confront institutional threats. In doing so, he relied heavily on
TVA's special status as a government corporation, endowed with "a degree
of autonomy and flexibility which ordinary Government departments do
not possess."[180] He reminded the skeptical that Congress intended TVA to
"have much of the essential freedom and elasticity of a private business
corporation."[181] He contended that TVA decentralized its programs in close
concert with the people it was serving. Critics called this an "organizational
myth."[182] But it was, for a time, highly effective propaganda.

Commonwealth & Southern lost the battle of the Tennessee Valley, but
private utility interests and conservative members of Congress prevented
replication of the TVA idea elsewhere.[183] The private utility industry survived the New Deal and went on to prosper in the postwar era. TVA's
enormous expansion as a power producer also continued, promoted by

defense-related demands of the Korean War and the cold war with the Soviet Union. During the 1950s more than half of TVA's power production served Atomic Energy Commission plants at Oak Ridge and Paducah.[184] Lilienthal's dedication to low-cost power production, originally intended to bring electricity to farmers and townspeople in the rural South, proved a sustaining legacy, although now applied in a far different industrial context.

Of equal importance was his continued interest in TVA's autonomy. This led him to propose, while at Lazard Frères long after leaving TVA's chairmanship, privatizing TVA's power system to free it from congressional appropriations at a time when TVA was losing political support for public funding of its rapidly growing power system.[185] Lilienthal's proposal did not gain traction, but TVA eventually realized a measure of the freedom he envisaged in legislation authorizing it to issue electric system revenue bonds, payable from its power proceeds.[186]

Lilienthal was a decisive administrator, quick study, ambitious self-promoter, and combative political infighter. His major accomplishment, seen in retrospect, was acquisition of an electric power market in the face of concerted opposition from private utilities serving the Tennessee Valley, then supported by TVA's chairman and Lilienthal's codirector A. E. Morgan. Equally important, Lilienthal demanded TVA market its power output primarily through municipalities and cooperative agencies that agreed to pass on to consumers TVA's low prices. Finally, he played a pivotal role, with White House support, in preserving TVA's internal independence in the face of serial federal and legislative encroachments, including Secretary Ickes's cynical efforts to swallow TVA within the Department of the Interior. Lilienthal proved indispensable to TVA; without him it would never have survived.

3 Bonneville Power: Overreach and Disaster

Prologue

In 1982 the Washington Public Power Supply System (WPPSS), a consortium of small public utilities in the state of Washington, was unable to pay for $2.5 billion of municipal bonds it had issued to finance two nuclear power stations. WPPSS' failure, a product of bureaucratic overreach, forecasting errors, and managerial incompetence, triggered the largest municipal bond default in U.S. history.

Organized in 1957 to consolidate public power efforts in the Pacific Northwest, WPPSS joined forces in the 1960s with the Bonneville Power Administration (Bonneville), a federal marketing agency for hydropower produced by dams on the Columbia River, to promote a hugely ambitious thermal power program. Bonneville forecast major power shortages in the Northwest during the next decade and beyond but could not, by law, build or own the power plants required.

Needing a surrogate, Bonneville tapped WPPSS, whose misplaced ambition far outstripped its capacity to deal with complex nuclear technology. WPPSS was unconcerned about the risks involved and agreed to finance, construct, and operate five nuclear plants. Bonneville guaranteed financing for three of the plants, but WPPSS raised money for the remaining two, plants four and five, on the strength of contracts with participating local public utilities—Bonneville's power customers—which agreed to pay for the plants whether or not they ever produced power. As it happened, only one of the five planned nuclear plants reached completion. The rest were abandoned, partially finished, at a loss of billions.

WPPSS issued tax-free municipal bonds to investors, many of them individuals seeking retirement income, to fund the nuclear program and went to market many times over a decade, becoming the largest issuer in the nation's revenue bond business. Its prowess in raising money was, unfortunately, not matched by its capability as a manager. The nuclear program encountered massive cost overruns, technical failures, labor disputes, and delays. Forecasts of imminent power shortage, an article of faith at Bonneville and WPPSS, proved wildly wrong. Justification for five nuclear plants vanished. The failure that followed inflicted serious damage on ratepayers and bondholders alike. It also raised searching doubts about the governance of the politicized bureaucracies in charge and, more broadly, about energy policy blindly pursued in the face of mounting countervailing evidence.

Donald P. Hodel was Bonneville's administrator during five critical years ending in 1977. An ambitious, politically connected lawyer, Hodel received a directive from the secretary of the interior to push Bonneville's thermal program but met concerted resistance from environmental activists, whom he famously dismissed as "prophets of shortage." When environmental litigation ended Bonneville's thermal program, Hodel redoubled his efforts to gain support for plants four and five, but many of the local utilities remained stubbornly unconvinced the plants were necessary.

In 1976, as a last resort, Hodel had Bonneville issue a notice of insufficiency, an official pronouncement that threatened energy curtailment unless plants four and five were built as planned. As Bonneville's power customers, the participating utilities realized they had no choice, signed apparently ironclad take-or-pay contracts offered by WPPSS, and assumed the risk that plants four and five might never produce electricity.

After WPPSS defaulted and a trustee for bondholders filed suit, the Washington Supreme Court declared the take-or-pay contracts void and unenforceable, provoking years of litigation that reallocated some losses but signally failed to fix accountability. Bondholders eventually recovered only one-quarter of their investment, Bonneville's ratepayers endured huge increases in the cost of electricity, and Bonneville itself was saddled with billions of dollars of debt for two of the unfinished plants. No manager at Bonneville or WPPSS accepted personal responsibility for the ill-fated nuclear power program.

Hodel, Bonneville's administrator and principal program enforcer, made an early and fortuitous departure and was not on-site when WPPSS defaulted, later serving as secretary of the Departments of Energy and the Interior under President Reagan. A forceful advocate for nuclear power as a principal hedge against anticipated energy shortfalls, Hodel remained rigidly committed to forecasts of shortage notwithstanding clear evidence regional demand had slowed. His decision to issue the notice of insufficiency compelled participation in plants four and five and set in motion the chain of events leading to default. At a House subcommittee hearing in 1984, when asked if Bonneville had pressured utilities to participate, Hodel said he had no recollection.[1] Intervention in the electricity marketplace as a federal official appeared to pose no conflict with his laissez-faire economic philosophy as a member of President Reagan's cabinet.

This is a story that begins with Bonneville's creation during the New Deal as a federal marketing agency, with distinctly limited authority and subject to political control through the Department of the Interior. Bonneville's inception witnessed fierce infighting between public power advocates and conservatives who opposed replication of the TVA in the Northwest. As a result, Bonneville was not self-governing and remained exposed to the variable winds of political pressure linked to federal subsidies. Faced with the prospect of power shortages, it relied, unwisely, on WPPSS to do indirectly what it could not do directly, lost control of its agent, and presided over the resulting regional disaster. In the wake of this monumental failure, the public power movement sustained a serious reversal. At the same time, alternative approaches to the nation's energy future took root in the ashes and gained a wider audience.

Early Years

While campaigning in the Pacific Northwest as a vice presidential candidate in 1920, Franklin Roosevelt glimpsed the mighty Columbia River from a railroad dining car. Impressed by the river's flow, he made a note on the back of a menu: "As we were coming down the river today, I could not help thinking, as everyone does, of all that water running down unchecked to the sea."[2] The river's potential then remained untapped; private power companies refused to bring electricity to the sparsely populated countryside to light "the desert for jackrabbits and rattlesnakes."[3] Critics insisted there was no market for power in the Northwest.[4] But Roosevelt harbored a different idea, one that became a pillar of progressive politics. Years later, in a famous speech in Portland, Oregon, during the 1932 presidential campaign, he called for a government power development on the Columbia River as a "national yardstick to prevent extortion against the public and to encourage the wider use of that servant of the people—electric power."[5] To private utilities it was an ominous message. Roosevelt, they believed, had one purpose in mind: socialization of the electric power industry.

The Columbia River is more than 1,200 miles long. From its source in British Columbia, it flows south through eastern Washington; is joined by the Snake River near Pasco, Kennewick, and Richland; turns west to form the border between Washington and Oregon; and merges with the Willamette River, reaching the Pacific near Astoria, Oregon. From headwaters in Canada it drops 2,650 feet, almost twice the decline of the Mississippi, and its stream flow is prodigious. Its potential for hydropower development had engaged the enthusiastic support of local boosters and the Corps of Engineers since the late nineteenth century but remained a dream until the New Deal. In 1933 Roosevelt made good on his Portland pledge, and the Public Works Administration funded construction of the Bonneville and Grand Coulee Dams.[6]

Bonneville Dam was an epic undertaking, built by the Corps of Engineers and planned as one of ten dams on the Columbia River and its tributaries. Anchoring the dam in the river's soft banks posed formidable technical problems, made more difficult by the rush of melted snowpack each spring. In 1936 the river broke through an earthen cofferdam above the Bonneville construction site, smashing into the partially completed dam. Nonetheless construction continued around the clock: "Night became day while work on the dam was at its height. For months the symphony ... of jackhammers and trucks and cats and riveters and aggregate buckets swinging from the highline was never stilled. The dam at night was like a strange factory run by a race of gigantic elves, its half-finished facades of smooth spillway piers rising sleek and gray under tens of thousands of candle power, and the ghostly forests of reinforcing steel towering insanely against the outer blackness."[7] Against all odds the Corps of Engineers finished Bonneville Dam on schedule. At its dedication in September 1937, two months after passage of the legislation authorizing the Bonneville Power Administration—the Bonneville Project Act—Roosevelt forecast a "date, not far distant, when every community in this area will be wholly electrified."

Political Logrolling

While construction of Bonneville Dam proceeded in a straight line, creation of the Bonneville Power Administration followed years of intricate legislative logrolling and, even after passage of the Bonneville Project Act, invited further intense bureaucratic warfare. Public power proponents wanted to replicate TVA on the Columbia River. The Corps of Engineers and Bureau of Reclamation, having little or no interest in public power and believing Bonneville should not seek its own customers in the first instance, planned to market electricity from Bonneville and Grand Coulee Dams, but only to fill local demand unmet by investor-owned utilities, which viewed government power as the entering wedge of socialism. "In all these respective localities," said the president of the Edison Electric Institute, "there is a far greater abundance of power now existing ... than is needed."[8] Private utility interests opposed TVA-style distribution of power to municipalities and nonprofit cooperatives. "Each dam," wrote one critic, "is a white elephant which tramples out legitimate business, eats the taxpayer's money, and cannot be sold or slaughtered because it is a sacred thing for which the public-ownership group will fight fanatically."[9]

Legislative proposals were similarly divided. In 1935 Senator James F. Pope of Idaho introduced a bill to establish a Columbia Valley Authority (CVA) embracing the entire Pacific Northwest.[10] Months later Republican senators from Oregon sponsored a substitute bill that, critics said, would have Bonneville's transmission lines carry power only to heavy industry and private utilities at tidewater.[11] The senators opposed a CVA for the Northwest and favored separation of Bonneville and Grand Coulee power. Their bill, supported by local chambers of commerce and private utilities, was not intended to spread the benefits of cheap power. Public opinion differed by state: Oregon and the headwater states of Montana, Wyoming, and Idaho opposed establishment of a CVA; Washington was more receptive. Congress adjourned before acting on either bill.[12]

When Congress reconvened in 1936, Bonneville was at the center of a complex legislative struggle to control the future of power in the Pacific Northwest. Ever diffident about resolving contested issues, Roosevelt instructed the National Resources Committee, chaired by Harold L. Ickes, secretary of the interior, to investigate future development of the Columbia River. The committee passed on to the president, with its endorsement, a report of the Northwest Regional Planning Commission (representing the state planning boards of Washington, Oregon, Idaho, and Montana). The report recommended a new government power agency to market Bonneville's electricity, a uniform rate policy, and a three-person administrative board.[13]

Although it stopped short of proposing a CVA, "with its ameliorative and philanthropic tasks," the report envisaged the power agency as an independent public corporation that would pay its own way. The secretary of war was a dissenting voice. He demanded mileage rates for transmission of power rather than the uniform postage stamp rates advocated by the committee and saw the Corps of Engineers as more than a mere construction firm. Under uniform rates the cost of power is the same regardless of the distance power travels to the customer; mileage rates increase depending on distance.[14] Having built Bonneville Dam, the Corps wanted to distribute its power and determine electricity rates but proposed building only two short transmission lines and giving industrial customers near the dam site concessional terms. The Corps could not comprehend low-cost power as the key to economic development of the Pacific Northwest.[15]

Fearful of an impasse, Roosevelt suggested establishment of a provisional agency to distribute power until Congress worked out a permanent solution. In Senate hearings in 1936, Frederic A. Delano, Chairman of the National Resources Committee, said the present Congress need not legislate finally for Bonneville "but could set up or suggest an organization which would explore the question, and perhaps at the next session of Congress further develop it." It was left to another witness to propose Bonneville as a cooperative wholesale purchasing and transmission agency to market low-cost power to independent and municipal retail distributors over a super-grid.[16] As 1936 came to a close, Roosevelt had to decide whether to seek an accommodation with private utility interests or back a national public power program based on the TVA experiment.[17]

In early 1937 the Bonneville dam was nearing completion and would soon begin to produce power. The administration needed, at the very least, a vehicle in place to provide for distribution of that power. It also had to find a pathway through a thicket of competing and contradictory legislative proposals. The course of future federal power policy was at stake.

Not content to rely on the National Resources Committee, Roosevelt formed a new Informal Committee on Power Policy, headed by Secretary

Ickes, to recommend legislation on Bonneville and formulate a federal power program. At the same time Senator George Norris of Nebraska launched an ambitious proposal for "enough TVAs to cover the entire country." After meeting with the president, Norris said he would draft legislation for multiple regional authorities modeled on TVA.[18]

Meanwhile the committee had prepared its own Bonneville bill. It entrusted power generation and transmission to an agency led by a civilian administrator, recommended uniform rates, and gave preference to public and cooperative distribution agencies. As a sop to Secretary Ickes, however, in sharp contrast to the autonomous organization of TVA, the committee recommended that Bonneville be made a bureau of the Department of the Interior. Ickes's effort to set himself up as a power czar cast a long shadow over Bonneville's future.[19] Senator Norris's competing plan to plant little TVAs across the land lost traction and the president's support when opposed by the secretary of agriculture and other dissenting voices within the administration.[20]

The committee's bill still faced opposition from the Corps of Engineers, which wanted to produce and transmit Bonneville power for sale to private utilities. Under pressure of time, a compromise bill emerged. Over Ickes's bitter objection, the Corps would operate Bonneville Dam and its generation facilities. It would then deliver power to Bonneville's civilian administrator, who would control its sale and distribution. Under the Bonneville Project Act, Bonneville was launched as a provisional power marketing agency with authority to set rates, enter into long-term sales contracts, build and operate transmission lines, and distribute power to public bodies and cooperatives on a preferential basis.[21]

Unlike TVA, an autonomous government corporation, Bonneville was an arm of the Department of the Interior, not charged with a public utility's obligation to serve[22] and unable to own or control the projects from which it marketed power, including, as a result of an executive order in 1940, power from Grand Coulee Dam.[23] Instead it acted as a jobber, wholesaling electricity at a price just high enough to recover costs.[24] Initially, Bonneville also lacked authority to make long-term purchases of new power sources.[25] These limitations did not discourage James D. Ross, Bonneville's first administrator, who viewed it as "Thomas Jefferson's dream of a 'great, free and independent empire on the banks of the Columbia.'"[26] Ross built a network of high-voltage transmission lines linking major population centers and helped form electric cooperatives and public utility districts in Washington and Oregon to take Bonneville's power.[27]

Other players were less euphoric. Bonneville's provisional organization invited a fierce bureaucratic struggle during the next five years between the proponents of a CVA, principally Senator Norris; advocates of local control; and Harold Ickes, who wanted Bonneville, TVA, and the Forest Service under his thumb in a new Department of Conservation that would run all power activities of the federal government. The president vacillated. In dedicating Bonneville Dam, he had warned of "dangerous national centralized control." Later, at Ickes's insistence, he supported the proposed Department of Conservation and, when that met resistance in Congress, a single-administrator bill placing Bonneville permanently under the Department of the Interior.[28]

"To make his control permanent," *Time* reported in 1941, "Ickes got a bill introduced in Congress setting up a [Columbia Power Authority] under the Interior Department, with a single administrator to be appointed (and removed) by him. To counter this move, the Norris forces introduced a bill setting up a CPA like TVA—with a three-man board, appointed by the President, with terms extending over a nine-year span."[29] Although rooted in TVA's successful practice, Norris's counter was ill-timed. The war effort ended any further consideration of the regional power program he favored.

Mobilization required top-down control. In 1942 the War Production Board ordered the interconnection of Bonneville and all other major public and private utility systems in the area, creating a Northwest Power Pool linked by the network of high-voltage transmission lines Ross had conceived. Private utilities were delighted; public power advocates saw the order as the "nose of the camel under the tent."[30] Between 1940 and 1944 Bonneville's transmission network expanded twentyfold.[31] But the reform era was over. Bonneville's mission had shifted from providing low-cost hydropower to farmers and local residents. It now had to meet the huge wartime electricity demands of aluminum companies, shipyards, atomic works, and other war industries receiving over 90 percent of its output.[32]

Public Utility Districts

Bonneville's preference customers were cooperatives, municipal utilities, and, most important for this narrative, public utility districts (PUDs). The initial purpose of the preference clause was to ration low-cost power in the event of a shortage. Bonneville would then "prefer" public to private users.[33] Bonneville produced so much power that preference customer energy purchases did not exceed those of private utilities until 1952.[34] Private users at first had no risk of power curtailment. In 1936 fifteen districts in Washington voted to form PUDs, a reflection of growing public power sentiment in the Northwest. By 1940 there were twenty-nine PUDs in the state.[35] Basic PUD governance consisted of a commissioner to handle business matters and an operating manager to deal with engineering concerns. The commissioner was an elected official, answerable to ratepayers, and a layperson required by law to hold an outside job. The manager was a hired hand. Over time managers eclipsed commissioners in importance.[36]

As preference customers, public utilities were more than Bonneville's distribution appendages. They also were in a favorable position to buy private utility company assets, either through negotiation or condemnation. "The purchasing of a private power concern that wishes to sell," said Bonneville's Ross, "not only ends a controversy in which neither side can win, but it follows the most economical line and brings the lowest possible rates for light and power."[37] To fund the purchase of operating assets, public utilities sought federal loans or planned to float tax-free revenue bonds repayable from future power sales (as opposed to municipal tax revenues).[38] By the late 1930s, public utilities had opened a relationship with a New York fiscal agent to assist in negotiating private utility buyouts.[39]

In early years, however, most PUDs were ramshackle, local affairs that operated "on a shoestring and a prayer; their allies in the Grange held potlucks and bake sales to raise money for paying legal bills or buying advertising or hiring engineers. Everyone knew that the power companies could match every dime of that money with a dollar, and often they did, particularly before an initiative vote or election, when the private interests would shell out huge sums of money in trying to defeat a referendum or candidate representing public power."[40]

Public power was a political cause, and PUDs were a natural constituency. Contending factions sought to control the Washington PUD Commissioners' Association. Ken Billington, the leader of one faction, the Public Power League, became the association's executive director in 1951. A PUD activist since the 1930s, Billington saw public power as a grassroots crusade to place electricity under direct control of individual consumers. When he took office, the association's membership was split between public utilities that owned their own power supplies and those wholly dependent on Bonneville power. Long-established municipal systems in Tacoma, Washington, and Eugene, Oregon, were often more interested in collaborating with private firms than in supporting nongenerating PUDs.

The postwar political climate had changed. New Deal reformism was a fading memory. Conservative legislators looked unfavorably on continued PUD influence in the state of Washington, where for more than a decade public utilities had carved up private firms' domains through negotiated purchases and condemnation proceedings. President Eisenhower, newly elected, opposed federal power development; his assistant secretary of the interior said, "It is time we get away from the idea of giving power away at the taxpayers' expense for the purpose of stimulating local public power."[41] The public power movement was at a crossroads. To compete with private companies, public utilities could no longer depend entirely on Bonneville but would have to develop large-scale projects on their own. This would require, Billington believed, a joint operating agency.[42] "It appeared logical to me," he said, "that some kind of legal entity was needed by which we could consolidate the financial strength of these small utilities to construct some of the larger needed projects."[43]

In 1952 the association sponsored legislation that would permit two or more PUDs to organize a separate municipal corporation to construct and operate generation and transmission facilities.[44] The founders wanted, above all, to keep Bonneville's transmission network in public hands. The board of the proposed entity would represent the interests of its member utilities, and its managers would carry out the board's decisions, effectively removing—despite Billington's grassroots sentiment—"by one more step the access that the consumers ... had to the electricity they owned."[45]

In 1955, after an intervening struggle with Governor Arthur Langlie, a conservative Republican, Billington secured a joint operating agency law vesting control in member PUDs. A year later, the directors of the association moved to create a new joint operating agency, the Washington Public Power Supply System (WPPSS).[46] Early in 1957 the state gave its stamp of approval.[47] WPPSS was a vehicle designed to minimize oversight and allowed individual utilities to escape accountability and criticism. Using tax-free revenue bonds, it had the legal right to borrow money without voter approval by action of its board of directors. The public would not feel the costs until much later. Although nominally a state agency, it was free of most fiscal and political constraints: its meetings were private, its spending was not budgeted by the state of Washington or any local government, and it was not answerable to citizen-ratepayers.[48]

Forecasts of Power Shortage

"World War II," wrote *Time*, "tripped off the biggest influx of newcomers in the Northwest's history; it had gained a million and a half people. The population of Washington jumped from 1,700,000 to 2,500,000 between 1940 and 1950, Oregon from 1,000,000 to 1,600,000. For the first time, the Northwest, risen from the raw wilderness in little more than a century, seemed to be within range of becoming an industrial dominion, rather than an outpost of Eastern manufacturing and finance."[49] From 1946 to 1970 electricity consumption in the Northwest grew at a compound rate of 7 percent annually. During the same period Bonneville's electricity prices, in real terms, fell by 2.6 percent annually.[50] Driven by demand from residential space heating and the aluminum industry, load growth continued in lockstep with advancing real output. In twenty years, loads tripled.[51] Planners expected demand for electricity in the Northwest to double every ten years.

Before the oil shock of the early seventies, energy forecasting simply projected past trends into the future on a regional basis in reliance on simple econometric models. For two decades the Pacific Northwest Utilities Conference Committee had issued annual load forecasts for Washington, Oregon, Idaho, and Montana. Each forecast was a composite of predictions made by more than one hundred member utilities, often based on estimates generated by Bonneville's staff. This self-referential methodology embedded the biases of individual utilities, which typically assumed a constant annual growth rate. Forecasters believed the future would be little changed from the past. Bonneville called future demand levels "requirements," cloaking them in the "rhetoric of inevitability." Its power planners matched forecast energy needs to the policies they wanted.[52] Ken Billington observed the same practice. "Since Bonneville had ongoing contracts ...," he wrote, "it had to make forecasts in order to determine its ability to meet those contracts."[53] An economist, describing the same behavior, would speak of the "political incentive that government agencies have to overestimate demand and thereby justify new plants."[54]

By the late 1960s planners believed hydropower could no longer meet the growing regional demand for electricity. Few feasible dam sites remained, and continued opposition by environmental interests had halted further dam construction on the Columbia River.[55] Since Bonneville had to serve public utilities first, their private counterparts, including those service industries that purchased power directly from Bonneville, feared losing access to its cheap electricity.[56] In the words of the *Northwest Ruralite*, a local trade paper for electric cooperatives, "Electric power is like love—nobody ever gets quite enough."[57] Bonneville, regional utilities, and industrial customers all began to look elsewhere for additional generating capacity and focused on a single supply possibility: central station thermal power.[58]

In 1966, David S. Black, Bonneville's administrator, was "looking toward the region's very imminent transition into a new era of thermal-electric generation." By 1975, he warned, the region would have developed most of the available hydropower sites and would need "at least one million kilowatts of new thermal generation each year thereafter." Without new thermal plants, Bonneville could not meet customers' demand after the mid-1980s and would gradually reduce and ultimately halt power sales to privately owned utilities. To meet future demand Black envisaged construction of huge thermal plants that would take advantage of economies of scale and solve the region's growing energy crisis. All that was lacking was a means of paying for the new plants.[59]

In 1968, following a series of closed meetings, Bonneville and the committee representing its 108 customers launched the Hydro-Thermal Power Plan. Ambitiously, it called for 26 nuclear and coal-fired plants to add more than 40,000 megawatts of capacity to meet anticipated demand through 1995 at a cost of $15 billion.[60] Although the federal government would pay for expansion of the hydro system, all utilities wanted to control their own power sources in anticipation of future shortage. "The lesson," said a former head of the Northwest Public Power Association, "is to get your own power supply or a very friendly power supply or in the alternative, fast or slow, your electric system will die."[61] In 1969 President Nixon approved the Hydro-Thermal Power Plan.

The dizzying prospect of nuclear power drew enthusiastic support. By the 1960s, aided by a statutory liability cap and promised federal support for reactor waste disposal, General Electric and Westinghouse were selling turnkey nuclear power plants to domestic utilities below cost and offering twenty-year contracts to supply cheap fuel. Later the manufacturers promoted large-scale plants up to 1,000 megawatts in capacity. By 1968 they were taking orders for plants six times larger than the largest one then operating. Construction of the new plants, sold on a cost-plus-fixed-fee basis, in time revealed huge operational difficulties. Average construction times doubled, capital costs ballooned, and regulatory oversight and litigation portended endless delays. Since utilities could not recover their costs until plants started running, these were mortal threats. Reality on the ground proved far different from the prediction of Lewis Strauss, commissioner of the Atomic Energy Commission, who famously once said of nuclear power "our children" will enjoy electricity "too cheap to meter."[62]

WPPSS Takes Command

To justify its formation and avoid PUD defections, WPPSS wanted to build its own projects. Otherwise, the board feared, state lawmakers might vote to repeal the joint operating agency law. "We better get pregnant," Billington warned, "or they'll vote to dissolve us."[63] In 1962 WPPSS started a small hydroelectric project at Packwood Lake, Washington, financed by tax-free revenue bonds and fraught with cost overruns, delays, and litigation. In 1966 a second WPPSS project began commercial operation at the federal government's plutonium reactor site at Hanford, Washington, also financed by revenue bonds. The project generated 860 megawatts of electric power from by-product steam, sold to PUDs and private utilities. Bonneville agreed to transmit the power.[64] "Only six and half years before," wrote one observer, "WPPSS had consisted of a piece of paper and a dream. ... Against sometimes overwhelming odds, [it] had managed not only to survive, but to earn the privilege of ushering the nuclear age into the Northwest."[65]

Although most of its board members were "farmers and small businessmen who were neophytes in the nuclear business,"[66] WPPSS expected to lead public power's nuclear development in the region. It hired an engineering consultant and, as Bonneville was developing the Hydro-Thermal Power Plan, proposed to build a light water nuclear plant at the Hanford site. The principal author of the proposal was Owen Hurd, WPPSS' first managing director. He promised "ample power at lowest cost to maintain the region's competitive position in serving large industrial loads."[67] Bonneville, he knew, was not able to realize this goal alone. By law it could neither build new power plants itself nor directly purchase electricity from nonfederal plants.[68] As a public body and proven power developer, however, WPPSS could do so and was the right vehicle, Hurd argued, "for securing maximum benefits resulting from joint action."[69]

WPPSS had launched a bold initiative, but a major obstacle remained. Its constituent utilities—Bonneville's preference customers—lacked the capital and credit required for large-scale nuclear projects. Without Bonneville's backing, WPPSS' proposal could not go forward, and private utilities would likely fill the void. But Bonneville was only a marketing agency and had no authority to purchase electricity from a third party or own power plants. To act on WPPSS' proposal and the Hydro-Thermal Power Plan, Bonneville had to find a legal loophole. Drawing on prior accounting practice, it conceived a scheme called net billing.[70]

Under net billing a preference utility participating in a thermal power plant (Bonneville's customer) would assign its share of the anticipated output of that plant (i.e., its "capability") to Bonneville, which would deduct from the utility's monthly power bill an amount based on the cost of the potential output assigned as an offsetting credit. The customer would then use the amount credited to pay WPPSS for the "capability" it had purchased and assigned to Bonneville.

Under this scheme Bonneville would bear the cost of constructing the plant and would do so whether or not it was completed, operable, or operating, effectively assuming what came to be called the "dry-hole risk." The preference utility would be able to offset its cost even if the plant never delivered power. Bonneville's administrator proposed that the sunk cost in an unsuccessful project be net billed immediately. Net billing therefore shifted all commercial risk to Bonneville, a federal government agency, which assured bondholders that project debt would be paid back from its power sales revenues. This was an offer too good to refuse. Bonneville had more than one hundred preference customers; only the city of Tacoma declined to participate.[71] Bonneville's ratepayers were not consulted.

Net billing was more than an accounting fix. It was a way for Bonneville to acquire electricity from a thermal plant without buying it directly or owning the plant. "Instead," said the Government Accounting Office, "[Bonneville] was paying for the right to receive a share of output from a power plant being built by a third party."[72] Bonneville did not actually buy the share and so did not own the net-billed plants. Net billing allowed participating utilities to avoid the financial risk of building plants on their own. Bonneville would pay for the WPPSS bonds through its general wholesale rates, spreading costs and financial risks among all Bonneville customers.

By assuming the utilities' shares, Bonneville also assumed their share of the debt and ensured repayment of the revenue bonds issued by WPPSS from Bonneville's power sales. Because Bonneville, a federal government agency, backed the WPPSS bonds, they carried a lower interest rate than if issued by WPPSS without Bonneville's guarantee. Net billing also allowed Bonneville to blend higher-cost thermal power with cheaper power from its hydro system. Bonneville's overall cost of power would increase, but each participating preference utility would not have to bear the full burden of expensive new thermal power. By increasing total supply, net-billed plants would also ensure the availability of power for Bonneville's direct-service customers, which ranked below preference utilities and feared losing cheap hydro power.[73]

Bonneville lobbied hard for net billing. Its administrator spoke of brown-outs, blackouts, and power rationing if new plants were not built. He said demand for power would overtake Bonneville's supply by 1975 and predicted dirt-cheap power from the new plants.[74] Congress approved Bonneville's net-billing agreements, including its acquisition of electricity from nonfederal plants under the Hydro-Thermal Power Plan. Congressional approval gave comfort to bond counsel and underwriters, who would rely on net-billing agreements to finance the plants and wanted Congress to "give express recognition to [Bonneville's] implied authority to acquire the power." Net billing also benefited private power companies, which agreed to support its use for public plants.[75]

But net billing was not a panacea. WPPSS' construction of nuclear plants cost much more than planned. In 1974 Bonneville had to raise its wholesale rates, only the second time since 1937 it had done so. Cost overruns at the net-billed plants drove a 27 percent increase. Although Bonneville's rates were still far below the national average, its customers were not pleased. Public support for the net-billed plants began to fade as WPPSS announced ever higher cost estimates to complete the plants.[76]

Construction of Nuclear Plants

Between 1969 and 1972, in reliance on net billing, WPPSS aggressively committed to build three large nuclear plants in Washington as part of a regional power program "whose economic costs were disguised and whose environmental costs were an afterthought."[77] The decision plunged WPPSS into the complex bureaucratic politics of nuclear energy and strained its fragile managerial resources.

WPPSS sited its first plant on the nuclear reservation at Hanford. Bonneville guaranteed the financing, $150 million in tax-free revenue bonds. The project's estimated cost approached $400 million, almost four times WPPSS' original expectation, but did nothing to contain its misplaced ambition.[78] A single project, however significant, would not establish WPPSS as an emerging public power leader in the Northwest, and it moved immediately to co-opt large municipal utilities in Seattle and Tacoma that might otherwise build their own nuclear plants.

WPPSS formed a seven-member executive committee of its large, unwieldy board and invited Seattle and Tacoma to join and assume permanent committee seats. Ken Billington emphasized "the need to balance a large utility interest with a smaller utility interest [and] … suggested that one board member be from Seattle City Light; one from Snohomish County PUD; one that would represent the other municipals, such as Tacoma and Richland; one that would represent the three public utility districts of Cowlitz, Clark, and Grays Harbor; and one that would represent the voluntary members of other State of Washington public utility districts."[79] Seattle and Tacoma soon joined WPPSS, firming its resolve to assume additional regional responsibilities.[80]

WPPSS undertook the next two nuclear projects in 1972 shortly after Bonneville's administrator, concerned about delays, urged public power "to take some definitive action" to get the program "back on schedule."[81] WPPSS agreed to build a second nuclear plant at Hanford, originally a power enhancement scheme that became a separate 1,250-megawatt facility, and a third 1,240-megawatt plant west of the Cascade Mountains at Satsop, Washington, to be 30 percent co-owned by private utilities.[82] Bonneville and most of its preference utilities signed financing contracts.[83]

Concurrent construction of three large nuclear plants severely strained WPPSS' resources. In two years its operating budget increased tenfold, topping $100 million; staff doubled and would continue to double annually.[84] Its inexperienced management confronted a formidable array of financing, permitting, engineering, environmental, and labor problems, complicated by factional local politics. "The sheer workload and pace of activity ... [were] staggering. Agendas for Executive Committee and Board of Directors meetings were many pages long and deliberations involving hundreds of million dollars were common."[85] WPPSS had to master arcane nuclear technology, ever-changing federal regulations, and the scheduling, construction and oversight of multiple complex power projects. Delays and cost overruns were inevitable. In time WPPSS found itself ridiculed as a "refuge for rubes where experts played on ambitions and gullibility of small-town business people."[86]

In August 1972, unexpectedly, net billing came to an end. The Internal Revenue Service denied tax-exempt status for bonds sold by publicly owned utilities to finance their power plants if more than 25 percent of the output was sold to a government agency such as Bonneville. The new rules grandfathered WPPSS' three existing net-billed nuclear plants, preserving its ability to issue tax-exempt bonds with Bonneville's guarantee, but eliminated net billing for all future projects.[87] This was a dagger in the heart of Bonneville's Hydro-Thermal Power Plan. To finance the next thermal plants on the drawing board, preference utilities would have to rely on their own credit without Bonneville's participation.[88] Its new administrator, Donald P. Hodel, took command as the crisis broke. He warned immediately of power shortages. "It is hoped," he said, "that a solution will be found and found soon to keep the unique Hydro-Thermal Power Program viable because the economic life and well-being of the entire region are at stake."[89]

Figure 3.1
President Roosevelt at dedication of Bonneville Dam, 1937. Credit BPA.

Figure 3.2
Hodel and Stein sign BPA WPPSS Hanford #1 contracts. Circa mid-1970s. Credit BPA.

Figure 3.3
Hodel at last staff meeting, December 15, 1977, with precipitation chart. Credit BPA.

Figure 3.4
WPPSS Nuclear Plant #4 construction. Circa late 1970s. Credit BPA.

Figure 3.5
Ken Billington, former WPPSS head, 1984. Credit BPA.

Hodel's Agenda

Hodel was a politically ambitious lawyer who had already served three years as Bonneville's deputy administrator and was deeply immersed in its power planning. A militant conservative, he was to become secretary of energy and secretary of the interior under President Reagan and, years later, president of the Christian Coalition of America among many other affiliations. Utility interests in the Northwest, concerned about Bonneville's leadership, welcomed Hodel as a young, dynamic executive who could deal with disarray in the Hydro-Thermal Power Plan now beset with unexpected cost increases and construction delays. Hodel was known to play hardball and had once told Bonneville's preference customers that "in a time of regional shortage the preference clause may not mean very much. For then it may come to a political decision as to who gets the power."[90]

At an all-hands meeting shortly after taking office, Hodel confirmed the demise of net billing and said future plants would urgently require a different approach. In ten years energy demand would exceed supply, he said, and the Northwest would experience mass power deficits. Hodel warned investor-owned utilities Bonneville would not offer them new power contracts when the current ones expired. For direct-service industries, which relied exclusively on Bonneville power, the future was bleaker still.[91]

Under Hodel's prod, Bonneville worked desperately with utility stakeholders to shore up the faltering Hydro-Thermal Power Plan and rethink its role as the region's central power authority. Hodel had received marching orders from Rogers Morton, then secretary of the interior, to tell Bonneville customers that "notices of power insufficiency ... would be issued ... unless the utilities and [Bonneville] develop a plan for carrying forward the [the Hydro-Thermal Power Plan] or some alternative procedure which would assure the region of a future power supply and minimize demands on the Federal Treasury."[92] A notice of insufficiency, if issued, would imply Bonneville's rationing of power after a specific date. Its customers would then have to wean themselves from dependence on cheap hydropower.

Bonneville still supported construction of nuclear plants, but the end of net billing meant its utility customers would have to underwrite new plants without Bonneville's financial backing. Most parties believed an energy shortage was around the corner and new power supplies were indispensable. Badly in need of a solution, Bonneville found an ally in the Public Power Council, which had already asked WPPSS to build a fourth nuclear plant to be financed collectively by the region's public utilities, warning that holdouts "may find themselves without ability to meet their load growth after the date of insufficiency."[93]

WPPSS readily agreed to the new assignment and thanked the council for its expression of confidence. Neither Bonneville nor WPPSS saw any reason to reappraise their dire energy forecasts. In the following year the council proposed that WPPSS undertake a fifth nuclear plant. WPPSS' largest member (Seattle) warned of political and financial risks, but WPPSS again agreed to go forward because its "sense of mission overcame reservations."[94] WPPSS regarded plants four and five, with 2,500 megawatts of generating capacity, as its contribution to the region's future power supply. Bonneville agreed. Hodel urged Bonneville's utility customers to sign up for power from plants four and five. "Any utility which needs additional power resources in the mid-1980s," he wrote, "will need to enter the participants' agreements with WPPSS at this time." Hodel predicted that by the mid-1980s, without the new plants, Bonneville might not be able to meet its firm-load commitments.[95]

Meanwhile, in November 1973, Bonneville announced Phase II of the Hydro-Thermal Power Plan, including massive additional coal-fired, nuclear, and hydropower plants financed by local utilities. In place of net billing, Phase II relied on participants' agreements under which each participating utility would assume a portion of a plant's debt in exchange for a share of its output (whether or not the plant was ever completed). Bonneville no longer had ultimate responsibility for repaying borrowed construction funds.

Under Phase II Bonneville would be a coordinator, not a financial guarantor; deal with its preference utilities as a technical and economic mentor; and act as an agent to purchase thermal plant power for preference customers.[96] To free up regional electricity reserves, Bonneville and its direct-service industrial customers also agreed that it would have the right to curtail their power to meet other commitments. In exchange they would receive extended industrial power sales contracts offering an extra decade of interruptible low-cost energy.[97] Bonneville and the aluminum industry, among others, had forged a special relationship, ensuring access to Bonneville's low-cost power and federal transmission lines.[98] In a deal using variable rates, Bonneville even agreed to share the commodity risk inherent in aluminum markets by tying the cost of electricity to the cost of aluminum.

But Bonneville ignored an inconvenient truth about nuclear power. By 1974 fourteen nuclear plants elsewhere in the country had been canceled, while WPPSS' existing nuclear plants, near to hand, were plagued by cost overruns and construction delays. Hodel was undeterred. In testimony before Congress in March 1974, he predicted power deficits in each of the next six years.[99] Some of Bonneville's preference utilities still believed nuclear plants were feasible and feared losing customers to investor-owned utilities if they did not participate or build their own plants.

But many smaller utilities, guaranteed their full requirements up to twenty-five megawatts, saw no need to risk buying into plants four and five. By mid-1974, only a handful of utilities said they would sign on. Hodel wrote personal letters to the commissioners of every public utility in the region, urging them to participate, and sent his managers on the road to follow up. At year end only forty public utilities, out of more than one hundred that were eligible, appeared willing to commit to plants four and five.[100] Concerned the Northwest was running out of power, Congress granted Bonneville explicit short-term authority to purchase electricity "to meet temporary deficiencies."[101]

A Fatal Interaction

Bonneville and WPPSS were promoting unsustainable, codependent programs, each premised on management's unshakable conviction that a regional power shortage was near and large nuclear plants were the road to salvation. The big investor-owned utilities, which had agreed to take a 30 percent ownership interest in WPPSS' fifth nuclear plant, were also on board. But smaller public utilities had grave doubts. They questioned continued forecasts of shortage and began to lose faith in nuclear power. Participation in plants four and five seemed an invitation to trouble. Public utilities saw higher electric rates, municipal debt stretching out for thirty years, and ownership responsibilities well beyond their management capability. The mayor of the city of Heyburn, Idaho, a typical small public utility, "was convinced that [its] participation in Projects 4 and 5 was unnecessary and that [its] needs and requirements ... could be adequately filled" by Bonneville.[102]

Many public utilities also recalled that voters in Eugene, Oregon, had recently approved a moratorium on development of a nuclear plant and the Seattle City Council had decided against participation of Seattle City Light—a WPPSS member and the largest municipal system in the Northwest—in plants four and five. Both actions were driven by environmental concerns. To settle litigation, Seattle's city government had commissioned a study of future energy demand, notable for reliance on econometrics to project the impact of rising electricity prices on consumption.[103] The study showed that more efficient electricity use could reduce Seattle's demand for power and even avoid new nuclear plants altogether. The study also predicted cost increases would reduce demand for power. Bonneville's forecasters simply assumed consumers would continue to buy the same amount of electricity regardless of cost. Having debunked the prevailing obsession with future shortages, Seattle chose to meet its energy needs largely through conservation and without participating in plants four and five. For Bonneville and WPPSS, that was unwelcome news.

The decisions in Eugene and Seattle were not isolated events but part of a rising tide of environmental activism in the Northwest that put an end to Bonneville's ambitious Phase II plan and further complicated the launch of plants four and five. The immediate change agent was a federal court case, *Port of Astoria, Oregon v. Hodel,* decided in 1975.[104] Alumax Pacific Corporation planned to build an aluminum smelter plant at Astoria and signed an industrial power sales contract with Bonneville. The Oregon Environmental Quality Commission objected, citing the risk of fluoride emissions. Rather than fight the local opposition, Alumax decided to build the plant in eastern Oregon.

The Port of Astoria, unwilling to lose the plant, sued Bonneville under a federal law that required it to file an environmental impact statement. The court, siding with the Port, ordered Bonneville to do so by broadly addressing its role in regional power supply. Bonneville took five years to complete the statement and meanwhile had to suspend all efforts to realize Phase II. That effectively ended its role as agent for planned sales of power from the Phase II thermal plants to its preference and direct-service industrial customers. Without Bonneville's participation, Phase II was dead.[105] Remaining were the grandfathered net-billed plants and, potentially, the three new nuclear plants sponsored by WPPSS.

To Hodel environmental attacks were more than an irritant; they were a threat to his stewardship of Bonneville's core programs, now undercut by litigation. In a speech at the Portland City Club in July 1975, one month before the *Port of Astoria* decision, he angrily lashed out at his environmental antagonists:

Over the past few years ... [the environmental movement] has fallen into the hands of a small, arrogant faction which is dedicated to bringing our society to a halt. They are the anti-producers, and anti-achievers. The doctrine they preach is that of scarcity and self-denial. I call this faction the prophets of shortage. Their tactics are those of confrontation rather than constructive dialogue. Their weapons are the injunction, the restraining order, and the challenge to the environmental impact statement. Their theatre of operations is the courtroom, where they are always the plaintiff, never the defendant ... [T]he anti-producers do it week in and week out, seldom winning a case but satisfied to keep progress at bay with their legal maneuvers. By halting the needed expansion of our power supply system, they can bring this region to its knees.[106]

The "prophets of shortage" speech, as it came to be known, was a major strategic blunder. In a single stroke, Hodel had crystallized environmental opposition. The National Resources Defense Council soon presented an alternative plan showing that, except for plants already approved, none of the thermal plants projected by Bonneville would be needed before 1995. The best low-cost resource, said the council, was conservation. The Oregon Department of Energy challenged the forecasting methods used by a local investor-owned utility, the same methods used by Bonneville. Montana and Oregon passed ballot measures constraining approval of nuclear plants.[107] Bonneville's efforts to revive net billing by further legislation went nowhere. In early 1976 Hodel issued a press release confirming that Phase II was in "shambles."[108] Counsel for WPPSS feared plants four and five would be "scrubbed and recognized as dry holes."[109]

Perhaps in response to environmental attacks, Bonneville engaged a consultant to review the potential of conservation. The consultant's study found that Bonneville could suppress the growth of energy consumption by more than 50 percent over time by such straightforward expedients as adoption of energy efficient building codes. Energy efficiency, it argued, would entail only a small fraction of the cost of nuclear power. This finding undermined the rationale for plants four and five and, unsurprisingly, was not well received. Hodel denounced the study, which was purged from Bonneville's archives and did not surface in its dealings with preference customers. Bonneville continued to act on its belief in an imminent power shortage and the need for massive thermal plants even if the region undertook an aggressive energy conservation program.[110]

Bonneville redoubled its efforts to get public utilities to buy into plants four and five by signing participants' agreements. At a meeting of its major customers in the ballroom of the Sheraton Hotel, Hodel painted a bleak picture of ever-increasing energy demand and looming power shortfalls. Unless the utilities supported WPPSS' plan to build two more plants, he said, Bonneville would not be able to supply future power needs.[111] Public utilities, particularly those relying on Bonneville for all their electricity, knew a threat when they heard one and could not ignore Hodel's ominous message.[112]

Even so, public utilities had good reason to be wary of entering into participants' agreements, without the protection of net billing, that would require them to invest in the "capability" and pay the costs of plants four and five, including debt service on bonds issued, by making payments to WPPSS whether or not the plants were completed or produced electricity or WPPSS performed—the so-called take-or-pay or dry-hole provision.[113] Each participating utility might have to pay its share of bond debt, amounting to millions of dollars, with no electricity to sell. The take-or-pay provision was in effect a financial guarantee, disguised as a power purchase agreement.[114] To overcome doubts, WPPSS said Bonneville's industrial customers would take excess power produced by plants four and five on a short-term basis. It then submitted participants' agreements to ninety-three public utilities in the region, to be signed as is. "Any changes ...," it said, "would be unacceptable."[115] Once an advocate of grassroots participation, WPPSS had become a command-and-control promoter.

In June 1976, Hodel issued the dreaded notice of insufficiency to Bonneville's preference customers. After 1982, he warned, Bonneville would be unable to guarantee their power needs. The notice was a grim and foreboding document for utilities without power generation of their own and forced commitment to plants four and five. The mayor of Bandon, Oregon, recalled that "it was only at the urging of [Bonneville] and the not very subtle threat of eventual blackouts if we didn't have a piece of the action that prompted Bandon to sign virtually at the last minute."[116] Without further legislative guidance, Bonneville faced an intractable long-range problem in allocating available power among its preference customers.[117]

When WPPSS' directors met in July, they learned that eighty-eight utilities had signed the participants' agreements, oversubscribing for the capacity of plants four and five. The utilities elected a seven-member participants' committee to approve bond sales, change orders, and make other major decisions.[118] WPPSS, propelled by Bonneville's notice of insufficiency, was now the sponsor of five nuclear plants. Hodel's sales job was done. Within a year, having set in motion an epic default, he left Bonneville for Washington, D.C., eventually to become President Reagan's secretary of energy. At his confirmation hearing the Sierra Club, among others, accused Hodel of promoting higher demand estimates to justify the need for nuclear plants, ignoring conservation, and pressuring municipal utilities to participate in plants four and five.[119] Much later, writing on energy policy and perhaps regretting his tenure at Bonneville, he opposed "federal intervention and control in the energy marketplace."[120]

The Nuclear Program Unravels

WPPSS' reach vastly exceeded its grasp. It had agreed to build five stagger-ingly complex nuclear plants but lacked even minimal management depth and experience. Its board members included a sheep rancher, an orchardist, a retired bank manager, and several small business owners.[121] To its defend-ers, WPPSS "was a victim of outside events and other factors beyond the recognition, understanding, or control" of its managers.[122] To its critics, and they were legion, WPPSS committed unforgivable errors of judgment, compounded by a stubborn unwillingness to recognize its own shortcom-ings. "Very little provision was made for disagreement," said its manag-ing director, "for how to handle things when there was disagreement and conflict."[123] Construction of multiple nuclear plants, ambitiously under-taken, was marred by strikes, equipment failures, escalating change orders, regulatory delays, and huge cost overruns—all made worse by WPPSS' own management failures. WPPSS consistently failed to meet construction dead-lines for the three net-billed plants, whose combined costs rose stratospher-ically from $2.25 billion to $12 billion before the projects were suspended in 1981.[124]

As signatories to the participants' agreements, small public utilities were exposed to enormous risk. WPPSS had told them at the time plants four and five would cost less than $2.5 billion and be completed by 1984. Only one month later, WPPSS announced a $540 million cost increase, caused by construction delays and unanticipated "contingencies." The cost increase was shocking news. It foretold a pattern of future construction problems and cost escalation, consistent with WPPSS' already woeful track record on the net-billed plants. WPPSS' budgets for all five plants understated costs and had only a small likelihood of success based on its own in-house risk assessment. Bonneville said little although its staff knew WPPSS was overextended. Others were more critical. Environmental groups predicted declining future energy demand and opposed building hugely expensive nuclear plants.[125]

Bonneville's forecast of power shortages, stubbornly maintained in the face of mounting contrary evidence, would soon prove wildly wrong. The 7 percent annual growth rate in demand, received wisdom in 1974, was no longer credible just a few years later. Even Bonneville's own assessment, filed with Interior in mid-1977, conceded that "any permanent reduction in anticipated electrical loads would likely result in reduced requirements for new generation."[126] In fact, between 1974 and 1980, estimates of 1981 electricity demand declined by almost 3,500 megawatts, roughly the capacity of three nuclear plants.[127] Conservation measures spurred by oil price spikes in the 1970s sharply reduced demand for electricity as did economic recession in the Northwest. The hypothetical need for five nuclear plants vanished, and Bonneville's reliance on WPPSS to build those plants proved a slow-motion disaster.[128]

As project sponsor, WPPSS could not manage construction of a single nuclear plant, let alone the unprecedented complexity of building five plants at the same time. An 1,100-megawatt nuclear plant required, by one estimate, thirty-eight million pieces of paper.[129] WPPSS became embroiled in conflicts with contractors, design professionals, consultants, labor unions, and Bonneville (with which it had a shifting and ever more contentious relationship). In building plants that employed both major types of reactor design (boiling water and pressurized water), it engaged three different architect-engineering firms, procured reactors from three different manufacturers, and used three different nuclear steam supply systems. Failure to standardize reactor design was a costly error, amplified as WPPSS contracted with hundreds of companies, supervised a workforce of more than eight thousand, and made continuing changes in concept and work plans. By the end of 1977 WPPSS had signed four hundred contracts relating to one plant alone. Although it had assumed the role of construction manager, WPPSS lacked line authority and could not control confusion in the field. Multiple change orders inflated contract costs, caused delays, and ate up management time.[130] WPPSS was adrift.

Bonneville viewed the managerial vacuum at WPPSS with dismay, citing a "complete lack of control procedures ... change orders being recalled and renegotiated ... and the terminations and transfers of key employees." Bonneville wanted greater oversight, but WPPSS resisted. In a letter to WPPSS, Bonneville's deputy administrator wrote: "Because the net-billed projects ... are financed on the credit of [Bonneville] and since we essentially purchase the entire output of the projects at whatever costs are finally incurred, ... our role must go beyond budget review and monthly reports so that we can assure ourselves, our customers, and Congress that the plants are being constructed as efficiently as possible."[131] Bonneville requested an outside audit, which found a near-total lack of fiscal control. WPPSS hired a succession of management consultants but could not cope with the nuclear program's unprecedented technical and logistical problems.

This became an acute source of concern as WPPSS issued bonds to finance the nuclear program. By 1978 all five plants were seriously delayed, and their costs had doubled to $8.5 billion. Newspaper accounts mentioned incomplete records, sloppy accounting, and unacceptable work quality. A General Accounting Office study, issued in 1979, doubted that "Bonneville is adequately prepared to protect customers from cost overruns on large power plants." By mid-1979 total project costs reached $11.75 billion, soon to go much higher; Bonneville had announced massive rate increases; and a day of reckoning was near.[132]

Financing the Fiasco

WPPSS paid for all the construction costs of plants four and five, including capitalized interest, through the sale of tax-free municipal bonds. As construction costs mounted and schedules stretched out, its financing needs far outpaced revenues received. WPPSS went to market for plants four and five fourteen times between 1977 and 1981, raised $2.25 billion, but required more than twice the additional financing at the end of that period than it did at the beginning.[133] The biggest problem WPPSS faced was the cost of money. In four years interest rates doubled, reaching more than 12 percent. WPPSS did not charge participating utility ratepayers while the plants were under construction. Instead it issued more bonds to finance the interest until the estimated completion "date certain" for each plant. WPPSS simply borrowed money to pay interest on the bonds it had sold earlier. By the time WPPSS sold its last bonds for plants four and five, 45 cents of every dollar borrowed went to capitalize its interest costs. For each of the net-billed plants, by contrast, Bonneville paid interest currently out of revenues after the date certain and then raised its rates to recoup.[134]

WPPSS needed ever-increasing amounts of money, and Wall Street had an unquenchable thirst for its high-yield bonds. In several years WPPSS bonds amounted to more than 20 percent of all gas and electric revenue bonds sold. As one financial observer noted, "Wall Street made tens of millions of dollars off [WPPSS]. Investment bankers and bond dealers became almost addicted to WPPSS bonds; with the vast supply and attractive yields, there seemingly was no end to the underwriter fees and dealer markups."[135]

Two underwriting syndicates bid on the offerings but did not conduct a due diligence review, accepting at face value disclosures in WPPSS' official statements that consistently overestimated demand—the basic rationale for forecasted power shortages and thus additional plants—and minimized the risk of budget shortfalls.[136] Having purchased bonds by competitive bid, the underwriters were coolly indifferent to negative information and focused on two things: high yields and investment grade ratings.[137] The rating agencies also failed to inquire deeply. It was a pattern to be repeated thirty years later in the securitized mortgage meltdown that triggered the recession.

By 1979 bonds for the net-billed plants were faring better in the market than those for plants four and five. A majority of the net-billed bonds were going to institutional investors, but underwriters, uncomfortable with declining load forecasts and construction cost overruns, began to sell plant four and five bonds to individuals through unit investment trusts, attracted by yield premiums and investment grade ratings.[138] The ranks of WPPSS' bondholders were filling with unsophisticated individual investors, recalling, to those with very long memories, the small bondholders of Insull's failed holding company empire in the early 1930s. Merrill Lynch, one of the underwriters, told WPPSS that "price is the cure to saturation." Discounted prices sold bonds, but raised interest rates and increased WPPSS' debt burden. Assured by the take-or-pay provision in the participants' agreements, bond dealers and investors shrugged off the prospect of default.[139]

Bond counsel blessed the legal validity and enforceability of bonds issued by WPPSS for plants four and five. Counsel's opinion relied on the participants agreements and, in particular, the take-or-pay provision they contained, although its validity was not supported by statute or any court decision. The take-or-pay provision required the participants to pay the costs of plants four and five, including debt service, whether or not the plants were completed or produced electricity, without granting the participants an ownership interest in the plants.[140] Bond counsel contended the participants had entered into an enforceable power purchase agreement, even though "the purchaser of power took the risk that it would not be delivered," but admitted under SEC questioning they had found no cases in point.[141] An alternative reading, dismissed by counsel, saw the take-or-pay provision as an unconditional guarantee of payment that put the participants in the "banking business" rather than the "power business."[142] Confident in its interpretation, counsel issued an unqualified opinion on the validity of seventy-two of the participants agreements without seeking a test case or legislation.[143] It was to prove a fateful decision.

Many participants did not at first understand they would be obligated even if the projects were not built; nor did they find out for several years that bond counsel's opinions failed to cover all participants agreements. A lawyer for Idaho Falls said he "did not have any understanding that this would finally be construed as a guarantorship, whether we've got any power or not, that we're going to pay these bonds out." By 1980, as project failure loomed, all eighty-eight participants faced the possibility they would have to pay their share of bond debt for plants four and five, amounting to billions of dollars, with no electricity to sell.[144] "Lose 4 and 5 ... ," they were advised, "[and] every single one of you are going to be looking at a possible downgrading of your system."[145]

Desperate for a solution, the participants approached Bonneville and its direct-service customers for relief. At a hardball negotiating session in October 1980, the participants threatened to "pay off what we owe and let you, Bonneville, decide how you are going to get power to meet your obligations." It was an empty gesture. Having signed apparently ironclad take-or-pay contracts, the participants had no leverage with Bonneville or its direct-service customers, who were purchasing extremely cheap power and saw the high-cost output of plants four and five as a millstone. Analysts warned Bonneville that a takeover of plants four and five would threaten viability of the net-billed plants. WPPSS tried to keep the intramural unpleasantness quiet. It agreed to consider a slowdown or even termination of plants four and five but concluded the cost of any delay would be prohibitively expensive.[146]

Crisis and Default

Construction delays and rising interest rates precipitated a crisis for WPPSS. The midyear budget estimate for 1980, presented at internal management meetings in November, revealed that all five nuclear plants would now cost $20.4 billion, nearly $4.5 billion more than the budget estimate published just four months earlier.[147] The executive committee was shocked. WPPSS had gone to the bond market almost thirty times since 1973 but had taken in less than half the money required. It was running faster but falling farther behind. Its financial advisor warned "it might be unable to raise the funds it needs to maintain construction cash flow at acceptable interest rate levels, or any interest rate level at all." Fearful of market reaction, WPPSS did not disclose the enormous cost increase to underwriters or rating agencies and used obsolete forecast figures in its last official bond statement.[148] The nuclear program had become a bottomless sinkhole.

By 1981, as WPPSS funded the net-billed plants at ever-higher interest rates, public support evaporated. Bonneville's customers were angered by a 50 percent increase in its wholesale rates and no longer believed predictions of energy shortage. Finally willing to entertain conservation as an alternative, Bonneville said it would defer a decision on acquiring the output of plants four and five for three years. Long-run demand growth was now expected to be 1.5 percent per year, a sharp reduction from previous forecasts.[149] Electricity use was going down in the region, not up as predicted. Plants four and five, each well under 20 percent complete, were suddenly without economic justification.

In March 1981 underwriters told WPPSS it would be difficult or impossible to market bonds for plants four and five without Bonneville's backing. WPPSS' managing director, desperate for help, told his board that the budget numbers were too large to handle without total commitment and support of the State and the region. In May, as overall costs reached an astonishing $24 billion (including $12 billion for plants four and five), WPPSS imposed a one-year construction moratorium and canceled the next bond issue with only six weeks of cash flow remaining. An analyst at Drexel Burnham Lambert guessed that plants four and five "probably will not be completed," and the rating agencies, at long last concerned, downgraded their bonds (which obligated the participants to pay $7 billion over the next thirty years).[150] Public indignation was quick to follow. A citizens' ratepayer group, Don't Bankrupt Washington, placed an initiative on the November ballot requiring a vote on financing new large power plants, including WPPSS' nuclear plants. It was approved by a wide margin but did not survive judicial review.[151]

Disarray and confusion followed. David Stockman, new director of the Office of Management and Budget in the incoming Reagan administration, fired the Bonneville administrator, who was replaced by a political ally of the president. The governors of Washington and Oregon appointed a panel to find a way to save plants four and five and avoid an uncontrolled termination, without avail. The Washington state legislature replaced the WPPSS executive committee with an executive board of four outside members, all of whom quit after several months. The participants committee said it would pursue all available options, including the purchase of power from plants four and five by Bonneville and acceptance of responsibility by all electric utilities, Direct Service customers, and Bonneville but an Oregon congressman dismissed a federal bailout as a "dead duck." Moody's suspended its bond ratings, and on January 22, 1982, WPPSS finally terminated plants four and five.[152] On termination, the participants were immediately responsible for interest payments on the outstanding bonds and had to raise their consumers' rates.[153] The net-billed plants, although backed by Bonneville, could no longer readily attract bond finance. Bonneville leaned heavily on WPPSS, which had no choice but to delay plants one and three indefinitely.[154] Bonneville was still obligated to pay bondholders of plants one, two, and three. A federal court ruling confirmed enforceability of the net-billed contracts.[155]

Ratepayers and municipalities, searching for a way out of the morass, were quick to contest the legality of the participants agreements.[156] As trustee for the plant four and five bondholders, Chemical Bank saw an immediate threat and sued in Washington state court, seeking a declaratory judgment that the participants were bound by the agreements' take-or-pay clause.[157] The participants contended they had been compelled to assume a debt prohibited by the Washington state constitution. The trial court ruled in favor of Chemical Bank, but on June 15, 1983, the Washington Supreme Court reversed on appeal, finding the take-or-pay clause unenforceable.[158]

"The unconditional obligation to pay for no electricity," said the court, "is hardly the purchase of electricity."[159] It was instead an *ultra vires* financial guarantee, the very interpretation previously dismissed by WPPSS' bond counsel without benefit of a test case, part of a "plan to mortgage the futures of ratepayers by requiring huge increases in electricity rates, in exchange for nothing, in violation of our statutes and state constitution."[160] In early August 1983 Chemical Bank declared the bonds in default. Most of the participants had already stopped payments to WPPSS, which acknowledged it could not pay $2.25 billion in bonds used to finance plants four and five.[161] Without the participants agreements, there was no source of revenue. The bonds were not the general obligation of WPPSS but were to be paid from funds generated by the terminated plants, guaranteed by the participants.[162]

The default triggered the largest municipal bond default in U.S. history. "The fiasco," wrote *Time*, "has robbed thousands of investors of their savings, shaken confidence in the municipal bond market, angered and humiliated the people of the Northwest, tarnished the reputations of some of Wall Street's leading institutions and provoked at least 70 lawsuits that will be clogging the courts for years to come."[163] WPPSS, once a grassroots institution, had become a bloated bureaucracy distant from ratepayers and indifferent to bondholders, many of whom were small individual investors. It had financed plants four and five on the backs of local utilities, using the threat of power shortage to induce them to bear the risk the plants would not be completed and never produce electricity. Promising power without cost, it delivered cost without power.

The comparison with Insull was inescapable. WPPSS had issued billions of dollars of bonds against invalid participant guarantees. Like Insull, WPPSS had overreached, driven by blind ambition and misplaced belief in dire forecasts of power shortage. Its insular leadership, mostly local small business owners, was ill-prepared to construct one nuclear plant, let alone five at the same time. It was nonetheless the chosen instrument of Bonneville, which used WPPSS to get around legal constraints on direct ownership of power plants and then lost control of its surrogate. Don Hodel, once Bonneville's administrator and now energy secretary, "having left the agency in financial shambles and the power system in chaos,"[164] was unrepentant. "The Administration strongly opposes any bailout," he said, "and I don't sense any sentiment for one in Congress."[165] Ratepayers and bondholders could fend for themselves.

Chemical Bank immediately filed suit for fraud, negligence, and breach of contract against WPPSS and other defendants associated with the collapse of plants four and five but did not name the bond underwriters, rating agencies, or bond counsel. The case became known as Multidistrict Litigation 551, consolidated individual bondholder suits, and continued for the remainder of the decade.[166] Plaintiffs included seventy-five thousand investors, most of whom were individuals, including ten thousand who had bought bonds directly with a face value of $1.24 billion for retirement income.[167]

When the case settled in 1988, the bondholders realized $590 million, about 26 cents on the dollar invested. Among other sources of funds, Bonneville contributed $35 million, the state of Washington $10 million, the city of Seattle $50 million, WPPSS members $181 million, and four major under-writing firms $92 million. WPPSS settled at no monetary cost by agreeing to make its managers available to bondholders' lawyers,[168] and its officials, despite huge losses and failure to disclose rising project costs, escaped SEC sanction.[169] In 1984 WPPSS finally completed plant two, the only one of five nuclear projects to go online, at a cost of $3.2 billion, almost ten times the original estimate.[170] To pass through its share of WPPSS costs between 1979 and 1983, Bonneville had to increase its rates sixfold. It also incurred $6.3 billion in debt (in 2012 dollars) for plants one, two, and three, requiring annual debt service of almost $650 million.[171]

Epilogue

Bonneville was not alone in promoting a failed nuclear venture. TVA had to cancel plans for eight nuclear plants by 1984, and the Long Island Lighting Company plant at Shoreham, New York, although virtually complete by 1983, fell victim to environmental and safety litigation, leaving a "$6 billion radioactive hulk to be dismantled in the 1990s."[172] But these disasters offered small comfort to citizens of the Northwest as they pondered the ruins of WPPSS' nuclear program. "The sheer magnitude of nuclear-power miscalculation is difficult to grasp," wrote the *Seattle Times*, "unless one walks through the abandoned plants, reactors that will never fire, turbines that will never run, control-panel dials that will never twitch, trays of cable that will never carry electricity. Cooling towers as high as a 50-story building. ... All to be sold off, dismantled or dynamited."[173]

Bonneville embodied President Roosevelt's populist vision. With hydro-power from huge government dams on the Columbia River, it electrified the countryside, serving publicly owned utilities as preference customers that in turn served farmers and households ignored by the region's investor-owned utilities. For years the supply of cheap hydropower seemed endless. Distribution, not generation, was the paramount concern. Bonneville had been organized as a federal marketing agency. It was not an autonomous, freestanding government corporation like TVA and did not have authority to develop or buy its own power supplies.

The politics of Bonneville's creation also placed ultimate control with the secretary of the interior, who could hire and fire its administrator and determine its agenda. TVA, by contrast, was run by a three-person board, appointed by the president for fixed terms and capable of fending off political interference, but its very success spawned political enemies. Congress was simply unwilling to replicate TVA in the Northwest. Bonneville's truncated role as power marketer was the direct result.

Bonneville's mission changed over time. Most of the power it sold went to industrial customers, notably aluminum companies, with voracious appetites for cheap electricity. Although Bonneville had enough power to sell to everyone, by the 1960s its planners forecast a shortage and began to think about thermal supplies.[174] This posed a problem, given Bonneville's limited charter. Deprived of in-house generation capacity when hydropower alone was thought insufficient to meet an expected power shortage, Bonneville fatefully turned to WPPSS to construct and operate a high-risk, multiproject nuclear program. Outsourcing proved a convenient fix, and Bonneville was able to navigate around its statutory mandate.

WPPSS wanted to be a regional player and, although woefully ill-equipped, was only too happy to accept the challenge. With origins stretching back to the 1930s, WPPSS, a consortium of local public utility districts, was a significant factor in public power politics. As a municipal entity chartered by the state, WPPSS could issue tax-free bonds and spend billions, unbudgeted by any state or local government and free of taxpayer approval or official oversight. Its managers were appointed, not elected, and accountable only to its board.[175] In short, WPPSS had the autonomy and freedom of action that Bonneville lacked. Together, Bonneville and WPPSS could use Bonneville's cheap hydropower to blend with the much more expensive thermal power output of the nuclear plants WPPSS was undertaking. Bonneville's ratepayers would bear the burden.

To raise the prodigious sums required, WPPSS became a latter-day "paper pyramid," issuing billions of dollars of bonds on the strength of Bonneville's guarantee as to the net-billed plants and the take-or-pay obligation of participating public utilities as to plants four and five. WPPSS' role as financier was ironic. It had

adopted the ways of one of its oldest and bitterest enemies, not only in its finances, but in its demeanor as well. It had grown distant from the ratepayers who owned it, just as holding companies had become aloof to the wishes of their stockholders. ... Originally so dedicated to the needs of its ratepayers, [it] was in the end obsessed with its own survival, defensive against the tide of popular criticism, and belligerent toward the federal agency that had for many years treated it as a favorite son among the region's utilities. Embodied in the bloated bureaucracy of WPPSS, the crusade looked into the mirror and saw Insull.[176]

Still, ultimate responsibility for the WPPSS disaster must rest with Bonneville, which set the monster in motion, was unable to control it, and thrust the enormous cost of failure on its own ratepayers, WPPSS' bondholders, and, ultimately, the federal government. Don Hodel, Bonneville's administrator during the critical window, played a central part in the drama. A zealous proponent of flawed shortage forecasts, he suppressed contrary findings, stigmatized environmental opponents, and, by issuing a notice of insufficiency, forced public utilities to enter into participants agreements, ultimately judged to be unenforceable *ultra vires* contracts.[177] Although Hodel acted at Interior's behest, he never questioned federal directives and took aggressive action to carry them out. His cameo appearance in the WPPSS disaster was decisive. Hodel left Bonneville, opportunely, before the deluge and later, as a federal official, was quick to dismiss the possibility of a bailout when the nuclear program foundered.

Hodel's tenure at Bonneville coincided with a seismic shift in the nation's energy economy, brought on by the oil embargo imposed by Mideast producers in 1973. It was no longer an unassailable fact that electricity demand would increase year after year, nor was it true that nuclear power would usher in a new age of completely reliable, low-cost power. Fixation on large-scale central station thermal power began to give way, and advocates for conservation, renewable energy, and the environment approached the mainstream. These changes came too late to alter the mindset at Bonneville and WPPSS but compelled a painful review of energy policy in the Northwest and the nation in the following decades. The public power movement, launched with such hope and fervor during the New Deal, revealed the same flaws of hubristic overreach and nonaccountability that had undone Insull's holding companies forty years before.

4   Paul Joskow and the Intellectual Blueprint for Industry Reform

Origins

New Deal legislation vastly expanded the reach of government-owned and financed electric power, dismantled giant interstate holding companies under the Public Utility Holding Company Act (PUHCA),[1] and enlarged federal regulation of investor-owned utilities by recasting the role of the Federal Power Commission, previously merely the overseer of hydroelectric projects on federal lands and navigable rivers.

The Federal Power Act,[2] passed in 1935, aimed to fill a glaring regulatory void left by the Supreme Court's 1927 decision in *Public Utilities Commission v. Attleboro Steam & Electric Co.*,[3] which held states had no jurisdiction to regulate wholesale electric power rates in interstate commerce. "Congress believed," wrote the Supreme Court years later, "that Attleboro and the related cases compelled ... comprehensive federal regulation."[4] To achieve this, the act gave the Federal Power Commission authority, for the first time, over interstate sales for resale and transmission of electricity between unaffiliated utilities but was careful to extend that authority "only to those matters which are not subject to regulation by the States."[5] Generation and local distribution of power remained beyond its reach,[6] as did regulation of market entry, supply planning, and facility construction.[7]

Framers of the act knew that regulation of wholesale electric rates, however important, would not alone achieve its purpose. More critical by far was the haphazard state of the private sector, which revealed "little interconnection between competing electric systems and between privately and publicly owned sources of power."[8] Such disarray cried out for a solution, and Representative Rayburn of Texas and Senator Wheeler of Montana introduced bills that would have imposed on public utilities an affirmative duty to serve, making them common carriers with an obligation, using their own wires, to transmit or wheel power for third parties.[9]

The initiative drew hostility from investor-owned utilities and did not survive further legislative deliberations. The Senate Committee on Interstate Commerce eliminated the duty to serve, preferring instead to rely on "voluntary coordination of electric facilities ... for the first Federal effort in this direction."[10] As adopted, the act directed the Federal Power Commission "to divide the country into regional districts for the voluntary interconnection and coordination of facilities for the generation, transmission, and sale of electric energy."[11] The Senate Committee expressed confidence that "enlightened self-interest will lead the utilities to cooperate with the Commission and each other in bringing about the economies which can alone be secured through the planned coordination which has long been advocated by the most able and progressive thinkers on this subject."[12]

Given the private sector's bitter opposition to New Deal policies, reliance on investor-owned utilities to provide "voluntary interconnection and coordination" was an exercise in wishful thinking. Under the act the Federal Power Commission could not order one utility to wheel power for another and had only limited and conditional authority to direct the interconnection of transmission facilities and compel a public utility to sell or exchange energy.[13] Its main focus was to prevent wholesale rate discrimination.[14] Electric utilities could largely decide for themselves whether to wheel or sell power at wholesale as they saw fit. A vertically integrated utility could therefore use its control over transmission lines to protect its own generation by preempting potentially competitive suppliers from wheeling power to serve customers on its system. For forty years the commission presided under this narrow grant of authority. Public power advocates introduced numerous bills in Congress to make utilities common carriers and enable the commission to order wheeling, all without success.[15]

There were nonetheless certain contraindications. Nuclear facilities were governed by a different statute, the Atomic Energy Act,[16] which provided for antitrust review before grant of a nuclear plant commercial license and, as later amended, on application for a construction permit.[17] The Nuclear Regulatory Commission could condition licenses to ensure that the applicant did not discriminate and was therefore able to impose commitments to wheel power for other utilities.[18] The Federal Power Commission, for its part, had limited power in principle to order wheeling on behalf of preference customers (municipals and cooperatives) of a federal hydroelectric project if the transmission facilities required for wheeling were a primary line of the project subject to commission licensing.[19]

Eventually all sales at wholesale by a public utility participating in an interstate power pool were deemed to be jurisdictional sales, making it unnecessary to trace power flows across state lines to establish federal jurisdiction.[20] Similarly, the Federal Power Commission was found to have plenary jurisdiction over all wholesale sales in interstate commerce, including sales by an investor-owned electric utility to a generation-dependent requirements customer in the same state.[21] These precedents greatly expanded the number of full and partial requirements contracts subject to regulation.

Power pools, which extended the scale and scope of individual utilities in both generation and transmission, also presented an important opportunity for assertion of federal regulation. Without ordering wheeling, the commission could still pass on the propriety of power pooling arrangements covering seasonal power interchange, reserve sharing, and transmission service, inducing at least one major power pool to open its membership to any electric utility, regardless of size or degree of vertical integration.[22] Power pools accommodated a portfolio of different kinds of generation plants (base, load-following, and peaking) and allowed member utilities to coordinate supply, demand, and reliability factors economically within a regional service area. Scalability and diversification enabled power pools to achieve significant economies in electricity generation and storage while enhancing reliability. By 1970, nationwide, there were more than twenty power pools established by formal pooling agreements and an additional network of informal coordinating organizations—all brought forward by Section 202 of the Federal Power Act, which directs the commission "to divide the country into regional districts for the voluntary interconnection and coordination of facilities for the generation, transmission, and sale of electric energy" and "to promote and encourage such interconnection and coordination within ... and between such districts."[23]

Notwithstanding such developments and reorganization of utility holding companies under the Public Utility Holding Company Act, passage of the Federal Power Act left the basic structure of the power industry largely unchanged from Insull's day. Investor-owned utilities continued to supply most of the nation's power requirements, each typically generating, transmitting, and distributing electricity under an exclusive franchise to serve captive retail and wholesale requirements customers within a defined territory at rates regulated by state commissions. As self-sufficient providers, vertically integrated utilities dispatched and transmitted their own power generation, distributed it at retail, and controlled the wires from power plant to ultimate consumer. Competition from other sources of power could not threaten their licensed monopoly status. Retail rates, based on a utility's operating and capital costs, remained under state regulation. Investor-owned utilities had every motive, and legal sanction, to use their high-voltage wires to protect the power they generated and the markets they served from third-party competition.[24]

Some called the regulatory response to natural monopoly an implicit compact, "a protective device rather than ... a promotional or developmental one."[25] As described by a federal court of appeals, "A monopoly on service in a particular geographical area ... is granted to the utility in exchange for a regime of intensive regulation, including price regulation, quite alien to the free market. ... Each party to the compact gets something in the bargain. As a general rule, utility investors are provided a level of stability in earnings and value less likely to be attained in the unregulated ... sector; in turn, ratepayers are afforded universal, nondiscriminatory service and protection from monopolistic profits through political control over an economic enterprise."[26] But the regulatory compact, even so described, did nothing to encourage competition in power generation or loosen each utility's stranglehold on transmission of power over its high-voltage wires. "Without regulation," wrote one contrarian economist, "the firm would face competition from neighboring firms which might encroach on its territory. ... Any removal of regulation would increase the elasticity of demand faced by a single firm above the elasticity of the market and so lead to lower prices."[27]

Otter Tail: A Crack in the Monopoly Monolith

In the 1960s Otter Tail Power Company, a small investor-owned utility, sold electric power at retail to customers in hundreds of towns and hamlets in western Minnesota and the eastern Dakotas over a large transmission grid. Otter Tail served each town under an exclusive municipal franchise that created a monopoly submarket for distribution and sale of electric power at retail. In addition to its own retail distribution, Otter Tail sold power at wholesale and wheeled power to independent municipal systems that in turn resold the power at retail. The rates and terms applicable to Otter Tail's sales and wheeling services were regulated by the Federal Power Commission. In a few towns it served at retail Otter Tail faced competition from municipalities seeking to create municipally owned distribution systems that would displace Otter Tail as power distributor within the municipalities' franchise areas.

When Otter Tail's twenty-year retail franchise in Elbow Lake, Minnesota, ended, the townspeople voted to establish their own municipal distribution system but still expected Otter Tail to wheel, over its own wires, low-cost power marketed by the U.S. Bureau of Reclamation (USBR) from nearby federal hydroelectric sites. Intransigent at the loss of its retail franchise and fearing further business erosion, Otter Tail refused to wheel USBR power to Elbow Lake or to sell it power at wholesale.[28]

In 1966 Elbow Lake petitioned the Federal Power Commission to order Otter Tail to interconnect and wheel power. The commission approved a temporary interconnection, upheld on appeal.[29] Later the commission confirmed the interconnection and ordered wholesale service, conceding it could not compel Otter Tail to wheel power under the Federal Power Act.[30] But the matter did not end there. In a parallel proceeding, a federal district court responded to an antitrust suit filed by the Department of Justice against Otter Tail. With "strategic dominance in the transmission of power in most of its service area,"[31] the court found, Otter Tail had violated Section 2 of the Sherman Act, frustrating establishment of municipally owned distribution systems by refusing to sell at wholesale or wheel power. The court ordered Otter Tail to offer wholesale and wheeling services on terms approved by the commission.[32] Otter Tail appealed to the Supreme Court.[33]

Otter Tail said the district court decision ignored forty years of practice under the Federal Power Act, which Congress could have addressed (but did not) by amending the act to provide for wheeling. The government saw the case as an opportunity to apply the antitrust laws, as fundamental national policy, to the electric power industry and said a utility could not coerce its retail customers in order to suppress competition for the municipal distribution franchise. The case suggested an inflection point in utility regulation and attracted amicus briefs from the Edison Electric Institute, American Public Power Association, and the commission.[34]

In a 4–3 decision, the Supreme Court agreed with the government. "The record makes abundantly clear," wrote Justice Douglas, "that Otter Tail used its monopoly power in the towns in its service area to foreclose competition or ... destroy a competitor, all in violation of the antitrust laws" and did so by leveraging its control over transmission, an essential facility, to cut off a potential municipal entrant from outside sources of electric power.[35] Otter Tail refused to sell or wheel power, the court said, in an attempt to monopolize, proscribed by Section 2 of the Sherman Act. Rejecting Otter Tail's claim that the antitrust laws did not apply, the court said "repeals of the antitrust laws by implication from a regulatory statute are strongly disfavored. ... There is no basis for concluding that the limited authority of the Federal Power Commission to order interconnections was intended to be a substitute for, or to immunize Otter Tail from, antitrust regulation for refusing to deal with municipal corporations."[36]

Otter Tail spawned an outpouring of commentary, much of it critical. Some observers sided with the dissent, which said that "the Court in this case has followed the District Court into a misapplication of the Sherman Act to a highly regulated, natural monopoly industry wholly different from those that have given rise to ordinary antitrust principles."[37] Others complained that *Otter Tail* and similar cases failed to explore "the social costs and benefits or the administrative costs of requiring the creator of an asset to share it with a rival"[38] and called the essential facilities doctrine "troublesome, incoherent, and unmanageable."[39] But the decision underscored a basic economic truth: wheeling power supplied by third-party generators was indispensable if isolated, dependent, and unintegrated distribution companies were to serve retail customers economically; given economies of scale in generation, such companies could not be expected individually to incur the cost required to build their own generating facilities in order to provide equivalent service.

Whatever its doctrinal and pragmatic shortcomings, however, *Otter Tail* confirmed that a competitive market in wholesale electricity requires transmission open to competing suppliers.[40] *Otter Tail* was the first major challenge to the electric utility industry's vertical monopoly business model, sheltered for decades by compliant state commissions. "Regulation is acquired by the industry and is designed and operated primarily for its benefit," said George Stigler, a leading economist, echoing Samuel Insull. "Every industry ... that has enough political power to utilize the state will seek to control entry ... and retard the rate of growth of new firms."[41] By controlling transmission, investor-owned utilities also controlled access to the grid and were able to foreclose competition in generation. *Otter Tail* looked at foreclosure through the lens of antitrust, disregarded the regulatory compact, and set the stage for further changes to come. Just a few years later, when Arkansas Power & Light Company filed a wholesale rate increase with the commission, several of its municipal wholesale customers in retail competition with the utility argued the increase should be denied as "'an attempt to squeeze [them] ... out of competition and to make them more susceptible to the persistent attempts of the company to take over the public[ly] owned systems in the State.'"[42] The Supreme Court agreed, holding that the commission must consider allegations of price squeeze in setting wholesale rates.[43]

PURPA and the Dawn of Competition

In October 1973, just months after the Supreme Court's decision in *Otter Tail*, the Organization of the Petroleum Exporting Countries (OPEC), angered by United States' military aid to Israel as Egypt attacked, reduced petroleum production and imposed a total embargo against the United States. The embargo disrupted world petroleum markets and reduced the availability of foreign crude oil. When it ended five months later, OPEC had raised the price of a barrel of oil almost sixfold. The price increase rippled through domestic energy industries, inflating fuel and power prices and altering lifestyles. "Thermostats were turned down in offices and homes," wrote the *CQ Almanac;* "gasoline was scarce and lines were long at service stations when it was available."[44] Residential and industrial utility rates rose sharply, and overall electricity sales declined. Within less than a year the stock market had lost almost half its value. The energy crisis demanded greater government intervention, but the nation lacked a coherent national energy policy.[45]

After years of inaction, President Jimmy Carter moved to meet the crisis. In April 1977, standing in the White House Rose Garden, he announced a National Energy Plan, the defining initiative of his presidency. "Our decision about energy," he said, "will test the character of the American people and the ability of the President and the Congress to govern this nation."[46] It was nothing less, he said, than the "moral equivalent of war." The plan proposed far-reaching initiatives, eventually contained in complex legislation called the National Energy Act of 1978,[47] which sought to reduce dependence on foreign oil, encourage conservation, and develop sustainable sources of energy. It also became, almost inadvertently, the entering wedge of change that was to remake the electric utility industry in the following decades.

When presented to the House of Representatives in May 1977, the plan took the form of a 283-page bill containing more than one hundred separate bits of legislation.[48] Among those initiatives, the plan gave the Federal Energy Regulatory Commission (FERC), successor to the Federal Power Commission, sweeping authority to order utilities to interconnect, sell, and exchange power and provide necessary transmission services.[49] This was, on its face, a fix squarely directed at the problem the Supreme Court had confronted in *Otter Tail*. On emerging from the legislative mill, however, the plan's interconnection and wheeling provisions were far more conditional. An interconnection or wheeling order could not result in "reasonably ascertainable uncompensated economic loss" and had to "preserve existing competitive relationships." As a result, FERC issued few such orders between 1978 and 1992, when further legislation granted unambiguous authority.[50]

Fierce lobbying by private utility interests also diluted many other provisions of the National Energy Act. But one lobbying effort went the other way. Wheelabrator-Frye, a New Hampshire manufacturer of environmental and energy systems, had built a waste-to-energy plant near Boston that burned garbage and sold heat to a nearby General Electric factory.[51] Wheelabrator considered using some of the heat to make electricity to sell to a local utility but knew, as an independent producer of power, it would face strong resistance in negotiating acceptable price and interconnection terms. To solve this problem, Wheelabrator needed at least three things: a realistic price formula, the right to require the purchasing utility to interconnect and take its plant's power, and exemption of its plant from state and federal utility regulation that would require it, among other things, to sell its power at cost plus an agreed rate of return. It hired Washington counsel and attracted the support of Senator John A. Durkin, a New Hampshire Democrat with an interest in hydroelectricity, small-scale power systems, and rate reform. Senator Durkin's help proved consequential.[52]

Section 210 of the Public Utility Regulatory Policies Act (PURPA), an obscure element of the National Energy Act, came to be the most significant of its many initiatives. As framed by Senator Durkin, Section 210 required utilities to purchase power from cogenerators, such as Wheelabrator, and small power generators at the utility's "avoided cost," defined as "the cost to the electric utility of the electric energy which, but for the purchase ..., such utility would generate or purchase from another source."[53] So defined, avoided cost included both the variable and capital costs of power plants built after 1978, when PURPA became law,[54] but became the subject of further debate and refinement in subsequent years. Section 210 also freed cogenerators from onerous utility regulation but gave them transmission rights comparable to those of utilities. FERC, accorded final authority to develop pricing and administrative rules, expanded application of the new law to its limits.

At one stroke, PURPA opened the electric utility industry to a new class of nonutility participants, called "qualifying facilities" or QFs. Exemption from utility rate regulation and an assured market for output proved to be powerful inducements, creating, out of whole cloth, an independent generating sector that would lead in time to development of a competitive bulk power market. Utilities could no longer exclude or dictate terms to nonutility generators but had to interconnect[55] and buy their power at the utilities' incremental or avoided cost. QFs now had a valuable contractual put. They could require utilities to buy their power at rates not subject to state regulatory review or based on the seller's own cost of production, whether low or high.[56] Life-of-loan power purchase agreements with creditworthy utilities assured a predictable stream of dollars sufficient to build power plants using highly leveraged, nonrecourse project finance. Legislative fiat had flattened barriers to entry in the power generation business.

Utilities saw a threat to their historic franchise and sued to overturn PURPA's displacement of state regulation and its rate incentives for cogenerators and small power producers. In two separate decisions the Supreme Court confirmed the constitutionality of the program and FERC's implementing rules.[57] Once these legal challenges were resolved, entrepreneurial developers responded quickly, saddling utilities with relatively high-cost power they could not refuse. In just a few years independent power producers were to account for more than half the utility industry's annual capacity additions.[58] This mushroom development appeared to fulfill the vision of

Senator Charles Percy, a legislative proponent of PURPA, who predicted "a new era in electric power production" based on "small energy-producing technologies, all of which would supply electric power in small amounts, be operated locally, and be owned by individuals or small companies instead of central electric utility companies."[59]

Insull's regulated monopoly model, which had survived the Depression and continued intact for decades thereafter, now confronted irreversible change.[60] Investor-owned utilities faced the prospect of competition in wholesale power generation just as the industry began to exhaust economies of scale.[61] Critics of conventional rate regulation were emboldened. Section 210 aside, President Carter's program of massive government intervention in the energy sector, including price controls, was widely seen as a failure, yielding record inflation and long lines at filling stations. It was time for a radical reassessment. Neoclassical economists deemed public utility rate structures inefficient and urged new pricing principles, based on marginal costs.[62] Alfred Kahn, an academic turned regulator, became an arch-proponent of market-based rates and, as chair of the New York Public Service Commission, pioneered time-of-day rate differentials for utilities,[63] while Milton Friedman, an iconic professor of economics at the University of Chicago, also attracted a following of true believers. "Centralized governmental control over the economy," Friedman wrote, "has never been able to achieve either freedom or a decent standard of living for the ordinary man."[64]

Paul Joskow: Herald of a New Order

Friedman's philosophy and Kahn's focus on marginal costs resonated with students of the electric utility industry, who found much not to like in its pervasive multijurisdictional regulation by federal and state agencies, in particular oversight of failed nuclear projects sponsored by the likes of Bonneville and TVA. "Evidence is mounting that the industry's investment decisions of the 1970's have produced economic losses measured in scores of billions of dollars," said one academic critic. "Regulatory allocation of losses in the electricity industry has threatened the financial viability of many utilities, forced the closure of many industrial plants, and exposed millions of consumers to the hardship and financial dislocation of 'rate shock'—a dramatic one-time increase in electric rates."[65] The central concept of natural monopoly, subject to cost-based rate regulation, was ripe for deconstruction. By the 1980s profound dissatisfaction with the existing state of affairs drove a search for market-based reform, based on fundamental changes in industry structure foreshadowed by *Otter Tail* and Section 210.

Prominent among industry analysts considering a new direction for the electric utility business was Paul Joskow, then a rising young economics professor at MIT, protégé of Alfred Kahn, and author or coauthor of several scholarly articles and books. In 1983 Joskow and Richard Schmalensee, professor of applied economics at MIT, coauthored a groundbreaking book, *Markets for Power: An Analysis of Electric Utility Deregulation,*[66] sharply critical of the electric power industry "in which most sellers have protected monopolies and regulated prices, so that they are insulated from the discipline of the marketplace."[67] Their book reimagined the industry as restructured and market-driven.

The most promising starting point, the authors found, was the utility-to-utility market for wholesale power, the industry's potentially competitive element (unlike transmission and distribution, monopoly functions that would require continuing regulation). In a competitive wholesale market an importing firm, like the municipal distribution utility in *Otter Tail*, could contract to have low-cost power wheeled from a remote power source to the utility's service area using—if accessible—the intervening wires of the wheeling utility. To do this, however, the importing firm would have to "transport power over transmission lines at appropriate rates and under appropriate conditions"[68]—an essential right not yet granted by federal regulation. The "transmission network ...," Joskow and Schmalensee wrote, "is the heart of the modern electric power system."[69] With Section 210 clearly in mind, the authors concluded that wholesale power competition, given open transmission access, "can promote production at minimum cost by encouraging low-cost suppliers to expand and by making these supplies available where they are most valuable."[70] Generation of power, unlike transmission, was not seen as a natural monopoly.[71]

To peer into the industry's future, the authors considered four different deregulation scenarios, predicted the probable agreements that would replace the internal arrangements of vertically integrated utilities, and established benchmarks to measure the likely success of each scenario.[72] Scenario Four, the most far-reaching change, envisioned a regulated regional power pooling and transmission entity that would own and operate the high-voltage transmission network. Enabled by open-access transmission, independent, large-scale generation companies would sell power into an unregulated market designed to call forth necessary quantities and types of generating capacity. The pooling-transmission entity would then physically deliver the power and provide a framework for settling the underlying purchase and sale transactions. Retail rates would remain subject to state regulation, and independent franchised monopoly distribution companies would provide retail service.[73]

Given what happened to the electric utility industry in the following decades, the authors were remarkably prescient, but hardly naive about the difficult problems deregulation would pose. Since Insull's day the industry had been dominated by vertically integrated utilities that owned and seamlessly operated generation, transmission, and distribution assets. Deconstruction of the vertically integrated model would require new institutional arrangements linking the industry's constituent elements. Joskow and Schmalensee shrewdly forecast the likely nature of those arrangements but expressed caution. "Deregulation is not a panacea for the electric utility industry," Joskow said at the time. "The kind of deregulation model that was applied to the airlines, the trucking industry, and even to the telecommunications industry is not relevant here."[74]

Essential to any deregulation scenario, the authors asserted, would be an open-access regional transmission-coordination system that interconnected and centrally dispatched generating plants, using command and control, a bidding or brokering scheme, or some combination of the two.[75] "Under each of the deregulation scenarios," they added, "some pooling and coordination entity will have to be created to serve as an intermediary (both physical and financial) between individual producers of electric power and wholesale customers (primarily distribution companies)."[76]

The exact characteristics of such an entity might vary, the authors predicted, but it would in any event dispatch generation in merit order, monitor power flows over the transmission system, rationally determine system expansion, and aggregate demand profiles of individual load-serving utilities. It would also serve as a clearinghouse to enable contractual relationships, much like a stock or commodities exchange. Joskow and Schmalensee thus anticipated the salient features of the regional transmission organizations that were to remake the power industry almost fifteen years hence.

But transformation of the vertically integrated monopoly electric utility industry, they warned, would not be a simple affair and would require pervasive structural, regulatory, and market design reforms.

Markets for Power was just the opening salvo in Joskow's career-long effort to shape the future of a bedrock industry. A prolific author and widely connected energy economist now the president of the Alfred P. Sloan Foundation, he was present at the creation of the restructured utility business, having (with a handful of others) laid down the essential markers for deregulation, which eventually influenced Congress and the regulators. "The basic reform model," he wrote many years later, "... has been (a) to separate (structurally or functionally) the potentially competitive segments from the monopoly/oligopoly network segments that would be regulated, (b) to remove price and entry regulation from the competitive segments, (c) to unbundle the sale of regulated network service from competitive services, (d) to establish transparent prices for access to and use of the network, and (e) to allow end-users (local distribution companies or consumers ...) to choose their suppliers of competitive services and have them arrange to have it 'shipped' to them over an open access network with a regulated cap on prices for providing transportation service."[77]

The theoretical blueprint in *Markets for Power*, however insightful, was not self-actuating. The path to realization had to overcome resistance by investor-owned utilities, especially those in high-cost states such as California, whose expensive assets would not allow them to sell electricity as cheaply as new entrants. By 1983 it was clear a utility operating a multibillion-dollar nuclear power plant would need to charge higher rates to recover its costs than an independent producer using a turbine generator fueled by cheap natural gas. If higher rates could not be passed on to its customers, such a utility would have incurred "stranded costs." In the dawning era of competition, the utility would still be responsible for paying off the cost of expensive equipment acquired earlier under regulation. Unless it could extract compensation from its ratepayers for stranded costs, it would not be able to compete with new low-cost providers.

"Every investment that we're charging for right now has gone through a prudency review at our state commission ...," said one utility executive. He continued:

And you want to now come around as an afterthought and say, "we're going to deregulate, allow this new technology to come in and undercut the old, and all those costs are going to be shoved on share holders, and millions of people across the country that own stocks in utilities are going to take it in the chops?" To say that they should eat that is really a violation of the regulatory compact that was agreed to. ... When utilities make [these] decisions they have a monopoly franchise, and they agree to a regulated modest rate of return in exchange for a reasonable return on their investment. Everyone realizes those are 20, 30, 40 year investments for these big power plants. In the middle of that we're going to change the rules? ... The stranded generating or above market costs need to be amortized as a surcharge that will be paid by the people who take advantage of the new world.[78]

Beyond the resistance of major stakeholders, deregulation of the electric power business also posed knotty structural problems unique to a network industry, as Joskow and Schmalensee had recognized in their book. In a system characterized by "transmission constraints that limit the geographic expanse of competition, generation ownership concentration within constrained import areas, the non-storability of electricity, and the very low elasticity of demand for electricity," Joskow wrote years later, generator market power was to prove a serious problem.[79] The transition to deregulation invited gaming and market manipulation, particularly under peak-load conditions. To deal with the problem, the proponents of competition focused intensely on market design. "The key technical challenge in relying on decentralized competition at the generation level," Joskow observed, "is to do so in a way that preserves the operating and investment efficiencies that are associated with vertical and horizontal integration while mitigating the significant costs that the institution of regulated monopoly has created."[80]

Joskow's career was in the ascendant. His research reflected a masterful blend of applied economic theory, detailed institutional analysis, and careful econometrics, eventually leading him to be selected as a Distinguished Fellow of the American Economic Association. At MIT, in just a few years, he rose to be head of the Department of Economics, was concurrently professor of economics and management at MIT's Sloan School of Management, held a named chair, and was director of the MIT Center for Energy and Environmental Policy. His publications were legion, and he served on corporate boards and as a member of industry task forces and advisory boards. This platform enabled him to speak with authority as deregulation progressed. Less an advocate than a clear-eyed analyst, he saw marketplace competition, whatever its likely shortcomings, as a better alternative for the utility business than top-down regulation. As a widely acclaimed scholar and lecturer, he helped frame public debate, but, as he well understood, renovating a regulatory scheme in place for almost fifty years was to prove a formidable task. Progress in the years immediately following publication of *Markets for Power* was not encouraging. "The electricity sector," he wrote, "... is stuck somewhere between the policy framework of 1935 and the vision for restructuring, competition, and regulatory reform."[81]

A Restructured Electricity Market Takes Form

The law was slow to change. A century of jurisprudence had established the basic principle that electric utilities are quasi-public entities, providing essential services at cost-based rates in exchange for legal monopoly.[82] The Federal Power Act, enacted in 1935, adopted this principle, including the requirement of "just and reasonable" rates, construed to mean provision of power at lowest reasonable cost.[83] FERC's more recent advocacy of rates determined by market efficiency, in the natural gas and oil pipeline industries, had met with withering scorn from courts of review focused on consumer protection, hardly a good omen for electric utility deregulation.[84] In a leading case, a federal court of appeals reaffirmed that "the most useful and reliable starting point for rate regulation is an inquiry into costs."[85]

FERC proceeded nonetheless. In 1985, using terms that could have been borrowed from *Markets for Power*, it started a notice of inquiry (NOI) "to evaluate its present policies toward wholesale electricity transactions and transmission service" and specifically "how its policies promote, or whether they impede, efficiency in electricity markets and to determine whether there are available alternatives."[86] FERC sought comments on utility-to-utility coordination services (interchange transactions and economy energy sales) and open-access transmission as a "necessary element to competitive electricity markets."[87] FERC also requested comments on marginal cost pricing as an alternative to the regulatory gold standard, average embedded cost of service.[88] These were topics of intense current interest to Joskow and other like-minded economists.

The NOI generated prolix comments and several conferences, but no action or policy declaration. Joskow supplied an explanation. "FERC's jurisdiction is limited," he wrote. "It can regulate the rates charged for transmission service, but except in extraordinary circumstances it cannot order a utility to provide such service. Thus most transmission arrangements are voluntary, reflecting regulatory and financial incentives, the availability of capacity to serve non-requirements loads, the historical cooperation between proximate integrated utilities, and the threat of anti-trust sanction."[89] Without authority to open the nation's high-voltage wires to all comers, FERC could not mandate a competitive wholesale power market. Instead it would have to build on the limited competition provided by QFs under PURPA as an entering wedge.

After a two-year hiatus, FERC moved forward. In a speech to the Edison Electric Institute FERC's chairman, acknowledging the rapid development of QF power, said it would explore competitive bidding for electric generating capacity supplied by QFs, utilities, and independent power producers as an alternative means of determining avoided cost rates.[90] Competitive pricing could be just and reasonable, the chairman said, where supporting markets for power exist.[91] There was at least some precedent for FERC's prospective reliance on competition. In 1983, the year *Markets for Power* was published, FERC had authorized four investor-owned utilities operating in a three-state area to buy and sell two electrical commodities, economy energy and block energy, at unregulated, market-based prices within a prescribed bandwidth for an experimental two-year period. As a precondition to creation of a competitive market, the participating utilities agreed to provide each other open-access transmission on a voluntary basis.[92] Not until Congress changed the law in 1992, however, was growth of the wholesale nonutility generating market assured.

In 1988 FERC issued notices of proposed rulemaking (NOPRs) that would, among other things, allow QFs to build or own interconnection facilities and transmission lines free of Federal Power Act jurisdiction if used to transmit power to a purchasing utility. The NOPRs also authorized competitive bidding to determine the avoided cost of capacity supplied by QFs, utilities, and independent power producers but did not make bidding dependent on transmission access since, in FERC's view, bidding was simply an alternative means of identifying avoided costs and would not increase a purchasing utility's market power.[93]

Without assured connection to numerous sellers and buyers via open-access transmission, however, FERC could not by rule call forth a robust competitive market for generation. A potentially important class of participants, independent power producers that were not QFs, remained subject to cost-of-service regulation and did not enjoy assured transmission access.[94] Charles A. Trabandt, an outspoken dissenter at FERC, defended the historic regulatory regime. "We ... were not commissioned to use this nation's interstate electric power system," he said, "to test new economic theories and regulatory concepts on a generic basis, as if that system were the world's largest micro-economic model. The Commission needs to ... refocus its attention on the American consumer rather than the primacy of economic efficiency in theory."[95] Against such resistance, and with no legal authority to order open-access transmission, it appeared FERC would have to defer fundamental change until Congress acted.

Joskow, who styled himself a noninterventionist, believed otherwise. "I am optimistic," he wrote shortly after FERC issued its NOPRs, "that the new wholesale markets are and will be competitive. ... Active markets for short- and medium-term power in excess of the current needs of integrated utilities have emerged in most areas of the country. Coordination and wheeling transactions have increased substantially. ... As a result of extensive inter-connections, coordination agreements and power-pooling arrangements and voluntary wheeling, ... these markets are often very competitive."[96] Joskow was not indifferent to the importance of transmission access or utilities' limited obligation under federal law to provide it. "Nevertheless," he said, "utilities voluntarily negotiate transmission arrangements with other utilities all the time."[97] And, drawing on his experience as a director of the New England Electric System, he noted that "extensive wheeling service has been made available in New England ... for QF power."[98] Joskow said power producers, using the implicit threat of potential antitrust sanction, could often get wheeling service through negotiation and without any special regulatory obligation.

To accelerate the shift to competitive power markets, however, he thought those markets should include more than QFs. "Ideally," he said, "a utility should be able to turn to the most economical supply sources, whether QF generating plants, independent non-QF plants, excess capacity and energy available from proximate utilities, or internal utility production."[99] To make competitive markets a reality, he concluded, independent producers, like QFs, would need to be free of FERC's traditional embedded cost-of-service accounting principles, and all producers ultimately would need access to open transmission. In such markets, Joskow speculated, a regulator would set target quantities of power and require "utilities to solicit competing bids to supply these quantities, choosing the most economical mix of bids submitted. The regulator sets the quantities and the market sets the prices."[100]

But exactly how would the market set the prices? The answer to that question depended on a theory of spot pricing taking into account the unique conditions of electric power systems, initially put forth by Joskow's MIT colleague, Fred Schweppe, and others,[101] and further developed by William Hogan, an influential economics professor at Harvard's Kennedy School.[102] Spot pricing makes no distinction based on the ownership or regulatory status of the generating unit or transmission system; "the formula is the same regardless of who owns and controls the generators, transmission/distribution system, and customers."[103] In a spot pricing world transmission between two locations on the system is simply the difference in spot prices at those locations, sometimes referred to as a congestion cost. "Transmission prices calculated according to optimal spot pricing theory," Hogan wrote in 1992, "incorporate the marginal cost of generation, the marginal cost of losses, and the opportunity cost created by congestion in the system. Economic dispatch calls for use of the cheapest combination of power plants needed to meet existing load. If all the plants and loads were located in the same place, then the plants would be dispatched in order of lowest to highest marginal cost. If plants are located in different places, and power must travel over the transmission grid, then the losses of power in transmission should enter the economic dispatch calculation."[104]

A heavily loaded transmission grid, Hogan explained, also often has congestion bottlenecks that prevent full use of the cheapest plants on the grid. The cost of system congestion is reflected in the different price of power at each bus, depending on its location, because thermal limits on the flow of power over individual lines prevent access to the cheapest power sources if they are upstream of the congestion. "It is possible to calculate the congestion cost induced by any thermal constraint," Hogan continued, "and thereby estimate the effect on the optimal spot prices throughout the network."[105] In this formulation transmission prices equal the difference between spot prices at different locations on the grid. For each source-to-destination option, there is a difference between the value of power delivered to the destination and the cost of producing that power at the source—a difference that defines the maximum a user would be willing to pay for transmission capacity. With an appropriately structured bidding system, Hogan concluded, "a set of bids for transmission capacity from bus to bus could be identified with an associated maximum price that could be paid for each right."[106]

Using a model based on Hogan's formulation, a grid operator, such as the one Joskow hypothesized in *Markets for Power,* would be able to determine the market clearing price at each bus within the grid for any given level of transmission capacity and the most efficient combination of power bids to supply current system load. The operator would then dispatch generation in accordance with the model and use a settlement system to manage financial payments among the participants. Promising as this forecast appeared in theory, however, it remained critically dependent on open-access transmission. "It is clear," wrote Hogan, "that adopting a transmission pricing regime that replaces contract paths with contract networks will require major institutional change."[107] Change was soon to come.

Figure 4.1
Paul Joskow at a lecture at the Center of Global Energy Policy at Columbia University titled "From Shortages to Abundance: Natural Gas: Past, Present and Future," October 29, 2013.

Figure 4.2
Paul Joskow at the Penn Program on Regulation as part of the Risk Regulation Lecture
Series, March 27, 2012.

The Energy Policy Act: Congress Acts at Last

With a stroke of the pen, President George H. W. Bush thrust the electric
utility industry into a new era. At a ceremony on an oil rig near Maurice,
Louisiana, Bush signed the Energy Policy Act of 1992, landmark legislation squarely aimed at the high-voltage transmission monopoly exercised
since Insull's day by the nation's investor-owned utilities.[108] At long last a
third-party power producer had the legal right, through the Federal Energy
Regulatory Commission as intermediary, to require a transmitting utility
to wheel its power to a wholesale buyer at just and reasonable rates.[109] As a
concession to investor-owned utilities, the act did not authorize the commission to compel retail wheeling—the sale of power from remote suppliers to retail customers—but still advanced the Bush administration's
free-market energy policy.[110] "We believe increased access to electric transmission facilities for wholesale buyers and sellers," said the deputy secretary
of DOE, "[will] increase economic efficiency, stimulate competition, and

Figure 4.3
Paul Joskow at the Penn Program on Regulation as part of the Risk Regulation Lecture Series, March 27, 2012.

ensure that the nation's industries, shops, and residences benefit from their local utility having access to electricity at the lowest reasonable cost."[111]

To do this, beyond opening transmission on the grid, the act exempted independent power producers—the group Joskow thought essential to competitive electricity markets—from the provisions of the Public Utility Holding Company Act that then governed the corporate structure of regulated power companies. These producers, called exempt wholesale generators, could now freely sell power at wholesale without regard to energy efficiency (unlike QFs under PURPA), unconstrained by cost-based regulation and other onerous restrictions imposed on public utilities since the New Deal. Fulfilling Joskow's prescription for competitive power markets, the act opened the utility system to a new class of independent players.

Investor-owned utilities were not enthralled by the new order of things and worked hard to blunt the act's competitive impact. Joseph Paquette, chief executive officer of Philadelphia Electric Company, among many other utility executives, opposed open-access transmission and wanted

Figure 4.4
Paul Joskow in Stockholm at the ceremony in December 2010 awarding the Nobel Prize in economics to Peter Diamond. From left, Messrs. Poterba, Diamond, Joskow, and Blanchard.

to keep the regulatory vise of the Public Utility Holding Company Act in place. Unleashing competitive forces, he argued, would turn a transmission system built for customers' benefit into a vehicle allowing private entrepreneurs to profit. "The only ones who will benefit are the independent power producers and their select customers. Outside of this small group, everyone else stands to lose through higher costs and less reliable service."[112]

This was, on its face, a brief for continuing regulatory protection that Insull would have embraced. It won the support of the Edison Electric Institute and many of the chief executives of its member utilities, who opposed opening the transmission system to nonutility companies. Forty investor-owned utilities formed the Electric Reliability Coalition, which lobbied against the act and warned it would "establish a new category of unregulated electric power producers that [consumers] would pay for through higher electricity bills." To be sure, a handful of contrarian utilities saw potential profit in new sources of power, selling surplus power to customers outside their franchise areas, and wheeling power for others.[113] But most investor-owned utilities viewed the act as a dire threat to their core business.

Although easily dismissed as naked self-interest, the argument advanced by Joseph Paquette found another, ostensibly neutral champion in Richard Cudahy, a federal judge on the Seventh Circuit Court of Appeals. "Disintegration," he wrote, "is bound to introduce costs as well as provide benefits. Who is to maintain reserves for the low-cost power obtained at distant markets, and what is the cost of maintenance of reserves and how should it be compensated? Vertically integrated utilities have had a great deal of experience in planning for a variety of system contingencies. This may mean drawing on spinning reserves, starting up idle plants, buying power from a neighbor or wheeling it from a distant source, or shedding load if necessary, all to be accomplished in the most reliable and economic way."[114]

The electric utility business, Judge Cudahy said, is an infrastructural industry whose members are affected with a public interest and have an obligation to serve. "... [I]t is uncertain," he added, "whether this kind of attitude can be maintained in the case of a utility whose best customers have been 'cherry-picked' by upstarts, leaving the less desirable customers for the utility."[115] Even Joskow and Schmalensee, proponents of competitive electricity markets, expressed caution. "There appear to be large potential efficiencies associated with vertical and horizontal integration, especially at the generation and transmission levels," they concluded. "While vertical and horizontal disintegration may increase the competitiveness of wholesale markets, significant costs may thus be associated with any such restructuring."[116] The years following passage of the act, as Joskow and Schmalensee had predicted, saw an intense regulatory effort to put in place new arrangements for an industry in flux.

The noisy opposition of investor-owned utilities aside, the act, although groundbreaking, was built around the traditional model of a regulated monopoly distribution company having exclusive rights to serve retail customers within its franchise area. The act did not require utilities to open their retail markets to competitive suppliers, nor did it require them to buy power from independent producers or exempt wholesale generators.[117] It did, however, authorize open-access transmission, and the Federal Energy Regulatory Commission lost no time in expanding opportunities for independent power producers to contract with utility buyers, even those located on another utility's transmission system.

In short order it required utilities to publish detailed information about transmission capacity on their systems, offer a full range of transmission services to wholesale buyers and sellers, and agree to file open-access transmission tariffs as a prerequisite to merger approval.[118] Although freeing up the balkanized grid, these initiatives did not, except in the merger context, require utilities to file generic open-access transmission tariffs or define the nature and pricing of the transmission services on offer. Still, the proposals were a clear sign FERC intended to pursue a pro-competitive agenda.

As further evidence of its intent, FERC adopted an idea Congress had explored in framing the act—voluntary formation of regional transmission groups, including both users and owners of high-voltage wires, to deal with transmission planning, operations, and pricing. A key requirement, in FERC's view, was that member utilities expand transmission to handle all wheeling requests.[119] Joskow and Schmalensee had anticipated FERC's interest in regional transmission groups. Their book, *Markets for Power*, paid special attention to tight power pools, alliances formed by independent utilities to coordinate operations and realize economies of scale. "Tight pools," they wrote, "impose the most extensive formal requirements and coordination upon pool members" including "capacity requirements, central dispatch of generating plants as a single system, and coordinated scheduling of maintenance and unit commitment."[120] Tight pools were therefore foundational precedents for the regional transmission groups FERC was proposing, but, as Joskow and Schmalensee foresaw, it would have to "formulate rules and regulations to structure the market ... [and] provide access to coordination and wheeling services on reasonable terms."[121] This was exactly the exercise FERC had begun.

California and FERC Order 888: Design for a Restructured Industry

Deregulation was meanwhile vigorously underway at the state level, with California a first mover. "High electricity rates became a major issue in California in the early 1990s," wrote Joskow several years later, "... stimulated by a severe recession and the loss of manufacturing jobs."[122] In fact, the state's electricity rates were 50 percent higher than the national average, driven by high-cost QF contracts and an undersupply of new utility capacity. Stung by the unrecoverable cost of nuclear plants, local utilities had little economic incentive to build new generation.[123] The California Public Utility Commission (CPUC) saw a pressing need to restructure the state's electric utility business. Under its brilliant, if imperious, president, Daniel William Fessler, the CPUC wanted to use free-market principles to bring down the cost of electricity. Its staff issued a 1993 report, called the Yellow Book, proposing, among other alternatives, that investor-owned utilities sell their generation assets. Retaining only their transmission and distribution functions, utilities would then earn money by transporting power from many independent suppliers to retail customers. This was a formula for retail wheeling, the ultimate fix excluded from the Energy Policy Act, and a clear threat to California's utilities. Southern California Edison (SCE), for one, said retail wheeling would leave it with stranded assets—high-cost investments with impaired economic value in a competitive marketplace. Its shareholders would suffer, SCE argued, unless it could recover the cost of stranded assets from its customers.[124]

In 1994 the CPUC issued a further policy statement, known as the Blue Book, looking to "markets and the private sector, rather than command-and-control regulation, as the preferred means to achieve the goals established and benefits identified."[125] The views of at least three of the CPUC commissioners were heavily influenced by privatization and restructuring of Britain's state-owned utility system (the CEGB and the Area Boards), driven by the privatization and free-market policies of the Thatcher government, which they studied during a visit before publication of the Blue Book.[126] The devil, as always, resided in the details. The CPUC thought customers should have a choice among competing generation providers and performance-based regulation should replace traditional cost-of-service regulation. It encouraged utilities to divest their power plants and rely instead on a competitive spot market in which to buy and sell electricity. Finally, persuaded by SCE's concerns, it said California utilities should recoup stranded costs through a nonbypassable "competitive transmission charge." The Blue Book stunned stakeholders with its audacity. Utility investors were convinced competition would reduce share values, and shortly after publication of the Blue Book power company stock prices sank and SCE cut its dividend by 30 percent.[127]

The Blue Book drew pushback from the state legislature, which sought a more substantive role in the restructuring process and required the CPUC to issue a further proposal. A schism emerged between two factions within the CPUC. The majority wanted a poolco model, in which generators would sell power into a centralized spot market for distribution to customers; the minority wanted a direct-access model, in which customers would purchase power from any source under bilateral contracts. In its final policy statement the CPUC proposed a power exchange that would run a day-ahead auction market among generators and purchasers for the next day's electricity and an independent system operator that would coordinate the scheduling and dispatch of power from suppliers and arrange transmission access for all bids meeting the spot price determined by the power exchange—features Joskow and Schmalensee had forecast in principle more than a decade before.[128] The final policy statement required all electricity to be provided through the spot market except for power purchased by retail customers dealing directly with suppliers using bilateral contracts. Customers electing to remain with the local utility would have their electricity purchased for them on the spot market. The policy statement also proposed that SCE and Pacific Gas & Electric, major California utilities, "voluntarily" divest 50 percent of their fossil-fueled generating assets.[129] Looking back, Joskow views the final model approved by the CPUC as a compromise. "Most of us," he recalls, "didn't really understand how challenging it would be to create well-functioning wholesale markets, and the arguments have not stopped."[130]

In August 1996 the California legislature enacted CPUC's final policy statement virtually unchanged but imposed a cap on retail rates at 10 percent below current levels for a period of four years to allow for stranded cost recovery. California entered the brave new world of electricity deregulation optimistically but with largely untried arrangements. Governor Pete Wilson, who signed the CPUC deregulation plan into law, said: "We are shifting the balance of power in California. ... We've pulled the plug on another outdated monopoly and replaced it with the promise of a new era of competition."[131]

The restructured California wholesale electricity market was a leap into the future. The new law created two wholly new institutions, the California Independent System Operator (CAISO) and a Power Exchange (PX). It required California investor-owned utilities to turn over operation of their transmission networks to CAISO and the PX and CAISO to operate public markets with transparent market-clearing prices for energy and related services. At the same time it allowed individual generator owners to supply energy and manage congestion in their own interests. It also required utilities to procure power in the volatile spot market, froze retail rates, caused the sale of fossil-fueled generating plants to merchant affiliates of out-of-state utilities, and discouraged use of bilateral long-term electricity supply contracts as a hedge against market volatility.

The implications of these market design decisions, when coupled with high natural gas prices and California utilities' decade-long shortfall in providing new generation capacity, were not immediately apparent but were to become so, disastrously, within a few years. "Generating firms able to sell power only on the spot market," Joskow and Schmalensee had warned years before in *Markets for Power*, "will be extremely vulnerable to opportunistic behavior."[132] The design of competitive electricity markets would therefore prove to be of paramount importance. A market that can be gamed, Murphy might have said, will be gamed.

California's restructuring had an impact far beyond its borders. As Joskow was to observe several years later, FERC realized that "its transmission access and pricing rules might have to support far more radical changes in the structure of the utility industry [including] the functional separation of generation of electricity from distribution service and the opening of retail service to competition."[133] The Energy Policy Act had established open-access transmission in principle, but case-by-case administration of the law was simply unworkable.[134] The industry still needed sweeping reform.

Finally, in April 1996, FERC issued Order 888. The order reflected a historic policy shift. Henceforth the transmission system would promote, rather than impede, competition in the wholesale power market.[135] In FERC's own words, the order was a "legal and policy cornerstone ... to remedy undue discrimination in access to the monopoly-owned transmission wires that control whether and to whom electricity can be transported in interstate commerce."[136] It was a remedy sixty years overdue. FERC's principal instrument was a pro forma open-access nondiscriminatory transmission tariff containing minimum terms and conditions of service.[137] Each public utility owning interstate transmission had to file a conforming tariff opening its wires to third parties on terms, conditions, and rates comparable to those charged its own generating units. Retail customers, excluded under the Energy Policy Act, were eligible for coverage under the pro forma tariff if a transmitting utility offered unbundled retail transmission service voluntarily or under state law. "The future is here," said FERC Chair Betsy Moler when issuing the order, "and the future is competition. It is a global trend, and in North America we are at the forefront. There is no turning back."[138]

Open-access transmission, although vitally important, depended largely on behavioral rules and left vertically integrated utilities intact. To promote competition in the power markets, however, FERC wanted structural separation of transmission and generation. This meant, according to Joskow, that "competitive services (e.g., generation) are to be separated from natural monopoly services (e.g., transmission and distribution), and the regulated monopoly services are to be made available and priced on an unbundled basis to retail consumers. ... All generators compete in unregulated wholesale markets to serve retail demand. Retail customers ... are guaranteed non-discriminatory access to monopoly transmission and distribution 'delivery' services at regulated rates so that they can shop directly in the wholesale market or through competing retail supply agents ... who purchase electricity in wholesale markets and resell to final consumers."[139]

FERC also sought to apply structural separation regionally, not simply to individual utilities. It therefore paid special attention to power pools—contiguous utilities that coordinate their operations to get greater efficiency—and in particular to tight power pools such as Pennsylvania–New Jersey–Maryland (PJM), whose pooling agreements were subject to FERC regulation. PJM, a group of eight separate utility systems linked by high-voltage wires, centrally dispatched the group's generating plants in order to reduce capacity reserves, lower operating costs, and enhance reliability—advantages similar to those once achieved by Insull's holding companies. PJM had detailed agreements and protocols governing relations among its constituent utilities. It operated within a single control area and served combined loads as one system.

Through a central dispatch center, PJM was able to monitor generation output and power flows to meet demand at lowest cost, subject to physical constraints such as transmission line loading and line losses. Power pools like PJM, FERC concluded, "involve agreements containing an intricate set of rights, obligations, and considerations among the members." The filing of an open-access tariff by each member "is not enough to cure undue discrimination in transmission if those public utilities can continue to trade with a selective group within a power pool that discriminatorily excludes others from becoming a member and that provides preferential intra-pool transmission rights and rates."[140]

FERC therefore ordered PJM, among others, to file a joint poolwide tariff. Members would then take service under the tariff, and the pool's wires would be open to any wholesale market participant, wherever located, on the same terms. [141] FERC's focus on power pools was potentially transformative. It also fulfilled the prediction of Joskow and Schmalensee, years earlier, that FERC would have to examine "pooling and coordination arrangements ... to determine whether these arrangements provide access ... on reasonable terms ... to promote wholesale power competition."[142]

To separate control of transmission from generation, FERC also encouraged power pools to adopt a new organizational entity, the independent system operator (ISO), which would operate, but would not own, the high-voltage transmission system previously run by the pool. Independent of all market participants, the ISO would provide open-access, self-scheduled transmission under a single, nondiscriminatory gridwide tariff. It would be responsible for short-term system reliability and exercise operational control over generation in order to regulate and balance power flows and relieve transmission constraints. It would also make system information, including available transmission capacity, public on an electronic network.[143] A further key function, said FERC, would be "to accommodate transactions made in a free and competitive market ... [including] a settlements system and operation of an energy auction."[144] FERC's ISO was the virtual embodiment of the "pooling and coordination entity," Joskow and Schmalensee had projected almost fifteen years before.[145] It remained to be seen whether theory could be reduced to real-world practice.

PJM: The Blueprint Realized

In July 1996, PJM's member utilities filed a massive restructuring plan at FERC intended to transform the existing power pool, formed originally in 1927, into an ISO that would administer a poolwide open-access transmission tariff and a competitive regional wholesale electricity market. PJM was well situated to make the transition. To interconnect their systems, the member utilities had put in place a high-voltage transmission ring enabling them to exchange power, share load, and render mutual assistance in emergencies. They had also established an office to conduct all pool operations, including interchange accounting, planning, and engineering, governed by a management committee representing each member company. The office centrally dispatched generation within the pool, acted as agent for the member companies, but had no ownership interest in operating equipment or transmission assets. The arrangements accommodated coordinated system operation and individual ownership. Each member utility had an equitable interest in the system's total generation capacity but retained first call on the availability of its own wires.[146]

The restructuring plan required further change as the member utilities faced the prospect of yielding control of their transmission assets to an ISO and providing it with necessary financial support and resources. The members were not about to give an untried entity carte blanche. An administrative committee was empowered to approve the ISO's capital budget and, if necessary, to remove the ISO and replace it with a new ISO. Nor were the members inclined to accept FERC's pro forma tariff. The PJM tariff, as adopted by the members, divided the PJM service area into ten zones, corresponding to existing individual service territories. Transmission customers would then pay for network service based on the revenue requirement of the owner in whose zone the load was located, but member utilities would provide each other reciprocal network system access at no charge. Critics of the restructuring plan argued that it undercut the independence of the ISO and failed to use a single, gridwide rate for network transmission services.[147]

PJM also tasked the ISO with running a regional wholesale market for bulk power. The market design drew heavily on a "poolco" model, previously advanced at FERC and similar to the spot market envisaged by Joskow and Schmalensee in *Markets for Power* and Hogan in his influential 1993 paper, "A Competitive Electricity Market Model." In the poolco model, the ISO would centrally dispatch generating resources at least cost on an hourly basis using bid prices submitted (rather than running costs) after accounting for transmission constraints. Generators would be paid the market-clearing price during each hour, not the bid price each generator submitted to the ISO. Spot prices would vary from one geographic location to another to reflect transmission constraints limiting movement of power from low- to high-cost areas.[148] The poolco model adopted by PJM used a two-settlement system. This allowed market participants the option of trading in a forward or day-ahead market for electrical energy based on generation offers, demand bids, and transaction schedules or a real-time energy market in which hourly clearing prices are determined by actual system operating conditions, calculated at short intervals and based on hourly quantity deviations from day-ahead scheduled hourly quantities and real-time prices integrated over the hour.

Under the restructuring plan, sellers into the regional market would submit priced offers for energy and related services on a day-ahead basis. Buyers would submit load forecasts or prices at which they were willing to make purchases. All market participants would also submit schedules for bilateral transactions and self-scheduled generation. The ISO would then determine the least-cost means of satisfying the projected hourly energy, operating reserves, and ancillary services required by market buyers, inform each seller whether its offer for the following day had been accepted, and publicly post its forecast locational marginal prices. The ISO would schedule and dispatch generation on the basis of day-ahead offers using bid-based, security-constrained dispatch.[149] The prices for energy bought and sold in the market would reflect the hourly locational marginal price at each load and generation bus, and the ISO would collect transmission congestion charges from all transactions causing or contributing to congestion. In PJM's market design, trading hubs and zones were based on mathematical aggregates rather than physical boundaries. As new areas of congestion developed, locational marginal prices would therefore reflect changing system constraints, and market forces would determine how transmission reservations were valued over time.

In November 1996 FERC rejected PJM's restructuring plan.[150] The proposed ISO, it found, lacked independence, while the PJM tariff's use of zonal transmission pricing did not square with the pro forma tariff. The PJM utilities confronted an organizational and policy crisis. A halfway solution would not fly. To satisfy FERC's independence concerns, the members formed a not-for-profit limited liability company as the de facto ISO, governed by an independent board, but reserved the right to file for certain changes in transmission services.[151] They also revised the PJM tariff to provide open-access transmission on a comparable basis throughout the pool. All firm transmission users would then pay a single rate. To hedge against congestion costs, firm customers would be awarded fixed transmission rights (FTRs) for specific receipt and delivery point reservations entitling the holder to receive compensation for transmission congestion charges that arise during peak-load hours when differences in locational marginal prices result from the dispatch of generators out of merit order to relieve congestion.[152]

The PJM interchange energy market started operations in April 1997, and shortly before the end of the year FERC recognized PJM as an ISO.[153] Unlike California, PJM's market design did not require utilities to divest generation assets, preserved the role of bilateral contracts, and was to become the gold standard for market design. In 2001, following further development, FERC approved PJM as a regional transmission organization.[154] Thereafter it grew rapidly in size, complexity, and membership. Today hundreds of different firms buy, sell, and trade electricity in PJM, which serves almost sixty million people in thirteen states.[155] Other power pools have also made the transition to become regional transmission organizations.[156] But serious questions remain, even among proponents of competitive power markets, whether restructuring has delivered promised benefits. "The transition to competitive electricity markets," wrote Joskow, "has been a difficult process in the United States ... [and] requires a commitment by policymakers to do what is necessary to make it work."[157]

Joskow Reflects

Although a visionary thought leader, Joskow has typically chosen not to play an advocate's role. He has instead, in books and articles written over decades, taken a holistic, analytical view, well aware that reinventing a century-old industry, dominated by vertically integrated utility monopolies, would not be an easy task. Like his mentor, Alfred E. Kahn, Joskow has used economic analysis to solve public policy problems in ways that recognize a broad array of economic and institutional imperfections.[158] Early in his prolific academic career, he predicted with remarkable accuracy the change that would overtake the electric utility industry years later and then, with a handful of others, sought to shape that change in the most effective way. But he was not the least bit naive about the costs and difficulties of restructuring or the massive political and economic forces at play.

Like many critics of the established order, Joskow saw a pressing need for change. "The system of regulated vertically integrated monopoly," he said in retrospect, "was plagued by cost overruns associated with nuclear power plants, poor operating performance for both nuclear and large fossil-fueled plants, poor fuel procurement decisions, wide price differences between neighboring areas, excess generating capacity, inefficient dispatch and economy energy trading between generating companies, regulatory incentives to keep old inefficient plants operating rather than retiring them, too many small utilities to take advantage of economies of scale, institutional and technological barriers to using the transmission network to access lower cost power, productivity lags, and inefficient retail prices."[159] The solution he and Schmalensee had offered in *Markets for Power* was a mixture of regulatory reform, structural reorganization, information collection, and deregulation, much of which eventually came to pass.[160]

But many intractable problems, uniquely characteristic of the electricity industry, made restructuring problematic, as Joskow had foreseen. A proponent of competition, he still expressed doubt that industry changes had benefited retail customers or mitigated the continuing exercise of market power. "The necessary linkages among participants in an electric power system," he and Schmalensee wrote long before the crisis in the California electricity market, "are too complex and pervasive, and the resultant opportunities for both collusion and socially wasteful opportunistic behavior are too numerous."[161] As a believer in structural solutions, Joskow also feared that continued regulatory intervention would undermine the effectiveness of competitive markets. He saw the need for freeing up the wholesale power market even if transmission and distribution remained regulated monopolies but lamented the lack of a coherent national policy for the electric power industry. Given his grasp of the underlying economic issues, he was not so much a tribune of the new order as a sober analyst reaching carefully hedged conclusions.

At the end of the day, following the epic collapse of California's electricity market, even Joskow had to question whether restructuring of the electricity industry in the United States had achieved its aims. "The overriding reform goal," he said, "has been to create new institutional arrangements … that provide long-term benefits to society and that an appropriate share of those benefits [is] conveyed to consumers through prices that reflect the efficient economic cost of supplying electricity."[162] To reach this goal, he argued, competitive wholesale markets were the touchstone. Competition would provide better incentives for controlling the costs of new and existing power plants, encourage innovation, and—most important—shift the risk of technology choice, construction cost, and operating errors to suppliers and away from consumers. Competing retail sellers would provide formerly captive customers with sophisticated service options, risk management, and demand management.[163] Despite this bright forecast, industry reform proved elusive, made more so by the uncertain impact of reform on costs, prices, innovation, and consumer welfare.[164] Joskow concluded that "creating competitive markets ... requires a commitment by policymakers to do what is necessary to make it work. That commitment has been lacking in the U.S."[165]

To complete the task of industry reform, Joskow said, "we need to stop dealing with the electric power sector by placing band aids on the Federal Power Act of 1935."[166] Under a national electricity policy, following the model of the natural gas regulation, FERC would have clear siting and planning authority over the high-voltage transmission grid; would mandate nationwide creation of regional transmission organizations (like PJM) to operate competitive wholesale electricity markets and large transmission networks; and would require existing vertically integrated utilities to separate generation from distribution facilities. As Joskow acknowledged, such far-reaching structural changes will confront entrenched resistance. "It will take significant political courage to design and implement a comprehensive electric sector reform program," he said, "because there are powerful interest groups that benefit from the status quo."[167] Investor-owned utilities accept change grudgingly, Joskow might have observed, and the ghost of Sam Insull still presides over the industry he created more than a century ago.

5 Ken Lay: Competition Betrayed

Prologue

Ken Lay's career echoed Sam Insull's. Like Insull, Lay grew up dirt poor but fired with ambition. He attracted well-placed mentors, made strategic corporate moves, and enjoyed spectacular early progress. Like Insull, he cultivated influential political players and, at several crucial turning points, turned lack of government oversight to his advantage. Ever alert to the flow of economic events, Lay seized on the wide-ranging commercial opportunities presented by deregulation of the natural gas industry and then applied lessons learned to the electricity business as well. While his company received massive government support for overseas projects, he remained an unapologetic supporter of laissez-faire government policy and nonintervention in the private sector. "I believe in God," he said, "and I believe in free markets."[1] The free markets Lay envisioned were not a state of nature but a "highly-crafted artifice, coolly manufactured on K Street and on Capitol Hill."[2]

Like Insull, who built his vast holding company empire in a regulatory vacuum, Lay worked, very successfully for a time, to secure exemption from government controls and supported a deregulatory agenda through massive political contributions. He lobbied policymakers to gain favorable treatment, cleverly exploiting decisions in his favor. He reconfigured Enron, originally a gas pipeline company, as an online trader in energy, broadband, and water and as a developer of electric power plants worldwide, eventually capturing a large slice of the relevant trading market for natural gas and electric power. Like Insull, however, Lay overreached, made shockingly bad business decisions, and saw his once successful company descend into financial ruin.

Indifferent to gritty operating details, accounting rules, and legal constraints, he delegated the management of his enterprise to superaggressive and predatory executives but did nothing to reverse its slide into criminality or its disastrous impact on investors, creditors, and energy markets. Lay "glided on the coattails of others and a Rolodex of influential relationships. ... When he sensed dangerous truths, he saw his job as one of containment, rather than showing courage or character."[3] He has been described as a "Gatsby of the pipelines, a minister's son from Missouri fueled with the desire for grandiose status."[4] In the end, like Insull, Lay avoided criminal judgment but certainly not the judgment of history, which holds him accountable for the paradigmatic corporate fraud of the early twenty-first century.

Early Years

Ken Lay grew up in a struggling Missouri farm family in a home without indoor plumbing. As a young man he worked at whatever job came to hand—running paper routes, raising chickens, baling hay. Early hardship spurred Horatio Alger–like ambition, and he plotted his future "riding around on a tractor on the flat plains of Missouri."[5] Lay was a serious and driven student with an intellectual bent. At the University of Missouri he fell under the spell of Pinkney Walker, a free-market economist and the first of several influential mentors who would shape his career. Lay earned a Phi Beta Kappa key, was president of the best fraternity, and showed exceptional skill at social networking, becoming "an inveterate collector of relationships."[6] He refined and drew on these talents as he rose in the business world.

Walker convinced his protégé to remain in school for a master's degree. Lay then worked for an oil company and, mindful of his résumé, took evening classes toward a doctorate in economics. Lay left Houston to serve as a naval officer. Instead of drawing sea duty, thanks to Walker, he worked at the Pentagon. As the navy tour came to an end, Walker, then a newly appointed member of the Federal Power Commission, summoned Lay to be his aide. It was the era of bundled natural gas transportation and commodity service, average cost pricing, and wellhead natural gas price ceilings for gas sold in interstate markets. Walker and Lay, contrarian economists in an agency dominated by lawyers and engineers, believed marginal cost pricing of gas and pipeline services, price deregulation, and competition were the best means of reversing shrinking interstate gas supplies.[7] Lay became indispensable to Walker, handling all matters for his boss and giving impassioned speeches in favor of deregulation and the benefits of a free market—the cause he would zealously pursue in coming years to liberate the energy industry, as he saw it, from the heavy hand of government control. In 1972 the Nixon White House, needing a point person on energy policy, appointed Lay deputy undersecretary in the Department of the Interior. He was just thirty years old.[8]

He served less than a year in his new office, but his short tenure coincided with the Arab oil embargo and the onset of a national energy crisis. Finding additional sources of oil and gas became a pressing national priority. Lay worked on President Nixon's 1973 energy message to Congress, which called for increased offshore drilling. At a hearing, Lay met Jack Bowen, head of Florida Gas Company.

Lay saw his opportunity and approached Bowen for a job. "I have been involved in energy policy making in Washington for the past two and half years," he wrote, using Interior Department letterhead. "I feel it is now time I begin thinking about returning to the private sector." Bowen hired Lay as vice president for corporate planning.[9] The job was Lay's portal of entry to the corporate world. "Here was this 30-year-old, without experience other than working for the president of Humble Oil and two jobs as an energy regulator," recalled a Florida Gas executive at the time. "He didn't have industry experience in corporate finance, capital budgeting, stockholder relations, or operations. Yet he told me as if it was written in stone. *I am going to be the CEO of a major energy company.*"[10]

Shortly after Lay joined Florida Gas, Jack Bowen left to become chief executive officer of Transco, a major gas pipeline company. Lay continued his rapid ascent at Florida Gas nonetheless. Two years later, as president of its pipeline subsidiary, Lay cut his teeth on difficult market, legal, and regulatory issues but also revealed a human touch. A colleague recalled "he would always remember your name, your wife's name, and ask how things were."[11] With his avuncular style, Lay proved adept at recruiting new employees, and many, including Richard Kinder and John Wing, would later join him at Enron. In 1979, after Continental Can acquired Florida Gas, Lay found working for a nonenergy conglomerate uncongenial. In 1981, in yet another example of extraordinary serendipity, Jack Bowen, his former boss at Florida Gas, offered Lay the presidency of Transco. Lay did not hesitate to seize the brass ring.[12]

With $4 billion in assets and over three thousand employees, Transco was much bigger than Florida Gas.[13] It operated interstate pipelines and sold gas to local utilities, petrochemical companies, and power plants.[14] Transco faced a chronic supply shortfall caused by price ceilings on natural gas but was able to take advantage of a new federal law—the beginning of deregulation of the natural gas industry—that raised ceiling prices and began unbundling sales of natural gas from transportation.[15] An energy industry boom followed. By 1980 Transco's stock price broke $60 per share, a sevenfold increase in five years.[16] Lay's timing was exquisite. He had made a transition to the big time (while also shedding an old wife and acquiring a new one).

At Transco Lay was a rising star, focused on natural gas reform and well versed in the politics of federal regulation. Transco had entered into long-term take-or-pay contracts with gas producers, guaranteeing it would purchase a specified minimum volume of gas. High gas prices reduced system demand, leaving Transco with an unmarketable surplus of 600 million cubic feet per day. To work through the take-or-pay problem, Lay proposed a market-based solution—an Industrial Sales Program (ISP)[17]—that allowed Transco's gas suppliers to sell directly to its customers. Transco arranged the sales and transported the gas to market. It also transported off-system gas supplies purchased directly by its customers. Although experimental and hedged about with restrictions,[18] the special marketing program was a success. By the end of 1983, Transco had reduced its take-or-pay obligations and was selling one-third of its pipeline gas at market rates. Lay had begun to attract favorable attention in the press. "Some analysts," wrote the *Houston Chronicle*, "attribute the strength of Transco's stock price to Lay's credibility and bold and unique accomplishments."[19] As the industry made a portentous shift toward deregulation, Lay was not looking for a professional change. Like many events in his remarkable early career, however, it would just happen.[20]

In 1984, Lay received an offer he could not refuse. Houston Natural Gas (HNG), a diversified gas supplier to major industrial customers on the Texas coast, needed a new chief executive officer. Its longtime chairman, Robert Herring, a mover and shaker in Houston's elite business and social circles, had died several years earlier, and his caretaker successor had barely fended off a corporate takeover attempt. A key HNG board member approached Lay to head HNG. Lay quickly accepted (but was careful first to get Jack Bowen's blessing). At forty-two he became chairman and chief executive officer of a major energy company, thrust forward by extreme ambition, talent, cultivation of powerful friends, and the blind luck of exceptional timing. As events turned out, HNG was just a way station on Lay's corporate journey. Within a year it became the foundation for Enron.[21]

In 1985 InterNorth, an Omaha-based gas pipeline company with a major system, had attracted the unwelcome advances of Irwin Jacobs, a feared corporate raider. To fend him off, InterNorth needed to grow bigger and incur more debt. By acquiring HNG, InterNorth's board reasoned, it could accomplish both objectives. While Lay cultivated the biggest stockholders and promised higher fees for board members, his chief negotiator, John Wing, orchestrated a corporate coup.

InterNorth acquired HNG at a huge premium to its market price, but by agreement HNG's management team was to run the combined enterprise and, after a suitable transition, Lay was to be chairman and chief executive officer. A few months after the deal closed, the board of the combined company fired its top officer and installed Lay in his place, resolving a power struggle between two strong-willed executives.[22] Lay now commanded the nation's largest gas transmission system with over 37,000 miles of pipeline and access to growing markets in California, Florida, and Texas. Not least, he reaped a $4 million windfall on the sale of his HNG stock.[23] Lay vowed to make the new enterprise "the premier integrated natural gas company in North America," a lofty goal for a company heavily burdened with junk debt.[24]

Lay immediately set to work, gaining control of the board, installing a close ally as head of the executive committee, raiding a workers' pension fund to finance a buyout of Irwin Jacobs's stock position, relocating company headquarters to Houston, and giving the company a new name, Enron, that was to become infamous years later. InterNorth had paid a huge premium for HNG, financed by $5 billion in new debt. With interest and principal payments draining cash, the company had to sell assets and keep borrowings off the balance sheet it presented to Wall Street and the world, thus forecasting its flight toward self-immolation. Enron reported a small loss for its first full fiscal year and, threatened with a takeover attempt, had to repurchase a chunk of its common stock at a premium.[25] Its birth pangs had been anything but easy.[26]

Enron Is Launched

Ken Lay's creation of Enron coincided with massive change in the gas industry. In 1985, FERC issued a landmark order[27] that allowed interstate pipelines to act solely as transporters of natural gas rather than as gas merchants. The order extended the advantages Lay's ISP had earlier afforded to industrial fuel-switching customers; allowed pipelines, on a voluntary basis, to offer transportation services to all customers who requested them on a first come, first served basis; and barred pipelines from discriminating against transportation customers to protect their own merchant services. It set transportation rates within a bandwidth that enabled pipelines to compete on price. Enron's pipelines, like most others nationwide, became open-access carriers. These regulatory changes prefigured similar changes in the electric power industry a few years later.

Customers could now purchase and resell natural gas, contract separately for its transportation, and conduct trading at spot prices much lower than those offered by the pipelines. Customers could also take advantage of a new secondary market in pipeline space, buying and selling contracts for released space in just the same way as they did natural gas. Specialized middlemen—gas marketers and other intermediaries—arose to service these transactions.[28] In 1989 Congress completely deregulated wellhead natural gas prices.[29] It was clear to Ken Lay that consumer-driven markets required new business strategies and placed a premium on skills not present in the regulated pipeline business. Open access was the new competitive space, but greater competition implied a general decline in prices and margins so long as natural gas was traded exclusively in a spot physical market.[30]

In the mid-1980s Enron desperately needed a new business strategy. Lay looked to Jeff Skilling in McKinsey's Houston office for advice. Skilling was a brilliant, if arrogant and abrasive, consultant. "Even by McKinsey standards," wrote one account, "he had been phenomenally successful, rising through the extremely competitive ranks with almost surreal speed."[31] Like Lay, Skilling welcomed the advent of deregulation but argued that natural gas would never be a source of reliable revenue for Enron as long as it was traded exclusively in a spot physical market for immediate delivery.[32]

The spot market was volatile and uncertain. Prices could swing violently, and industrial customers could not be assured of continuing supply. Skilling had a better idea. His key insight was to have Enron aggregate supplies from gas producers and then guarantee reliable delivery to utilities and other large-scale consumers using a portfolio of long- and short-term fixed-price purchase and supply contracts to eliminate supply risk and minimize price fluctuations. "I felt the solution lay in new ways of creating portfolios of natural gas," he said, "which would allow us to eliminate our need to own all the assets and use other people's assets to provide a reliable delivery service." To hedge against volatility, he foresaw development of a derivatives-driven gas futures market in which consumers could control price risk by purchasing gas today at a fixed price for future delivery and entering into option contracts that enabled them to purchase or sell gas at a fixed price in the future. He called his idea the Gas Bank.[33]

In 1987 Skilling broached the Gas Bank concept to Enron management, initially without success. But after a famous "come-to-Jesus" meeting a few months later, in which Ken Lay demanded an entirely new way of doing business, he and Rich Kinder continued to rely on Skilling for strategic advice. The Gas Bank was not dead but needed refinement. Producers were reluctant to sign long-term contracts to deliver gas at a low fixed price, leaving Enron still reliant on the volatile spot market to fulfill commitments on the supply side. Enron's gas marketing department had little enthusiasm for a plan that might saddle the company with wildly unprofitable supply contracts. Lay knew that, for the plan to work, Skilling had to join the company. "I had just been made a director at McKinsey," Skilling recalled, "but I knew this thing was big. I had to show how it could work." In 1990, after months of negotiations, Skilling joined Enron as chief executive officer of Enron Finance (EFC). Like Ken Lay, he burned with ambition and vowed Enron would become the "world's first gas major"—the natural gas equivalent of Exxon or Shell.[34]

To solve the gas supply problem, Enron became a lender. At a time when banks were reluctant to finance producers, Enron offered them capital in return for forward commitments of their production, in effect making secured loans (called Volumetric Production Payments) against and repayable in kind from gas reserves, whose output it had typically presold under long-term fixed-price contracts. To fund the resulting debt and keep it off Enron's balance sheet, Skilling's recently hired finance whiz, Andy Fastow, unbundled the risks implicit in Enron's production loans, repackaging development risk, production risk, price risk, and interest rate risk for sale as specialized securities to banks, insurance companies, and pension funds. As counterparties to Enron's long-term fixed-price delivery and price risk management contracts, customers were able to manage exposure to falling prices. Enron acted as a market maker, buying and selling gas at fixed and floating prices or swapping one for the other. It became the primary supplier of liquidity to the market, capturing the spread between bid and offer prices as a fee. Enron also learned to extract profit from the relationship between the physical and derivative markets. The Gas Bank began to work. Producers signed long-term contracts. With supply and price guaranteed, utilities found natural gas an environmentally friendly alternative to coal and began building gas-fired plants.[35]

Skilling had a further innovation. Fixed-price contracts to buy and sell natural gas, he realized, could be traded if the contracts had standardized terms and there were enough participants to create liquidity. By 1990 gas trading had reached critical mass, and the New York Mercantile Exchange began making a market in gas futures—contracts to buy or sell gas at a later date at a specified price. As the natural gas market became more integrated and coherent, Enron remained a dominant player, supplying liquidity to standardized markets and retaining first-mover advantage in the customized over-the-counter derivatives business. Skilling's Gas Bank transformed natural gas from a physical commodity to a financial commitment. Instead of owning hard assets, Enron could own a portfolio of contracts that would allow it to control the underlying resources. Skilling called this Enron's "asset-lite" strategy. "In the early days we were printing money," said one of his lieutenants. "We saw things no one else could see."[36] The insight gained from natural gas was soon to have profound implications for the electricity business as well.

In 1991 Skilling made another transformative change by convincing the SEC to allow Enron to book trading revenues using mark-to-market accounting. Like other energy companies, Enron carried its gas contracts at historic cost, recognized revenues as they were received, and calculated profits accordingly. If Enron had a ten-year contract to supply natural gas to a utility, it would record revenues received as the utility made payments over the contract term. Mark-to-market accounting, by contrast, allowed Enron to book all future revenues on the day it signed a contract although cash payments would trickle in over time. Investment banks, holding financial assets that fluctuate in value, used mark-to-market accounting, but no energy company had ever done so. Skilling said Enron's trading assets resembled financial assets and deserved the same accounting treatment. This might have made sense for short-term, standardized contracts but did not for complex, long-term agreements where market quotes were unavailable. Mark-to-market accounting allowed Enron to use complex models to estimate the value of those contracts, based on assumptions that could range from future gas prices to the pace of energy deregulation to trends in interest rates. "As the deals came to maturity," said a Senate report after Enron's collapse, "... the assumptions underlying the valuations in many cases proved incorrect and the contracts had to be revalued."[37]

The SEC nonetheless reluctantly acquiesced to Skilling's relentless advocacy.[38] Enron was then free to apply mark-to-market accounting to long-term contracts involving assets in thinly traded markets, where price information was of limited use, and ultimately to every portion of its merchant investment business. By 2000, over 30 percent of Enron's assets received mark-to-market treatment that created a timing gap between recognition of net income and receipt of associated cash. Enron used special-purpose entities to mask the resulting cash-flow gap.[39]

Early on, however, Skilling's Gas Bank looked like a masterstroke. Enron Gas Services (EFC's successor, combining EFC with Enron Gas Marketing, a unit dealing in spot market gas sales) sold $800 million worth of gas in one week's time and over a billion cubic feet per day. Even before the new accounting protocol, by mid-1991, Enron had long-term contracts with more than thirty-five natural gas producers and fifty users. One contract ran for twenty-years and was worth more than $3.5 billion. By 1992 Enron was the largest natural gas merchant in North America, and the gas trading business had become a major contributor to its net income. Skilling's strategy was "get in early, push to open markets, position ourselves to compete, and compete hard when the opening comes." This strategy suited his boss. Ken Lay was attracted to "ruthless, brainy alter egos such as Jeff Skilling and Andrew Fastow, who could act out Lay's ambitions while he played Mr. Congeniality."[40] The synthesis of Lay and Skilling put Enron at the "confluence of major political and financial currents. The deregulation of energy markets ... and Skilling's foray into energy trading came just as financial institutions were unleashing exotic investment tools—a flow of money looking for opportunities."[41]

Lay avoided personal conflict, but gave Skilling, who relished confrontation, free rein to run his division. Skilling transformed Enron's culture. The Southern, good-old-boy ethos of the highly regulated pipeline industry gave way to a hypercompetitive, survival-of-the-fittest system populated by bright, ambitious graduates of elite business schools, motivated by stock options and pay-for-performance bonuses. Enron itself was repositioning itself as a growth company and could no longer be described as a "somewhat sleepy natural gas utility."[42] Enron Gas Services, soon to be renamed Enron Capital and Trade Resources (ECT), became a developmental platform for financially linked products and services, run by traders and focused on financial instruments. Skilling wanted people who would bring new thinking to a tradition-bound business, then subjected them to ruthless performance review. Fierce internal competition prevailed, and Skilling's division replaced 15 percent of its workforce each year. Within just a few years Skilling saw his embryonic Gas Bank group encompass a full-service merchant organization. ECT was a "hotbed of entrepreneurial activity and an engine of growth," spanning more than a dozen business units, "each offering a unique, specialized set of financial products and energy services to customers at both ends of the gas pipeline."[43]

Lay was not content to dominate domestic markets. He wanted to make Enron the first great international utility, pipeline, and energy-trading company. In 1993 Rebecca Mark, Skilling's most formidable executive rival, convinced Lay to establish Enron International, of which she became the first president. Mark did not adopt Skilling's asset-lite strategy but instead contemplated large capital-intensive projects, particularly in markets, like Margaret Thatcher's United Kingdom, where energy was being deregulated. The new unit's first major project was construction of a huge electricity cogenerating plant in Teesside, England, fueled by North Sea gas and initially seen as a major success. Projects in Eastern Europe, Africa, the Middle East, India, China, and Latin America followed, massively supported by billions in subsidized public loans and guarantees from the World Bank, the U.S. Export-Import Bank, and the Overseas Private Investment Corporation.[44]

Enron enlisted cabinet secretaries and U.S. ambassadors to intercede with foreign governments and recruited relatives of heads of state as investors and lobbyists. But Enron's ambitious grasp exposed it to political risk, improvident deals, and the limits of its organizational competence. "A lot of our capital-intensive international deals," said Enron's chief risk officer, "started looking a lot less attractive after we factored in things like currency risk and default probability."[45] The Dabhol power project in India, a $2.9 billion white elephant, never operated, typifying Enron's troubled international power investments. "Instead of realizing its dream of opening the Indian subcontinent to a vast energy market and then dominating it, Enron faced the reality of a huge, idle power facility on its balance sheet and major write-offs."[46] Such outcomes, dimly perceived, if at all, at Enron International's inception, precipitated Enron into the "nether world of Special Purpose Equity Financing"[47] as a means of masking failed deals, a subterfuge that led to its bankruptcy in 2001.

The Electricity Market

"The constant theme in Mr. Lay's career ... [was] his understanding of the symbiotic relationship between business and politics and his willingness to aggressively play the game."[48] Nowhere was that relationship more important than in deregulating the electric power industry, whose size dwarfed the natural gas business. Electricity was a target of opportunity that enabled Enron to extend its trading expertise, developed in the natural gas industry, to an essential, interrelated business. Lay believed Enron could make more money trading electricity contracts and derivatives than it could by producing electricity.[49] "[A] power plant with a contract," said Jeff Skilling, "is really just a gigantic short position for natural gas."[50] By 1992 Enron had begun using derivative contracts to set future prices of electricity and natural gas.

Like many proponents of electricity deregulation, Enron wanted to deconstruct the vertically integrated utility business into its constituent parts: power generation, long-distance transmission, and distribution. Power generation, potentially a competitive market, would be owned separately from transmission and distribution, its regulated monopoly elements. Competition in power generation was expected to drive down electricity prices, and businesses and residential customers could then be induced to leave their utility suppliers.[51] Enron's business model, as it evolved, was to acquire physical capacity in the electric power market and leverage that investment through flexible pricing structures, using financial derivatives to manage risk. Enron became, in effect, two companies—an energy supply company that acquired electric power plants and other physical assets and a financial dealer in wholesale energy derivatives transactions.[52]

To free electricity as a speculative commodity, Enron needed to remove government oversight of its trading practices so that it could exploit market deficiencies to manipulate prices and supply. Lay was a persistent advocate of deregulated energy markets, supported by a powerful lobbying arm and strategic political contributions to both parties. His object was to rewrite the rules of the energy business to Enron's advantage. He preached free-market economics but sought—and eventually obtained—near monopolistic control of gas and electricity trading nationwide.[53]

Lay's timing, as usual, was propitious. In 1992, the Energy Policy Act (for which he had lobbied intensely) opened wholesale electricity markets for nonutility generators, mandated open-access transmission of wholesale power, and gave FERC responsibility for transforming the wholesale power generation segment of a regulated industry into a competitive market in which electricity could be generated and sold much like any other commodity. FERC increasingly relied on market forces to contain wholesale prices and, commencing in the 1980s, approved almost one thousand applications submitted by intermediaries wishing to sell power competitively in wholesale markets with little oversight.[54] Competitive markets, it believed, were more efficient than traditional cost-based regulation in electric generation and supply.[55] In modeling electricity deregulation on the deregulated gas industry, however, FERC paid scant attention to critical differences. Electricity cannot be stored and is more difficult to trade and transport. Electricity prices are also more volatile and, at times of peak load or scarcity, open to manipulation by aggressive market players.

Enron's political contributions smoothed the course of deregulation. Ken Lay had learned, as a fundamental rule of politics, that contributions made friends of elected officials. Between 1989 and 2001 Enron and its executives gave nearly $6 million to political parties and candidates, mostly to Republicans, and from 1993 to 2001 became the largest single source of campaign contributions from any corporation in the energy sector. Lay and his wife personally gave almost $900,000. Senator Phil Gramm of Texas, a strategic beneficiary, received almost $100,000.[56] The senator's wife, Wendy Gramm, was chair of the Commodity Futures Trading Commission (CFTC), an agency with nominal jurisdiction over energy derivative contracts and interest rate swaps, both matters of acute interest to Enron, whose business expansion depended on use of over-the-counter (OTC) energy derivatives—nonstandardized vehicles that do not trade on a regulated exchange.[57] In the OTC market firms act as dealers, trading individually negotiated contracts with utilities, banks, hedge funds, and energy companies that seek to reduce their risk exposure to energy prices.[58] Enron wanted to use OTC derivatives without interference from federal regulators.

In November 1992 Enron asked for a ruling that would exclude energy derivative contracts and interest rate swaps from the CFTC's oversight.[59] Two of the commission's five seats were vacant. To reach a decision before Bill Clinton took office, Wendy Gramm orchestrated a fast-track rulemaking without consulting her co-commissioners. In January 1993 the CFTC voted 2–1 to grant Enron's request. A week later Gramm resigned as CFTC's chair and within a month took a seat on Enron's board. The CFTC's ruling allowed Enron to create its own unregulated in-house derivatives exchange. Within a year Enron's price risk management activities expanded by almost a third and continued their mushroom growth for the balance of the decade. Sheila Bair, the lone dissenting CFTC commissioner, called the ruling "a dangerous precedent." Critics said cash-settled derivative contracts were uniquely susceptible to manipulation. But Enron, encouraged by its success, "assembled a special interest machine unprecedented in the energy industry."[60]

Enron also wanted relief from the Public Utility Holding Company Act,[61] a Depression-era statute designed to eliminate abuses by multistate electricity and natural gas utility holding companies, over which the SEC had jurisdiction. Enron aggressively sought exemptions from the act or "no-action" rulings that proposed activities would not bring it within the definition of a public utility holding company. In 1993 Enron approached the SEC on behalf of Enron Power Marketing, a wholly owned subsidiary of Enron Gas Services, needing assurance that power marketing—the purchase and resale of electricity—would not subject it to the registration and other requirements of the act. Under political pressure, the SEC granted Enron Power Marketing the exemption it sought, the first power marketer to receive absolution from the act.[62] Enron was to make effective use of the resulting regulatory vacuum, without which, critics later said, regulators "would have identified and prevented Enron's ill-fated activities."[63]

Enron was now free to build a portfolio of products and services for the power industry similar to those it had created for the gas sector without disclosing the price, volume, or terms of transactions. "The more we looked at the two industries," said Lay, "... we increasingly could see their convergence over time, primarily because natural gas would be the swing fuel in power generation. ... And we realized that our services—such as risk management and financial services—could be transferred easily from gas to electricity."[64] The company became a giant intermediary and market maker. Traders bought and sold forward contracts, initially over the phone (and later online), from and to energy companies needing to hedge against price volatility. Enron quickly became a key player in the wholesale power business, selling primarily to utilities and municipalities, dominating a field of more than forty entrants. In 1997 it sold electricity worth $4 billion, almost one-fifth of the North American wholesale market, but generated little of it, relying instead on its mastery of swaps, collars, caps, floors, and hybrids.[65]

Enron's initial success masked underlying problems. Electricity traders found it difficult to induce large-scale companies to sign profitable long-term contracts; many prospective customers were unwilling to provide access to their transmission lines; and, under the law in many states, Enron could not trade electricity unless it owned power plants. The incumbent utility industry was unwilling to cede its valuable turf easily to an aggressive newcomer. Enron had reached the limits of Skilling's asset-lite strategy.[66] "The electricity guys were scared to death of Enron," said Skilling. "It was very hard to break into the electricity market."[67]

To do so Enron had to join the club. In 1996, after approaching dozens of utilities, Enron signed a contract to acquire Portland General, a midsize utility in Oregon, for a premium of almost 50 percent to its market price. Enron wanted to combine its gas trading, risk management, and logistics expertise with Portland General's capacity in power generation, transmission, and distribution. A particular focus was spark spread trading that would allow Enron to hedge the difference in price between gas and electricity. It closed the deal a year later, but only after offering Oregon customers a large rate cut. With the purchase of Portland General, Enron gained entrée to California's power grid, a supply of electricity to trade, and access to the industry's secret playbook. Shortly after, Enron recast itself as "The World's Leading Energy Company."[68]

Between 1996 and 2000 Enron appeared to fulfill the hype. Its revenues rose from $13.3 billion to $100 billion, bracketing the company with super-majors such as BP and ExxonMobil. Driving the increase was a proprietary website, EnronOnline, that captured for Enron as the sole counterparty nearly one-quarter of all gas and electricity trades nationwide. By mid-2000 Enron was doing billions of dollars of business daily and needed huge amounts of cash to support the float. Enron's stock price and reported earnings took a quantum leap, driven by frenetic trading activity and exceptional revenue growth (to which Enron's interstate pipelines, once the core of its business, contributed only a small fraction). *Fortune* listed Enron, now styled as a logistics company, among the world's most innovative and admired corporations. A Goldman Sachs analyst wrote that "Enron has built unique and, in our view, extraordinary franchises in several business units in very large markets."[69]

But for those looking more closely at Enron's opaque financial reports, there were countervailing signs. Enron had vastly increased its reported revenues by exploiting two revenue recognition rules. Mark-to-market accounting enabled it to accelerate the presumed benefits of long-term energy contracts into current period income, and merchant accounting reported the entire value of each trade on EnronOnline as revenue rather than just trading or brokerage fees. These techniques artificially inflated Enron's revenues and cost of goods sold, creating the illusion of a much larger company. Without mark-to-market and merchant accounting, in 2000 Enron would have had reported revenues of $6.3 billion, not $100 billion. Enron's reported profits were microscopic relative to revenues and reflected a steady decline in net profit margin.[70]

Even more ominous was a catalog of financial reporting manipulations eventually revealed at Enron's bankruptcy: failure to disclose the extent and nature of transactions with partnerships operated by its chief financial officer, Andy Fastow; excluding from Enron's balance sheet massive debt incurred by special-purpose entities; removing poorly performing assets from the company's books without transferring the risks of ownership; disguising loans as commodity trades and treating them as trading liabilities rather than debt; failure to disclose debt that would become due if Enron's stock price or credit rating dropped; issuing stock for notes recorded as assets; and engaging in sham hedging transactions. Between 1997 and 2000 Enron overstated its reported net income by more than

$1.5 billion and shareholders' equity by $2.6 billion. The eventual restatement sharply reduced earnings per share and return on assets and increased debt-to-equity ratios.[71] "The tragic consequences of the related-party transactions and the accounting errors," a postbankruptcy report concluded before criminal prosecution of Lay, Skilling, and Fastow, "were the result of failures at many levels and by many people: a flawed idea, self-enrichment by employees, inadequately designed controls, poor implementation, inattentive oversight, … accounting mistakes, and overreaching in a culture that appears to have encouraged pushing the limits."[72] Ken Lay's fingerprints were all over the report.

The Retail Gamble

Enron's dramatic demise seemed a most unlikely outcome as the Energy Policy Act of 1992 and FERC's Order 888, passed in 1996, opened electricity generation markets at the state level and offered the prospect of retail competition, allowing individual consumers to choose between the local utility and a third-party supplier for electric power. The transmission grid no longer served the interest of its owners but became a common carrier system for electricity. Some states (California and Pennsylvania) unbundled their local distribution networks in order to introduce retail competition for generation services for all customers at the same time; others introduced retail competition first for large customers, then gradually extended it to smaller customers.

For Ken Lay, whose company had already captured a significant slice of the wholesale electricity market, the lure of dominating the much larger retail market was compelling. In 1997 he predicted that, within five years, Enron's retail business alone would equal or exceed its then total revenues of $20 billion. "Retail markets are just going to explode," he said. "As states open up their electricity markets to competition and customer choice, it will enable Enron to become more profitable, faster."[73] By 1998 twenty-four states had adopted some form of utility restructuring. The combined markets for retail electricity and gas were estimated at over $300 billion. For each percent of that market it gained, Enron believed it could increase its profit by $300 million.[74]

In 1997, shortly after becoming Enron's president and chief operating officer, Skilling formed Enron Energy Services (EES) to capture the retail side of the domestic energy market. Its mission was to enter into customized energy contracts with large industrial users like Owens Corning, whose energy needs Enron agreed to supply nationwide for ten years, guaranteeing $60 million in savings. The University of California, Lockheed Martin, IBM, and Chase Bank were other clients. Enron traders concluding such billion-dollar deals earned large bonuses upfront, closed transactions quickly, and entered into what proved to be many losing contracts. Originators received bonuses on how profitable a deal appeared to be at signing, not how it eventually worked out. Typical deals offered few economies of scale and swamped Enron's limited administrative capabilities. To conceal possible losses, EES booked deals based on the total cost of energy outsourced over the life of a contract, not on profit. "Total contract value" accounting suited Lay and Skilling, who expected to cash in large grants of phantom equity by taking the new enterprise public. Just two years after its formation, Enron sold 7 percent of EES' equity to two pension funds for $130 million, establishing its value at $1.9 billion and allowing Enron to realize a $61 million profit.[75]

Even before EES, Enron had mounted an intense lobbying campaign to promote deregulation in Texas, Oregon, Pennsylvania, New York, Massachusetts, Rhode Island and California, among many other jurisdictions, supported by heavy campaign contributions to more than seven hundred candidates in twenty-eight states and a nationwide advertising campaign extolling free-market electricity. Although he gave to both parties, Lay had especially close ties with both Bushes; he was cochairman of the senior Bush's reelection campaign in 1992 and chairman of the Republican National Convention that summer. "For more than a decade," said *Time,* "Enron spent lavishly to untether itself from government oversight."[76] It also became a pervasive factor in electric industry restructuring at the state level, most intensely in Texas, California, and Pennsylvania.[77]

Lay framed this campaign as a fight against "cozy monopolists" and advertised Enron as a national alternative to local utilities. But his rhetoric did not match results. Utility interests fought back and slowed deregulation to a crawl in many states. In 1996 Enron lost $35 million on its retail energy business and the following year reluctantly quit signing up new residential customers. States were not deregulating fast enough to justify the expense. "When it came to the simple realities," said the company's newly hired marketing consultant, "Enron simply didn't get it."[78] In one state, however, Enron continued to see a huge profit opportunity from restructuring. California's revised electricity market—a comprehensive and fatally flawed regime—attracted commercial predators of every stripe. Enron led the way. "Our activism in the political and regulatory process," said Ken Lay, "is essential to our continued success."[79]

California

Enron targeted the California electricity market early on. Jeff Skilling approached the California Public Utilities Commission (CPUC) many times before the onset of deregulation in 1996, claiming it would yield potential cost savings in the billions and arguing for specific rules that would favor Enron's trading activities as power marketer. "Enron's sophisticated lobbying efforts," said a member of the state senate, "helped create the very market it would later exploit."[80] But this was far from clear in the run-up to deregulation, called by one observer "the age of market triumphalism."[81] Deregulation appeared to have universal appeal. To those on the right it promised to undercut government regulation and promote consumer choice; to those on the left it reduced the influence of monopolistic utilities and also promised consumer choice. The chief proponents in California were large industrial users that wanted lower power prices.[82] California's retail rates were 40 percent higher than the national average and exceeded out-of-state wholesale prices at the California-Oregon border. Industrial users pushed hard for access to low-priced wholesale energy.[83]

Two institutions shaped deregulation in California: the CPUC, which undertook deregulation and restructuring initiatives from 1992 to 1996, and the state legislature, which intervened to modify the CPUC's proposals by adopting a negotiated package of legislation. The final bill (AB 1890)[84] was a political compromise, offering something to everyone but ignoring the industry's technical complexity and regulatory history. A witness at congressional hearings in 2001, with the benefit of hindsight after the California market had imploded, described its design as "a recipe for disaster."[85]

Both the CPUC and the legislature were divided. One faction preferred a "poolco" model (Hogan's proposal for a tight power pool with price bidding and central dispatch) and a rival faction wanted bilateral trading outside the power pool. "The end result," said Paul Joskow, "was the most complicated set of wholesale electricity market institutions ever created on earth and with which there was no real world experience."[86]

AB 1890 established two independent bodies to run the California market, the nonprofit Power Exchange (PX) and the Independent System Operator (ISO). California's three major investor-owned utilities had to sell off their fossil-fuel power plants and buy all their power through a single transparent market run by the PX. The merchant generators that purchased the power plants from the utilities became profit-maximizing sellers of wholesale power outside the control of state regulation; but the incumbent utilities, discouraged from entering into long-term forward energy contracts as a hedge against volatility, were left with few instruments for managing price risk. Instead they were required to buy power through the PX—a day-ahead market where buyers and sellers would submit bid curves (indicating how much power they proposed to buy or sell at various prices) one day before delivery at prices geared to hourly segments during the next day. The ISO would run the transmission system, still owned by the utilities and still regulated under cost-of-service ratemaking by FERC or the CPUC, monitor the physical flows of electricity, and balance electricity supply and demand in real time throughout the entire transmission system.[87]

The PX solicited hourly output bids (amounts and prices) from all generators a day in advance and also solicited estimates of hourly demand from the three major California utilities (Pacific Gas & Electric, Southern California Edison, and San Diego Gas & Electric) and from independent marketers of electricity like Enron. The PX accepted supply bids in ascending order of price until supply equaled expected demand. The cost of the most expensive unit of power needed to meet expected demand in any given hour set the price for all the power the PX purchased for that hour. In the California market, therefore, most transactions were scheduled before the actual hour of delivery. To ensure that supply and demand remained in continuous equipoise, the ISO ran an imbalance energy market to handle real-time deviations from amounts bid. Like the PX, the ISO set a uniform price based on the offer of the marginal supplier. A market participant whose delivery or consumption of power deviated from its final schedule was charged or paid the ISO imbalance energy price for the hour in question depending on whether the participant was long or short in real time. The utilities were expected to purchase most of their demand through the PX and use the ISO to cover imbalances caused by last-minute deviations. In fact, the separate real-time market weakened the PX, depriving it of exclusive access to pool prices and demand.[88]

Sellers soon realized the ISO would, if necessary, pay higher prices than the utilities would pay in the PX, just to keep the grid operating. At times of expected scarcity sellers incurred little risk in declining to participate in the PX day-ahead market or demanding extremely high prices for their power since the ISO, pressed to balance system supply and demand, could be expected the next day to offer a higher price.[89] Sellers therefore abandoned the PX day-ahead market for the ISO real-time market whenever they thought the ISO would need to buy power at the last minute the next day. This reduced the amount of power offered through the PX and made the ISO a buyer of last resort under urgent conditions. The ISO became a market maker rather than a transmission system manager, and sellers were incentivized to withhold power from the PX day-ahead market to induce scarcity or demand extremely high prices when scarcity was likely. The decision to separate the PX and the ISO created a systemic arbitrage opportunity that Enron, among others, was quick to seize.[90]

Enron was a direct-access provider to large institutional users like the University of California; a trader and marketer of electricity; and, through EnronOnline, an unregulated auctioneer in the electricity and natural gas markets where it viewed every bid, every ask, and every trend in those markets. As a "risk manager" Enron sold protection against volatility to market participants in California and worked to undermine the PX in order to establish itself as the primary market maker. Price stability in the PX cut against Enron. If the PX operated efficiently, players would not need protection against volatility, nor would they have recourse to the ISO imbalance market. By offering to sell its electricity only at unacceptable, high prices in the PX day-ahead market or simply withholding, Enron forced buyers (primarily the three major investor-owned utilities) to seek a better deal in the ISO market. As real time approached under conditions of peak-load scarcity, however, a better deal was not to be had. Enron knew the ISO would have to buy power without regard to price.[91]

The framers of AB 1890 did not anticipate gaming of the new pricing system. Instead they thought wholesale electricity prices, driven by competition, would fall dramatically. Merchant generators, they believed, could sell power far cheaper than the incumbent utilities. If the market were allowed to find its own level, however, the utilities would not be able to recover expensive investments, called stranded costs, they had made under regulation in contracts for alternative energy and nuclear power plants. To address this problem, AB 1890 fixed the maximum retail price utilities could charge for electricity at about 6 cents per kilowatt-hour, then thought to be an artificially high level, until 2002 or until the utility had recovered its stranded costs, whichever came first. The recovery mechanism was a Competition Transition Charge, which customers would pay the utilities in addition to the wholesale price actually set by the market at a level expected to be much lower than 6 cents. To make this compromise more palatable to retail customers and small businesses, the maximum retail price reflected a 10 percent rate cut financed by state bonds. AB 1890 gave no thought to what might happen if the wholesale price exceeded the capped retail price, perhaps by a large amount, so that a utility could not pass the increase along to customers, recover its stranded costs, or even preserve its assets.[92] Constrained to buy power in volatile day-ahead and spot markets, stripped of most of their generating capacity, discouraged from entering into long-term forward contracts, and confronting a retail price freeze, California's utilities willingly accepted the new regime but were blind to the disaster that lay ahead.

FERC also played a major part in the forthcoming drama. Beginning in 1996, it issued orders approving proposals by the three utilities, and later by trustees for the ISO and the PX, to implement the state's plan.[93] These authorized transfer of control of the utilities' transmission systems to the ISO, operating rules and governance for the ISO and the PX as jurisdictional public utilities, and limits on utilities' exercise of market power.[94] FERC also granted requests by the buyers of former utility power plants for authorization to sell wholesale electricity at market-based rates. In granting these requests, FERC looked only at the share of generation capacity controlled by each generator and its affiliates in a geographic market and did not consider overall supply and demand projections or how the restructured market would function under real-world conditions.[95]

With minimal analysis FERC deregulated the wholesale price of electricity in California. It treated the state as one big market instead of distinct north–south markets formed by a transmission constraint; failed to identify load pockets at times of high energy use; deregulated ancillary services; accepted on faith, without any concrete plan, that "must-run" plants would mitigate market power; and rubber-stamped industry rules on transmission capacity availability and load relief that were incapable of preventing market manipulation. FERC then refused to police the markets it had deregulated. It defended the secrecy of spot-market bidding, refused to requisition bidding records after price spikes, and approved high rates without subjecting them to refund.[96]

Deregulation in Action

The state's deregulated electricity market opened for business in March 1998. Given its embedded structural flaws, the California market was an inviting prospect for Enron and other players, who sensed a historic profit-making opportunity, particularly in times of scarcity. "We believe in markets," said Ken Lay. "Sometimes there's an aberration. But over time, markets figure out value."[97] Enron's West Coast traders, one hundred strong and housed in the Portland World Trade Center, focused on vulnerable market rules, not value. Enron's Wholesale Energy unit now accounted for 90 percent of the company's $40 billion in revenues. Traders were on a roll. "If they're going to put in place such a stupid system," said a senior Enron executive, "it makes sense to try to game it."[98] The essential principle was to take advantage of scarcity. Without elasticity of demand, Enron knew, tight supply conditions in electricity markets would allow sellers to exercise market power and raise prices virtually without limit.[99]

For its first two years, however, the new system appeared to function smoothly. California had excess capacity, and average wholesale electricity prices remained low (although higher than the marginal cost of production). So long as wholesale prices were less than retail rates, the public was unconcerned. But sellers began to test the market to see if they could exercise market power. In July 1998 the price for reserve power, which had been one dollar, spiked as high as $9,999 per megawatt-hour. Dynegy, a power marketer, had offered to supply power at that price, and the ISO, with few other offers and facing high demand, had no choice but to accept. Its chief executive officer was appalled. "All of us saw those numbers," he said, "and realized ... there was nothing to stop someone from bidding to infinity." The ISO sued to reverse Dynegy's market-based pricing authorization but was denied by FERC, which advised the ISO simply to reject bids "in excess of whatever price levels it believes are appropriate." Given official carte blanche, market players conducted further tests to gain strategic information about market structure and competitive behavior for later use.[100]

Enron began probing for weaknesses. In May 1999, Tim Belden, a leader among the company's West Coast traders, put in motion a price manipulation scheme to test the profit potential in the division between California's day-ahead and real-time markets. He submitted bids, accepted by the PX, to sell 2,900 megawatts to meet peak demand the next day. Power was to flow from a source in Nevada through a terminal at Silver Peak for transmission to Southern California. The Silver Peak lines, Belden knew, could handle only fifteen megawatts. The transaction therefore was physically impossible, and the PX suddenly confronted a huge shortfall in expected power. The ISO had to meet the deficit by buying makeup power at prices 70 percent higher than normal. Enron and others made money in the real-time market, but its game cost users in California an additional $7 million. In the ensuing investigation, Belden told the PX he had done the state a favor by pointing out a structural flaw. Ken Lay wrote a letter to the PX claiming Enron "believes in the highest ethical standards." Enron eventually paid a $25,000 fine without admitting or denying a violation of market rules, which remained unchanged. Belden's experiment revealed an ill-conceived system vulnerable to gaming with virtually no regulatory oversight.[101]

As the California market drama unfolded, Enron was reaching the peak of an exceptional corporate rise. Its revenues had grown from $13.5 billion in 1991 to $101 billion in a decade, it had delivered more than a 700 percent cumulative total return to shareholders, its stock price had soared from $10 to $90 per share, and it had been recognized by *Fortune* as the nation's most innovative company—for the fifth consecutive year. Nearly one-quarter of all gas and electric trades nationwide went through EnronOnline, which did billions of dollars of trades in multiple products daily. In just two years Ken Lay had realized almost $175 million from open-market sales of stock awards, sales of stock back to Enron, and exercised options.[102]

But Enron's apparent success hid profound problems, disguised by misleading financial statements. Enron was getting bigger but less profitable as its cash from operations and return on equity declined. It had made disastrous deals on the hard asset and nonenergy sides of its business, including the Dabhol plant in India, a failed investment in privatizing water markets in England and Argentina, and an ill-advised attempt to sell broadband capacity. The most important fact about Enron was how poorly the company was doing in many branches of its business even as Wall Street thought it was thriving. By the late 1990s Enron had lost approximately $2 billion investing in broadband, $2 billion in a Brazilian utility, $2 billion in water investments, and another $1 billion in Dabhol. Enron Energy Services was also losing money on many of its long-term contracts subject to mark-to-market accounting. Operating and capital losses in electric power, water, and broadband exceeded $6 billion. To maintain its critically important share price, Enron hid underperforming assets, called "nuclear waste" by insiders, in special-purpose entities to keep debt off its books. Enron's energy trading was exorbitantly profitable, accounting for over 90 percent of its overall revenues in 2000. While it was making billions trading derivatives, however, it was losing billions on virtually everything else and using special-purpose entities and its expertise in derivatives to hide massive debts and losses.[103]

Aware that many of his company's diverse businesses were failing, Lay saw the California market as an enormous, and possibly redeeming, profit opportunity. For one thing, California's excess generation capacity had vanished. Economic growth required more power, but the state's environmental laws delayed major new plants. Electricity consumption increased by almost 9 percent in two years just as low-cost imports from hydropower in the Northwest and coal and nuclear power in the Southwest were no longer available. Almost overnight, California's former surplus became a shortage. The ISO, initially tasked with simply balancing supply and demand, had to supply a quarter of the state's total energy needs at increasingly high prices. The market logic was inescapable. Enron's traders, who controlled 30 percent of all action at West Coast hubs, took a huge long position in electricity.[104]

The traders, led by Tim Belden, also devised artfully titled ways to game California's dysfunctional power market and make money in the process. In "Load Shift" Enron scheduled power deliveries in the day-ahead market that it never intended to execute, using a north–south transmission corridor that could be easily congested. When the anticipated congestion prevented delivery, Enron canceled the transaction in the real-time market and collected payments for relieving the very congestion it had created. Payments for alleviating congestion (up to $750 per megawatt-hour) exceeded capped electricity prices ($250 per megawatt-hour) in the real-time market. In "Death Star," Enron scheduled transmission to relieve congestion but did not generate additional power. Instead it imported power from outside the ISO's service area to collect congestion relief payments or simply failed to provide any electricity at all. The ISO paid the congestion relief charge, which was greater than the penalty for not delivering scheduled power, in advance and did not ask for its money back. In "Ricochet," a further adaptation, Enron sold exported California power back into the state's real-time market to evade price controls, a technique called "megawatt laundering." "Fat Boy" was a strategy to exploit demand differences in the day-ahead and real-time markets. When demand in real time was greater than the PX forecast, the ISO had to buy additional power at prices higher than those in the day-ahead market. Anticipating greater real-time demand, Enron traders overstated the demand of its customers and scheduled generation to meet that demand in the PX day-ahead market. Requiring less power than it had scheduled in the day-ahead market, Enron received credit for excess generation at the higher real-time price. "Get Shorty" was a similar arbitrage strategy, used when the real-time price was lower than the day-ahead price.[105]

Years later FERC released evidence suggesting Lay and Skilling must have known of these scams. "We have now moved out of the gray area ... ," Belden told Enron's chief lobbyist and vice president of regulatory affairs. "There's a lot of political risk. ... If Jeff Skilling has to go in front of some commission and explain the activities of the West Coast Group, that's probably not so great for my career." Despite Belden's explicit warning, no one told him to stop. Between 1999 and 2001 revenues of his trading unit rose from $50 million to $800 million. The California market was a gold mine.[106]

Enron's manipulation of the California market involved far more than arbitrage and exploiting regulatory loopholes. Enron traded electricity among five of its commonly managed subsidiaries at prices as high as $3,300 per megawatt-hour when the price cap in the real-time market was $250. "These trades were sham transactions," said the president of the CPUC after Enron's collapse. He continued,

Enron was selling the same megawatts back and forth to itself, causing the price to rise with each supposed sale, all under the rules they had helped create. ... The selling ... created the illusion of an active, volatile market, appearing to the rest of the world as though massive trading was occurring on Enron's online trading floor. ... Since Enron used accounting methods that let them book as revenue the value of every trade, not just the profit, they were able to create false value in their company with every affiliate trade. ... The prices that were reported on Enron's Internet-based trading site, EnronOnline, became the benchmark in the market for wholesale bids into the California Power Exchange and the California ISO. These purchases and sales were only possible ... because there was no regulation of this market. There were no rules imposed by the CFTC or the FERC to prohibit ... sham transactions between affiliated entities.[107]

By 2000 30 percent of Enron's trades were among its own affiliates.[108] Other market players also used round-trip trades to boost revenue growth, manipulate prices, and gain market share.[109]

Enron traders dominated the state's natural gas market as the price of natural gas increased exponentially. Higher gas prices meant higher prices for electricity generated by gas-fired plants. EnronOnline, launched in November 1999, was the major trading platform for natural gas transactions at the California border and the primary source of price discovery in California's gas markets. It established bid and asked prices and posted, executed, settled, and cleared every trade. As FERC staff later concluded, "Enron had access to trading histories, limit orders, and volumes of trades, and therefore understood the liquidity of the market. ... Because the [EnronOnline] platform was wholly controlled by Enron, there were no fixed rules. The [EnronOnline] operator had an infinite ability to manipulate what was posted."[110]

Traders could buy and sell natural gas at spot prices unrelated to actual cost and without making physical delivery. Financial positions were settled for cash, not product. EnronOnline became a key enabler of churn trading, and, with proprietary knowledge of market conditions and use of derivatives, Enron traders were able to manipulate the thinly traded physical gas market and realize huge profits in associated financial markets.[111] In one instance, Enron moved the price of gas in the physical markets by only 10 cents per million BTUs but earned a $3 million profit in the financial markets.[112] Meanwhile the CPUC relieved large corporate customers and utilities of gas storage obligations as the latter fought against increasing pipeline capacity into the state.[113] Given the impact of high gas prices on the price of gas-fired electricity in California, its power market was ripe for manipulation.

In 1999 and 2000 Enron spent $5 million lobbying Congress and federal agencies to deregulate the trading of energy futures. This would allow EnronOnline, using the floor of its own energy auction, to buy and sell electricity, natural gas, and other commodities in huge volumes without disclosing prices or quantities. Enron's point person was Senator Phil Gramm, a close friend of Ken Lay and major beneficiary of Enron campaign contributions, whose wife was an Enron director. In December 2000 Congress passed the Commodity Futures Modernization Act as part of an omnibus spending bill. The act expanded and codified the CFTC's decision exempting energy contracts from oversight and, even more important, removed electronic trading from CFTC jurisdiction. Enron could now bypass regulated trading auctions. Free of federal and state regulation, it gained effective leverage over California's energy supply.[114]

The California Market Implodes

In May 2000 hot weather and withholding of electricity converged to escalate electricity prices in the California market. Generating units were "unavailable" at a rate many times the industry average. The merchant generators that had acquired the units from local utilities took many of them offline, idling nearly a quarter of the state's generating capacity. The ISO knew which power plants could meet demand but lacked authority to compel the owners to turn them on or sell their output to the grid at a reasonable price. Physical withholding empowered predatory merchant generators, which extracted billions in excess of competitive baseline revenues. Average PX prices for wholesale power reached the previously unthinkable level of $166 per megawatt-hour. Annual statewide electricity costs totaled $27 billion, compared with $7 billion in 1999. Governor Davis urged the ISO and the PX to ask FERC for extended authority to establish price caps. The California legislature imposed retail price controls in San Diego (where the local utility was not subject to the existing retail rate freeze).[115]

The ISO declared a Stage 2 emergency and curtailed service to retail customers, but price spikes continued, rising sharply with the onset of winter. Caught between spiraling wholesale prices and the state-imposed freeze on retail rates, Pacific Gas & Electric (PG&E) and Southern California Edison (SCE) borrowed enormous amounts simply to maintain operations and meet demand. As their debts mounted, the utilities' power suppliers required security to ensure payment, and the ISO could not find willing sellers in the real-time market. The CPUC granted a 40 percent increase in retail rates and authorized the utilities to enter into long-term bilateral contracts outside the PX but would not ensure recovery of contract costs. In December the secretary of energy issued an emergency order directing certain generators and marketers to make sales to the ISO. The order did little to abate the crisis. Desperate to avoid blackouts and system outages, the ISO had no choice but to buy power in the real-time market at virtually any price.[116]

During the winter of 2001 the California system was in free fall. Rolling blackouts and huge price spikes disrupted business and people's lives. The ISO called Stage 3 alerts (required when power reserves, typically 15 percent or more, fall to less than one-tenth that amount) and curtailed service to interruptible retail customers. By early 2001, both utilities were in crisis mode and could not repay billions in debt incurred to purchase power in the spot market. SCE defaulted on a payment obligation of more than $250 million, while PG&E failed to pay even larger amounts owed to the ISO and PX. Unrecovered purchased-power costs of both utilities topped $12 billion. With billions appropriated from the state's General Fund, the Department of Water Resources (DWR) finally stepped in to buy power on behalf of the cash-strapped utilities, but could not halt the inexorable rise in whole-sale power prices. Lacking a portfolio of long-term procurement contracts, DWR had to purchase six million megawatt-hours of power each month in volatile spot markets subject to rotating outages. Merchant generators were quick to extract inflated market prices, often embedded in and amor-tized over long-term contracts that perpetuated elevated costs for years. In January 2001 the CPUC announced a $5.7 billion rate increase, and Gov-ernor Davis declared a state of emergency. "Never again," he said, "can we allow out-of-state profiteers to hold Californians hostage. Never again can we allow out-of-state generators to threaten to turn off our lights with the flick of a switch." The FERC, he added, had "shirked its responsibilities to protect ratepayers from this legalized highway robbery."[117] On May 2001 Lay met with Arnold Schwarzenegger, then a likely successor to Gray Davis, the incumbent governor, to discuss "fixing" California's energy crisis by raising electricity rates, ending state and federal investigations, and cancel-ing plans to reregulate volatile electricity markets in the state. The meeting was the spearhead of a carefully orchestrated public relations campaign.[118]

Meanwhile Governor Davis negotiated with the state's desperate utili-ties to provide some form of relief. For months, the utilities had warned they were running out of cash and demanded that rates be increased to cover their costs. In a televised speech on April 6, 2001, Davis reversed his stand against electricity rate increases, acknowledging that consumers would have to pay more. The governor's office was also negotiating to keep the utilities solvent by buying their transmission lines.[119]

The next day PG&E, the state's largest utility, filed for bankruptcy, citing "unreimbursed energy costs which are now increasing by more than $300 million per month, continuing CPUC decisions that economically disadvantage the company, and the now unmistakable fact that negotiations with Governor Davis are going nowhere."[120] PG&E contended the energy crisis and rate freeze had prevented it from recovering $9 billion in electricity procurement costs. "The regulatory and political processes have failed us," said its chairman, "and we are now turning to the court."[121] SCE resisted bankruptcy, and it eventually reached a settlement under which the CPUC kept its retail rates at elevated levels for several years to enable it to pay its debts. San Diego Gas & Electric avoided bankruptcy and was largely able to pass its wholesale costs on to its retail customers.[122]

The California market was a zero-sum game. As PG&E and SCE sank under unsustainable debt, Enron's revenues spiked. In 1999 Enron's Wholesale Services generated revenues of $35 billion, rising to $93 billion just one year later. It was no mere coincidence that in 2000 thousands of megawatts of in-state generating capacity were offline, almost five times the total during the previous year. Enron seized on scarcity. An Enron manager confessed: "There were days when we were making $100 million. When you're making that kind of money, you have to ask yourself, 'Are we the market?'"[123]

Although Enron did not own a single power plant in California, the answer to that rhetorical question was clear. By 2000 EnronOnline had gained control over a significant share of the California energy market, aided by Senator Gramm's legislation, the Commodity Futures Modernization Act. From December 21, 2000—the date Enron was allowed to operate an unregulated trading auction—until re-regulation of the market in June 2001, California suffered thirty-eight Stage 3 emergencies (rolling blackouts) compared to only one before that date. "Phil Gramm's [commodities deregulation law], for which Enron was the primary lobbyist," said Public Citizen, "allowed Enron's unregulated energy trading subsidiary ... to threaten millions of California households and businesses with power outages for the sole purpose of increasing the company's profits."[124] Overall, in 2000, Enron's North American trading desk made $2.2 billion and Belden's West Coast power division almost $500 million. The profits were so large that Enron had to book $1.5 billion as a reserve to hide the extent of its gain and avoid a potential political firestorm.[125]

Regulatory Aftermath

Mindful of the dollar-spinning market it was exploiting, Enron lobbied furiously against price caps and mounted a public relations campaign to convince federal regulators that California's crisis was a simple matter of supply-and-demand economics, made worse by a seriously flawed restructuring scheme. Lay was dismissive. California's system, he told Enron's employees, "was doomed to failure at the beginning. ... We think they ought to be trying to make the system work effectively with competition and with markets." Lay took his arguments public in speech after speech, denying Enron's manipulation and blaming lack of new power plants instead. At a meeting with DWR's David Freeman toward the end of 2000, Lay went even further. "In the final analysis," he said, "it doesn't matter what you crazy people in California do. I've got smart guys out there who can always figure out how to make money."[126]

Until mid-2000 FERC took no action. Finally, in August, responding to a utility complaint, FERC opened an investigation into California wholesale prices, setting a date, sixty days later, after which sales would be subject to potential refund (but refusing to require retroactive refunds and thereby insulating prior overcharges).[127] FERC also considered separate requests to impose price caps and set cost-based rates for sales into the ISO and PX.[128]

On November 1 FERC issued an order finding California's market structure to be seriously flawed.[129] Because sellers could "exercise market power when supply is tight," it deemed the resulting higher electric rates "unjust and unreasonable."[130] California's requirement that utilities buy and sell all their energy through the PX, FERC found, had induced overreliance on spot markets and prevented incumbent utilities from using forward contracts. FERC proposed to abolish the mandatory buy-sell rule, limit bids above $150 per megawatt-hour, and penalize certain purchases in the real-time market. Beyond tinkering with the market mechanism, however, FERC stopped short. The Federal Power Act, it said, was not created "to redress traumatic and inequitable circumstances ... but to provide rate certainty in a relatively static monopoly environment."[131] During the California energy crisis, FERC failed to take enforcement action against any generator operating in the California market;[132] to communicate with the CFTC and the SEC, agencies with nominal oversight of the power market; or to understand the linkage between the physical and financial markets in energy and energy derivatives.[133] A University of California economist said its policy "amounted to religious faith in markets."[134]

FERC also declined to cap wholesale prices. "In choosing our price mitigation approach," it said, "it is our intent to guide these markets to self-correct, not reintroduce command and control price regulation."[135] On December 15, seven months after the crisis began, FERC adopted its November 1 proposals but refused to contemplate retroactive refunds and forbade the utilities to sell power into the PX.[136] In framing its relief, FERC vindicated Ken Lay's free-market philosophy. "We reject proposals to return to cost-based regulation," it said. "Prices based upon traditional cost of service are incompatible with fostering a competitive market. ... The one thing California needs most is new supply, and a return to traditional cost of service ratemaking will not encourage supply to enter the California market."[137] FERC ignored the advice of ten prominent economists, including Paul Joskow, who predicted its "failure to act now will have dire consequences for the State of California and will set back, potentially fatally, the diffusion of competitive electricity markets across the country."[138]

FERC's rhetoric was hardly a surprise. Enron had launched a ferocious attack on the California market, aided by a successful public relations campaign and well-placed political allies, notably Senator Gramm.[139] "As they [Californians] suffer the consequences of their own feckless policies," the senator said early in 2001, "political leaders in California blame power companies, deregulation and everyone but themselves, and the inevitable call is being heard for a federal bail-out. I intend to do everything in my power to require those who valued environmental extremism and interstate protectionism more than common sense and market freedom to solve the electricity crisis without short-circuiting taxpayers in other states."[140] The CPUC took a different view. "There is no factual basis," it said, "upon which FERC can reasonably conclude that the California markets are sufficiently workable to produce reasonable prices in the absence of hard price caps."[141] It was not surprising that FERC's December 15 order failed to limit price increases or stabilize the market in which Enron continued to make huge profits.

Enron vehemently opposed hard price caps and, as his largest campaign donor, pressed its advantage with President Bush. Ken Lay was among the first people to meet with the newly inaugurated president, who promptly declared his opposition to price caps on wholesale electricity and urged California to relax its environmental regulations. He attributed California's market problems instead to its failure to build enough power-generating plants. Between February and April 2001, as the California crisis continued, Lay also met in secret five or six times with Vice President Cheney, whose task force was formulating energy policy for the Bush administration. In April Lay delivered a memo outlining Enron's policy suggestions. It urged the administration to "reject any attempt to deregulate wholesale power markets by adopting price caps." Although Cheney may not yet have known it, Enron was near collapse, heavily dependent on income derived from unregulated energy markets in California and other western markets where its traders were creating shortages through illegal market manipulations. A day later Cheney initiated an interview with a reporter for the *Los Angeles Times*. "Price caps provide short-term relief for politicians," he said, "but they do nothing to deal with the basic, fundamental problem. ... Once politicians can no longer resist the temptation to go with price caps, they usually are unable to muster the courage to end them."[142]

The war of words mattered. FERC's December 15 order was toothless. The California ISO said the rigged power market had cost consumers billions and again asked for price caps.[143] In April, FERC issued a tepid and technical response, once again declining to cap wholesale energy prices. "We are now eleven months into the California calamity," said a dissenting FERC commissioner, "and there is no end in sight." He noted the "high cost of natural gas delivered into California is ... used to justify high wholesale electricity bids into the ISO market"—a critical linkage in view of later findings that El Paso and others had manipulated and misreported prices in the California gas market.[144] FERC's April order drew intense criticism from the California agencies, which argued for price caps and a return to cost-of-service ratemaking.

FERC's continued inaction drew political pushback. Senator Feinstein of California called for an investigation of Enron's influence at FERC, prompted by media reports Ken Lay had pressured Curtis Hebert, FERC's chairman, to deregulate in ways favorable to Enron and then, dissatisfied with Hebert's response, had moved to replace him with Pat Wood, a Texas utilities commissioner thought to be more friendly to Enron. "Since FERC has refused to ... restore 'just and reasonable' electricity rates," Feinstein said, "we need to ask whether undue influence by the companies that FERC regulates has resulted in its failure to act. ... In California, the total cost of electricity in 1999 was $7 billion. This climbed to $28 billion in 2000 and is predicted to reach $70 billion this year. At the same time, with FERC refusing to act, power generators and marketers have made record profits. The people of our nation deserve an investigation."[145] The entire California delegation agreed, claiming "energy companies ... have wrung billions out of California consumers by squeezing supply to create artificial shortages."[146]

Finally, by order issued in June 2001, FERC set a hard price cap and prohibited megawatt laundering—shipping electricity out of state and then reselling it in California to avoid price mitigation. Neither measure reflected ideological retrenchment. Cost-of-service ratemaking, said FERC, did not provide "proper incentives for generators to become more efficient."[147] The June order was nonetheless immediately effective. Average spot prices dropped immediately by 75 percent, followed by further declines in later months. FERC's action, however grudging, resolved an epic market failure, much of it traceable to Enron, gas pipeline suppliers, and predatory merchant generators. As the California market returned to normal, Enron's profit gusher subsided. It had expected electricity prices would remain high for at least another two years. FERC's June order was a dagger in Enron's heart and ended its last chance to escape bankruptcy.[148]

The debacle in California provoked heated debate. Ken Lay blamed the weather, reduced hydro supplies, flawed market rules, dominance of the short-term market, absence of new power plants, and environmental regulation.[149] Paul Joskow and Alfred Kahn said a prime cause was "withholding of supplies from the market" in an exercise of "supplier market power."[150] Other economists took notice of abnormally high gas prices in California that amplified the market power of generators and triggered class-action antitrust suits against El Paso Natural Gas, Southern California Gas, and San Diego Gas & Electric.[151] Robert Nordhaus, a regulatory lawyer, cited "the lack of any effective mechanism to preclude 'pivotal bidders' from setting a market clearing price well in excess of competitive levels."[152] Joseph Dunn, a California state senator, said Enron worked to "undermine the CalPX in order to establish itself as the primary market maker," gain market power, and raise electricity prices.[153] And the U.S. Senate found that FERC "was no match for a determined Enron," displaying "a shocking absence of regulatory vigilance ... and a failure to structure the agency to meet the demands of the new market-based system that the agency itself has championed."[154]

Enron's End

In December 2000 Enron announced that Jeff Skilling would succeed Ken Lay as chief executive officer, and Enron's common stock closed above $83 per share, almost doubling its price in one year. Earnings for the year reached $1.3 billion, and Lay and Skilling each received multimillion-dollar payouts. Enron was no longer an asset-laden producer of natural gas. It had become a financial intermediary trading not just electricity and natural gas but pulp and paper, metals, and broadband services and selling derivative-based risk management products. Enron promoted itself as a "new-age" logistics and trading company but was in fact an accident waiting to happen. It had pledged shares of its common stock as collateral for off-balance debt incurred by affiliated special-purpose entities that had purchased its problematic assets. Enron was exposed to massive risk. A falling stock price would immediately erode credit guarantees secured by the pledged shares. Enron's operating businesses also concealed huge guarantee obligations that surfaced only after its bankruptcy. Enron had in fact consistently invested in unprofitable and marginal businesses, driven by "commercial naivete, deal orientation, and lack of financial discipline," and had incurred publicly reported operating losses of over $6 billion in electric power, broadband, and water. It had also grossly misrepresented its true financial condition, as subsequent restatements would reveal.[155]

In February 2001 Lay announced his retirement and named Skilling as his successor. In the company's annual conference with Wall Street analysts that month, Skilling bragged that Enron's stock was worth $126 per share, more than 50 percent above its current level. But the bull market was over, and Enron's stock price soon began to fall as Internet-related and telecommunications stocks lost favor with investors. In February *Fortune* magazine, previously a cheerleader, published a critical article about Enron, and Enron canceled a video-on-demand deal with Blockbuster. In May Enron withdrew from Dabhol, the failed power generating project in India, and from the

$10 billion Dolphin gas export project in the Persian Gulf. Also in May Cliff Baxter, a key executive who was later to commit suicide, left the company after a clash with Skilling over Enron's partnership transactions as senior management continued to sell their stock in Enron. Lay alone sold $70 million of Enron stock to the company to pay off loans it had made to him. In June Enron's stock price declined sharply as FERC imposed price caps in California. Despite an apparently profitable second quarter, the stock price continued to fall. Short sellers noticed Enron had added $3.9 billion of debt in 2000 and reported negative cash flow of $1.3 billion for the first two quarters of 2001. Between March and the end of June four institutional investors sold more than twenty-one million shares of Enron stock.[156]

In August Jeff Skilling resigned as chief executive officer, having realized millions from selling Enron stock in little more than a year, and was replaced by Ken Lay. In a conference call with analysts and investors Skilling claimed he had made an entirely personal decision. There are, he said, "no accounting issues, trading issues or reserve issues." Ken Lay confirmed that "the company is in the strongest shape it's ever been in."[157] But Skilling's sudden resignation created ripples, not least within the company. Sherron Watkins, an Enron vice president, sent an anonymous letter to Lay. "Skilling's abrupt departure," she wrote, "will raise suspicions of accounting improprieties and valuation issues. ... I am incredibly nervous we will implode in a wave of accounting scandals." Her letter and a later memo laid out serious problems affecting Enron's hedging transactions with special-purpose entities. "My concern," she said, "is that the footnotes don't adequately explain the transactions. If adequately explained, the investor would know that the 'entities' described in our related party footnote are thinly capitalized, the equity holders have no skin in the game, and all the value in the entities comes from the underlying value of the derivatives (unfortunately, in this case, a big loss) and Enron stock." Lay transferred Watkins to another department and had Enron's counsel research the legal implications of firing her.[158]

Watkins's letter addressed truths Lay did not wish to hear. Enron had entered into swaps with related-party special-purpose entities (SPEs) to hedge its downside risk on large block positions of publicly traded stock held in its merchant portfolio and had funded the SPEs with its own stock, the only asset available to cover any loss. When the portfolio stocks lost value, the Enron stock used to support the swaps also fell below the SPEs' exposure on the swaps, rendering the SPEs technically insolvent as counterparties. Enron had also guaranteed billions of affiliates' debt with Enron stock and would become liable to repay the debt if its share price fell below a certain threshold. "Enron was issuing its own common stock to itself," said one commentator, "to cover its own income statement loss."[159]

The *Powers Report,* submitted after Enron's bankruptcy by a special investigative committee of its board, concluded that "Enron engaged in transactions that had little economic substance and misstated Enron's financial results." It concluded that Lay had approved and was responsible for flawed related-party transactions.[160]

October was a portentous month. Enron agreed to sell Portland General Corp., the electric utility it had purchased in 1997, at a loss of $1.1 billion; announced a third-quarter loss of $618 million; and took a $1.2 billion write-down of stockholders' equity. *The Wall Street Journal* reported a $30 million payment to Fastow, the intermediary between Enron and its SPEs, whose termination quickly followed. Days later the SEC opened an investigation of conflicts of interest among Enron, its directors, and its special partnerships. Between October 15 and the end of the month the price of Enron stock sank from $33 to just under $14 per share, which triggered immediate payment of billions of dollars of contingent obligations and forced Enron to borrow $1 billion collateralized by its pipeline assets, the only viable asset remaining. Drawing on his political connections, Lay called Treasury Secretary O'Neill and Commerce Secretary Evans without avail. At the end of the month a desperate Enron entered into merger negotiations with Dynegy, Inc., an energy marketer in Texas, and signed a merger agreement a few weeks later. Throughout October Lay insisted Enron had access to cash and that the company was "performing very well."[161]

November brought further bad news. Enron restated its financials for the previous four years, driving its earnings for the period down by almost $600 million and increasing debt for 2000 by $658 million. Enron also reported a third-quarter loss of more than $600 million. Enron tried to prop itself up with new borrowing, including $1.5 billion from Dynegy secured by an option to acquire Enron's pipeline system. As revelations about Enron's finances unfolded, Dynegy cut the merger price in half. Uncertain the deal would be consummated, credit agencies downgraded Enron's debt to junk bond status, suddenly making it liable to retire $4 billion in debt, removing liquidity, reducing Enron's stock price to mere pennies per share, and compelling Dynegy to opt out. "If there was any hope of the merger," said Dynegy's president, "that put a nail in the coffin."[162] By late November Enron owed almost $19 billion to its trading customers. Its trading business, dependent on huge amounts of credit, quickly faded away. On December 2, Enron filed for bankruptcy in New York. At the time it was the largest bankruptcy, financial fraud, and audit failure in U.S. history.[163]

Enron's Chapter 11 filing had seismic consequences. The company's twenty thousand employees lost most of their life savings and pension plans as management in the final weeks locked down 401(k) plans, 60 percent invested in Enron stock. Creditors had billions at risk, eventually recovering no more than 40 cents on the dollar. Postbankruptcy management wrote down the value of Enron's assets by $14 billion and acknowledged a restatement would require a further multibillion-dollar write-down of risk management assets. In January 2002 Ken Lay resigned under pressure as Enron's chairman and chief executive officer, even as he claimed to be a victim of corrupt underlings and clung to his board seat for a few more weeks, until the *Powers Report* tagged him with "ultimate responsibility" for the Enron disaster as "captain of the ship." Jeff Skilling denied "the company was in anything but excellent shape" and said it had failed as a result of a "classic run on the bank" and a "liquidity problem." But Lay and Skilling had clearly seen the disaster coming a long way off. They had realized millions from sales and redemptions of Enron stock. Shareholders who held on to the end were left with nothing.[164]

Reckoning

The company's collapse unleashed a frenzy of analysis, finger-pointing, and litigation.[165] Critics identified deregulation, corporate greed, auditing failures, derivatives, lax board oversight, and complicit banks, among other causes. One commentator identified "senior executives' serious misreading of similarities between the natural gas business and the power generation, broadband, and water businesses" and Enron's belief in "one successful business model that can be applied to any market, leading to huge investment losses outside Enron's original gas business."[166] Another described Lay as "an extraordinary, mile-a-minute political capitalist" who overbuilt his company on government favor and minimal oversight.[167] But causation theories, however plausible, were all after-the-fact explanations, nowhere to be seen when Enron was riding high.[168]

Twenty-two Enron executives and partners pleaded guilty or were convicted of criminal charges for their roles in Enron's collapse. Enron's auditor, Arthur Andersen, was found guilty of fraud (although its conviction was overturned on appeal, too late to save it from dissolution). Determined to convict Lay and Skilling, the Justice Department created an Enron Task Force, staffed with selected prosecutors from across the country. Indictments followed in 2004, alleging conspiracy and fraud, among other charges. The case against Lay turned on his actions after returning as chief executive officer, when he misrepresented the true state of Enron business. He was not charged with approving Enron's off-the-books partnerships that hid billions of dollars of debt, and, unlike Skilling, he was not charged with insider trading. Between indictment and trial in 2006, Lay took his

Figure 5.1
Kenneth Lay, left, stands with his attorneys George "Mac" Secrest, center, and Mike Ramsey after they finished their closing arguments in his fraud and conspiracy trial on Tuesday, May 16, 2006, in Houston. (AP Photo/Pat Sullivan.)

case public and portrayed himself as uninvolved in accounting details and fraudulent deals. At trial, however, the government produced testimony from Enron executives who had warned Lay of problems only to have him paint an optimistic picture for investors.[169]

Lay had failed, prosecutors alleged, to disclose massive problems he knew about, including billions in hidden Enron debts and a loan secured by Enron's pipelines. He had also professed the "highest faith and confidence" in Enron's chief financial officer, Andrew Fastow, who the next day took a permanent leave of absence. Lay said he was unaware of Fastow's activities. He testified to being "on the battlefront" as Enron spiraled out of control and blamed its collapse on Fastow and a witch hunt led by the *Wall Street*

Figure 5.2
Law enforcement officials escort Enron founder Kenneth Lay and his wife Linda away from the courthouse after his fifth day on the stand in his fraud and conspiracy trial, Monday, May 1, 2006, in Houston. (AP Photo/Pat Sullivan.)

Figure 5.3
On October 23, 2006, former Enron CEO Jeff Skilling, left, leaves the federal court-house with his attorney Daniel Petrocelli, right, after being sentenced to twenty-four years in federal prison. (AP Photo/David J. Phillip, File.)

Journal and short sellers. At trial Lay was arrogant and contentious. He also played the Horatio Alger card. "Like Nixon," wrote one account, "Lay's face naturally falls into a frown. On the stand, his brows come together. His tongue flicked back and forth hitting the corners of his mouth. He tried to win the jury over during direct examination by telling about the three paper routes he had growing up and summers laboring on farms in Missouri. Lay, once a multimillionaire, also testified that he drives a thirteen-year-old car and all his savings are gone." The prosecutor pointed out that Lay had made secret sales of Enron stock and spent millions on an extravagant lifestyle. In May 2006, after sixteen weeks of trial, the jury found Lay guilty as charged and Skilling guilty on nineteen of twenty-eight counts. Both faced years in prison.[170]

Little over a month after his conviction and before he could mount an appeal, Ken Lay died of a heart attack in Aspen, Colorado, and his conviction was, as a matter of constitutional law, extinguished. "It's as if he was never charged and convicted," explained a Houston criminal lawyer. "This is the law. There may have been a moral victory for the government, but there's no longer a legal victory." His obituary compared Lay to Icarus, the figure in Greek mythology who had wings of feathers and wax but fell into the sea when he flew too close to the sun. "The Enron and Ken Lay stories are best told in an English literature class, or a classics class," it said, "where you are trying to explain what hubris is all about."[171]

6 Amory Lovins: Prophet of a New Order

Prologue

In 1976, when Bonneville was aggressively promoting nuclear power projects, Ken Lay had yet to form Enron, and Paul Joskow was still years away from conceiving the blueprint of a restructured utility industry, Amory Lovins, then a twenty-nine-year-old consultant physicist, published a now-famous article, "Energy Strategy: The Road Not Taken," in *Foreign Affairs*.[1] Drawing on Robert Frost's poetic image, he saw two contrasting energy paths the nation might follow over the next fifty years: a hard path relying on centralized fossil fuel and nuclear power stations to increase energy supply and a soft path based on efficiency and renewable energy sources.

"The hard path," he wrote, "sometimes portrayed as the bastion of free enterprise and free markets, would instead be a world of subsidies, $100 billion bailouts, oligopolies, regulations, nationalization, eminent domain, corporate statism."[2] The soft path, using distributed solar power, windpower, and biomass, would be "flexible, resilient, sustainable, and benign."[3] The choice between the two paths was seen as a struggle between new stakeholders and entrenched interests over how to manage power systems and industrial utilities and, more broadly, a conflict over competing conceptions of modern life and identity: decentralization versus centralization, consolidated versus dispersed control over natural resources, and conventional cost accounting versus consideration of environmental externalities.[4] Among those externalities is climate change. "The commitment to a long-term coal economy … ," Lovins prophesied, "makes the doubling of atmospheric carbon dioxide concentration early in the next century virtually unavoidable, with the prospect then or soon thereafter of substantial and perhaps irreversible changes in global climate."[5]

Once described as the *"enfant terrible* of the energy left,"[6] Lovins grew up near Washington, D.C., the grandchild of immigrants from the Ukraine and son of a polymath engineer who designed and built scientific instruments. "At three or four years of age," Lovins recalled, "I liked taking old watches to bits and putting them back together."[7] His mother read him poetry, taught him phonics, and had him reading before age four. By age seven he had devoured the entire *Encyclopaedia Britannica*. After two years at Harvard, he spent another two at Magdalen College, Oxford, where he studied music, classics, math, linguistics, some law, and a little medicine. "I picked up economics later," he said. "It's really very simple once you learn the terminology."[8]

In 1969, at age twenty-one, he became a Junior Research Fellow at Oxford, but only after receiving his master of arts degree by special resolution because he did not meet the formal requirements. In 1971, finding it was too soon to be allowed to do a doctorate in energy at Oxford, Lovins resigned from his fellowship to work for David R. Brower, a conservationist and head of the Friends of the Earth Foundation, on energy, which was "about to become a major and persistent global problem."[9] Ever prolific, by 1975 Lovins had produced essays and analyses on energy and several books, including *Non-Nuclear Futures: The Case for an Ethical Energy Strategy,* that foreshadowed his *Foreign Affairs* article. Publication of that article launched a far-ranging career that promoted an alternative vision based on efficient use and sustainable supply. His urgent recommendations were often dismissed by utility and nuclear interests as unworkable but were eventually assimilated as part of mainstream energy policy. Starting as an outlier, Lovins became a widely acclaimed authority on energy, founded the Rocky Mountain Institute as an energy think tank, and accumulated laurels and honors.

Lovins's energy policy rests in part on core assumptions about comparative fuel costs. Early on he urged an end to fossil fuel subsidies and advocated a severance royalty, now called a carbon tax, in order to place renewables—wind, solar, and biomass—on an equal footing and to have all energy sources reflect their true long-term costs, including the costs of externalities such as pollution and climate change. He characterized renewables as "soft technologies," at once more participatory and less coercive than "hard technologies" run by remote, centralized facilities. "Soft technologies," he argued, "use familiar, equitably distributed natural energies to meet perceived human needs directly and comprehensibly."[10] Certain critics, unimpressed, were quick to seize on Lovins's "technological utopianism,"[11] labeled him a "libertarian and technocrat,"[12] and called his proposals "discourse-by-declaration."[13] In fact, by including externalities, his early views can be seen as traditional, with an intellectual debt to A. C. Pigou, the famous early twentieth-century Cambridge economist, who argued for internalization of the social cost of pollution by government regulations or taxes.[14]

Many of Lovins's recommendations are in fact pragmatic and quantifiable. But his preference for local, distributed sources of renewable power runs squarely counter to more than a century of development in the U.S. utility business, whose principal architects, Edison and Insull, were devout believers in size, monopoly, economies of scale, and central power stations. To their followers and heirs, Lovins's prescriptions seem heretical, or at least unpersuasive; to a growing audience of true believers, however, he has charted a path to the energy future.

Nuclear Power

Nuclear power—a particular Lovins bête noire—was long seen by U.S. policymakers as the main alternative to fossil fuels and from its inception was heavily subsidized and regulated. The government indemnified private companies in the nuclear power industry against the risk of catastrophic loss caused by major accidents.[15] It also subsidized the cost of nuclear fuel and conducted research and development, without charge, at national labs to assist private industry.[16]

The Atomic Energy Commission, charged with the conflicting tasks of regulating and promoting nuclear power, gave way in 1974 to the Nuclear Regulatory Commission (NRC), whose mandate is to oversee the safety and security of nuclear power, including the initial licensing of reactors, handling of radioactive materials, and storage and disposal of spent fuels. The mandate is broad but ill-defined. Congress did not require definitive reactor safety and siting standards or provide a framework for managing nuclear wastes.[17] Tons of spent nuclear fuel, scattered in dry casks and storage pools in locations throughout the United States, continue to pose an intractable problem.

By the late 1970s it became difficult to site nuclear plants. Community activists launched legal challenges in federal and state courts, causing construction delays and reshaping public attitudes about nuclear power. Friends of the Earth, David Brower's green organization, became a spearhead in the worldwide antinuclear movement and urged that all reactors be shut down "until the environmental and genetic safety of their operation can be proved and until a safe method is found for keeping high-level radioactive waste separated from the environment. ..."[18] The industry, well entrenched, deflected such environmental challenges.

By 1974 there were fifty-four operating reactors in the United States and close to two hundred on order. U.S. coal prices had reached record levels in real terms, and utilities were forecasting steady compound annual growth in electricity demand for decades. The Atomic Energy Commission predicted that, by the turn of the century, half of all electricity generation would come from nuclear power. Instead, after 1974, utilities suspended existing reactor orders and stopped placing new ones. Fewer than half the reactors on order were ever completed.[19] Several hard realities drove the reversal of fortune. Nuclear plants encountered regulatory delays and huge cost overruns; demand for electricity leveled off; and, by the early 1980s, the price of fossil fuels fell dramatically.[20] "The doubtful economics of ... [pressurized water reactors]," wrote Lovins in 1978, "uncertainties about demand, reliability, and safety, and the macroeconomic problems of capital intensity 10 to 30 times greater than North Sea oil capacity have together led to ... the most dramatic collapse of a major industrial enterprise in history.'"[21]

Nuclear safety—for Lovins an oxymoron determined "not by our care or ingenuity but by our inescapable fallibility"—also played a critical role in halting the industry's momentum.[22] In 1979, as if to prove the truth of Lovins's insight, a reactor at the Three Mile Island plant in Pennsylvania came within an hour of total meltdown, averted only by manual shutoff of a pressure-operated relief valve that had been open for two hours. Pennsylvania officials had to put in motion contingency plans to evacuate 650,000 people within twenty miles of the plant.[23] The incident became a cause célèbre, focused attention on human error, and crystallized public opposition to nuclear power. When the Chernobyl disaster occurred in 1986, expansion of the U.S. nuclear power industry had come to a halt. The Shoreham nuclear power station on Long Island, the target of antinuclear activists, shut down, stranding a $5.6 billion investment before it produced a single kilowatt-hour of power. "Three-fifths of the ordered plants were abandoned," Lovins said in retrospect. "Many others proved uncompetitive. Steep debt downgrades hit four in five nuclear utilities. Some went broke. Through 1978, 253 U.S. reactors were ordered (none since). Only 104 survive. Two-fifths of those have failed for a year or more at least once."[24]

Notwithstanding this checkered history, the nuclear power industry survived and quite recently appeared to be on the cusp of a renaissance. In 2007 the NRC received the first new license application in almost three decades, followed within a year by sixteen additional applications for twenty-four proposed reactors. The Energy Policy Act of 2005 offered loan guarantees, production tax credits, and other subsidies for new nuclear plants worth an estimated $13 billion,[25] while streamlined federal safety review and licensing procedures cut regulatory lead times.[26] Over intervening decades since 1978 the nuclear power industry had upped its game, increased capacity factors to around 90 percent, reduced unit operating costs below those for fossil-fueled plants, and improved safety metrics. Also in nuclear power's favor for a time were volatile fossil fuel prices, climate change policies that promised to place constraints on carbon dioxide emissions, and a national policy to reduce oil imports from unstable areas of the world.[27] The chairman of the NRC declared the "nuclear renaissance is here," and Senator Hagel of Nebraska saw the industry's immediate future as an "almost golden time of possibilities."[28]

But a nuclear renaissance was not to be. Newly abundant shale gas supplies drove natural gas prices down sharply; the recession reduced electricity demand; legislation to limit carbon emissions stalled in Congress; and in 2011, echoing the Chernobyl disaster twenty-five years earlier, an earthquake and tsunami damaged the Fukushima Daichi nuclear plant in northern Japan, causing reactor meltdowns and large-scale releases of radioactive steam.[29] After 2009 the NRC received just one additional license application, and few of the pending applications moved forward. The chairman of one of the largest U.S. nuclear companies said he would not proceed until the price of natural gas doubled and carbon emissions cost $25 per ton.[30] Existing nuclear plants remained in place, subject to license extensions.

New facilities face a stubborn reality. "Nuclear plants," said Lovins almost thirty years ago, "are fundamentally uneconomic."[31] More recently, he inveighed against "shockingly large" subsidies for new nuclear plants built by private companies and certain state laws that compel utility customers to finance new reactors in advance "whatever they cost" and "whether they ever run" plus "a return to the utilities for risks they no longer bear." Despite massive government-financed incentives, he noted, the sponsors of new nuclear plants have been unable to raise private capital "because there's no business case. Subsidies can't reverse business fundamentals."[32] Investment in new nuclear plants presupposes major changes in the status quo, including a significant price on emissions of carbon dioxide, high fossil fuel prices, and a solution to long-term disposal of nuclear waste.[33] Such changes are not on the immediate horizon, and without them new nuclear plants may not be economically competitive.[34] Existing nuclear plants nonetheless remain a significant source of low-carbon power and are expected to continue to provide a meaningful share of generation in the U.S. market in coming decades.[35]

Lovins's brief against nuclear power does not rest on economics alone. He also believes nuclear power is the "main driving force behind proliferation" since "every form of every fissionable material in every nuclear fuel cycle can be used to make military bombs, either on its own or in combination with other ingredients made widely available by nuclear power." Nuclear power generates vast flows of materials, equipment, skills, and knowledge that, in Lovins's view, create do-it-yourself bomb kits. "Every known civilian route to bombs," he concluded as early as 1980, "involves either nuclear power or materials and technologies ... [that are] a direct and essential consequence of nuclear fission power."[36] A collateral concern is sabotage and terrorism. "The huge radioactive inventories in nuclear reactors and spent fuel facilities," he wrote in 1983 long before the events of September 11, 2001, "place the fallout potential of a sizable nuclear arsenal in the hands of anyone with the simple means required to cause a major release."[37] At bottom, Lovins believes, the risks of nuclear proliferation and terrorism cannot be contained by diligence alone but reflect the imponderable "impact of human fallibility and malice on highly engineered systems."[38] Lovins's concerns are hardly theoretical. The essential ingredients required for making a nuclear weapon exist in many countries; no binding global standard exists for securing weapons-grade nuclear material; and there have been many reported incidents of nuclear smuggling.[39]

Renewables

"Soft technologies" is a core concept, connoting, in the Lovinsian vocabulary, renewable power sources provided by sun, wind, and vegetation that imply fundamental changes in "the technical and sociopolitical structure of the energy system."[40] Diverse, locally accessible, and scaled to meet end-use needs, renewables are expected to gain market share by reducing infrastructure costs and virtually eliminating the costs of energy conversion and distribution.[41] Lovins predicted, in the 1970s, that soft technologies would meet "virtually all needs in 2025"[42] and that a "largely or wholly solar economy can be constructed in the United States with straightforward soft technologies that are now demonstrated."[43]

These were grandiose forecasts, driven more by advocacy than hard fact. To Lovins renewable power sources imply permanence and ecological discipline; conventional sources, mineral extraction and profit making. "One system is dying," he believes, "and others are struggling to be born."[44] At bottom, in Lovins's view, the true contest between large-scale, fossil-fueled generation plants and decentralized renewable systems is philosophical: "Each path entails a certain evolution of social values and perceptions that makes the other kind of world harder to imagine."[45]

Despite recent encouraging trends, Lovins's sweeping predictions have not yet come to pass. Renewable energy confronts economic, policy, and technical barriers. "The primary public policy argument for promoting electricity generation from solar, wind, and other renewable sources," writes Severin Borenstein, a professor of business economics at the University of California, "is the unpriced pollution externalities from burning fossil fuels."[46] The best way to price externalities, most economists agree, would be a tax on emissions, sometimes called a carbon tax, or a tradable permit system. For the most part, however, regulators in the United States and elsewhere have promoted renewable power through subsidies or mandates. Even with government support, the relatively high direct cost of renewable power still limits it to a fairly modest market share. Coal and natural gas, also subsidized, remain the lowest-cost, and still dominant, sources of power.[47]

Levelized cost is the principal metric used in comparing renewable and fossil fuel technologies, which have different temporal and spatial production profiles. Although a useful starting point, levelized cost does not take account of the costs of intermittency. Solar power is produced only during sunlight hours and peaks at midday, at the same time as the highest demand, therefore commanding a higher-than-average price. Windpower is also intermittent, peaks in evening hours, and is worth as much as 10 percent less than average output would be.[48] Grid operators tend to solve the intermittency problem by adding reserve generation and charging the cost of reserves to the system as a whole. Windpower, typically sited remotely and requiring long transmission lines to reach markets, also faces locational constraints. Who should bear the cost of long-line transmission to serve windpower generation remains a vexing policy question. Residential solar generation avoids transmission investment but does not bear its share of the cost for the utility's distribution system.[49] "Advocates of wind generation who argue that it is at grid parity in some locations," says Borenstein, "generally do not adjust for the timing, location, and intermittency factors that can make wind substantially less valuable." Similarly, advocates of grid parity for solar photovoltaic power "do not consider that the retail electricity rate [i.e., the rate typically paid by the local utility for net-metered electricity sold back to the grid] pays for much more than the energy that the solar generation replaces."[50]

Levelized cost comparisons are approximations. They do not include project-specific soft costs, such as land acquisition and permitting, tax subsidies, or the costs of new transmission. Nor, most critically, do levelized cost comparisons reflect fossil fuels' externality costs related to air pollutants (sulfur dioxide, nitrous oxides, mercury, and greenhouse gas emissions), which are subject to command-and-control regulation, technology mandates, and subsidies for green power but not a monetizable tax or a tradable permit program. Even if the generally accepted cost of externalities were included, renewables would not necessarily reach economic parity. "Residential solar would be cost competitive on a social cost basis," writes Borenstein, "only if the cost of carbon dioxide emissions were greater than $326 per ton," three times the prevailing forecast price (which is, in any event, not applied on a comparative basis). Because a carbon tax remains uncertain in the immediate future, energy markets in the United States fail to price in environmental externalities, leaving renewable power at a competitive disadvantage despite subsidies.[51] Wind and solar supply less than 5 percent of all electricity generation in North America (although significantly more in Europe).[52] Free-market critics have noted "extremely high capital costs, spotty power output, environmental complications, serious NIMBY opposition, and struggling economics."[53]

Lovins, characteristically, is undeterred. "Renewable technologies generally have had higher capital costs than fossil-fueled power plants," he wrote recently, "but their fuel is free, their energy price is locked in for decades, and their capital costs are falling. ... Quick and substantial ongoing cost reductions will be the key to continued growth."[54] Lovins sees such reductions in the solar photovoltaics industry, driven by technological advances and economies of scale, and cites a prediction by GE's global research director that electricity from photovoltaics "may be cheaper than electricity generated by fossil fuels and nuclear reactors within three to five years."[55] A glut of photovoltaic panels, sourced mostly from China, is expected to continue to drive prices down.[56]

Similar technological progress in wind turbine technology is cutting windpower costs per kilowatt-hour. As for renewables' variability and uncertainty, grid operators can mitigate those factors through diversity of supply and demand and bulk power storage. Variable renewable supplies, Lovins believes, could therefore account for 30 percent or more of all grid power in the United States and has already reached that threshold in parts of Germany.[57] But embedded problems exist. To support windpower growth, a large investment in new high-voltage transmission lines would be required, and Lovins does not convincingly explain how that would come about.[58]

He is nonetheless unfailingly bullish about the prospects for renewables. "In California last year [2012]," he notes, "the state's three largest shareholder-owned utilities generated 19.8 percent of their electricity from renewables ... ; Texas, leading the nation in installed wind capacity ... , generated more than 10 percent of its electricity from renewables in 2012 ... , and in early 2013 was nearing 30 per cent." Recently, he added, California utilities soliciting bids for solar power received enough to meet the state's entire peak load.[59] Lovins envisages a system in which there will be more low-carbon and intermittent energy sources, more suppliers, fewer coal and nuclear plants, better storage, distributed renewable power, and more energy traded to bolster supply and mitigate environmental problems. It is a sanguine view of the energy future that may turn, in the last analysis, on government intervention.

U.S. energy policy has been problematic, cyclical, and event-driven. It supported renewable power under President Carter but virtually eliminated funding for renewable energy research and terminated federal tax credits for renewable energy under President Reagan. Early support for renewable energy faded by the mid-1980s during an era of cheaper fossil fuels and overt hostility from investor-owned utilities. Federal legislation in 1989, 1990, 1992, and 2005 again promoted renewables, including the production tax credit, a major boost for windpower, that initially expired in 1999 but was later expanded and extended by several other laws.[60] Neither the Department of Energy, which is largely engaged in research and development, nor the NRC or FERC, both regulatory agencies, is a consistent source of energy policy, which has emerged instead through a complex mix of federal and state legislation and regulation. The states have, by default, often become policy innovators.[61]

With authority over retail electricity service, many states have enacted renewable portfolio standards (RPS) that require utilities to purchase a specific percentage of their energy requirements from renewable sources. To promote its windpower industry, in 1999 Texas adopted one of the nation's first RPS, mandating installation of 2,800 megawatts of renewable energy in ten years. Texas reached its goal in 2005 and increased the threshold to almost 6,000 megawatts by 2015 and 10,000 megawatts by 2025. Even though "utilities kicked and screamed the first time we passed a mandate ... in 2005," said the head of the Environmental Defense Fund's Texas office, "they didn't even bother to oppose the stricter requirements, because they saw they could actually make money off it."[62] But Texas is an exception. Overall program targets are modest, compliance with RPS requirements is often honored in the breach, and the base from which new renewable capacity is growing is low. Recent efforts to adopt a federally mandated RPS failed.[63] With certain important exceptions, many state RPS programs appear aspirational. "The recent history of renewables," according to a prominent academic critic, "leads to a conclusion that existing and proposed mandates are better viewed as special interest legislation than as rational responses to climate change and fossil-fuel power plant emissions."[64]

Still, RPS programs have encouraged energy entrepreneurs. In 2008, testifying before the Senate Energy and Natural Resources Committee, T. Boone Pickens, the Texas oilman, appeared as a persuasive, if unlikely, advocate for wind energy. He told the committee his company, Mesa Power, had just placed the largest single turbine order ever given and the Mesa Pampa Wind Project in Texas, when completed at a cost close to $10 billion, would generate 4,000 megawatts—enough energy to power 1.3 million homes. He also noted a potential pitfall: "The large, flat open areas with adequate wind are usually located a long way from where electricity is needed. Since we can't do much about where nature has put the wind, we have to do something about transmission to move electricity to market."[65]

Less than two years later, Pickens abandoned his project, saying he would build a wind farm in the Panhandle when transmission is built. Pickens's change of fortune illustrates a wind energy problem. The United States is home to vast clean energy resources but lacks a modern interstate transmission grid to deliver carbon-free electricity to customers in highly populated areas. Many wind projects with output that potentially could meet a significant fraction of the nation's energy needs—must wait in line to connect to the grid until there is enough transmission capacity to carry their power.[66]

Texas is not the only part of the country where local generation exceeds local load and must rely on high-voltage transmission lines to carry power to distant urban markets. Windy states such as Wyoming, Kansas, and Nebraska are generation-rich, demand-poor, and without energy-dependent industry. To reach distant urban markets local generators cannot rely on existing high-voltage transmission lines, constrained by limited capacity, to traverse a balkanized national grid. Yet construction of new connecting lines, although sorely needed, confronts technical, jurisdictional, and cost allocation barriers.

The price tag for expanding power lines to reach offshore and remote land-based wind turbines alone could reach $150 billion. Who should pay for an upgrade of that magnitude poses a knotty regulatory problem, of particular importance since over half of all new resources expected to be added to the bulk power system within the next decade will be wind and solar.[67] Accommodating green power requires change—"not in the physics of how grids work," says Lovins, "but in the strategies, rules, and procedures operators use to run them—a big institutional challenge."[68]

Historically, transmission planning has been a bottom-up process. The local utility would assess its need for new transmission within or connecting to its service area, based on considerations of reliability and the need for power to service its own customers; it would have little incentive to build new transmission lines to reach distant renewable projects owned by others. The local utility would also have a right of first refusal to build, own, and operate any lines built within its service area. Outside transmission developers often hesitated to undertake transmission projects the local utility could unilaterally decide to control and build itself. A leading energy consultant identified over one hundred planned transmission projects nationwide with a total cost of $180 billion, many of which, it said, would not be built because of deficiencies in transmission planning and cost allocation.

Capital-intensive transmission projects, it has become clear, require a more top-down process of approval and cost allocation. With jurisdiction over interstate transmission of electricity, in 2011 FERC finally mandated important changes in the planning of transmission facilities and how their costs are assigned to customers.[69] Under the new rules existing transmission owners no longer have a right of first refusal to build regional transmission projects, must engage in regional transmission planning, and must also allocate costs regionally since long transmission lines (particularly those connecting remote windpower projects) are likely to benefit customers over a wider geographic area than the service territory of a single utility. FERC's overriding cost allocation principle assigns costs on a basis "roughly commensurate" with project benefits.[70]

FERC's standard, although rooted in common sense, faced a judicial test on parallel facts. In 2010 MISO, the Midwest regional transmission organization, sought FERC's approval to impose a tariff on its members to fund construction of new high-voltage transmission lines for electricity generated by remote wind farms. Every state in MISO's region encourages or even requires utilities to obtain a specified percentage of its electricity supply from renewable sources, mainly wind farms. Most of the states expect or require utilities to obtain between 10 and 25 percent of their electricity needs from renewable sources by 2025. MISO proposed to allocate the cost of new transmission lines in proportion to each utility's share of the region's total wholesale consumption of electricity. Previously, MISO would have allocated the cost to utilities nearest a proposed transmission line because they would presumably benefit most. MISO decided instead to allocate the cost among all utilities drawing power from the grid according to the amount of electrical energy used, placing most of the cost on urban centers where demand for energy is greatest. FERC approved MISO's rate design, precipitating petitions for review before the Seventh Circuit Court of Appeals.[71]

Illinois objected to MISO's plan. It contended all MISO members would be forced to contribute to the cost of transmission projects that benefit only a few. Illinois' argument provoked a sweeping rejection in words that could have been authored by Amory Lovins had he been sitting on the bench. "The promotion of wind power deserves emphasis," the court said through Judge Richard Posner. The court continued:

deserves emphasis. Already wind power accounts for 3.5 percent of the nation's electricity ... and it is expected to continue growing. ... The use of wind power in lieu of power generated by burning fossil fuels reduces both the nation's dependence on foreign oil and emissions of carbon dioxide. And its cost is falling as technology improves. No one can know how fast wind power will grow. But the best guess is that it will grow fast and confer substantial benefits on the region served by MISO by replacing more expensive local wind power, and power plants that burn oil or coal, with western wind power. There is no reason to think these benefits will be denied to particular subregions of MISO. Other benefits ..., such as increasing the reliability of the grid, also can't be calculated in advance ..., yet are real and will benefit utilities and consumers in all of MISO's subregions.[72]

Michigan utilities also objected. They said MISO's program would force them to pay for costly new power lines carrying out-of-state renewable energy contrary to Michigan's Clean, Renewable and Efficient Energy Act, which forbids utilities to count out-of-state green power against the minimum required RPS percentage. Judge Posner said the Michigan statute trips over "an insurmountable constitutional objection" and cannot, "without violating the commerce clause ... of the Constitution, discriminate against out-of-state renewable energy."[73] Since most state RPS programs also favor in-state generation, the court's decision could have far-reaching implications. In the end, however, the economic case must still be made for transmitting renewable energy over long distances from one region of the country to another. This means generation costs must decline and capacity factors for green lines, now no more than 40 percent, will need to rise. Judge Posner's "best guess" as to the benefits of windpower must still be regarded as an unproven expectation.

Efficiency

In 1989, at the Green Energy Conference in Montreal, Lovins gave the keynote address, "The Negawatt Revolution—Solving the CO_2 Problem."

Figure 6.1
Amory Lovins of the Rocky Mountain Institute addresses the Vermont legislature in Montpelier on January 11, 2007. (AP Photo/Toby Talbot.)

It was a bravura performance, part dazzling array of facts and part novel prescriptions for the energy future. "The relevant question," he said, "is not simply where to get more energy, of any kind, from any source, at any price. Rather, it is a series of inter-linked questions. What do we want the energy for? What are the end uses we are trying to provide, such as comfort and light and torque? And how much energy, of what kind, at what scale, from what source, will meet each of these end use needs in the cheapest way?"[74] The bottom line, for Lovins, was energy efficiency, driven by new technologies (e.g., improved lighting, electric motors), regulatory change, and new ways to finance and deliver benefits. "To allocate society's capital efficiently to meet its electrical service needs," Lovins theorized, "requires that all ways to make or save electricity be compared with each other on an equal footing, at the same discount rate. One obvious way is to have the utility invest on your side of the meter to save electricity whenever it's cheaper to do that than for them to run or to build ... capacity."[75] Electric utilities therefore need to determine whether it is less expensive to pay customers to reduce consumption or to build and maintain a supply-side resource. Lovins believed foregone consumption less costly than increasing electricity supply.

He then made an intellectual leap, suggesting a market in what he called negawatts, a theoretical unit of power representing an amount of energy saved (measured in watts) as a direct result of energy conservation or increased efficiency or, stated differently, an imputed quantity calculated against a counterfactual baseline. Negawatts in this formulation are a commodity, tradable across time and space in a secondary market that reallocates electricity from one consumer to another and allows users to lower their usage in return for compensation. "If I ... run a paper mill in Quebec and I want cheap electricity," he speculated by way of example, "I ought to be able to come here and fix these ridiculous lights over our heads ... and then have Hydro-Quebec sell my paper mill the same amount of electricity I saved here—wheel it back to me in effect—but sell it to me at a discount so that I share the saved operating costs between myself and other customers."[76]

Having propounded a radical reordering of the electricity marketplace, Lovins next turned his attention to regulation. Prevailing regulatory practice, then and now, sets rates to allow recovery of operating expenses and fixed costs at an anticipated revenue threshold. Once the rate has been set, a utility can increase its profits by exceeding that threshold. There is a direct relationship between a utility's sales volume and its profits. Until the advent of demand-side management, the utility was rewarded for selling more and penalized for selling less. Conservation programs that reduce sales also generally reduce profits and therefore encounter resistance from managers of investor-owned, profit-maximizing utilities.

Lovins identified a completely new principle of utility regulation, then being explored by Puget Power and Boston Edison among others, that would decouple utilities' profits from their sales. "That way," he explained, "if they sell less than expected they're not in the hole, and if they sell more than expected they don't benefit from it. They're indifferent, then, to whether they sell more or less. If they do something smart to cut your bill, let them keep part of the saving as extra profit, or in some other way give them an exemplary reward for efficient behavior so they really have an incentive to be efficient." Utilities, he concluded, should sell less electricity and more efficiency, becoming competitors in the energy service market-place rather than mere commodity vendors.[77] Lovins envisioned a 75 percent increase in end-use efficiency at an average life-cycle cost of only 0.6 cents per kilowatt-hour (kWh) saved.[78]

Lovins's vision of a repurposed energy marketplace and utility industry did not escape the scrutiny of energy analysts, notably Paul Joskow—as we saw in chapter 4, an MIT economist and coauthor of *Markets for Power,* a treatise on the restructured electric utility industry then emerging. Joskow and a colleague surveyed the electricity conservation programs of ten utilities to calculate the cost of a negawatt and found it to be much higher than Lovins's estimate. "What does a negawatt really cost when it is purchased by a utility?" they asked in a famous article authored in 1992. "The honest answer is that neither we nor anyone else knows with any precision! We do know that ... [a negawatt] is likely to have actual costs that are significantly understated ... by most of the utilities whose programs we have examined."[79] Joskow's careful empirical inquiry revealed that utilities had lowballed the cost of conserved energy by failing to report all relevant costs, relying on engineering estimates rather than ex post measurement of actual savings, and failing to adjust for free riders, customers receiving utility incentives who would have undertaken the efficiency investment in any event. Joskow noted the "great optimism" implicit in Lovins's cost estimates and suggested utilities were subsidizing conservation because, as regulated monopolies, they could easily pass the associated costs on to customers. He called the process taxation by regulation.[80]

Lovins was not long in responding to Joskow's frontal assault. Joskow , he said, "used highly aggregated data from a small group of utilities with wildly divergent programs, installing efficiency improvements often inferior in design or execution to modern standards." Lovins denied relying on "assumptions" or "estimates" and referenced "empirical cost and performance data" used by more than one hundred utility companies in thirty-five countries. "Vigilant regulators ...," he advised, "ensure that utilities do not waste customers' money for long."[81]

Unchastened, Joskow restated his criticism in a 1993 MIT white paper, noting that Lovins's numbers "drastically understate the true costs of energy conservation programs" and "were becoming an embarrassment to the energy conservation community because they had no relationship to reality."[82] Utilities spending general ratepayer money to finance energy conservation, he argued, "are going to have to pull their socks up." Joskow urged a more serious effort to estimate conservation costs and energy savings achieved. "Placing the utility in the position of deciding how millions of customers should use electricity, and then using general ratepayer funds to subsidize consumers so that they behave in ways that some engineering model says they should behave reflects a central planning mentality that is doomed to failure."[83]

Joskow followed the white paper with a further published letter in the pages of *Science*, observing that Lovins's cost data "are based on many assumptions about the generality of usage conditions, marketing, installation, [and] monitoring costs." As a result, he suggested, many utilities have been led to fund "inefficient energy conservation programs, whose costs are recovered through higher electricity rates" and treat conservation as a "utility resource rather than as a market-driven, customer resource."[84] This was not an isolated view. Other critics found Lovins's work to be "replete with misleading conclusions, errors in calculation, factual inaccuracies, and wildly speculative assumptions" and claimed Lovins "had distorted and/or fabricated virtually all of his 'evidence.'"[85]

Despite such doubts, energy conservation has gained political traction, finding expression in state law, the National Energy Conservation Policy, PURPA, the Energy Policy Act of 1992, and the Energy Policy Act of 2005, among other legislation. The principal conservation medium, demand-side resources, contemplates direct utility investment in efficient end-use products such as residential weatherization and fluorescent lights.[86] "Energy conservation," writes one critic, "is the great political tonic. Both Republicans and Democrats prescribe government-mandated energy conservation as the magic cure for perceived economic and environmental ills ranging from impending energy scarcity, foreign oil dependence, and decreasing international competitiveness to global warming and air pollution."[87] Negawatts, Lovins's coinage, neatly encapsulated the concept of energy efficiency and attracted formidable proponents, including the McKinsey Global Institute and the International Energy Agency, which foresaw profitable energy-efficiency investments in the billions of dollars[88] and expected the demand for energy efficiency to grow alongside global energy demand, with buildings offering the largest uncaptured efficiency potential.[89] In a recent book Lovins and the Rocky Mountain Institute forecast $1.4 trillion in net present value energy savings for building stock by 2050.[90]

Capturing the most obvious opportunities to improve efficiency has in fact forced a decline of 2 percent a year in energy intensity—the amount of energy required to generate each dollar of output. Before the first oil shock in 1973 energy intensity fell by a fraction of that rate. Improved efficiency since then has avoided massive costs that would otherwise have been incurred.[91] Yet there are still hundreds of billions of dollars' worth of unfulfilled energy opportunities. "The biggest problem," Lovins believes, "is that the path to making money from energy savings isn't always clear."[92] Market failures and distortions discourage investment in efficiency. One critic describes these obstacles as "the energy conservation paradox."[93]

Investment in energy efficiency confronts the irrationality of human nature. "Often," explains *The Economist*, "consumers are poorly informed about the savings on offer. Even when they can do the sums, the transaction costs are high: it is a time-consuming chore for someone to identify the best energy-saving equipment, buy it and get it installed. It does not help that the potential savings, although huge when added up across the world, usually amount to only a small share of the budgets of individual firms and households. Despite recent price increases, spending on energy still accounts for a smaller share of the global economy than it did a few decades ago."[94] Electricity prices that do not reflect the cost of externalities are also a fundamental market distortion. If electric power appears too cheap to be worth saving, consumers are less likely to make an efficiency investment. Accurate price signals presuppose government intervention in the marketplace, including a carbon tax, which has to date encountered political resistance.[95] But the universe of potential investment opportunities is very large. In the housing sector alone, Lovins notes a "vast sea of leaky, inefficient row houses, apartments, McMansions, shops, warehouses, factories, tenements, hospitals, schools, and skyscrapers."[96] Unfortunately, as Lovins also acknowledges, the path to achieving those savings will be long and winding.

A collateral problem, couched in the arcane terminology of economics, is the price inelasticity of electricity—that is, the historic inability of many end-use customers to reduce power consumption in the face of price increases. The demand for and wholesale price of electricity vary widely over time, and peak demand may be a multiple of the lowest demand on a single day. Since it cannot be stored, electricity is "the ultimate 'just in time' manufacturing process, where supply must be produced to meet demand in real time."[97] In competitive wholesale electricity markets, locational marginal prices reflect fluctuations in supply and demand at each hour and each node on the grid, enabling most wholesale buyers to respond by reducing electricity purchases when prices are high.[98] Residential rates, on the other hand, are often fixed and do not fluctuate during peak periods. Most retail utility customers pay prices determined by contract and therefore lack incentive to curtail demand at times of peak load. Time-of-use and interruptible pricing, designed to discourage consumption during high-demand periods, have been advanced in pilot programs but have not gained wide adoption among retail customers, who typically have meters that record only aggregate consumption between periodic readings.[99]

Demand response, a further adaptation of real-time pricing, allows end-use customers to change their normal pattern of consumption in response to changes in the price of electricity over time or to incentive payments made to reduce consumption when wholesale prices are high or peak-load use threatens grid reliability.[100] Under demand response, the incentive to build new generation capacity "should be the same with respect to placing the generator on the consumer side of the meter versus [the utility's] side of the meter."[101]

Demand response is not new. By the mid-1980s several utilities had started curtailment or peak-load shaving programs to control air-conditioning loads, using a radio frequency switch to shut off participating customers' units intermittently during peak periods and paying a flat fee for the right to do so. More recently, utilities have programmed responsive loads to provide contingency reserves and even minute-to-minute regulation.[102] Demand response is now embedded in both state and federal law. At the state level demand response programs are driven by such factors as customer mix, market penetration of central air-conditioning equipment, perceived cost-effectiveness, and deployment of smart meters that gather hourly or subhourly data. At the federal level the Energy Policy Act of 2005 authorizes FERC to promote use of demand response and distributed generation. In 2011 FERC issued an order requiring payment to retail customers for reducing purchases of electric energy during peak demand periods.[103]

Following the California energy crisis, observers realized that even modest amounts of demand response could lead to significant reductions in wholesale prices at times of peak load. Over twenty years, one consultant has speculated, reducing U.S. peak demand by 5 percent would save consumers $35 billion.[104] Decades previously, Lovins had suggested "thriftier technologies to produce exactly the same output of goods and services ... as before, substituting other resources ... for some of the energy we formerly used."[105] It was a kernel of thought that over time became mainstream policy and now also underpins the smart grid—the concept that a modernized electricity grid can optimize operation of its interconnected elements "from the central and distributed generator through the high-voltage transmission network and the distribution system, to industrial users and building automation systems, to energy storage installations, and to end-use customers, and their thermostats, electric vehicles, appliances, and other household devices."[106]

Climate Change

In any discussion of energy policy, climate change is the elephant in the parlor—huge, menacing, and unavoidable. Lovins anticipated today's acute concern almost forty years ago. The catalog of climate change consequences is long and dire. It includes sea-level rise, ocean acidification, droughts, increased storm intensity, health impacts, and species extinction. Once released into the atmosphere, carbon dioxide stays there a long time; today's actions (or inactions) therefore have profound effects far into the future.[107]

In pursuit of his early formulation, Lovins recently provided a detailed blueprint in his book *Reinventing Fire*.[108] "To reinvent fire across the U.S. economy," he believes, "our electricity system must accelerate the transition already under way to become renewable, diverse, distributed, resilient, and customer-oriented. ... This more interactive, informed, rapidly evolving electricity system is not centrally planned from the top down. Rather, it can evolve at least equally from the bottom up through radically broadened, deepened, and accelerated innovation and competition."[109]

Lovins envisages several different possible scenarios for the future of the U.S. electricity system. In the "Business-as-usual scenario" the industry continues to rely predominantly on coal, natural gas, and nuclear fuel generated by large, centralized plants and sent over hundreds of miles of high-voltage transmission lines to lower-voltage distribution lines that finally connect to the customer. The prevailing regulatory regime rewards building a large asset base and selling more electricity. It presides over a system that presently accounts for 40 percent of the nation's fossil fuel carbon emissions and, if unchanged, will increase those emissions significantly by 2050. "Business-as-usual," Lovins argues, cannot cope with falling demand, aging infrastructure, and environmental constraints. Many coal plants predate and cannot comply with Clean Air Act requirements; most have no scrubbers, nitrogen oxide reducers, or modern controls for particulate and mercury emissions. The enormous cost of complying with environmental regulations falls disproportionally on the oldest and dirtiest plants, drives up the cost of burning coal, and forces utilities to scrap coal-fired generators. "Coal-fired generation," one banker concludes, "is a dead man walking."[110]

The "Migrate" scenario contemplates retirement of older, carbon-emitting plants and construction of new nuclear plants and combined-cycle coal-fired plants equipped with carbon capture and sequestration (CCS) technology. It is an alluring prospect, says Lovins, that would solve electricity's climate problem while preserving existing utility business models and saving the coal-mining industry. Lovins estimates such a build-out would reduce the electricity sector's carbon emissions significantly by 2050 but would require installation of three new nuclear plants and nine CCS-equipped coal plants each year for the next forty years at a total present value cost of $6.5 trillion. Investment in such large, capital-intensive, long lead-time plants would require assured capital recovery and expose utilities to financial risk. The problematic history of nuclear power and the cost impact of still unproven CCS technology, despite government subsidies and grants, are red flags. "Migrate" would lower carbon emissions but would not position utilities to meet the disruptive economic threat posed by renewables that makes "fossil-fueled generators run fewer hours, reducing wholesale prices and fueled plants' profits."[111]

"Renew" charts a future in which, by 2050, centralized renewables—solar, wind, geothermal, biomass, and hydropower—account for 80 percent of U.S. electricity generation and reduce carbon emissions by replacing fossil-fueled plants and avoiding the environmental and climate risks of coal. Lovins makes the best case for renewables, despite their relatively high cost, variability, and intermittency. To integrate centralized renewables into the grid, "Renew" presupposes construction of new high-voltage transmission lines costing $166 billion by 2050. At the same time it recognizes the extreme difficulty of financing, siting, and permitting new lines. "The increased requirement for transmission to interconnect the best renewable regions with distant load centers," he writes, "poses a significant risk."[112]

"Transform," Lovins's fourth scenario, embodies concepts first set forth in "Energy Strategy: The Road Not Taken" and envisions a radical change in the centralized grid architecture that has existed since Edison first promoted central stations in the nineteenth century. Distributed resources—rooftop solar, fuel cells, and small-scale wind coupled with smart meters—can create interlinked microgrids that run in conjunction with the grid or seamlessly disconnect. In typical breathless prose, Lovins foresees that "Transform" will displace top-down power with local power by combining distributed generation, intelligent demand devices, and digital infrastructure. "This represents," he says, "a transition from a centrally planned system to a market-based system that can govern and stabilize itself through millions of smart chips in intelligent conversation."[113] The transition depends on competitive power markets, time-varying price signals, and reliable communications that can "securely choreograph supply- and demand-side resources nearly in real time."[114] It is a description borne in part of passionate advocacy, reflecting Lovins's utopian social goals.

How does Lovins's preferred scenario relate to climate change? The answer lies in the market-based system he visualizes. "Most efforts to hedge climate risks," he believes, "have made four main errors: assuming solutions will be costly rather than ... profitable; insisting they be motivated by concerns about climate rather than about security, profit, or economic development; assuming they require a global treaty; and assuming U.S. businesses can do little or nothing before carbon is priced." In this formulation Lovins appears to have abandoned his early reliance on a carbon tax as the avenue to cost parity and finds that climate protection will depend more on "efficiency and clean energy's economic fundamentals than [on] possible future carbon pricing of unknown ... likelihood and price."[115] His prescription defies conventional economic wisdom.

William Nordhaus, Sterling Professor of Economics at Yale and perhaps the world's leading economic thinker on climate change, offers a different view. "The economics of climate change is straightforward," he writes. "Virtually everything we do involves, directly or indirectly, the combustion of fossil fuels, which results in emissions of carbon dioxide (CO_2) into the atmosphere. The CO_2 accumulates over many decades, changes the earth's climate, and leads to many potentially harmful effects. The problem is that those who produce the emissions do not pay for the privilege, and those who are harmed are not compensated. ... One important cost is not covered: the damage caused by the CO_2 that is emitted. Economists call such costs externalities because they are external to (i.e., not reflected in) market transactions." Markets, Nordhaus notes, are not a solution. "In the case of harmful externalities like CO_2, unregulated markets produce too much because markets do not put a price on external damages from CO_2 emissions. ... Therefore, governments must step in and regulate or tax activities with significant harmful externalities. Global warming is no different from other externalities. It requires affirmative governmental actions to reduce harmful spillovers."[116]

The easiest way to put a price on CO_2 emissions, Nordhaus observes, is to impose a carbon tax. The costs of generating electricity from coal would then rise sharply; costs from natural gas would rise somewhat less. A $25 per ton carbon tax would raise the wholesale price of coal by more than 130 percent and electricity by more than 30 percent. The prices of carbon-intensive goods would rise relative to low-carbon goods, leading consumers to buy less of the former and more of the latter. "The higher the carbon price, the more CO_2 emissions will be reduced. This 'law of downward-sloping demand'—meaning that quantity demanded goes down as price goes up—is one of the universally confirmed findings in all of economics."[117] A carbon tax of $25 per ton in 2015, rising to $53 per ton in 2030, would raise substantial revenues (1 percent of GDP) and cause U.S. emissions to stabilize at about the 2000 level. If met by parallel policies in other countries, a carbon tax would limit global temperature increase to around 2½ degrees Celsius. "Markets alone will not solve this problem," Nordhaus concludes. "There is no genuine 'free-market solution' to global warming."[118]

John Holdren, president of the American Association for the Advancement of Science, agrees. "Amory has been more energetic, more persistent, and more creative in thinking about ways to make this happen than anyone else," he said. "But Amory has always believed—seemed to believe—that free-market economics alone, rationally applied, will solve the problem. And I don't believe that."[119]

Nordhaus acknowledges that nations are at a stalemate in negotiations on climate change. Neither the Kyoto Protocol of 1997 nor its successors have resulted in an effective international agreement on CO_2 emissions. The key to policy harmonization, Nordhaus believes, is making the price of CO_2 emissions the same in each country, either through an international cap-and-trade program or agreement on a minimum harmonized carbon price. "The simplicity of a single carbon price compared to country-specific emissions caps," Nordhaus observes, "is an important but elusive point. ... Once the price is set, there is no need for any further negotiations about the differentiated prices for each country. ... The minimum price regime is a friendly approach, more like agreements on tariffs or tax treaties that countries already engage in. It is less likely to trigger nationalistic jealousies and taboos than the highly intrusive cap-and-trade approach of the Kyoto Protocol."[120] Major U.S. companies, including the big five oil companies, appear to agree and are planning future growth on the expectation the government will force them to pay a price for carbon pollution as a way to control global warming. Exxon-Mobil anticipates a carbon price of $60 a ton.[121]

Lovins's primary emphasis on efficiency, grid restructuring, and market-driven solutions, however attractively argued, finds few blind adherents in the economics academy. Professors Joskow, Borenstein, and Nordhaus, among others, have directly or indirectly disagreed with what they see as his overstated claims and flawed methodology. "The central question going forward," says Nordhaus, "is the prospect for economical low-carbon electricity. Wind is the only mature low-carbon technology. It is 50 per cent more expensive than the best existing technology. Moreover, its capacity is limited in the United States. The other promising technologies with the possibility of large-scale deployment are, from least to most expensive, advanced natural gas with carbon capture and storage (CCS), advanced nuclear power, and advanced coal with CCS. These are 50 to 100 percent more expensive than the most economical existing technology. Moreover, they are still a long way from being ready for large-scale deployment."[122] Without the spur of a carbon tax, Lovins's "Migrate" scenario therefore appears to be a nonstarter. Investments in the low-carbon technologies he prefers in scenarios three and four are depressed because the market price of carbon is below its true social cost. At the same time, Nordhaus would affirm, "development of low-carbon technologies is the last refuge for achieving our climate goals."[123]

Epilogue

Lovins is a paradox. In his early years, as an intellectual outlier, he launched a penetrating critique of U.S. energy policy that still resonates today. "Energy Strategy: The Road Not Taken" remains his essential manifesto. His "soft path" of small local energy systems, freed from remote, impersonal, and centralized utilities, evokes the "grassroots" sentiment (if not the infrastructure) of Lilienthal's TVA. The "soft path" is as much a philosophical expression as a technical prescription.

Recently, however, Lovins has courted mainstream support. His latest treatise, *Reinventing Fire*, carries endorsements from President Clinton, the former secretaries of state, treasury, and labor, the national security advisor to President Reagan, and a partner in a leading Silicon Valley venture capital firm, among others. Marvin Odum, president of Shell Oil Company, and John W. Rowe, chairman and CEO of Exelon Corporation, a nuclear utility, each contributed a laudatory foreword. "Burning fossil fuels," Rowe stated, "is not free, and it is imperative that as a nation we address this problem head on."[124] But neither Odum nor Rowe mentions a carbon tax, and Lovins, as noted above, is a proponent of the economic case to be made for clean energy without the benefit of problematic carbon pricing. Is it possible that Lovins, wishing to attract conservative establishment support for his views, has shrunk from the political consequences of a Pigovian tax even as the green-eyeshade folks at major oil companies have factored it into their business plans?

From the very beginning of his estimable career, Lovins has been a promoter of and indefatigable salesman for his core ideas, articulated and restated in an endless cascade of books, articles, and public appearances. As a first mover on energy efficiency, renewable power, and decentralization, he opposes entrenched features of the U.S. electric utility industry, which at first viewed him as an annoying and marginal critic and, to proponents of nuclear power, a bitter antagonist as well. But, over time, renewable power and efficiency have become integral to U.S. energy policy. Meanwhile Lovins's recommendations, no longer marginal, are widely seen as a major part of the regulatory solution.

The New York Public Service Commission recently issued a report, *Refining the Energy Vision*,[125] that parallels Lovins's concepts. The report envisions a radically different electric system, driven by decentralized production of renewable, intermittent energy sources like solar power or windpower. Instead of distributing electricity, New York utilities would direct traffic, coordinating distribution of electricity produced by a multitude of smaller entities. The commission hopes to make energy efficiency and other distributed resources a primary tool in the planning and operation of an interconnected modernized power grid in which markets and tariffs enable customers to reduce and optimize their energy usage.

In his zeal to advance the cause, Lovins has encountered the skepticism and, in certain instances, the scorn of economists who, analyzing data with cool detachment, have pronounced unwelcome findings about the cost-effectiveness of renewables and the essential importance of a carbon tax to price externalities correctly. Lovins's panglossian vision, helpful in attracting public attention and support, differs from the dour conclusions of economists focused relentlessly on comparative costs. Lovins would argue, perhaps, using the New York Public Service Commission's report as proof, that promoting a worthy but uphill agenda leaves little time for satisfying all critics and that the larger ends to be served are now fully validated by mainstream action.

7 Jim Rogers and the Politics of Accommodation

Prelude

In 1988 environmental, economic, and political stars aligned. George H. W. Bush, the Republican presidential candidate, placed the environment at the center of his campaign and promised to cut acid rain in half. Sulfur dioxide from coal-fired utilities in the Midwest was killing the forests and lakes of the Northeast, and state representatives demanded action. Standing on the shore of Lake Erie, Bush declared "the time for study has ended" and vowed to remove "millions of tons" of sulfur dioxide from coal plant smokestacks. Command-and-control environmental regulation had fallen out of favor in the Reagan administration. Bush wanted to improve air quality at least cost to industry and, borrowing ideas from the Environmental Defense Fund (EDF) and thinkers such as Ronald Coase, favored a market-based solution. The utility industry and many environmentalists were opposed, but Boyden Gray, White House counsel and a key Bush advisor, invited EDF's president, Fred Krupp, to develop a plan.[1] Gray liked the marketplace approach. Even before the Reagan administration had come to an end he put EDF staffers to work drafting legislation. It was an unlikely alliance between Gray, a conservative multimillionaire, and environmental activists consistently thwarted by the president he worked for.[2]

The best way to clean up the nation's air and water, many economists believed, would be to develop a market allowing companies to trade rights to emit pollution. Coal-fired electric utilities, reformers' principal target, accounted for 70 percent of SO_2 emissions. Drawing on academic proposals and the EPA's experiment with small-scale emissions trading programs, EDF came up with an outline. The government would set an overall emissions cap for SO_2 and a limit for each major source or plant, which would receive tradable allowances within that limit. If a plant's emissions exceeded the assigned limit, its owner could buy allowances or reduce emissions. The EPA would cut the aggregate cap and number of individual allowances year by year. Overall pollution would decline, but each company would be free to figure out how to meet its individual target. "We need to give plants flexibility," said EDF's economic consultant; this is not "just about mandating scrubbers on smokestacks." EDF envisioned allowances as de facto property rights, a tradable commodity that would let the most innovative companies successfully reduce SO_2 emissions at least cost.[3]

Cap and trade encountered an array of skeptics. The EPA mistrusted market-based methodology, had seen little success in previous small-scale emissions-trading experiments, and thought the program was focused on low cost rather than effective cleanup. Congressional subcommittee members found it hard to believe there could be a market for worthless emissions. Utility executives feared allowances might trade at $500 to $1,000 per ton, costing the industry as much as $25 billion a year. Industry opposition was nearly universal, and utilities refused to trade until TVA did the first deal at $250 per ton. Except for EDF, environmentalists also harbored doubts, saw emissions trading as a scheme that would allow polluters to buy their way out of fixing the problem, and accused EDF of the "twofold sin of having talked to the Republican White House and having advanced this heretical scheme."[4]

In July 1989, intent on advancing his environmental agenda, President Bush proposed major amendments to the Clean Air Act, legislation enacted two decades earlier to reduce airborne pollution. Title IV of the amendments was a strategic departure from previous command-and-control regulation that focused on emissions rates from individual sources and mandated specific control technologies and performance standards. Instead, Title IV addressed quantities of SO_2 emitted rather than emissions rates and imposed an aggregate cap on SO_2 emissions nationwide. Bush proposed cutting permitted emissions in half and required a ten-million-ton-per-year reduction in SO_2 emissions from 1980 levels by the year 2000. As the aggregate cap ratcheted down each year, utilities would incur billions in new compliance costs. To co-opt coal-fired utilities in the Midwest and their representatives in Congress, Title IV allocated free allowances, measured in tons of SO_2 emissions, to power plants covered by the law. If a plant's annual emissions exceeded its allowances, the utility could buy allowances or reduce emissions by installing controls, changing its fuel mix, or cutting back output. If a plant reduced emissions below the allowed level, the utility could sell the extra allowances or bank them for future use. Title IV placed no restrictions on reduction technology or who could buy or sell allowances. Cap and trade created an incentive to reduce SO_2 emissions. Regulated utilities, it was assumed, would pass the value of free allowances on to consumers, although free allowances would otherwise generate windfall profits.[5]

Utility opposition to Title IV remained a serious problem, but one industry player took a different approach. Jim Rogers, whose Southern charm could "talk the down off a duckling,"[6] was then the forty-year-old chief executive officer of PSI Energy, a coal-burning utility on the brink of bankruptcy. Rogers defied industry logic and supported the new program just as other utility executives lobbied fiercely against it. "It wasn't merely that they tended to resist regulation," the *New York Times* reported. "They also didn't believe it would work: they didn't trust that the necessary technology would evolve fast enough. If it didn't, they worried, very few firms would have extra allowances to sell, and the price of those on the open market would skyrocket. Companies might go broke trying to buy extra allowances to meet their cap."[7]

Rogers loved the market-based elegance of cap and trade and had faith technological solutions would emerge. His credentials were atypical for the insular utility industry. A lawyer who earned his law degree while working nights as a reporter for Kentucky's *Lexington Herald-Leader*, Rogers had clerked for the state Supreme Court, worked as a consumer advocate in the Kentucky attorney general's office, served as deputy general counsel of the Federal Energy Regulatory Commission for litigation and enforcement, and become a partner at Akin Gump Strauss Hauer & Feld, an influential Washington, D.C., law firm, where he helped start the U.S. Natural Gas Clearing House. His high profile attracted the attention of Ken Lay, who hired him to run the gas pipeline business for Houston Natural Gas, an Enron predecessor.

After four years working with Lay, Rogers took the helm at PSI Energy, then struggling to recover from the $2.7 billion write-off of a nuclear plant bitterly opposed by local environmental groups. Rogers saw that PSI Energy needed to integrate environmental risks into its decision making. Prior management, he believed, had not recognized those risks as legitimate until it was too late.[8] Having decided acid rain was a problem he could help solve, Rogers surprised the environmentalists by agreeing to talk. "You need to listen to adversaries and understand where they are coming from," he said. "Then find a way to find common ground with them."[9] As it happened, PSI Energy spent only $250 million to clean up its SO_2 emissions and found allowances to be cheap and plentiful.[10] "By 1995," Rogers recalled, "we had also reduced our SO_2 emissions by 30%."[11]

Rogers saw cap and trade as a smart and creative compromise. "It departed from uniform regulations that failed to consider the generating portfolios and geography of individual utilities," he wrote years later. "It generously allocated allowances to utilities in coal-dependent states in the early years and provided incentives to open low-sulfur coal mines. Most important, it enabled utilities to modernize their plants and meet aggressive emissions targets without sending prices skyrocketing."[12] In the decade following 1995, SO_2 emissions from electric power plants decreased by almost 40 percent even though electricity generation from coal-fired plants increased by 25 percent over the same period. The program achieved its long-term annual emissions goal by 2006 and cost less than command-and-control regulation. Utilities paid $3 billion annually to comply, not $25 billion as feared.

The program brought down abatement costs by providing incentives for innovation and encouraging trading of allowances. "Utilities learned how to burn cost-effective mixtures of different types of coal, how to take allowance prices into account in operating decisions, and how to build more cost-effective flue gas desulfurization devices."[13] By reducing airborne sulfate particles the program also generated unexpectedly large health benefits, estimated to be more than $100 billion per year.[14] It is ironic that cap and trade, successfully launched by a Republican administration despite environmentalists' opposition, should twenty years later, when applied to reduction of carbon dioxide, be passionately supported by the greens and viciously attacked by Republicans. "In most cases," it has been observed, "politics trumps science and economics."[15]

Wing Walking

Like Ken Lay, his one-time boss, Rogers was an adept corporate strategist, agile as a mountain goat and intently focused on the main chance. In 1993 he arranged a merger between PSI Energy and Cincinnati Gas & Electric.

He now headed Cinergy, a large Midwest power company with regional scope. Ninety percent of its power came from coal-fired plants that released seventy million tons of carbon dioxide annually.[16] Keenly aware of his company's vulnerability to environmental attack, Rogers drew on his formative experience at PSI Energy. "Among my first actions as CEO of Cinergy ...," he said, "was to create an updated environmental charter, which was adopted at the first meeting of the board."[17] In testimony before the Senate in 2001, he advocated setting limits for carbon dioxide emissions as part of comprehensive national emissions-reduction legislation—well in advance of the coming war over climate legislation.[18]

Rogers's environmental outreach generated favorable headlines but was inconsistent with his company's track record. Five years after he took control, Cinergy had yet to install scrubbers in coal-fired plants in Indiana and Ohio. In 1999 the Justice Department filed suit against Cinergy and other utilities in the Midwest and South, charging they had illegally released massive amounts of air pollutants for years and violated the Clean Air Act by modifying their plants without installing equipment required to control smog, acid rain, and soot. The lawsuits sought to force the utilities to use state-of-the-art control technology to reduce emissions. In 2000 Cinergy signed a $1.4 billion consent decree, agreeing to clean up or repower with natural gas its coal-fired plants, pay an $8.5 million civil penalty, and add scrubbers to four plants in future years at a cost of $580 million. Rogers said the settlement provided "certainty regarding future operations and expenditures."[19]

Like other coal-fired utilities, however, Cinergy still hoped to halt the government's drive to clean up aging coal-fired power plants. It supported an intensive campaign to elect an industry-friendly president, fill federal regulatory posts with former utility executives, and hire lobbyists to slow the EPA's Clean Air Act enforcement cases and soften existing and prospective rules. In 2000 Cinergy contributed almost $300,000 to the Republican National Committee and the Bush campaign and was able to place a Cinergy executive at the Energy Department as assistant secretary. In 2001, with a Republican administration in control, Cinergy withdrew from its settlement with the Justice Department. In 2003, the EPA issued modified rules that allowed utilities to spend up to 20 percent of a generating unit's replacement cost annually without tripping the new-source review threshold. This meant a utility operating a coal-fired power plant could freely modify a $1 billion plant, without installing scrubbers, as long as it did not spend more than $200 million a year on the plant. A federal court stayed the new-source review rules, questioning their legality and effectively suspending the government's program. Pending cases were weakened or dropped. While the court deliberated, Cinergy and other utilities deferred meaningful pollution control.[20] Rogers welcomed this chain of events. "The greatest risk we face," he said, "is 'stroke of the pen' risk, the risk that a regulator or congressman signing a law can change the value of our assets overnight. If there is a high probability that there will be regulation, you try to position yourself to influence the outcome."[21]

In 2006 Duke Energy acquired Cinergy in an all-stock deal valued at $9 billion, and Rogers—once again adroitly emerging in command—became president, chairman, and chief executive officer of the combined company, which generated more than 60 percent of its electricity from coal. The acquisition created the third largest utility in the nation with 5.4 million customers, 54,000 megawatts of electricity generation, and operations in two-thirds of the United States, as well as Canada and most of South America. As the merger was announced in 2005, Rogers predicted environmental benefits. "There will come a day when we have to retire some of our 50-year-old coal plants," he said, adding that "the deal gives us [Cinergy] an option we never had before."[22] Environmental critics were encouraged Rogers might be an ally in the mounting climate change debate as the three merged companies—PSI, Cinergy, and Duke—eventually spent more than $5 billion to scrub SO_2 from thirty coal-fired plants, passing most of the cost to consumers through higher rates. Rogers's real focus was on economics. "You make money by investing in hardware," he said, "and [scrubbing] turned out to be a money maker for us." At bottom, Rogers's environmental instincts were tempered by shrewd pragmatism. He remained intently focused on his company's bottom line. The cost of scrubbers was included in Duke Energy's rate base, enabling it to earn a return on remedial equipment. Rogers was therefore inclined to view climate change as a business opportunity. "I made money on sulphur," he said, "and I'll make money on carbon."[23]

Cap and Trade Revisited

"A well-documented rise in global temperatures has coincided with a significant increase in the concentration of carbon dioxide in the atmosphere," wrote Justice Stevens in the opening sentence of *Massachusetts v. EPA*, a landmark 5–4 Supreme Court decision affirming the EPA's authority under the Clean Air Act to regulate motor vehicle greenhouse gases.[24] The case reflected mounting national concern about climate change. In 2006 General Electric, encouraged by EDF's Krupp, agreed to form a corporate coalition, the Climate Change Initiative, to support climate change legislation using cap and trade. The founding members, an amalgam of blue chip companies and mainstream NGOs, included, among others, General Electric, Alcoa, Florida Power & Light, EDF, and the Natural Resources Defense Council. Also included was Duke Energy, "the third largest emitter of CO_2 among corporations in America" by Rogers's own description.[25]

As Duke Energy's CEO and the newly installed chairman of the Edison Electric Institute, Rogers was an indispensable member of the coalition, "a high-emitting, smooth-talking, coal-fired power boss willing to buck the rest of his industry."[26] His condition for joining the coalition, drawn from his experience with acid rain years earlier, was clear: any climate change cap-and-trade legislation supported by the coalition would have to give Duke Energy enough free allowances to make the transition to clean electricity affordable and avoid a rate shock for its customers. "You've got to help me smooth out the trajectory," Rogers told his colleagues. "There's going to be a backlash if rates go up." When the Climate Change Initiative (renamed the US Climate Action Partnership or USCAP) issued its first public statement, a *Call for Action*, it included the requirement that "a significant portion of allowances should be initially distributed free to capped entities."[27] Distrusted by environmentalists on the left and the utility industry on the right, Rogers had carved out a strategic path between the two. Anyone aware of public opinion on climate change, he believed, could see the government would eventually have to limit carbon emissions. Rogers hoped to influence the debate and mitigate the pain. "I wanted to get out ahead of it," he said. "If you're not at the table, you're going to be on the menu."[28]

In June 2007 Rogers made his case in testimony before the U.S. Senate, urging adoption of "an economy-wide, market-based cap-and-trade program."[29] Rogers's testimony was a forceful piece of advocacy, focused squarely on allowance allocations. Although "some have taken the position that all or most allowances should be auctioned rather than granted ...," he argued, the auction approach is "contrary to the methods Congress and the

EPA have successfully used in the past to reduce emissions, and ... should be avoided in climate change legislation." Duke Energy's customers, he said, depend on coal-fired generation from plants built decades ago, long before anyone raised carbon concerns. "To run those plants, we will need allowances. Again, requiring our customers to pay disproportionately higher fleet modernization costs, and at the same time pay the cost of allowances until the fleet can be de-carbonized, is an unfair double punch. The rate shock to customers and the disproportionate damage to the economies in the 25 states that depend on coal are neither reasonable nor equitable."[30]

Rogers's testimony was politically astute but did not tell the whole story. While it was clear regulators could give away allowances free, auction them, or use a combination of free allocation and auctioning, the choice would affect the distribution of wealth. In theory, no matter how allowances were distributed, the process of trading under a declining cap would ensure an overall reduction in emissions. But more recent economic analysis offered a different view. "By yielding government revenue," wrote a Stanford professor of environmental and resource economics, "auctioning has the potential to reduce the government's reliance on distortionary taxes. ... Auctioning can reduce the costs of meeting a given target for emissions reductions by almost half compared to a program with free permits. ... Rents from 100 percent free allocation would substantially overcompensate firms for the costs they would otherwise face."[31] Owners of coal-fired generation would then receive a valuable asset financed by ratepayers, who would pay for free allowances through higher energy prices.[32] Alert to the risk of granting windfalls to major polluters, some in Congress were understandably averse to free allowances in framing legislation. To decarbonize his coal-fired utility, however, Rogers needed as much federal assistance as he could extract.

In December the Climate Security Act of 2007, sponsored by Senators Joseph Lieberman (I-CT) and John Warner (R-VA), was reported out of committee.[33] Its stated purpose was to "avert catastrophic impacts of climate change and to do so while preserving robust economic growth." The bill called for the electric power, transportation, and industrial sectors to cut emissions to 70 percent below 2005 levels by 2050 and implemented the declining emissions cap through an allowance system. The cap started at 4 percent below the 2005 emissions level in 2012 and lowered year by year at a constant gradual rate. Emissions allowances declined in tandem. The electric power and industrial sectors were to receive 40 percent of all allowances in 2012 but end up with 12 percent in 2030. The bill allowed companies to trade, save, and borrow emissions allowances. Crucially, however, it required 18 percent of allowances to be auctioned in 2012 and increased the auction allocation thereafter by 2 percent annually, reaching 73 percent by 2026 and remaining at that level until 2050. Carbon allowances would become a new and valuable form of property, the biggest new source of cash in years. The government envisioned a steady stream of income from the sale of allowances—as much as $6.7 trillion over forty years.[34]

"Joe Lieberman and John Warner were under no illusion that their climate bill would pass in 2008," according to one account. "They simply wanted to demonstrate that the politics of global warming could be tamed, domesticated, *detoxified*. ... They wanted to write a climate bill that drew support from the political center, one that forged a grand bargain by cutting the deals necessary to bring in other Republicans alongside Warner. ... Only the gathering momentum of that process ... would force outside stakeholders—corporations, associations, unions, states, the full panoply of interest groups—to engage."[35]

In fact, the bill attracted concerted conservative opposition. Senator Inhofe, the ranking member of the Committee on Environment and Public Works, launched a broadside attack, citing increased costs to consumers, expansion in the size and scope of the federal government, bypass of the appropriations process, and use of auction revenues in support of favored programs to predetermine winners and losers in the marketplace.[36] The Heritage Foundation warned of "arbitrary restrictions predicated on multiple, untested, and undeveloped technologies [that] will lead to severe restrictions on energy use and large increases in energy costs."[37] The National Association of Manufacturers predicted that by 2030 the bill would drive up gasoline prices by almost 150 percent and cost the average family about $4,000 per year.[38] Opponents also appeared on the left. MoveOn.Org, an advocacy group, charged that the bill would give windfall profits to polluters. The free ride for dirty coal, it argued, had to end.[39]

For Jim Rogers, a vocal supporter of cap and trade and through Duke Energy a key member of USCAP, Lieberman-Warner was shaping up as a disaster. Initially, the bill would give away only around 80 percent of the allowances, auctioning the rest, and year after year the percentage to be auctioned would steadily rise. "Having to obtain allowances for existing coal plants through an auction," he said, "is nothing more than a carbon tax."[40] Rogers calculated Duke Energy would spend $2 billion in the first year alone and would have to raise its rates by 40 percent. Unlike the acid-rain legislation, the bill would not give coal-fired utilities special treatment. Instead it would allocate a large number of allowances to nuclear and hydroelectric utilities that produced very little carbon dioxide and could therefore sell their allowances for a profit. Duke Energy, on the other hand, would have to spend heavily for a decade to reduce emissions and would meanwhile need all the allowances it could get. In no way could it sell them for massive profits. "I will pass every single cent directly on to my customers," Rogers vowed.[41]

Rogers also objected to how the government would spend the cash it raised from selling allowances. He called it a money grab. "Politicians have visions of sugarplums dancing in their head with all the money they can get from auctions," he said. "It's all about treating me as the tax collector and the government as the good guy. I'm the evil corporation that's passing through the carbon tax so Senator Boxer can be Santa Claus!" If the government was going to collect cash from carbon auctions, Rogers believed, at least it ought to invest that money in technology research. "A billion dollars for deficit reduction," he vented. "A billion dollars! What is she [Senator Boxer] smoking? I thought we were solving carbon here."[42] Rogers, the green coal baron, was off the reservation, USCAP was bitterly divided, and environmental support had splintered. The Office of Management and Budget opposed the bill, warned President Bush would veto it, and said it assumed "the use of technologies not yet developed or demonstrated to be economically feasible."[43]

On June 6, 2008, Lieberman-Warner—the first climate change bill to be debated in Congress—died a procedural death on the Senate floor when the Democratic leadership could not rally the sixty votes necessary to move the bill from debate to a vote. Republicans were overwhelmingly in opposition. The minority leader called the bill a tax. The central feature of the bill—increasing the price of carbon as the indispensable means of reducing greenhouse gas emissions—had been obliterated by partisan political rhetoric and watered down by its sponsors in ways that won little or no support.[44] "Lieberman-Warner was strangled in its crib," wrote one observer, "because moderate Democrats weren't ready to go that far, because Boxer and the enviros weren't willing to compromise on their core issues, and because the opponents of global warming legislation remain strong."[45] The bill's proponents remained optimistic nonetheless. "We will have the Senate next year," said Senator Boxer, "and we will have a President who will be hospitable to this subject."[46]

The demise of Lieberman-Warner provoked a more searching analysis of the economic implications of cap and trade with particular attention to allocation of allowances. The Brookings Institution and the Brattle Group, a consultancy, authored white papers.[47] As the annual cap ratchets down, Brookings noted, the carbon price will increase, but covered firms will ultimately pass nearly all their costs to consumers through higher prices, a feature fundamental to the efficiency of cap and trade. Whoever gets the allowances or revenue from a government auction will receive a transfer from those paying the price on carbon. If the government auctions the allowances, it will receive revenue it can spend or rebate by lower taxes. If allowances are given away, firms will receive both allowances and higher prices for their products reflecting the scarcity of rights to emit. In either case the cost of abating emissions will remain a real resource cost, not a transfer, but there will be little economic reason to allocate free allowances to firms other than to accelerate adoption of the program. Costs at coal-fired power plants, Brattle said, will increase by more than power prices, negatively impacting the performance and balance sheets of companies with coal-fired generation. Brattle called this "a natural byproduct of pricing designed to reflect fuel-dependent environmental costs more accurately."[48] It was also a signal that Rogers's key objection to Lieberman-Warner would trouble similar legislative initiatives when Obama succeeded Bush as president.

Waxman-Markey

In his first State of the Union message President Obama asked Congress for "legislation that places a market-based cap on carbon pollution."[49] His budget request urged Congress to establish a greenhouse cap-and-trade program to reduce emissions and called for auctioning all the allowances industry would need to "ensure that the biggest polluters do not enjoy windfall profits."[50] He planned to spend $150 billion of the auction revenues for clean energy technologies and return the balance to consumers in the form of a tax cut, "especially vulnerable families, communities and businesses to help the transition to a clean energy economy."[51] Coal-fired

Figure 7.1
Jim Rogers, CEO of Duke Energy, gestures as he speaks during a discussion on climate change at the Brussels Forum, in Brussels, Belgium, on March 15, 2008. (AP Photo/ Thierry Charlier.)

electric utilities, with Duke Energy in the forefront, saw a looming economic threat. At a meeting with senior corporate executives in March 2009, aware of the pushback, Obama appeared to retreat from the 100 percent auction demand in his budget request, conceding his plan had little chance of congressional approval without strong support from business and industry. "We're going ... to make sure that it works for you," he assured his skeptical audience, following advice from the Senate Budget Committee chairman, who had warned Obama his plan as proposed would not get enough votes to clear the Senate. "I find it unlikely," the chairman said, "that climate-change legislation will pass that doesn't have some allocations reserved for especially hard-hit industries."[52]

Eager to influence the debate, Jim Rogers testified before the House Energy and Commerce Committee in January 2009 to promote USCAP's *Blueprint for Legislative Action,* which gave the power sector 40 percent of all allowances for free. He told the committee that allocation of no-cost

Figure 7.2
Duke Energy CEO Jim Rogers, second from left, testifies on March 20, 2007, before the House Energy and Air Quality Subcommittee hearing on climate change and energy security. From left are PNM Resources Chairman, President, and Chief Executive Officer Jeffry E. Sterbat; Rogers; MidAmerican Energy Chairman and Chief Executive Officer David Sokol; American Electric Power President and Chief Executive Officer Michael G. Morris; Old Dominion Electric Cooperative President Jackson E. Reasor; and CPS Energy General Manager and Chief Executive Officer Milton B. Lee. (AP Photo/Manuel Balce Ceneta.)

allowances should be viewed as a transitional measure, "a bridge to the point in time at which we can decarbonize our economy" by developing new technologies. "A full auction starting on day-1 of the program ...," he said, "takes away the transitional bridge to a low-carbon economy and creates nothing more than a cap-and-tax program, which will increase the cost to electricity consumers. ... The environmental integrity of the program is ensured by the cap, not whether allowances are auctioned or allocated at no cost."[53] Rogers's testimony squarely opposed the president's plan to auction allowances and was a warning shot across the bow of its sponsors in Congress. Buying allowances for the 2.4 billion tons of carbon dioxide the nation's utilities had released in 2007 would cost $39 billion.[54]

Figure 7.3
On May 5, 2009, Democrats serving on the Energy and Commerce committees leave
the White House after meeting with President Obama to discuss energy independence, healthcare reform, and other legislative priorities. The key House architects
of the climate change plan were Henry Waxman, D-CA, left, and Ed Markey, D-MA,
right. At center left, Bart Stupak, D-MI, and center right, Betty Sutton, D-OH. (AP
Photo/Ron Edmonds.)

Henry Waxman, who had replaced John Dingell as chair of the House
Energy and Commerce Committee, and Ed Markey, chair of its Environment Subcommittee, took the lead in framing a climate bill. "Waxman
and Markey are way to the left of us on this deal," Rogers warned some
committee members, "and if that bill comes out of your committee and
you weren't able to shape it, this ain't gonna be a happy thing."[55] In fact,
Waxman was a tough, pragmatic, and patient legislator who knew how to
compromise to advance his agenda. Waxman canvassed every Democrat
on the committee, including conservative members from Pennsylvania and
Virginia coal country, and explained he had come to view allowances as the
key to containing costs, avoiding rate shocks, and cementing the political
deal. He was not about to be sandbagged from the right.[56]

The Waxman-Markey bill established a cap-and-trade system for heavy greenhouse gas producers, including electric utilities, oil refiners, natural gas suppliers, and certain manufacturers. Under the program the EPA would cap the total amount of pollutants that could be emitted and require each company to hold enough allowances to account for its emissions. Starting in 2012, covered companies would have to present an emissions allowance for each metric ton of carbon dioxide produced. The total amount of greenhouse gas emissions and number of allowances could not exceed the cap, starting at 3 percent below 2005 emissions levels and progressively decreasing thereafter over time until reaching 42 percent below 2005 emissions levels in 2030 and 83 percent below by 2050. The number of extant allowances and overall pollution would decrease in tandem. A company unable to reduce its emissions could buy allowances from another company in surplus. The buyer would pay for the right to pollute, and the seller would be rewarded for making efficient reductions. Regardless of how allowances were distributed initially, the need to surrender valuable allowances to cover any emissions and the opportunity to trade those allowances would create a price signal for emissions.[57]

Waxman-Markey was nothing if not ambitious, authorizing new programs to promote clean energy, reduce mobile source greenhouse gas emissions, and foster smart grid technology. It also proposed lowering the cap and related allowances from a peak of 5.4 billion tons of emissions in 2016 to a little over one billion tons in 2050. "It is uncertain," wrote one critic, "whether the scale of the transformation envisaged is even technically achievable."[58] To reach its intermediate reduction goal by 2030, the power industry estimated it would have to build forty-five new nuclear plants, cut electricity consumption by 8 percent, and quadruple the amount of renewable power.[59]

The proposed bill would also have to address a host of potentially contentious technical and policy issues, including sources covered, the timetable for reaching specific CO_2 reductions, distribution of emissions allowances, regulation of the emissions trading market, use of auction revenue, realizing program flexibility through offsets, reserves, and banking and borrowing of allowances, and creation of other federal programs going beyond cap and trade (e.g., renewable energy standards, carbon capture and sequestration, and smart grid advancement and transmission planning).[60] Waxman knew he would have to give away free allowances to get industry backing, but any deal he cut on allowances would also have to take account of other pivotal issues—targets for emissions reduction, number and kind of offsets, performance mandates for carbon capture and storage, and size of the strategic carbon reserve (a pool of allowances that could be auctioned if the carbon price escalated). These variables, ultimately contained in a 648-page bill, were of intense interest to coal-fired utilities and would determine the cost and availability of carbon allowances over time.[61]

When Waxman unveiled the draft bill at the end of March 2009, he left the section on allowances blank, shrewdly declining to reveal whether emissions allowances would be auctioned or given away for free. Drawing on recent experience with the Lieberman-Warner bill, Waxman knew zealous critics would attack whatever allocation he made. To gain negotiating leverage, he did not commit. The hole in the draft bill worried Rogers, who testified again before Waxman's committee in April. Rogers called attention to the bill's missing pages. "Those are the ones," he said, "that contain the critical decision on how allowances will be distributed. Those pages, for Duke Energy and its customers, are the key to … protecting consumers from prices that increase so rapidly they disrupt livelihoods. … While [a full auction] may provide a steady revenue stream to the federal government, it will impact customers in coal-dependent states disproportionately by requiring utilities and their customers to buy allowances just to keep current facilities running."[62] Rogers saw cap and trade as a zero-sum game, pitting heartland coal states against those on either coast.

Allocation of allowances, however important to Rogers and the electric power industry, was only one element of a complex, articulated bill with broad economic impact, covering downstream emitters such as power plants, midstream sources such as local distribution companies, and upstream sources including producers and importers of petroleum-based and coal-based liquid fuels, all regulated above a minimum annual emissions threshold.[63] Simply to get his bill before the House, Waxman had to engage in serious legislative horse trading. To keep energy costs down, the power sector wanted free transitional allowances during the early years of the program. It also feared auctioning allowances would be "an invitation to Wall Street speculators to develop new schemes to manipulate the market, turn emission allowances into just another commodity like pork bellies and essentially allow Wall Street to determine electricity prices."[64] Supporters of an auction approach, on the other hand, believed polluters should pay. An auction, the president said, "ensures that all industries pay for every ton of emissions they release."[65] Waxman needed to reconcile these sharply opposed opinions.

But his first concern was Jim Rogers and a cadre of Rogers's influential colleagues at the Edison Electric Institute. In a conversation with Waxman early in May 2009, Rogers stressed the importance of "getting the transition right," by which he meant that electric utilities needed at least 35 percent of all allowances (enough to cover 90 percent of emissions) and a 17 percent reduction target by 2020. Waxman, who had kept his powder dry for just this negotiation, agreed. The Waxman-Markey bill, as passed by the House, distributed approximately 80 percent of the allowances without charge between 2012 and 2025 but only six years later required about 70 percent to be auctioned. For the decade beginning in 2016, as Rogers had asked, it allocated 35 percent of all allowances to electric utilities and 9 percent to the natural gas industry. But it directed the allocations to local distribution companies, which are subject to cost-of-service regulation, and specified that they pass the economic value of the allowances on to consumers through lump-sum rebates rather than reduction in electricity rates, thereby compensating consumers for increases in electricity prices without altering the retail price signal.[66]

Waxman could fairly take credit for a clever legislative compromise, having preserved the declining cap while agreeing to allowances and offsets, subsidies, and incentives with a consumer-oriented twist. "Given the nature of the allowance allocation in the Waxman-Markey legislation," wrote one observer, "the best way to assess its implications is not as 'free allocation' versus 'auction,' but rather in terms of who is the ultimate beneficiary of each element of the allocation and auction. ... On closer inspection, it turns out that many of the elements of the apparently free allocation accrue to consumers and public purposes, not private industry."[67]

In late June 2009 the Waxman-Markey bill passed the House by an uncomfortably close vote of 219 to 212. "A truckload of old-fashioned politicking was required to drag the bill home," said one reporter, "small political payoffs negotiated and announced by Waxman on the floor during the debate."[68] The bill had provoked a lobbying frenzy and wildly different economic estimates. "The bill contains everything you'd expect from an *Al Gore* wish list," said Rush Limbaugh, the right-wing radio commentator. "I don't know how this thing will not raise energy prices to crippling levels."[69]

The National Center for Public Policy Research and the Heritage Foundation claimed the bill would cut millions of jobs, burden households with over $1 billion in costs, mostly borne by the poor, and have the greatest economic impact on poorer Southern and Southwestern states (while most Democratic supporters of the bill represent wealthier coastal states).[70] The EPA and the Congressional Budget Office estimated its cost at less than 50 cents per household per day but were no match for the naysayers.[71]

Passage of the bill did nothing to calm the intense war of words launched by its enemies. The American Enterprise Institute struck an exposed nerve with its critique. "Perhaps the most astonishing aspect of the Waxman-Markey bill," it wrote, "is that so many environmentalists support it. ... Not only is Waxman-Markey a titanic giveaway to the very people that environmentalists have blamed for destroying the planet, it will prevent the EPA from regulating GHGs under the Clean Air Act."[72] The *New York Times,* ordinarily a reliable supporter of liberal legislation, claimed the bill had grown "fat with compromises, carve-outs, concessions and out-and-out gifts."[73] An energy partner in a New York law firm observed that "H.R. 2454 relies almost entirely on the efficacy of, and revenues from, an emission-trading scheme that is complex, manipulable and unproven at anything like its proposed scale."[74]

Jim Rogers, for his part, supported the bill throughout its tortured House passage. His intense lobbying had paid off for Duke Energy, which got more allowances from Waxman-Markey than it had from Lieberman-Warner. But Rogers could do nothing to stem widespread political opposition on the right. As the Senate prepared to leave Washington for its August recess, Senator Harry Reid hoped to "cobble together the pieces and get the package to the floor late in the fall."[75] Other observers were less sanguine. Rahm Emmanuel, the White House chief of staff and a consummate political player, thought cap and trade would not fly and concluded the fight for climate change legislation was unwinnable in the Senate.[76]

Kerry-Lieberman

In 2009 the Democrats held a majority in the Senate but did not have a "filibuster-proof" majority of sixty votes. After Waxman-Markey had barely passed in the House, an unlikely coalition of three senators formed to develop a bill that could pass in the upper chamber. Joe Lieberman, an Independent who voted with the Democratic caucus, had worked on climate change since the 1980s and recently introduced three global-warming bills.[77] Lieberman shared a wish to author "a bill that would fundamentally change the American economy and slow the emission of gases ... causing the inexorable, and potentially catastrophic, warming of the planet." Senator John Kerry, who had held that office for twenty-five years but had never written a landmark law, also needed to prove he "could be in a major, really historic piece of legislation." Lindsay Graham, the lone Republican, cross-aisle deal maker and middleman for business interests, saw an "opportunity to boost the nuclear industry and expand oildrilling." Graham also faced political pushback from angry constituents, attacks from the Tea Party right, and the displeasure of the then Senate minority leader, Mitch McConnell, who had vowed to thwart the president's agenda. To gain political support for their bill, the sponsors were prepared to offer major concessions to industry: loan guarantees for nuclear power, increased offshore drilling, and curtailment of EPA's power to regulate emissions.[78]

Kerry and Graham announced their partnership in an op-ed piece in the *New York Times*. The article aimed to defuse industry opposition. The authors said:

Nuclear power needs to be a core component of electricity generation if we are to meet our emission reduction targets. We need to jettison cumbersome regulations that have stalled the construction of nuclear plants ... while allowing utilities to secure financing for more plants. ... We must recognize that for the foreseeable future we will continue to burn fossil fuels. ... The United States should aim to become the Saudi Arabia of clean coal. For this reason, we need to provide new financial incentives for companies that develop carbon capture and sequestration technology. In addition, we are committed to seeking compromise on additional onshore and offshore oil and gas exploration. ... Finally, we will develop a mechanism to protect businesses—and ultimately consumers—from increases in energy prices. The central element is the establishment of a floor and a ceiling for the cost of emission allowances.[79]

In framing the bill's objectives, its sponsors proposed a cut in carbon pollution "in the range of 17%" by 2020 and 80 percent or more by 2050, matching the House bill; envisioned a comprehensive, bipartisan, multipurpose bill rather than an energy-only bill; and rejected both a carbon tax and command-and-control legislation. Lieberman described the group's proposal as a "market-based system for punishing polluters previously known as cap-and-trade."[80] Kerry used the phrase "pollution reduction incentive." Graham, making clear that most Republicans did not favor unlimited carbon pollution, endorsed a mechanism to set a carbon price. The sponsors hoped to put together a working coalition of progressive Democrats, conservative Democrats from coal states, and Republicans interested in energy independence.[81]

Environmental players were skeptical, but Jim Rogers saw an opportunity to win in the Senate as he had in the House. He mobilized USCAP's support behind Kerry, Lieberman, and Graham, whose plan would promote three mechanisms instead of an economywide cap: a carbon cap for the power sector only, a "carbon fee" for oil companies that would be geared to the price of allowances in the power sector, and, for steelmakers and other energy-intensive industries, a cap that would phase in gradually over several years. The plan would also, Rogers knew, favor offshore oil and gas drilling and massive subsidies for clean coal and nuclear power. He wanted those subventions as well as a predictable carbon price. "We're going to be replacing our fleet either way," he said, "and rates are going up no matter what. So we need a policy that forces industry to do the right thing."[82]

Bitter partisan divisions in the Senate and the prospect of forthcoming midterm elections, Rogers sensed, could prevent even a compromise bill. Together with other energy executives, he launched a lobbying blitz. A dozen CEOs—including Rogers, Shell Oil's Marvin Odum, and NRG Energy's David Crane—met with senators and administration officials as Kerry, Lieberman, and Graham were formulating their bill. "Comprehensive climate change legislation is not part of the liberal agenda," said Crane. "It's a decidedly centrist thing. We reduce carbon emissions, and we reduce our dependence on Middle Eastern oil. Both parts of the political spectrum should come together on that." The president appeared to agree, having blessed an expansion of nuclear energy in his State of the Union speech and submitted a budget calling for a $36 billion increase in loan guarantee authority for nuclear construction projects. A strong nuclear plank was critical to Graham and potentially a lure for other Republicans. Crane and his colleagues wanted to "see if we can help expand the Lindsey Graham circle. That's what we are going to try to do."[83] Once the president tripled loan guarantees for nuclear power, however, he gave away a concession Graham could have used to attract Republican votes.

Public support for environmental protection was fading quickly as the recession thrust economic concerns to the forefront. Conservative groups began attacking Graham for supporting "cap and tax" and referred to climate science as "climate-gate." At a townhall meeting in South Carolina, his constituents accused Graham of "making a pact with the Devil." One heckler shouted, "You're a traitor, Mr. Graham! You've betrayed this nation and you've betrayed this state!" Graham felt the political heat and warned Kerry and Lieberman they needed to negotiate the bill "before Fox News got wind of the fact that this was a serious process."[84] The search for incentives and giveaways accelerated as Graham pronounced the demise of economy-wide cap and trade in favor of a cap only for utilities. "Economywide cap and trade died of ... natural causes in Washington," said Fred Krupp of EDF. "The term became too polarizing and too paralyzing in the effort to win over conservative Democrats and moderate Republicans."[85] By the end of April 2010, as negotiations peaked and the oil spill at the BP platform in the Gulf of Mexico became the largest in history, Senator Reid, then the majority leader, decided the Senate would take up immigration in advance of the climate bill. Graham summarily abandoned the coalition, leaving Kerry and Lieberman as sponsors of a bill that called for expansion of offshore drilling at a moment when the newspapers were filled with photographs of birds soaking in oil. Once a potent bargaining chip when coupled with subsidies for nuclear power and clean coal, offshore drilling had become politically toxic.[86]

On May 12, 2010, Kerry and Lieberman unveiled the American Power Act—the product of contentious negotiations with environmentalists and the energy industry, among many others. Their bill established a carbon cap to reduce greenhouse gas emissions 17 percent below 2005 levels by 2020 and 80 percent below those levels by midcentury. To reconcile the sharply conflicting agendas of environmentalists and energy executives, it provided more than $50 billion in loan guarantees for up to twelve nuclear plants, granted free allowances to the utility industry and other heavy carbon emitters, and imposed upper and lower limits on the price of carbon in a trading market. The bill initially auctioned just under 25 percent of allowances and allocated the balance freely to local distributors of electricity and natural gas, "trade-exposed" industries, alternative fuel vehicle producers, companies engaged in carbon capture and sequestration, and others. In later years the bill slowly reduced the share of free allowances and increased the auctioned share, eventually auctioning 100 percent of allowances by 2035. Electric utilities and merchant coal generators initially received more than half of all allowances, worth $870 billion over the life of the bill—a tremendous transfer of wealth to a single industry. The bill required local electricity distribution companies to use free allowances for the benefit of consumers, but utilities were thought likely to divert a significant fraction of economic value to utility shareholders.[87]

Jim Rogers and other energy executives were present as Kerry and Lieberman introduced the bill. Rogers, whose company operated more than a dozen coal-fired plants, had every reason to be pleased. "Today," he said, "I am here as an advocate for Duke Energy's four million customers in five states in the Midwest and Carolinas who depend on coal for the majority of their electricity. ... Senators Kerry and Lieberman's bill helps 'get our transition right' to clean modern energy. ... It also gives our electric industry the policy roadmap we need to invest tens of billions of private capital to retire and replace aging power plant fleets with modern, efficient and clean plants." [88] Many environmentalists saw things differently. Greenpeace and Friends of the Earth said the bill was too weak to meet the demands of climate science and contained too many giveaways to the fossil fuel industry. "Without dramatic improvements," said the Friends of the Earth president, "this bill should not be passed." [89]

Most important, however, Republican support was nowhere to be seen. During a speech in early June, the president said he knew "the votes may not be there right now, but I intend to find them in the coming months." He never found them and did not appear to be looking very hard. On climate change the president was diffident, "leaving the dysfunctional Senate to figure out the issue on its own."[90] Waxman-Markey had received less than 5 percent support from Republicans and Kerry-Lieberman none at all. Conservatives (largely Republicans and some coal-state Democrats) had launched a successful campaign to demonize cap and trade, historically their own market-based creation, despite its proven performance.[91] Rogers supported cap and trade, but only if he could manage the costs of decarbonizing Duke Energy's plants without incurring the wrath of customers forced to pay higher electricity prices. Free allowances would insulate his company until long after his tenure as chief executive officer. In negotiations with Congress, Rogers used his pivotal position to get what he wanted only to see cap and trade blown away by hard economic times, extreme partisan division, and effective right-wing opposition. To his environmental critics, Rogers was a "greenwasher," saying all the right things so that he could wear the mantle of revolutionary without having to make hard sacrifices.[92]

Although undeniably a shrewd business diplomatist, Roger is more than a "greenwasher," given the conservative (at times, reactionary) industry in which he worked. Twenty years before Kerry-Lieberman, the Edison Electric Institute together with the National Coal Association and the Western Fuels Association formed the Information Council on the Environment with a mandate to discredit climate science on a grassroots basis. American oil interests (Chevron, ExxonMobil, and the American Petroleum Institute) were also notable climate skeptics at the time. To his credit Rogers took a different tack. Early on he saw the need to engage environmental advocates in a debate, and Duke Energy, a carbon-intensive company, became a linchpin member of USCAP, seeking to shape but not oppose legislative action on climate policy. The Edison Electric Institute, with Rogers at its head, reversed its climate policy opposition and also supported the Waxman-Markey bill. These were significant shifts.

Duke Energy's 2009 annual report offers a clue to Rogers's thinking. It saw a "growing consensus that some form of regulation will be forthcoming at the federal level with respect to greenhouse gas emissions."[93] Given the threat of legislation, Rogers tried to mitigate its risks. "When you see a parade form on an issue in Washington," he said, "you have two choices: you can throw your body in front of it and let them walk over you, or you can jump in front of the parade and pretend it's yours."[94] Liberal environmentalists were not amused. A cap-and-trade program that gave out free carbon allowances, they thought, was nothing more than a subsidy to coal-fired utilities. They wanted the government to auction allowances, invest some of the revenue in clean energy, and return the rest to consumers to cover higher electric bills. Rogers saw free allowances as the key to political acceptance.

In the end Rogers got his free allowances, but political support for climate change legislation, however favorable to industry, evaporated. Despite its free-market roots, historic success, and broad industrial support, cap and trade—the climate bill's central pillar—fell victim to recession, an inconvenient oil spill, and bitter partisanship. Conservative critics called Waxman-Markey and Kerry-Lieberman a redistribution scheme and a carbon tax. It is an irony that their broadside attack effectively tarnished cap and trade as an instrument of public policy, leaving future federal initiatives to potentially heavy-handed EPA regulation.[95]

End Game

Congress' failure to pass cap and trade did not discourage Jim Rogers, who emerged from the war on Capitol Hill as an energy sage. His company's website called him "a CEO statesman" for his effort to straddle the worlds of business and government. He propounded a nuanced view of regulation and believed that, for electric utility companies, market rules determine investment. By setting environmental standards, he said, the government forces companies to balance affordability, reliability, and external impacts. "Should we build clean coal plants? Should we build nuclear plants? Should we build natural gas? How much should we invest in wind and solar?" he asked. "Those choices will be made in the context of regulation. ... The important thing is for the government to have clear goals, clear regulations so we can make investments."[96]

The clear goals Rogers favored would allow coal-fired utilities like Duke Energy to decarbonize over time without price shock or prematurely stranded investments. "I know there will be a price on carbon ...," Rogers said recently. "I factor in a carbon price into every decision on what I build."[97] As evidence of his business strategy, his company began to replace old coal-fired power plants with new gas-fired units and a coal-gasification plant even as Congress' failure had left a regulatory void. "At the end of the day," Rogers said, "they will have to put a price on carbon. That can't be done by the EPA. That can only be done by Congress, and they need to act."[98] For the foreseeable future, however, congressional action seems unlikely. On June 2, 2014, the EPA moved to deal with climate change by issuing a new rule to cut carbon emissions from the power sector by 30 percent below 2005 levels nationwide. Having learned from the failure of Waxman-Markey, the EPA adopted a "bottom-up" approach and will set different emissions targets for different states, allowing electric utilities in each state room to decide how to meet the reduction targets, whether by deploying more renewable energy, scaling up energy efficiency, or joining regional cap-and-trade systems like California's Global Warming Solutions program or the Northeast's Regional Greenhouse Gas Initiative.[99]

Not content to rest on his laurels, Rogers also continued his careerist path, devoting full attention to Duke Energy's growth and diversification agenda. In 2010 he targeted Progress Energy, a cross-state rival, as a possible acquisition. Progress Energy was carrying too much debt, and one of its nuclear plants had been out of service for a year. Rogers called Bill Johnson, Progress Energy's CEO, who was open to the overture and later attended a Duke Energy board meeting by invitation, striking the Duke Energy board members as aloof. In early 2011 the companies jointly announced Duke Energy's plan to acquire Progress Energy for $13.7 billion in stock (a premium of only 5 percent over market valuation) and assumption of $12.2 billion in debt. At a teleconference with Wall Street analysts Rogers confirmed that "Bill is going to be the CEO, and he is going to be making the calls." Rogers explained the modest premium as a trade-off. "I effectively gave up the CEO job to pay a lower premium," he said, suggesting Johnson had agreed to sell his company at a discount so he would be named CEO. Johnson later testified he was "furious" at the suggestion.[100]

In early July 2012 Duke Energy's board gave its final approval for the acquisition of Progress Energy. Bill Johnson, Progress Energy's CEO, was to become CEO of the combined company, and Rogers, sixty-five, was to be named executive chairman, a step toward retirement. A few minutes later the Duke Energy board elected Johnson CEO. Two hours after that it took another vote and ousted him, with an exit package worth $45 million, and reinstalled Rogers in the top job.

The beneficiary of an extraordinary boardroom coup, Rogers now found himself the head of the nation's largest utility with $106 billion in assets and more than seven million retail customers. A registered Democrat and soi-disant intellectual who was often seen at Davos and the Aspen Institute, Rogers had ascended the corporate heights by force of personality, close attention to the bottom line, and willingness to challenge orthodox industry thinking. He saw himself as an enlightened enterprise builder, a latter-day Sam Insull (without the disastrous ending), whose career he had studied carefully. To his detractors, however, he was a slippery self-promoter. "I'd like to believe him when he says nice things about building a bridge to a cleaner energy future," said Jim Warren, executive director of North Carolina Waste Awareness and Reduction Network. "But with all the dirty coal he burns, I have to conclude he's more concerned with public relations and image than anything else. The Progress CEO thing looks like part of the pattern we've seen from Rogers for a long time. Progress and the utility commission got taken so Rogers could get his merger."[101]

This judgment does not define Rogers's legacy. Postmerger, Duke Energy has invested billions in control equipment for existing coal plants and will spend additional billions over the next decade to comply with environmental regulations, diversify away from coal, and invest in renewable power.[102] At bottom Rogers understands that his company, like other utilities, remains enmeshed in regulation, uniquely vulnerable to legislative fiat. His advocacy for cap and trade was primarily a risk management strategy. He saw the regulatory risk of emissions trading as less than that of a carbon tax.[103] But some form of regulation, he believes, is inevitable. Duke Energy's present agenda is practical recognition of that fact.

In pursuit of corporate self-interest, Rogers had long sought to anticipate and shape regulatory response to his company's advantage and was able to extract major concessions from Congress by occupying the strategic middle ground. Although his first loyalty was always to his company, he was not blind to the ultimate interests at stake. If there had been greater governmental will to attack climate change and other environmental problems, he would have had to respond accordingly. As regulatory power declined based on election results and shifts in public opinion, however, he took the ground as he found it and charted his company's course toward a less carbon-intensive future. But he left passionate advocacy to the environmentalists with whom he had sparred for many years.

8 Conclusion

Through streams of legislation, spending, and minutely detailed regulations, frequent application of moral persuasion, and various other means, the government is now present—either in person, or somewhat like Banquo's ghost, in disturbing spirit—at every major business meeting.[1]

The history of the electric power industry in the United States, created by entrepreneurs, is also the history of the exercise of political power. Electric utilities are a special kind of enterprise, said by courts to be engaged in a business affected with a public interest and subject to an obligation to serve. Their customers, ratepayers passively dependent on electricity as an essential service, were early on seen to require regulatory protection to avoid or at least mitigate the worst consequences of predatory behavior. One theme of this book is the ongoing struggle between investor-owned utilities and the government to determine the limits of acceptable corporate behavior, pursued through legislation, litigation, obscure regulatory proceedings, and broader appeals to public opinion. Another theme is the decisive but inconsistent role of the government in framing markets for power, directly through competition and subsidy and indirectly through regulation. A third theme explores how a handful of extraordinary individuals, driven by ambition and competitive zeal, organized and shaped a bedrock business indispensable to an advanced industrial society.

Edison and Insull largely determined the structure of the electric power industry in the United States. Edison's coal-fired central stations, connected to remote users, and Insull's exclusive regulated monopoly franchise became industry hallmarks, still recognizable to this day. The founders were risk-taking entrepreneurs, focused on technological and commercial innovation. Their industry blueprint became the base case from which later revisions have sprung. In a sense, the subsequent history of the industry, spanning a period of enormous social and technological change, can be read as a series of reactive efforts at modification. In the long course of that history, as this narrative chronicles, the electricity business has attracted powerful leaders, drawn to it by the prospect of controlling a huge national market for electricity, an essential product. The quest for private control of that market inevitably evoked a regulatory response. The state intervened, first as countervailing monitor and later as competitor, financier, and market maker.

In the nineteenth century, as Insull left Edison's side to seek his fortune in Chicago, nascent electric utility companies were little more than municipal pawns. To conduct business and extend their wires utilities needed a city franchise and rights of way—privileges within the discretionary control of venal local politicians. Utility promoters like Insull instantly recognized their vulnerability to the vagaries of political preference, a risk that drove him and his successors to seek the safe harbor of exclusive utility franchises, limited regulation at the state level, and protection against ruinous competition. For decades thereafter, spurred by technological advances and rapid industrial growth, investor-owned utilities determined the basic features of the industry and the electricity market. Regulation was weak, providing only nominal oversight of a business that concentrated economic power in a small cadre of corporate empire builders. Spurred by industrialization and urbanization, Insull's utility holding companies quickly outgrew municipal boundaries and the purview of local government.

Regulatory response was slow to follow, leaving a vacuum at the federal level that allowed highly leveraged utility pyramids to flourish until the onset of the Depression. Regulation then moved beyond mere policing and rate-setting authority. The New Deal commenced a broader, more intrusive role for government, leading it to create new markets, set standards and "yardsticks," and enforce industry rationalization as a means of undoing what Insull and others had built and extending electricity to the underserved hinterlands.[2] The state became a competitor, guarantor, channeler of financial flows, and enforcer of rules under which market participants engaged one another.[3] State action redefined a complex industry but still left intact its vertical monopoly structure and cost-based price regulation. The oil shock of the 1970s signaled the start of a decades-long government effort to reinvent the electric utility industry as a competitive business less dependent on fossil fuels. Unceasing demand growth plateaued. The most adept private companies tried to manage emerging electricity markets to their advantage. Rather than merely resisting government-sponsored change, they sought to co-opt it.

Each of the principal actors in this narrative, from Insull through Rogers, saw the government's rules of engagement as an opportunity and a platform. Historic development was contrapuntal; thrust was met by counterthrust. Insull, as the founder and early proponent of the private utility industry in the United States, sought and obtained state-sanctioned monopoly in exchange for regulation, built a corporate edifice on debt, and invited aggressive government intervention. Lilienthal, at the Tennessee Valley Authority in the 1930s, competed directly with private power producers and changed the way electricity was priced, delivered, and sold. TVA's business model of high-volume, low-cost electricity fundamentally altered the national market for electricity. Bonneville Power Authority, a government marketer of cheap hydropower, served and competed with private utilities in the Northwest but overreached as the sponsor of failed nuclear plants, precipitating an epic municipal bond default. It too altered the national market for electricity, prompting deregulation and industry restructuring that eventually became a profit-making opportunity for power merchants. Enron, under Ken Lay, promoted a competitive marketplace for energy and then, with the acquiescence of federal and state regulators, proceeded to game the rules it had lobbied to put in place, extracting huge profits in the California electricity market. Others concerned with market rules included Jim Rogers, the head of Duke Energy, who saw in federal climate change legislation a dire threat to his coal-burning utility and lobbied effectively to limit its impact. The thought leaders, Paul Joskow and Amory Lovins, each proposed radical changes to the established order, now carried forward through regulation, to reset the rules of engagement.

Each of these protagonists had strong views about competition. Insull urged electric utilities to sell their product "at a price which will enable you to get a monopoly" and "look to make your money out of the large business."[4] For many years Insull's companies did both. For Lilienthal, a fierce public power advocate, competition with private monopoly meant TVA's survival. He believed in cheap and abundant electric power and viewed

"TVA as a righteous sword to revolutionize rate-making and energy consumption practices throughout the nation."[5] As public power zeal faded in the postwar years, Bonneville Power Authority under Hodel used its dominant market position in the Northwest to promote ill-considered nuclear power plants, disregarding at its peril the usual constraints of private competition. A free-market economist, Joskow saw competition among suppliers of electric power as the key to reform of an inefficient, vertically integrated monopoly industry but knew that restructured electricity markets would require a continuing government presence. Joskow's cautionary judgment proved well founded as Enron under Ken Lay, although nominally pro-competition and a supporter of deregulated electricity markets, engaged in politically aided market rigging on a massive scale. Lay's rent-seeking corporate practice and professed ideology were violently at odds. Lovins became a tribune for the competitive future of distributed wind and solar power, which, he argued, would soon lower green electricity costs sufficiently to displace power generated by fossil-fueled central power stations through normal market processes. At Duke Energy Rogers agreed green energy costs would be competitive in the long run but feared the rate impact of a government anti–fossil fuel mandate in the short run. He was, at bottom, a skillful pragmatist who sought to defer and soften the consequences of government cap and trade.

Americans, it is said, are divided between Jeffersonians (who think that he governs best who governs least) and Hamiltonians (who favor active government).[6] Leaders of the private power industry may talk like Jeffersonians but are constrained to act like Hamiltonians. The history of the industry has not been one of free enterprise, except perhaps for several decades following its inception. Utilities are uniquely creatures of regulation, as are even the ostensibly competitive markets in which they function. The government's influence and importance will only increase over time in further development of a critical industry, still largely fossil-fueled but marked by decentralization, decarbonization, demand response, and ever more sophisticated trading markets in power.

To enable a green industrial revolution in response to climate change, the government will have to incentivize transformation of the nation's energy infrastructure and support "development of clean technologies ... through to commercial viability." These goals presuppose the political will to "prepare, organize, and stabilize a healthy 'market,' where investment is reasonably low risk and profits can be made."[7] Government will have to make or assist the most capital-intensive investments (as it has often done with nuclear power, solar power, and windpower) and put in place coherent and systematic policy signals.[8] In doing so, it will drive change as a prime mover. "The important thing for Government," John Maynard Keynes once said, "is not to do things which individuals are doing already, and to do them a little better or a little worse, but to do those things which at present are not done at all."[9]

Notes

Introduction

1. Robert J. Bradley Jr., *Edison to Enron: Energy Markets and Political Strategies* (Hoboken, NJ: Wiley, 2011), 493.

2. Federalist No. 44, January 25, 1788.

3. *Proceedings*, National Electric Light Association, 1898; Richard Munson, *From Edison to Enron: The Business of Power and What It Means for the Future of Electricity* (Westport, CT: Praeger, 2005), 5.

4. Amory B. Lovins, "Energy Strategy: The Road Not Taken?," *Foreign Affairs*, November 1977, 5.

5. Rogers quotation, *New York Times*, May 12, 2014, A18.

Chapter 1

1. See, for example, Mark Granovetter and Patrick McGuire, "The Making of an Industry: Electricity in the United States," in Michel Callon, ed., *The Laws of the Markets* (Oxford: Blackwell, 1998), 155; Jeff Clymer, "Modeling, Diagramming, and Early Twentieth-Century Histories of Invention and Entrepreneurship: Henry Ford, Sherwood Anderson, Samuel Insull," *Cambridge Journal of American Studies* 36, no. 3 (2002): 508.

2. Clymer, ibid., 511.

3. Thomas P. Hughes, *Networks of Power: Electrification of Power in Western Society, 1880–1930* (Baltimore: Johns Hopkins University Press, 1983), 205.

4. Samuel Insull, *Central Station Electric Service* (Chicago: n.p., 1915), 155.

5. Forrest McDonald, *Insull: The Rise and Fall of a Billionaire Utility Tycoon* (Frederick, MD: Beard Books, 1962), 10.

6. Ibid., 13.

7. Quoted in Robert J. Bradley, *Edison to Enron: Energy Markets and Political Strategies* (Hoboken, NJ: Wiley, 2011), 166.

8. Insull, *Central Station Electric Service*, 29.

9. Bradley, *Edison to Enron*, 35.

10. Insull, *Central Station*, 31.

11. McDonald, *Insull*, 23.

12. Insull, *Central Station Electric Service*, 31.

13. Quoted in Bradley, *Edison to Enron*, 38.

14. Alfred Tate, quoted in ibid., 39.

15. Granovetter and McGuire, "The Making of an Industry," 150.

16. Ibid.

17. McDonald, *Insull*, 29.

18. Maury Klein, *The Power Makers: Steam, Electricity, and the Men Who Invented Modern America* (London: Bloomsbury, 2008), 202. .

19. Quoted in John Wasik, *The Merchant of Power: Sam Insull, Thomas Edison, and the Creation of the Modern Metropolis* (London: Palgrave, 2006), 35.

20. William J. Hausman and John L. Neufeld, "The Market for Capital and the Origins of State Regulation of Electric Utilities in the United States," *Journal of Economic History* 62, no. 4 (December 2002): 1055. See also Werner Troesken, "Regime Change and Corruption: A History of Public Utility Regulation," in Edward Glaeser and Claudia Goldin, eds., *Corruption and Reform: Lessons from America's Economic History* (Cambridge, MA: NBER, 2006), 268.

21. McDonald, Insull, 30.

22. Hausman and Neufeld, "The Market for Capital," 1056.

23. Chi-nien Chung, "Networks and Governance of Trade Associations: AEIC and NELA in the Development of the American Electricity Industry 1885–1910, *International Journal of Sociology and Social Policy* 17, no. 7/8 (1997): 52–110.

24. Patrick McGuire and Mark Granovetter, "Business and Bias in Public Policy Formation: The National Civic Federation and Social Construction of the Electric Utility Industry Regulation, 1905–1907," white paper, 1998, 3, http://www.samuel-insull.com/7_31_05RTOCarTalk3.pdf.

25. Ibid.

26. Granovetter and McGuire, "The Making of an Industry," 154.

27. McDonald, *Insull*, 37–38.

28. Insull, *Central Station Electric Service*, 50.

29. McDonald, *Insull*, 38. .

30. Harold L. Platt, *The Electric City: Energy and the Growth of the Chicago Area, 1880–1930* (Chicago: University of Chicago Press, 1991), 67.

31. Bradley, *Edison to Enron*, 46–47.

32. Quoted in Insull, *Central Station Electric Service*, 52.

33. Hughes, *Networks of Power*, 77.

34. "Henry Villard," 2003, http://www.schwab-writings.com/hi/vl/1.html.

35. Bradley, *Edison to Enron*, 54; Hughes, *Networks of Power*, 77; McDonald, *Insull*, 41.

36. Insull, *Central Station Electric Service*, 55.

37. Klein, *The Power Makers*, 293.

38. Bradley, *Edison to Enron*, 57.

39. Jill Jonnes, *Empires of Light: Edison, Tesla, Westinghouse, and the Race to Electrify the World* (New York: Random House, 2003), 242.

40. Bradley, *Edison to Enron*, 59.

41. McDonald, *Insull*, 52.

42. Insull, *Central Station Electric Service*, 62–63.

43. McDonald, *Insull*, 53–54; Bradley, *Edison to Enron*, 60–62.

44. Insull, *Central Station Electric Service*, 62.

45. Ibid., 58.

46. Ibid., 66.

47. Hughes, *Networks of Power*, 201.

48. Dreiser, *Sister Carrie*; quoted in Wasik *The Merchant of Power*, 61.

49. Wasik, *The Merchant of Power*, 59.

50. Ibid.

51. Platt, *Electric City*, 68.

52. Richard D. Cudahy and William D. Henderson, "From Insull to Enron: Corporate (Re)Regulation After the Rise and Fall of Two Energy Icons," *Energy Law Journal* 26, no. 35 (2005): 42.

53. David Skeel, *Icarus in the Boardroom: The Fundamental Flaws in Corporate America and. Where They Came From* (New York: Oxford University Press, 2005), 82.

54. Samuel Insull, *The Memoirs of Samuel Insull: An Autobiography* (New York: Transportation Trails, 1992 [reissue]), 75; McDonald, *Insull*, 56–58; Cudahy and Henderson, "From Insull to Enron," 42; Platt, *Electric City*, 77; Bradley, *Edison to Enron*, 72.

55. John T. Flynn, "Up and Down with Sam Insull," *Collier's*, December 3, 1932; 10, quoted in Cudahy and Henderson, ibid., 43.

56. Klein, *The Power Makers*, 402–403.

57. Ibid.; McDonald, *Insull*, 62.

58. Quoted in Platt, *Electric City*, 77.

59. McDonald, *Insull*, 62.

60. Klein, *The Power Makers*, 402.

61. Bradley, *Edison to Enron*, 74.

62. Hughes, *Networks of Power*, 121–122, 208; McDonald, *Insull*, 69–70; Klein, *The Power Makers*, 407; Bradley, *Edison to Enron*, 70; Insull, *Central Station Electric Service*, 353.

63. McDonald, *Insull*, 63.

64. Insull, *Central Station Electric Service*, 73.

65. Hausman and Neufeld, "Time-of-Day Pricing in the U.S. Electric Power Industry at the Turn of the Century," *RAND Journal of Economics* 15, no. 1 (Spring 1984): 116.

66. McDonald, *Insull*, 64; Bradley, *Edison to Enron*, 75.

67. Insull, *Central Station Electric Service*, 25.

68. McDonald, *Insull*, 65–66.

69. Ibid.

70. Valery Yakubovich, Mark Granovetter, and Patrick McGuire, "Electric Charges: The Social Construction of Rate Systems," *Theory and Society* 34 (2005): 586–587.

71. McDonald, *Insull*, 67–68.

72. Ibid. The load factor indicates the degree to which investment in fixed costs is utilized rather than idle during the period measured. The fixed or standing costs imposed on customers are higher for lower load factors to compensate central stations for their unused investment—financed by interest-bearing loans. The lower the load factor, the higher the proportion that fixed costs are of customers' total costs, and the higher the cost of capital per unit of electricity produced (Yakubovich, Granovetter, and McGuire, "Electric Charges," 589).

73. Quoted in Bradley, *Edison to Enron*, 76–77. Despite the clarity of Insull's conceptualization, the origin of two-part ratemaking entails a far more complex narrative than his principal biographer suggests. The author of the first clear published account of a rate system with demand and operating components was British engineer John Hopkinson, who in 1892 distinguished between fixed and operating costs,

asserting that customers must pay both for their share of fixed costs and for actual consumption. Charges for fixed costs were assessed according to "connected load"— the amount of equipment customers had connected, even if actual consumption had not yet commenced. Such pricing systems were in use as early as the 1880s, "making it highly implausible that that they could have been unknown to Insull in 1894." Hopkinson's use of "connected load" discouraged customers from installing more lamps than necessary, since they would have to pay for the load even if rarely used. Wright's system, by contrast, defined maximum demand as the actual maximum during the billing period rather than as Hopkinson's connected load. Wright's system removed the disincentive for customers to purchase lightbulbs and other electrical equipment.

But neither Wright's nor Hopkinson's system considered the time of day when the customer demands maximum load. To address this problem, William Barstow of Brooklyn Edison designed an alternative rate system that differentiated standing charges based on time of consumption. When system load is highest (as, for example, at night in systems providing illumination), customers are required to pay higher rates for standing costs. Barstow's time-of-day pricing was intended to shift consumption to times of lighter usage, thereby flattening the demand curve and mitigating central stations' need to invest in additional fixed assets to meet peak load. Barstow promoted a meter that captured not only maximum load, as did Wright's, but also the time of day when maximum usage occurred. The Wright and Barstow systems, each supported by an innovative meter, framed the basic alternatives within the emerging electric industry during the mid-1890s. The Wright system promoted growth; the Barstow system promoted efficiency. One strand of economic theory, developed early in the twentieth century, favored a pricing system that encouraged off-peak electricity consumption relative to on-peak consumption, thereby improving the efficiency of the utility's overall operation. (See Yakubovich, Granovetter, and McGuire, "Electric Charges," passim.).

74. Yakubovich, Granovetter, and McGuire, "Electric Charges," 600.

75. Ibid., 591–599. Ferguson is quoted on p. 599.

76. Klein, *The Power Makers*, 406–407.

77. Ibid., 604.

78. José Gomez-Ibanez, *Regulating Infrastructure: Monopoly, Contracts, and Discretion* (Cambridge, MA: Harvard University Press, 2003), 178.

79. McDonald, *Insull*, 84. Also see Carter Harrison II (Chicago's mayor from 1897 to 1905), quoted in Robert Loerzel, *Privatize Public Transit: The Lessons in Chicago* (Chicago: Chicago Transport Workers Solidarity Committee, 2010), 11.

80. McDonald, *Insull*, 86.

81. Gomez-Ibanez, *Regulating Infrastructure*, 176; McDonald, *Insull*, 88.

82. McDonald, *Insull*, 82–83. Also see Hausman and Neufeld, "The Market for Capital," 1056; Gomez-Ibanez, *Regulating Infrastructure*, 174.

83. McDonald, *Insull*, 88–90.

84. Bradley, *Edison to Enron*, 85; McDonald, *Insull*, 91.

85. Werner Troesken, "Regime Change and Corruption: A History of Public Utility Regulation," in Edward L. Glaeser and Claudia Goldin, eds., *Corruption and Reform: Lessons from America's Economic History* (Chicago: University of Chicago Press, 2006), 261.

86. See, for example, Rogers Park Water Co. v. Fergus, 178 Ill. 571 (1899), aff'd, 48 L.Ed. 702 (1901); Mills v. City of Chicago, 127 Fed. 73 (1904).

87. "Notes on Municipal Government: The Relation of American Muncipalities to the Gas and Electric Light Service: A Symposium," *Annals of the American Academy of Political and Social Science* 27 (1906): 205.

88. McGuire and Granovetter, "Business and Bias in Public Policy Formation," 2.

89. See, for example, Charles E. Merriam, "The Case for Home Rule," *Annals of the American Academy of Political and Social Science,* vol. 57, Proceedings of the Conference of American Mayors on Public Policies as to Municipal Utilities (1915), 170–174.

90. William J. Hausman and John Kelly, "The Economic Role and Effectiveness of Local, Government Electric Utilities in the United States: Past and Present," white paper presented at the 4th International Conference on the Public Sector, University of Ljubljana, Slovenia, 2006, 25.

91. Insull, *Central Station Electric Service*, 44–45.

92. Ibid., 44–45; Cudahy and Henderson, "From Insull to Enron," 46. To deter monopoly abuse, a municipality would have the right to purchase the utility's assets "at a fair price."

93. Ibid., 44–45; Hausman and Neufeld, "The Market for Capital," 1058.

94. Ibid., 1051.

95. Economic theory has aggressively challenged the validity of natural monopoly. See, for example, Peter Z. Grossman and Daniel Cole, eds., *The End of a Natural Monopoly: Deregulation and Competition in the Electric Power Industry* (Boston: JAI Press, 2003); George L. Priest, "The Origins of Utility Regulation and the 'Theories of Regulation' Debate," *Journal of Law and Economics* 36, no. 1 (1993): 289–323; Christopher Knittel, *The Origins of State Electricity Regulation: Revisiting an Unsettled Topic*, working paper, University of California Energy Institute, 1999; Christopher Knittel, "The Adoption of State Electricity Regulation: The Role of Interest Group," *Journal of Industrial Economics* 54, no. 1 (June 2006): 201–222; Harold Demsetz, "Why Regulate Utilities," *Journal of Law and Economics* 11, no. 1 (1968): 55–65. If a single dominant firm is the natural outcome in a market with natural monopoly characteristics, the critics argue, why is it necessary to eliminate potential competition by granting a government-enforced monopoly? The benefits of potential competition are thereby foreclosed, and incentives to minimize costs and develop cost-sparing technological improvements are eliminated or reduced. (See R. Richards Geddes, "A Historical Perspective on Electric Utility Regulation," *Cato Review of Business & Government Regulation*, Winter 1992, 80.).

96. McGuire and Granovetter, "Business and Bias in Public Policy Formation," 10.

97. Quoted in Cudahy and Henderson, "From Insull to Enron," 50.

98. McGuire and Granovetter, "Business and Bias in Public Policy Formation," 14.

99. Ibid.

100. Gregg A. Jarrell, "The Demand for State Regulation of the Electric Utility Industry," *Journal of Law and Economics* 21, no. 2 (1978): 27–71. The Wisconsin statute served as a model for much legislation after 1907. It (1) converts all existing utility franchises to indeterminate franchises; (2) requires a certificate of convenience and necessity for new public utilities; (3) authorizes the state commission to establish service standards, to fix rates in accordance with accepted valuation principles, and to investigate rates on complaint and on its own initiative; and (4) empowers the commission to control the capitalization and issuance of securities by public utilities. (Ibid.)

101. 169 U.S. 466 (1898).

102. Ibid., 547.

103. Granovetter and McGuire, "The Making of an Industry," 14.

104. Hausman and Neufeld, "The Market for Capital," 1065.

105. McDonald, *Insull*, 177–182.

106. Patrick McGuire and Mark Granovetter, "Using Public Policy-Making to Lock In an Industry Structure; Social Construction of the Electric Utility Industry via the National Civic Federation Study of Electric Utilities, 1905-1907, white paper (1999), 4, available at uac.utoledo.edu/.../2000/Regulation-Public-Policy-Industry-Lock-in.pdf.

107. According to McGuire and Granovetter, Insull and his colleagues intentionally biased policy-making processes to create provisions which rewarded their preferred template of firm and industry and undermined alternative forms such as publicly-owned and privately-owned multi-use firms that sold electricity. Ibid., 1.

108. Insull, *Central Station Electricity Service*, 478.

109. Ibid.; Werner Troesken, "Economists and Regulation during the Gilded Age and Progressive Era," an H-SHGAPE GAPEBIB essay, May 11, 1997, 3.

110. Joseph P. Tomain, "The Persistence of Natural Monopoly," *Natural Resources & Environment* 16, no. 4 (2002): 242.

111. Gomez-Ibanez, *Regulating Infrastructure*, 178.

112. Lincoln L. Davies, "Power Forward: The Arguments for National RPS," *Connecticut Law Review* 42, no. 5 (July 2010), 1348–1349.

113. Insull, *Central Station Electric Service* (1915), 127.

114. Platt, *Electric City*, 119.

115. Ibid., 121.

116. Ibid., 164.

117. Insull, *Central Station Electric Service*, 116–117.

118. David E. Nye, *Electrifying America: Social Meanings of a New Technology* (Cambridge, MA: MIT Press, 1990), 233.

119. Bradley, *Edison to Enron*, 90–92 ; Wasik, *The Merchant of Power*, 84.

120. Platt, *Electric City*, 109.

121. McDonald, *Insull*, 98–101; Bradley, *Edison to Enron*, 92–94.

122. McDonald, *Insull*, 99.

123. Insull, *Central Station Electric Service*, 136.

124. Bradley, *Edison to Enron*, 94.

125. Platt, *Electric City*, 118.

126. Insull, *Central Station Electric Service*, 354.

127. Wasik, *The Merchant of Power*, 86.

128. Munson, *From Edison to Enron*, 54; Bradley, *Edison to Enron*, 94–95.

129. Insull, *Central Station Electric Service*, 148.

130. McDonald, *Insull*, 122.

131. Platt, *Electric City*, 131.

132. "The Systems of Operating Practice of the Commonwealth Edison Company," *Electrical World and Engineer* 51 (1908): 1023; quoted in Nicholas G. Carr, "The End of Corporate Computing," *MIT Sloan Management Review* 46 (Spring 2005): 69.

133. Hughes, *Networks of Power*, 214.

134. McDonald, *Insull*, 103–104.

135. Insull, *Central Station Electric Service* (1915), 239.

136. Insull, *Memoirs*, 95.

137. Platt, *Electric City*, 188–189.

138. McDonald, *Insull*, 138–140; Klein, *The Power Makers*, 420–421; Bradley, *Edison to Enron*, 96, 105–107; Insull, *Central Station Electric Service*, 358–377.

139. Paul Jerome Raver, "Municipal Ownership and the Changing Technology of the Electric Industry: Trends in Use of Prime Movers," *Journal of Land & Public Utility Economics* 6 (August 1930): 244.

140. Insull, *Central Station Electric Service*, 400.

141. Ibid.

142. Platt, *Electric City*, 189.

143. Schewe, *The Grid* (2007), 80.

144. Klein, *The Power Makers*, 420–423; McDonald, *Insull*, 143–144; Bradley, *Edison to Enron*, 115.

145. Platt, *Electric City*, 183.

146. Insull, *Central Station Electric Service*, 388.

147. Bradley, *Edison to Enron*, 115.

148. Insull, *Memoirs*, 98–99.

149. John H. Gray, "The State Abdicates: Utilities Govern Themselves," *Government Ownership of Power and Light Utilities* (1924), 105; quoted in Robert L. Bradley Jr., "The Origins of Political Electricity: Market Failure or Political Opportunism?," *Energy Law Journal* 17, no. 1 (1996): 80.

150. Kateena O'Gorman, "Remembering the Concept of the Corporation," white paper presented at the Stanford/Yale Junior Faculty Forum, May 29, 2009, 20–23; Stephen Holland and John Neufeld, "The Evolution of Government Policy and the Structure of the U.S. Electric Power Industry," white paper presented at the University of North Carolina, Greensboro, May 20, 2009, 3.

151. Quoted in Bradley, *Edison to Enron*, 118–119.

152. McDonald, *Insull*, 155–156.

153. Hughes, *Networks of Power*, 226.

154. Bradley, *Edison to Enron*, 117.

155. Insull, *Memoirs*, 117.

156. McDonald, *Insull*, 169.

157. McDonald, *Insull*, 201–202.

158. Ibid., 172, 182; Cudahy and Henderson, "From Insull to Enron," 52; Bradley, *Edison to Enron*, 141.

159. Quoted in Bradley, *Edison to Enron*, 173.

160. Cudahy and Henderson, "From Insull to Enron," 53; McDonald, *Insull*, 204–205.

161. Speech by Bernard Mullaney, Insull's public relations chief; quoted in Marion L. Ramsey, *Pyramids of Power: The Story of Roosevelt, Insull, and the Utility Wars* (Cambridge, MA: Da Capo Press, 1937), 136.

162. McDonald, *Insull*, 248.

163. Quoted in McDonald, *Insull*, 247.

164. Testimony by Congressman Rayburn, *Hearings Before Committee on Interstate and Foreign Commerce on H.R. 5423*, 74th Cong., 1st Sess, 343 (1935).

165. Adolf A. Berle Jr. and Gardiner Means, *The Modern Corporation and Private Property* (New York: Macmillan, 1933), 4–5.

166. Platt, *Electric City*, 235, 240.

167. Maury Klein, *The Genesis of Industrial America, 1870–1920* (New York: Cambridge University Press, 2007), 103.

168. Herbert Hoover, *The Memoirs of Herbert Hoover: The Cabinet and the Presidency*, 2nd ed. (New York: Macmillan, 1952), 47.

169. Holland and Neufeld, "The Evolution of Government Policy," 2–3. See W. S. Murray et al., *A Superpower System for the Region between Boston and Washington* (Washington, DC: USGPO, 1921); Morris Llewellyn Cooke and Judson C. Dickerman, *Report of the Giant Power Survey Board to the General Assembly of the Commonwealth of Pennsylvania* (Harrisburg, PA: Telegraph Printing Co., 1925).

170. Quoted in *Time*, April 18, 1932.

171. Bradley, *Edison to Enron*, 163.

172. Carl D. Thompson, *Confessions of the Power Trust* (New York: Dutton, 1932), 56.

173. Quoted in Bradley, *Edison to Enron*, 162; Thompson, ibid., 127–133.

174. Quoted in Cudahy and Henderson, "From Insull to Enron," 54n107.

175. Ibid., 59n134.

176. Aggressive investment bankers also formed holding companies to capture lucrative fees for underwriting bond offerings. See text at note 223.

177. Holland and Neufeld, "The Evolution of Government Policy," 3.

178. 273 U.S. 83 (1927).

179. 16 U.S.C §824 (1935). See generally *New York v. FERC*, 535 U.S. 1, 5–7 (2002) (tracing the history of the Federal Power Act). The Federal Water Power Act of 1920 created the Federal Power Commission, the predecessor to the Federal Energy Regulatory Commission, with jurisdiction over the siting, construction, and maintenance of hydroelectric dams on navigable waters and backstop authority to regulate rates and other matters related to electricity generated by federally licensed dams if the relevant state had not established a public utility commission with appropriate jurisdiction. See Federal Water Power Act, ch. 285, Section 30, 41 Stat. 1077 (1920) (current version at 16 U.S.C. Section 791 (2006)).

180. Duke Power Co. v. FERC, 401 F. 2d 930, 934 (D.C. Cir.1968).

181. Holland and Neufeld, "The Evolution of Government Policy," 3–4.

182. *The Power Industry and the Public Interest* (New York: Twentieth Century Fund, 1944), 16.

183. Charles Sillman Morgan, *Regulation and the Management of Public Utilities* (Boston: Houghton Mifflin, 1923), 11.

184. Thompson, *Confessions of the Power Trust*, 126.

185. Quoted in Bradley, *Edison to Enron*, 176.

186. The commission submitted its report on February 21, 1927, as Senate Document No. 213.

187. Insull, *Central Station Electric Service*, 151.

188. Cudahy and Henderson, "From Insull to Enron," 59–60; McDonald, *Insull*, 262–263; Bradley, "The Origins of Political Electricity," 83.

189. McDonald, *Insull*, 265.

190. Quoted in Anne M. Butler and Wendy Wolff, *United States Senate Election, Expulsion, and Censure Cases, 1793–1990*, S. Doc. 103–133 (Washington, DC: GPO, 1995).

191. *Congressional Record*, January 2, 1925, 68th Cong., 2nd Sess., pp. 1101–1107.

192. Quoted in McDonald, *Insull*, 267.

193. Quoted in Thompson, *Confessions of the Power Trust*, 8.

194. Ibid., 41.

195. Ibid., 127.

196. *Summary Report of the Federal Trade Commission on Utility Corporations*, Senate Document 92, 70th Congress, 1st sess., 840–841.

197. Bradley, *Edison to Enron*, 176; Thompson, *Confessions of the Power* Trust, 71–127. The Federal Trade Commission's conclusions are set forth in Section 1 of the Public Utility Holding Company Act and provided the factual predicate for deconstructing giant interstate holding companies (Cudahy and Henderson, "From Insull to Enron," 61).

198. McDonald, *Insull*, 249–251.

199. Skeel, *Icarus in the Boardroom* (2005), 87; McDonald, *Insull*, 251–252; *Time*, April 15, 1932.

200. Arthur R. Taylor, "Losses to the Public in the Insull Collapse, 1932–1946," *Business History Review* 36, no. 2 (Summer 1962): 189; *Time*, April 15, 1932; McDonald, *Insull*, 275.

201. Insull, *Central Station Electric Service*, 170.

202. Ibid., 188.

203. Ibid., 188–189; McDonald, *Insull*, 279–280; Cudahy and Henderson, "From Insull to Enron," 62.

204. McDonald, *Insull*, 281, quoting from company press release.

205. Ibid.

206. Dawson, "Insull on Trial," *The Nation* 139 (November 28, 1934): 611–612.

207. Ibid., 281–282; Cudahy and Henderson, "From Insull to Enron," 62–63; *Time*, April 18, 1932.

208. *New York Times*, November 18, 1929, 2; quoted in Cudahy and Henderson, "From Insull to Enron," 63.

209. McDonald, *Insull*, 283–285.

210. Ibid., 285–86; Bradley, *Edison to Enron*, 189; Klein, *The Power Makers*, 436–438.

211. Quoted in McDonald, *Insull*, 247.

212. Quoted in Bradley, *Edison to Enron*, Internet appendix 4.5,"Was Cyrus Eaton a Threat to Insull's Empire," at www.politicalcapital.org/Book2/Chapter4/Appendix5 .html.

213. McDonald, *Insull*, 286–294; Cudahy and Henderson, "From Insull to Enron," 65; Bradley, *Edison to Enron*, 193.

214. Insull, *Memoirs*, 198–199.

215. McDonald, *Insull*, 293.

216. Ibid., 294.

217. Insull, *Memoirs*, 209.

218. Ibid.

219. McDonald, *Insull*, 297.

220. Ibid.; Bradley, *Edison to Enron*, 193–194; Cudahy and Henderson, "From Insull to Enron," 67; Insull, *Memoirs*, 213–218.

221. Lincoln Printing v. Middle West Utilities Co., 74 F.2d 779, 788 (7th Cir. 1935).

222. Ibid., 786. ("Those three public utilities formed the foundation upon which the Insull utilities organization had been constructed. They were solvent, were paying dividends, and their capital stock was widely distributed and held by hundreds of thousands of individuals throughout the nation, and were regarded as quite valuable and substantial assets.")

223. Insull, *Central Station Electric Service*, 221–222.

224. McDonald, *Insull*, 301–304.

225. Taylor, *Insull*, 188, 191–193.

226. McDonald, *Insull*, 309–310.

227. Cudahy and Henderson, "From Insull to Enron," 68.

228. Franklin Roosevelt, Portland, Oregon, speech of September 21, 1932; reprinted in *The Public Papers and Addresses of Franklin D. Roosevelt*, vol. 1, 1928–1932 (New York City: Random House, 1938), 727.

229. "The Crime Hunt in Insull's Shattered Empire," *Literary Digest*, October 15, 1932, 12; Cudahy and Henderson, "From Insull to Enron," 68–69; McDonald, *Insull*, 305–313; Insull, *Central Station Electric Service*, 232–240; Bradley, *Edison to Enron*, 442.

230. Insull, *Central Station Electric Service*, 283; McDonald, *Insull*, 316–317; Cudahy and Henderson, "From Insull to Enron," 70; Bradley, *Edison to Enron*, 442.

231. Quoted in Cudahy and Henderson, "From Insull to Enron," 70n204.

232. Quoted in Cudahy and Henderson, "From Insull to Enron," 70.

233. "Samuel Insull Faces the Bar of Justice," *Literary Digest*, October 13, 1934, 4; Cudahy and Henderson, "From Insull to Enron," 70.

234. McDonald, *Insull*, 325.

235. Dawson, "Insull on Trial," 612.

236. Quoted in Cudahy and Henderson, "From Insull to Enron," 71.

237. Ibid.; McDonald, *Insull*, 320–330.

238. McDonald, *Insull*, 332.

239. Cudahy and Henderson, "From Insull to Enron," 71.

240. *Time*, August 31, 1938.

241. Ibid.

242. McDonald, Insull, 337.

243. Taylor, *Insull*, 200.

244. Insull, *Central Station Electric Service*, 270.

245. 77 Cong. Rec. H2935 (daily ed., May 5, 1933); Cudahy and Henderson, "From Insull to Enron," 74.

246. *Report of the National Power Policy Committee on Public Utility Holding Companies*, House document No. 137, 74th Cong., 1st Sess. (March 12, 1935), 4–9.

247. Bradley, "The Origins of Political Electricity," 84.

248. Paul W. White, "The Public Utility Holding Company Act of 1935," http://paulwwhite.com/the-public-utility-company-act-of-1935_316.html.

249. Michael Parrish, *Anxious Decades: America in Prosperity and Depression, 1920–1940* (New York: Norton, 1992), 344; Cudahy and Henderson, "From Insull to Enron," 75–76.

250. Arthur Schlesinger, *The Age of Roosevelt: The Politics of Upheaval* (Boston: Houghton Mifflin, 1958), 312.

251. White, "The Public Utility Holding Company Act of 1935," 8–24.

252. 15 U.S.C. Section 79(b)(1)(2000).

253. 15 U.S.C. Section 79(b)(2)(2000).

254. Cudahy and Henderson, "From Insull to Enron," 77.

255. Bradley, "The Origins of Political Electricity," 85.

256. Dewing, *The Financial Policy of Corporations* (1953), quoted in ibid.

257. Section 201(a), 49 Stat. 847.

258. Section 202(e), 49 Stat. 849.

259. Section 205(a), 49 Stat. 851; Section 301(a), 49 Stat. 854; Section 302(a), 49 Stat. 855.

260. Platt, *Electric City*, 276.

261. Skeel, *Icarus in the Boardroom*, 87.

262. Ibid., 89.

Chapter 2

1. Kenneth F. Davis, *FDR: The New York Years* (New York: Random House, 1985), 275–276.

2. Franklin D. Roosevelt, *Public Papers and Addresses*, Volume 1: *The Genesis of the New Deal (1928–1932)* (New York: Random House, 1938), 737–739.

3. Ibid., 739–740.

4. Ibid.; Arthur Schlesinger, *The Crisis of the Old Order* (New York: Houghton Mifflin, 1957), 424.

5. Franklin D. Roosevelt, "The Real Meaning of the Power Problem," *Forum*, December 1929, 327–332.

6. Quoted in Davis, *FDR*, 95.

7. Thomas K. McCraw, *TVA and the Power Fight, 1933–1939* (Philadelphia: Lippincott, 1971), 29.

8. Ibid., 31.

9. *New York Times*, March 5, 1931.

10. Section 124 of the National Defense Act of 1916; *United States Statutes at Large* 39, 166.

11. See Norman Wengert, "Antecedents of the TVA: The Legislative History of Muscle Shoals," *Agricultural History* 26, no. 4 (October 1952): 142–144.

12. See generally Preston J. Hubbard, "Origins of the TVA: The Muscle Shoals Controversy 1920–1932," *Indiana Magazine of History* 58, no. 2 (1961): 166–168.

13. Wengert, "Antecedents of the TVA," 145–146. The first Norris bill was proposed in the 67th Congress, 2nd Session (1922), S. 3420; the second, 68th Congress, 1st Session (1924), S. 2372; the third, 69th Congress, 1st Session (1926), S. 2147; the fourth, 69th Congress, 2nd Session (1927), S. J. 163; the fifth, 70th Congress, 1st Session (1928, S.J. 46; the sixth, 71st Congress, 1st Session (1929), S.J. 49; the seventh, 72nd Congress, 1st Session (1931), S.J. 15. The eighth became the TVA Act.

14. *New York Times*, January 22, 1933; Hubbard, "Origins of the TVA," 314.

15. Edwin C. Hargrove, *Prisoners of Myth* (Princeton: Princeton University Press, 1994), 20–21.

16. Ibid.

17. Roosevelt, *Public Papers and Addresses,* vol. 1, 888–889.

18. See Richard Lowitt, *George W. Norris* (Urbana: University of Illinois Press, 1978), 16–22.

19. U.S. House, Committee on Military Affairs, *Muscle Shoals,* 73d Cong., 1st Sess. (1933), 159, 225. See McCraw, *TVA,* 36.

20. See *Congressional Record,* 73rd. Cong., 1st Sess., May 8, 1933, 2984–2985.

21. P.L. No. 32, 73d Cong., 1st Sess. (1933); 48 Stat. 58, 16 U.S.C. Sec. 831.

22. James MacGregor Burns, *Roosevelt: The Lion and the Fox* (New York: Harcourt, Brace, and World 1956), 179. See generally, George D. Haimbaugh, "The TVA Cases: A Quarter Century Later," *Indiana Law Journal* 41, no. 2 (1966): 197 et seq.; "The Tennessee Valley Authority Act," *Yale Law Journal* 43, no. 5 (1934): 815 et seq.; Steven M. Neuse, *David E. Lilienthal* (Knoxville: University of Tennessee Press, 1996), 69; McCraw, *TVA,* 39.

23. Arthur E. Morgan, *The Making of TVA* (Amherst, NY: Prometheus Books, 1974), 2.

24. See Arthur E. Morgan, *The Philosophy of Edward Bellamy* (Whitefish, MT: Kessinger Publishing, 1944).

25. Arthur E. Morgan, *Nowhere Was Somewhere* (Chapel Hill: University of North Carolina Press, 1946), 12.

26. Quoted in J. P. Moeller, "The Making of the TVA" [review of the book], *The Historical Journal* 19, no. 1 (March 1976): 308–309.

27. David E. Lilienthal, *The TVA Years, 1939–45,* vol. 1 (New York: Harper & Row, 1964), 66–67.

28. Neuse, *David E. Lilienthal,* 62–63; McCraw, *TVA,* 42–43; Lilienthal, *The TVA Years, 1939–45,* 38.

29. McCraw, *TVA,* 46.

30. See, for example, David E. Lilienthal, "The Regulation of Public Utility Holding Companies," *Columbia Law Review* 29 (1929): 404 et seq.; David E. Lilienthal, "The Federal Courts and State Regulation of Public Utilities," *Harvard Law Review* 43 (1930): 379 et seq.

31. See, for example, *Smith v. Illinois Bell Telephone Co.*, 282 U.S. 133 (1930) (a case before the U.S. Supreme Court that resulted in a $20 million refund to customers who had been overcharged).

32. Neuse, *David E. Lilienthal*, 34–38.

33. Ibid., 42.

34. Neuse, *David E. Lilienthal*, 42–52; McCraw, *TVA*, 45.

35. McCraw, *TVA*, 45.

36. David E. Lilienthal, Memphis State Oral History Project, February 6, 1970, 4; quoted in Hargrove, *Prisoners of Myth*, 36–37.

37. Quoted in McCraw, *TVA*, 47.

38. Quoted in Hargrove, *Prisoners of Myth*, 40.

39. Lilienthal, *The TVA Years, 1939–45*, 39.

40. Neuse, *David E. Lilienthal*, 78–79.

41. John Braeman, "The New Deal and the 'Broker State': A Review of the Recent Scholarly Literature," *Business History Review* 46, no. 4 (Winter 1972): 415.

42. *Annual Report (TVA)*, House Doc. No. 83, 74th Congress, 1st Sess. for year ending June 30, 1934.

43. David E. Lilienthal, "Business and Government in the Tennessee Valley," *Annals of Political and Social Science* 172 (March 1934): 46.

44. McCraw, *TVA*, 61.

45. Memorandum to the New York State legislature accompanying transmittal of the *Report of the St. Lawrence Power Development Commission*, January 19, 1931, 187; memorandum to the New York State legislature concerning the bill to develop St. Lawrence hydroelectric power, March 4, 1931, 194.

46. Lilienthal, "Business and Government in the Tennessee Valley," 47.

47. Neuse, *David E. Lilienthal*, 76. Lilienthal also established the Electric Home and Farm Authority as a vehicle to encourage increased use of electric appliances and a mass market for electric power. It was one of the first attempts to implement a growth-oriented economic agenda within the New Deal. See Gregory B. Field, "'Electricity for All': The Electric Home and Farm Authority and the Politics of Mass Consumption, 1932–1935," *Business History Review* 64, no. 1 (Spring 1990): 32–60.

48. Robert W. Harbeson, "The Power Program of the Tennessee Valley Authority," *Journal of Land & Public Utility Economics* 12, no. 1 (February 1936): 25.

49. McCraw, *TVA*, 63.

50. Lilienthal, *The TVA Years, 1939–45*, 712–713; McCraw, *TVA*, 63; Hargrove, *Prisoners of Myth*, 44; Neuse, *David E. Lilienthal*, 82.

51. Lilienthal, *The TVA Years, 1939–45*, 712–713.

52. Ibid., 713.

53. McCraw, *TVA*, 64.

54. Lilienthal, *The TVA Years, 1939–45*, 7, 14.

55. McCraw, *TVA*, 65.

56. Joseph C. Swidler, *Power and the Public Interest: The Memoirs of Joseph C. Swidler*, University of Tennessee Press (2002), 32–34.

57. Walter Isaacson, ed., *Profiles in Leadership: Historians on the Elusive Quality of Greatness* (W.W. Norton 2010), 233.

58. Bennett, "Roosevelt, Willkie and the TVA," 28 *Tennessee Historical Quarterly* 28, no. 4 (Winter 1969), 391. Statement of John D. Battle, Executive Secretary of the National Coal Association, before the Committee on Military Affairs, House of Representatives (7th Congress, 1st Session, 1935).

59. Quoted in Ellsworth Barnard, *Wendell Willkie: Fighter for Freedom* (Marquette: Northern Michigan University Press, 1966), 89–90.

60. McCraw, *TVA*, 70. The economic rationale of the yardstick was open to question. TVA had deconstructed the power business as conducted by integrated private companies by dividing the wholesale from the retail business. TVA dams were intended to promote multipurpose river development (e.g., flood control, navigation, and hydroelectricity) and thus required arbitrary apportionment of the cost for yardstick purposes, a methodology TVA did not finalize until 1937–1938 (McCraw, *TVA*, 70–71; see also Harbeson, "The Power Program of the Tennessee Valley Authority"; Horace M. Gray, "The Allocation of Joint Costs in Multiple-Purpose Hydro-Electric Projects," *American Economic Review* 25 (June 1935): 224–235).

61. 9 F.Supp. 965 (N.D. Ala. 1935).

62. Ashwander v. Tennessee Valley Authority, 297 U.S. 288, 291–92 (1936).

63. Hargrove, *Prisoners of Myth*, 46.

64. The *Ashwander* suit had a profound effect on power revenues, which declined from $826,000 in 1934 to less than half that amount the following year (Neuse, *David E. Lilienthal*, 89).

65. Quoted in Barnard, *Wendell Wilkie*, 89.

66. McCraw, *TVA*, 115.

67. Tennessee Valley Authority v. Ashwander, 78 F.2d 578 (1935).

68. See Cushman, "Rethinking the New Deal Court," *Virginia Law Review* 80 (1994), 201.

69. 297 U.S. 288, 340 (1936). In view of the litigation TVA's board obtained amendments to the TVA Act empowering TVA to issue bonds and confirming its constitutional power to engage in the utility business.

70. Lilienthal, *The TVA Years, 1939–45*, 59.

71. Ibid.

72. By 1937 ninety-two suits had been entered against Public Works Administration allotments for power projects, fifty-eight against the Securities and Exchange Commission challenging the Public Utility Holding Company Act, and thirty-four against the TVA (McCraw, *TVA*, 109).

73. Haimbaugh, "The TVA Cases," 207.

74. Rexford Tugwell and Edward Banfield, review of Philip Selznick's "TVA and the Grass Roots: A Study in the Sociology of Formal Organization," *Public Administration Review* 10, no. 1 (Winter 1950): 50.

75. Lilienthal, *The TVA Years, 1939–45*, 80.

76. "Power: TVA Clear," *Time*, January 31, 1938. Swidler also turned to industrial power contracts to provide a market for TVA's increasing supply of low-cost power. Shortly after the *Ashwander* decision, TVA and TEPCO found themselves locked in competitive negotiations with Monsanto Chemical Company. TEPCO offered lower rates than TVA but could not provide a performance guarantee for the full contract term since the state public service commission retained oversight of pricing provisions that appeared to have discriminated against other TEPCO customers. TVA prevailed in the competition and sold power on similar terms to other companies in the next few years, realizing revenues in excess of the cost of production as required by statute. Monsanto was a breakthrough for TVA and launched a period of rapid expansion (Swidler, *Power and the Public Interest*, 35–40).

77. Alabama Power Corporation v. Ickes, 91 F.2d 303 (D.C. Cir. 1937); 302 U.S. 464 (1938).

78. Neuse, *David E. Lilienthal*, 90; McCraw, *TVA*, 91–93.

79. Quoted in McCraw, *TVA*, 95.

80. Ibid., 93–95.

81. Tennessee Electric Power Company v. TVA (TEPCO), 21 F. Supp. 947 (1938); 306 U.S. 118 (1939).

82. Quoted in Schlesinger, *Crisis of the Old Order*, 367.

83. Quote attributed to Francis Biddle, Roosevelt's attorney general, in Kenneth F. Davis, *FDR into the Storm, 1937–1940* (New York: Random House, 1993), 175–176.

84. Arthur M. Schlesinger, *The Age of Roosevelt*, Volume 3: *The Politics of Upheaval, 1935–1936* (New York: Houghton Mifflin, 1960), 366.

85. Lilienthal, *The TVA Years, 1939–45*, 62.

86. Ibid.

87. Charlotte Muller, "Aluminum and Power Control," *Journal of Land & Public Utility Economics* 21, no. 2 (May 1945): 111–112.

88. Swidler, *Power and the Public Interest*, 41.

89. Ibid., 41–42.

90. McCraw, *TVA*, 95–96; Schlesinger, *The Age of Roosevelt*, Volume 3, 366.

91. Lilienthal, *The TVA Years, 1939–45*, 65.

92. McCraw, *TVA*, 91–102.

93. Quoted in Schlesinger, *The Age of Roosevelt*, Volume 3, 369.

94. 21 F.Supp. 947 (E.D. Tenn. 1938).

95. 306 U.S. 118, 139–40 (1939). See Haimbaugh, "The TVA Cases," 199–200.

96. Quoted in Hargrove, *Prisoners of Myth*, 47.

97. Arthur M. Schlesinger, *The Age of Roosevelt*, Volume 2: *The Coming of the New Deal, 1933–1935* (New York: Houghton Mifflin, 1958), 331.

98. Quoted in Neuse, *David E. Lilienthal*, 99.

99. "Power: Great Schism," *Time*, January 25, 1937.

100. Arthur E. Morgan, "Public Ownership of Power," *Atlantic Monthly*, September 1937, 344–346.

101. Neuse, *David E. Lilienthal*, 101.

102. Neuse, *David E. Lilienthal*, 102–103.

103. Lilienthal, *The TVA Years, 1939–45*, 70.

104. Ibid., 72.

105. Neuse, *David E. Lilienthal*, 104.

106. The Joint Committee was created by Pub. Res. No. 83 (75th Cong., c. 61, 3d Sess., S. J. Res. 277), with a membership of five senators and five representatives. See "Power: Morgan v. Morgan Lilienthal," *Time*, March 14, 1938.

107. Quoted in Neuse, *David E. Lilienthal*, 10.

108. Lilienthal, *The TVA Years, 1939–45*, 75.

109. Arthur E. Marlett, "The TVA Investigation," *Journal of Land & Public Utility Economics* 15, no. 2 (May 1939): 221–224.

110. Davis, *FDR into the Storm, 1937–1940*, 178–179.

111. Swidler, *Power and the Public Interest*, 48.

112. McCraw, *TVA*, 133.

113. Swidler, *Power and the Public Interest*, 49; McCraw, *TVA*, 134; Braeman, "The New Deal and the 'Broker State.'"

114. McCraw, *TVA*, 130–134.

115. Barnard, *Wendell Wilkie*, 121.

116. Swidler, *Power and the Public Interest*, 49. Swidler later chaired the Federal Power Commission, and Krug became secretary of the interior.

117. Barnard, *Wendell Wilkie*, 122; McCraw, *TVA*, 136.

118. *New York Times*, June 18, 1939.

119. Lilienthal, *The TVA Years, 1939–45*, 96.

120. 53 Stat. 1083 (1939), 16 U.S.C. Sec. 831n-2 (2012). See Barnard, *Wendell Wilkie*, 123; McCraw, *TVA*, 136–137; Swidler, *Power and the Public Interest*, 51; Neuse, *David E. Lilienthal*, 109–113. The original TVA Act of 1933 authorized the sale by TVA of up to $50 million of bonds for construction of dams, steam plants, and other power facilities. In 1935 the act was amended to authorize the sale of an additional $50 million of bonds to permit TVA to lend money to municipal and cooperative electric systems for the purchase of existing distribution facilities. In 1939, the act was again amended, repealing all previous bond authorizations but providing authorization for $61.5 million in bonds to finance the acquisition by TVA of local electric systems in Tennessee, Alabama, and Mississippi. Under the 1939 amendment, during 1939 and 1940 TVA issued to the Treasury $56.5 million of bonds, later repaid out of power revenues. See Arthur R. Jones, "The Financing of TVA," *Law and Contemporary Problems* 26, no. 4 (1961): 729–730.

121. Lilienthal, *The TVA Years, 1939–45* (1964), 119–120. The balance of $33,696,795 was delivered by representatives of twenty-two Tennessee cities and eleven cooperatives. See Jones, "The Financing of TVA," 736; *Time*, August 26, 1939.

122. Neuse, *David E. Lilienthal*, 111–113.

123. Lilienthal, *The TVA Years, 1939–45*, 120–121.

124. Horace M. Gray, "The Passing of the Public Utility Concept," *Journal of Land & Public Utility Economics* 16, no. 1 (February 1940): 13–14.

125. Quoted in Neuse, *David E. Lilienthal*, 112–113.

126. McCraw, *TVA*, 137; *Time*, July 31, 1939.

127. Clayton R. Koppes, "Interior and Exterior Man: The Enigma of Harold L. Ickes" (review of *Righteous Pilgrim: The Life and Times of Harold L. Ickes, 1874–1952* by T. H. Watkins), *American History* 19, no. 4 (December 1991): 545–550.

128. *New Yorker*, June 5, 1954, 128–129.

129. Philip J. Funigiello, "Kilowatts for Defense: The New Deal and the Coming of the Second World War," *Journal of American History* 56, no. 3 (December 1969): 604–620.

130. Ibid.

131. The Reorganization Act of 1939, Pub.L. 76–19, 53 Stat. 561, enacted April 3, 1939, codified at 5 U.S.C. § 133, gave the president the authority to reorganize the executive branch (within certain limits) for two years subject to legislative veto and was the first major, planned reorganization of the executive branch of the government of the United States since 1787. The act led to Reorganization Plan No. 1, which created the Executive Office of the President.

132. Hargrove, *Prisoners of Myth*, 51.

133. Neuse, *David E. Lilienthal*, 126.

134. Ibid.

135. Lilienthal, *The TVA Years, 1939–45*, 126–128.

136. Ibid., 136.

137. Ibid., 136–137.

138. Ibid.

139. David E. Lilienthal, "The People's Business," *Annals of the American Academy of Political and Social Science* 201 (January 1939): 59–60.

140. David E. Lilienthal, "The TVA and Decentralization," *Survey Graphic* (1939), http://newdeal.feri.org/survey/40c17.htm.

141. Howard Segal, "Down in the Valley: David Lilienthal's TVA: Democracy on the March," *The American Scholar* 64, no. 3 (Summer 1995): 427; Neuse, *David E. Lilienthal*, 130–131; Lilienthal, *The TVA Years, 1939–45*, 149–150; Hargrove, *Prisoners of Myth*, 53. Lilienthal also resisted efforts to place TVA under the civil service and by the General Accounting Office to impose fiscal controls (Neuse, *David E. Lilienthal*, 132).

142. Lilienthal, *The TVA Years, 1939–45*, 359.

143. Ibid., 360–361.

144. Neuse, *David E. Lilienthal*, 129–130; Lilienthal, *The TVA Years, 1939–45*, 365–366, 375.

145. Lilienthal, *The TVA Years, 1939–45*, 372; Neuse, *David E. Lilienthal*, 149–153.

146. Lawrence L. Durisch, "The TVA and the War Effort," *Journal of Politics* 8, no. 1 (November 1946): 532.

147. Muller, "Aluminum and Power Control," 112–113.

148. Quoted in Neuse, *David E. Lilienthal*, 153–154.

149. Hargrove, *Prisoners of Myth*, 56.

150. Ibid., 56–57; Neuse, *David E. Lilienthal*, 155–159.

151. Lilienthal, *The TVA Years, 1939–45*, 396–397.

152. Ibid.

153. Ibid.

154. Neuse, *David E. Lilienthal*, 158.

155. Lilienthal, *The TVA Years, 1939–45*, 572–573.

156. Neuse, *David E. Lilienthal*, 158.

157. Lilienthal, *The TVA Years, 1939–45* (1964), 425.

158. Ibid., 482.

159. Ibid., 483; Hargrove, *Prisoners of Myth*, 58.

160. Hargrove, *Prisoners of Myth*, 58–59.

161. Lilienthal, *The TVA Years, 1939–45*, 498.

162. Ibid., 381–382.

163. Hargrove, *Prisoners of Myth*, 60–61; Aaron Wildavsky, "TVA and Power Politics," *American Political Science Review* 55, no. 3 (September 1961): 579; Jones, "The Financing of TVA," 732–733; Durisch, "The TVA and the War Effort," 532; Lilienthal, *The TVA Years, 1939–45* (1964), 528.

164. Lilienthal, *The TVA Years, 1939–45* (1964), 394.

165. Wildavsky, "TVA and Power Politics," 579–580.

166. Ibid., 395.

167. Braeman, "The New Deal and the 'Broker State,'" 416.

168. Tugwell and Banfield, review of Selznick's *TVA and the Grass Roots*, 47–55; Steven M. Neuse, "TVA at Age Fifty—Reflections and Retrospect," *Public Administration Review* 43, no. 6 (November 1983): 491–499.

169. Segal, "Down in the Valley," 424.

170. Lilienthal, *TVA: Democracy on the March* (1944), 79, 91.

171. Ibid., 150–151.

172. "The use of the region as an autonomous unit of development was a deliberate 'experiment'" (ibid., 156).

173. Tugwell and Banfield, review of Selznick's *TVA and the Grass Roots*, 48.

174. Philip Selznick, *TVA and the Grass Roots: A Study in the Sociology of Formal Orga-nization* (Berkeley: University of California Press, 1949). Page references are to the 2011 reprint edition.

175. Ibid., i–vi, 237–253; Tugwell and Banfield, review of Selznick's *TVA and the Grass Roots*, 47–55; Segal, "Down in the Valley," 423–427.

176. Hargrove, *Prisoners of Myth*, 171–177.

177. Lilienthal, *The TVA Years, 1939–45* (1964), 638–639.

178. Thomas K. McCraw, review of Hargrove, *Prisoners of Myth: The Leadership of the Tennessee Valley Authority, 1933–1990, Technology and Culture* 36, no. 4 (October 1995): 1008.

179. William M. Emmons III, "Franklin D. Roosevelt, Electric Utilities, and the Power of Competition," *Journal of Economic History* 53, no. 4 (December 1993): 880–897. See also Emmons, "Implications of Ownership, Regulation, and Market Struc-ture for Performance Evidence from the U.S. Electric Utility Industry Before and After the New Deal," *Review of Economics and Statistics* 79, no. 2 (May 1997): 279–299 (publicly owned firms charged rates between 10 and 20 percent less than those of private firms, even after controlling for the effects of subsidies, tax differentials, and lower capital costs).

180. David E. Lilienthal and Robert H. Marquis, "The Conduct of Business Enter-prises by the Federal Government," *Harvard Law Review* 54, no. 4 (February 1941): 558.

181. Ibid.; H. R. Rep No. 130, 73d Cong., 1st Sess. (1933), 19. Congress eventually sought to curtail the freedom of government corporations in the Government Corporation Control Act of 1945 (Public Law No. 248, 79th Cong.; 31 U.S.C. Sec. 841 et seq.; Marshall E. Dimock, "Government Corporations: A Focus of Policy and Administration," *American Political Science Review* 43, no. 5 (October 1949): 899–921).

182. Hargrove, *Prisoners of Myth*, 48.

183. William E. Leuchtenburg, "Roosevelt, Norris and the 'Seven Little TVAs,'" *Jour-nal of Politics* 14, no. 3 (August 1952): 433–434.

184. McCraw, *TVA*, 159.

185. Swidler, *Power and the Public Interest*, 85.

186. The Revenue Bond Act of 1959, 73 Stat. 280 (1959), 16 U.S.C. Sec. 831n-4 (Supp. II).

Chapter 3

1. James Leigland and Robert Lamb, *WPP$$: Who Is to Blame for the WPPSS Disaster?* (Cambridge, MA: Ballinger, 1986), 190–191.

2. Quoted in Herman Voeltz, "Genesis and Development of a Regional Power Agency in the Pacific Northwest, 1933–43," *Pacific Northwest Quarterly* 53, no. 2 (April 1962): 65; Richard L. Neuberger, *Our Promised Land* (New York: Macmillan, 1938), 3.

3. Daniel Pope, *Nuclear Implosions* (New York: Cambridge University Press, 2008), 9.

4. Arthur M. Schlesinger, *The Age of Roosevelt*, Volume 3: *The Politics of Upheaval, 1935–1936* (New York: Houghton Mifflin, 1960), 377.

5. Franklin D. Roosevelt, *Public Papers (1928–1932)*, Volume 1: *The Genesis of the New Deal* (New York: Random House, 1938), 733.

6. Pope, *Nuclear Implosions*, 8–9.

7. Hugh A. Scott, "Reminiscence: Hugh A. Scott on Bonneville Dam and the Boom Era," *Oregon Historical Quarterly* 88, no. 3 (Fall 1987): 283.

8. Schlesinger, *The Politics of Upheaval*, 376.

9. Kendall Hoyt, "The New Deal Policy Aimed at Socialization of the Nation's Power Resources," *The Annalist*, June 5, 1936, 839; Wesley Arden Dick, "When Dams Weren't Damned: The Public Power Crusade and Visions of the Good Life in the Pacific Northwest in the 1930s," *Environmental Review* 13, no. 3/4 (Autumn–Winter 1989): 134.

10. S. 869; 74th Cong., 1st Sess., *Congressional Record* (January 14, 1935), 407.

11. S. 3330, 74th Cong., 1st Sess., *Congressional Record* (July 29, 1935), 11944; Philip J. Funigiello, *Toward a National Power Policy* (Pittsburgh: University of Pittsburgh Press, 1973), 175.

12. Funigiello, ibid., 175; Herman Voeltz, "Genesis and Development of a Regional Power Agency in the Pacific Northwest, 1933–43," *Pacific Northwest Quarterly* 53, no. 2 (April 1962): 64–66.

13. "Organization for the Operation of Public Works," National Resources Committee, *Regional Planning*, Part I: *Pacific Northwest* (Washington, DC, 1936), 175–192.

14. *Columbia River Power for the People: A History of the Bonneville Power Administration* (hereafter, *BPA History*), https://archive.org/details/columbiariverpow00unit, 79–86.

15. Funigiello, *Toward a National Power Policy*, 176–179; Voeltz, "Genesis and Development," 68; *Navigation and Flood Control Hearings: Bonneville, 1936*, 74th Cong., 2nd Sess., 17; Pope, *Nuclear Implosions*, 10.

16. Ibid.

17. William E. Leuchtenburg, "Roosevelt, Norris, and the 'Seven Little TVAs,'" *Journal of Politics* 14, no. 3 (August 1952): 420.

18. Leuchtenberg, ibid., 418–421; *New York Times*, April 1, 1937.

19. Funigiello, *Toward a National Power Policy*, 183–186; *Columbia River: Bonneville Dam*, 1937 Hearings, 141–143.

20. Leuchtenberg, "Roosevelt, Norris, and the 'Seven Little TVAs,'" passim.

21. Pub. L. No. 75–329, 50 Stat. 731 (codified at 16 U.S. C. Sec. 832 (2012)); Funigiello, *Toward a National Power Policy*, 190–193; Bayard O. Wheeler, "The Production and Distribution of Bonneville Power," *Journal of Land & Public Utility Economics* 14, no. 4 (November 1938): 359 et seq.; *BPA History*, 55–62. See generally *The Evolution of Preference in Marketing Federal Power*, GAO-01–373 (February 2001).

22. "BPA was originated as a wholesale power marketing entity. Congress has added to BPA's duties and public utility characteristics since 1937 by extending the power marketing authority from one project to 30, broadening and defining BPA's service area, authorizing some long-term purchase of power through net billing, directing BPA to wheel non-Federal power and authorizing BPA to issue revenue bonds to finance construction of transmission facilities. But BPA could not build generating plants and basically did not have a legal public utility responsibility" (*BPA History*, 185).

23. *BPA History*, 124.

24. James A. Luce and Janet W. McLennan, "Acquisition of Energy Resources under the Northwest Electric Power Planning and Conservation Act: A Look at the Future," *University of Puget Sound Law Review* 5, no. 1 (1981): 71.

25. Ibid., 71.

26. Quoted in *Bonneville Power Administration, History*, http://www.nwcouncil.org/history/BPAHistory.

27. Craig Holstine, "Power to the People: Construction of the Bonneville Power Administration's 'Master Grid,' 1939–45," *Pacific Northwest Forum* 2 (Spring 1988): 35–46.

28. See Voeltz, "Genesis and Development," 70–74.

29. *Time*, November 17, 1941.

30. Voeltz, "Genesis and Development," 94–95.

31. *BPA History*, 127.

32. Donald Balmer, "From Symbiosis to Synergy: A Case Study of Public and Private Power in the Northwest," *Environmental Law* 13 (Spring 1983): 644.

33. Peter D. Cooper, "The Bonneville Power Administration: The Worst Mess by a Dam Site," *Cato Policy Analysis* 66 (February 8, 1986): 1.

34. *BPA History*, 76.

35. Ibid. Formation of a district is initiated by a petition signed by a small fixed percentage of the voters registered in the proposed district area. The proposal is then voted on at the next general election. On approval by the voters the district is established. See "Power Districts: An Emerging Device for Low-Cost Energy," *Yale Law Journal* 60, no. 3 (March 1951): 490. Oregon's law was less favorable to PUD formation than Washington's.

36. D. Victor Anderson, *Illusions of Power* (New York: Praeger, 1985), 26.

37. Quoted in Funigiello, *Toward a National Power Policy*, 205.

38. In 1940 and again in 1946 a coalition of private power companies backed state initiatives in Washington to restrict the ability of PUDs to issue revenue bonds by requiring voter approval. The initiatives were defeated at the polls (Anderson, *Illusions of Power*, 31; Ken Billington, *People, Politics and Public Power* (Olympia: Washington Public Utilities District, 1988), 20–30).

39. Billington, ibid., 23–24; Funigiello, *Toward a National Power Policy*, 200.

40. Anderson, *Illusions of Power*, 25–26.

41. *BPA History*, 193.

42. Pope, *Nuclear Implosions*, 15; Anderson, *Illusions of Power*, 28–32.

43. Billington, *People, Politics and Public Power*, 69.

44. Ibid., 70.

45. Anderson, *Illusions of Power*, 34.

46. Ibid., 36–37.

47. Pope, *Nuclear Implosions*, 38.

48. Ibid., 39; James T. Bennett and Thomas J. DiLorenzo, "The Nation's Largest Municipal Bankruptcy: The Tip of the Off-Budget Iceberg," white paper, National Center for Policy Analysis, August 14, 1981, 1; Daniel Goldrich, "Democracy and Energy Planning: The Pacific Northwest as Prototype," *Environmental Review* 10, no. 3 (Autumn 1986): 206.

49. *Time*, May 15, 1950.

50. Andrew N. Kleit and Richard L. Stroup, "Blackout at Bonneville Power," *Regulation* 11, no. 2 (1987): 32.

51. Daniel Pope, "Demand Forecasts and Electrical Energy Politics: The Pacific Northwest," *Business and Economic History* 22, no. 1 (Fall 1993) ("Pope Forecasts"): 236; Pope, *Nuclear Implosions*, 50–51.

52. Pope Forecasts, 235–237.

53. Billington, *People, Politics and Public Power*, 412.

54. Richard J. Pierce, "The Regulatory Treatment of Mistakes in Retrospect: Canceled Plants and Excess Capacity," *University of Pennsylvania Law Review* 132, no. 3 (March 1984): 533n196.

55. Balmer, "From Symbiosis to Synergy," 651. Additional hydropower was made available by building storage dams on the Columbia River in Canada. This required an international treaty with Canada, long-term power sales contracts with public and private power systems, and construction of intertie lines linking the Pacific Northwest and California (ibid., 649–650).

56. The default power sources for direct-service industries were coal-fired power imported from Wyoming or nuclear plants (Steve Weiss, "The Aluminum Lobby," *Forum* [Spring 2002]: 68).

57. Quoted in Pope, *Nuclear Implosions*, 51.

58. Pope Forecasts, 237; Goldrich, "Democracy and Energy Planning," 200–201.

59. Northwest Power and Conservation Council, *2012 Briefing Book ("NPCC Briefing Book")*, 8.

60. Pope Forecasts, 237; "Hydrothermal Power Plan," *Columbia River History*, https://www.nwcouncil.org/history/HydroThermal, 3. Phase I of the Hydro-Thermal Power Plan included seven projects: two coal plants and five nuclear plants to be built over a period of ten years. Bonneville expected WPPSS to build at least one of the nuclear plants.

61. Quoted in Pope, *Nuclear Implosions*, 50.

62. William Lanouette, "Atomic Energy, 1945–1985," *Wilson Quarterly* 9, no. 5 (Winter 1985): 109

63. Quoted in Anderson, *Illusions of Power*, 55–56.

64. Leigland and Lamb, *Who Is to Blame for the WPPSS Disaster?* 4–6.

65. Anderson, *Illusions of Power*, 65.

66. Charles P. Alexander, "Whoops! A $2 Billion Blunder: Washington Public Power Supply System," *Time*, August 8, 1983.

67. Pope, *Nuclear Implosions*, 53.

68. Consistent with Bonneville's original property disposal role, Congress denied it authority to own or control directly the projects from which it markets power (Luce and McLennan, "Acquisition of Energy Resources," 71).

69. Ibid., 53; Leigland and Lamb, *Who Is to Blame for the WPPSS Disaster?*, 8.

70. David L. Shapiro, *Generating Failure* (Lanham, MD: University Press of America, 1989), 24.

71. Ibid., 24–25; Pope, *Nuclear Implosions*, 56–57; Anderson, *Illusions of Power*, 75; *SEC Staff Report on the Investigation of Transactions in Washington Public Power Supply*

System Securities ("SEC Report"), September 1988, 290; letter dated August 2, 1983, from the comptroller general of the United States to the chair, Subcommittee on Mining, Forest Management and Bonneville Power Administration, 3.

72. *Government Accounting Office,* 1979, 4; quoted in Shapiro, *Generating Failure,* 27.

73. Pope, *Nuclear Implosions,* 58–59; *NPCC Briefing Book,* 9.

74. *NPCC Briefing Book,* 8.

75. *Public Works Appropriation for Water, Pollution Control, and Power Development and Atomic Energy Commission Act, 1970,* Pub. L. No. 91–114, 83 Stat. 323 (1969); *Public Works Appropriation for Water, Pollution Control, and Power Development and Atomic Energy Commission Act, 1971,* Pub. Law No. 91–439, 84 Stat. 890 (1970). See Luce and McLennan, "Acquisition of Energy Resources," 75, 80; also see letter dated August 2, 1983, from the comptroller general of the United States to the chairman, Subcommittee on Mining, Forest Management and Bonneville Power Administration. The first nuclear steam plant was sponsored by Portland General Electric, which negotiated the right to bank enough power surplus with Bonneville to meet the needs of private power companies in the Pacific Northwest. In exchange, the private power companies agreed to support Bonneville's net-billing arrangements for the publicly financed thermal plants (Billington, *People, Politics and Public Power,* 270).

76. *NPCC Briefing Book;* Port of Astoria, Oregon v. Hodel, 595 F.2d 467 (9th Cir. 1979).

77. Michael Blumm, "Risk Management and Northwest Electric Power Planning: Some Lessons from the Rearview Mirror," *Environmental Law* 13, no. 739 (Spring 1983): 756.

78. Pope, *Nuclear Implosions,* 62–70; Anderson, *Illusions of Power,* 84.

79. Billington, *People, Politics and Public Power,* 303.

80. Ibid., 304.

81. Pope, *Nuclear Implosions,* 70.

82. Ibid., 70–71; Anderson, *Illusions of Power,* 85; Leigland and Lamb, *Who Is to Blame for the WPPSS Disaster?,* 9.

83. Leigland and Lamb, ibid., 9. Bonneville and preference utilities signed contracts for WPPSS' 1,100-megawatt project at Hanford on January 4, 1971; for its 1,250-megawatt project, also at Hanford, on February 6, 1973; and for its third

net-billed project at Satsop, Washington, on September 25, 1973. These three WPPSS projects, along with two coal plants and another nuclear plant, comprised the six net-billed projects of Phase I of the Hydro-Thermal Power Plan (*NPCC Briefing Book*, 9).

84. Gary K. Miller, *Energy Northwest* (Bloomington, IN: Xlibris, 2001), 191.

85. Ibid., 191.

86. Richard White, *The Organic Machine* (Hill and Wang, 1996), 75.

87. Treas. Reg. Sec. 1.103–7; Pope, *Nuclear Implosions*, 73–74; Anderson, *Illusions of Power*, 86–87; Billington, *People, Politics and Public Power*, 335.

88. Bonneville would also exhaust its net-billing capacity with respect to existing plants if the cost of nuclear power exceeded the revenue collected from customer utilities and available for offset. Early in 1973 Bonneville estimated that by 1981 the revenues derived from the sale of federal hydropower to preference customers would amount to $145 million while the annual cost of the thermal plants would then have mounted to $135 million, over the net billing limit of 85 percent (Anderson, *Illusions of Power*, 85–86).

89. Quoted in Anderson, *Illusions of Power*, 88; *NPCC Briefing Book*, 10.

90. House Committee on Interior and Insular Affairs, Subcommittee on Mining, Forest Management and Bonneville Power Administration, *Bonneville Power Administration, Financial Fallout from Termination of WPPSS Nuclear Projects 4 and 5* (February, 14, 1983), 98th Cong., 1st Sess., Serial No. 98–1, 152; Pope, *Nuclear Implosions*, 91.

91. Anderson, *Illusions of Power*, 87–89. Direct-service industries had been buying excess electricity from Bonneville for thirty years at lower than wholesale cost because it was interruptible—that is, it was whatever was left over after preference customers and contracted investor-owned utilities had been served. By 1973 it appeared there would be no remaining power for aluminum companies and other similar industries (ibid., 89).

92. Quoted in Anderson, *Illusions of Power*, 94; Pope, *Nuclear Implosions*, 92.

93. *NPCC Briefing Book*, 10.

94. Pope, *Nuclear Implosions*, 80–81.

95. *NPCC Briefing Book*, 12; Shapiro, *Generating Failure*, 30.

96. Under the agent approach, Bonneville would obtain the lowest-cost power available, deliver it to preference customers requesting it, and charge those customers for the cost of the power and the expenses of transmission (Comptroller General of the United States, *Pacific Northwest Hydro-Thermal Power Program—a Regional Approach to Meeting Electric Power Requirements*, Report to Congress, 1974, 21).

97. Ibid., 82–83; Anderson, *Illusions of Power*, 90–91. Bonneville's arrangements with its direct-service industry customers are described in *Port of Astoria v. Hodel*, 595 F. 2d 467 (9th Cir. 1979), as follows: "In the past, it has been [Bonneville's] policy to obtain from industry a portion of the reserve power used as backup for its firm power commitments by providing industrial customers with restrictable grades of power. The reliance on industry increased under Phase I in order to protect firm power commitments in the event that construction of thermal plants fell behind schedule or the plants initially operated below capacity. In 1971 [Bonneville] adopted an industrial sales policy that eventually came to fruition in December 1974 with the introduction of the proposed industrial firm power contracts. ... Although the industrial firm power contracts provide a more restrictable grade of power, [Bonneville] seeks to make them attractive by offering to extend their terms to 1994."

98. Roger H. Coupal and David W. Holland, "Economic Impact of Deregulation on the State of Washington: A General Equilibrium Analysis," *Journal of Agricultural and Resource Economics* 27, no. 1 (July 2002): 245.

99. Miller, *Energy Northwest*, 224.

100. Pope, *Nuclear Implosions*, 84–85; Anderson, *Illusions of Power*, 91.

101. *The Columbia Transmission System Act*, 16 U.S.C. sec. 838i(b)(6)(i). The act gave Bonneville the authority to spend its revenues on transmission system upgrades, to borrow up to $1.25 billion from the federal treasury for that purpose, and to issue bonds.

102. Quoted in Pope, *Nuclear Implosions*, 93.

103. Goldrich, "Democracy and Energy Planning," 203.

104. Port of Astoria v. Hodel, 8 ERC 1156 (D. Or. 1975), 595 F. 2d 467 (9th Cr. 1979).

105. Pope, *Nuclear Implosions*, 86–87.

106. Quoted in Anderson, *Illusions of Power*, 99; *NPCC Briefing Book*, 12; Goldrich, "Democracy and Energy Planning," 204. Hodel did not moderate these views in

later years. Writing in 1997, he said, "I define radical environmentalism as a mechanism for permitting the collectivist mentality to feed its impulse to control society" (*Religion & Liberty* 7, no. 2 (March–April 1997): 1).

107. Goldrich, "Democracy and Energy Planning," 205.

108. Pope, *Nuclear Implosions*, 86–87.

109. Ibid., 89.

110. Miller, *Energy Northwest*, 234–235; *NPCC Briefing Book*, 11.

111. Kleit and Stroup, "Blackout at Bonneville Power," 34.

112. Springfield, Oregon, was a reluctant participant in plants four and five in contrast to Seattle, which rejected participation and found no truly attractive central-station generating options available. (Daniel Pope, "Seduced and Abandoned?: Utilities and WPPSS Nuclear Plants 4 and 5," *Columbia Magazine* 5, no. 3 (Fall 1991): 5.

113. *SEC Report*, 277, 287. The costs in question, based on terminology taken from the oil and gas industry, are referred to as "dry-hole costs." Investment in "capability" was not tantamount to ownership of the plants or electricity as such. Under the participants' agreements "capability" meant "the amounts of electric power and energy, *if any*, which the Projects are capable of generating at any particular time (including times when either or both of the Plants are not operable or operating or the operation thereof is suspended, interrupted, interfered with, reduced, or curtailed, in each case in whole or in part for any reason whatsoever), less Project station use and losses" (*SEC Report*, 278n468 [emphasis added]).

114. Ibid., 362–363.

115. Pope, *Nuclear Implosions*, , 95, 102–103.

116. Miller, *Energy Northwest*, 212.

117. In response Congress enacted the Pacific Northwest Power Planning and Conservation Act of 1980, 16 U.S.C. Secs. 839–839h, which transformed Bonneville from an agency that merely sold whatever power was available from generating facilities in the Federal Columbia River Power System to one charged with the responsibility for meeting the region's future power needs, promoting energy conservation, and enhancing fish and wildlife affected by the power system in the Columbia River

Basin. The act also sought to avert disputes over power allocation by requiring Bonneville to enter into an initial set of power sale contracts with different categories of customers, including direct-service industries. Under the act Bonneville was authorized to make four types of resource purchases, including billing credits. (See Luce and McLennan, "Acquisition of Energy Resources," 82–88.)

118. Ibid., 212–213.

119. "The Senate Confirmed Donald Hodel as Energy Secretary Last Week," *Nucleonics Week* 23, no. 50 (December 16, 1982): 5.

120. Donald P. Hodel, "The Theory of Energy Policies and Programs," *Natural Resources & Environment* 6, no. 2 (Fall 1991): 10. President Reagan's Department of Energy proposed increased funding for breeder reactor development, deregulation of fuel costs, eased licensing procedures for nuclear plants, and deep cuts in conservation research and development (Pope, *Nuclear Implosions*, 163n50).

121. Pope, *Nuclear Implosions*, , 161n44.

122. Billington, *People, Politics and Public Power*, 418.

123. Quoted in Pope, *Nuclear Implosions*, 125.

124. *SEC Report*, 45.

125. Ibid., 5–6; *NPCC Briefing Book*, 13.

126. *Draft Environmental Impact Statement* (DES-77–21-App. B), July 22, 1977, X-6.

127. *SEC Report*, 128.

128. Alexander, "Whoops! A $2 Billion Blunder"; Miller, *Energy Northwest*, 333.

129. Theodore Barry & Associates, *Management Study of the Roles and Relationships of the Bonneville Power Administration and the Washington Public Power Supply System* (Portland, OR: Bonneville Power Administration, January 1979), VII-2.

130. Pope, *Nuclear Implosions*, 125–132.

131. Miller, *Energy Northwest*, 270–271.

132. Ibid., 272–284.

133. *SEC Report,* 89–92.

134. *NPCC Briefing Book,* 15; Miller, *Energy Northwest,* 318–319.

135. Howard Gleckman, quoted in Anderson, *Illusions of Power,* 136.

136. *SEC Report,* 62–66, 123–124.

137. Ibid., 232. The underwriters contended that neither law nor industry custom required them to conduct a due diligence review of the issuer in competitive bond sales. If the sales had been negotiated, antifraud provisions of federal securities law would have applied (Pope, *Nuclear Implosions,* 156–158).

138. By June 1981, Merrill Lynch had purchased almost a quarter of a billion dollars of bonds for plants four and five for unit investment trusts it sponsored, more than 10 percent of all such bonds issued by WPPSS (*SEC Report,* 255).

139. *SEC Report,* 230–232; Pope, *Nuclear Implosions,* 157.

140. *SEC Report,* 285–287.

141. Ibid., 298–299.

142. Ibid., 307, 312.

143. Counsel had doubt that the remaining participants, collectively representing only 4 percent of the total subscription, were legally authorized to enter into the participants' agreements but assumed their shares could be absorbed by other participants, if necessary, through a step-up provision (*SEC Report,* 161, and *NPCC Briefing Book,* 15; see also *SEC Report,* 313). The net-billed plants stood on a different legal footing, having been expressly authorized by legislation (*Public Works for Water, Pollution Control, and Power Development and Atomic Energy Commission Appropriation Bill, 1971; Hearings on Pub. L. No. 91–439 Before the Subcomm. on Public Works of the House Comm. on Appropriations,* 91st Cong., 2d Sess. 867–68 (1970); Pub. L. No. 91–439, 84 Stat. 890 (1970)).

144. Miller, *Energy Northwest,* 331; *SEC Report,* 362–363.

145. *SEC Report,* 117n167.

146. Ibid., 155–164; Pope, *Nuclear Implosions,* 167.

147. Pope, *Nuclear Implosions,* 160–161.

148. Ibid.; Miller, *Energy Northwest*, 327, 345.

149. Pope, *Nuclear Implosions*, 190.

150. Ibid., 163–164, 175; Miller, *Energy Northwest*, 345–350; *NPCC Briefing Book*, 16.

151. *NPCC Briefing Book*, 16. WPPSS, Bonneville, and the banks serving as bond trustees for the net-billed plants succeeded in having a federal district court declare the initiative unconstitutional on impairment-of-contract grounds (Pope, *Nuclear Implosions*, 171–173).

152. Miller, *Energy Northwest*, 341–350, 355, 357; Pope, *Nuclear Implosions*, 170, 174–175.

153. R. L. Tamietti, "Chemical Bank v. WPSS, a Case of Judicial Meltdown," *Natural Resources Lawyer* 17, no. 3 (1984): 377.

154. Pope, *Nuclear Implosions*, 178–179; Anderson, *Illusions of Power*, 133. WPPSS and Bonneville suspended construction at plant one in May 1982 when it was 65 percent complete and plant three in July 1983 when it was 76 percent complete. Bonneville continued to pay the costs of mothballing the plants but finally terminated them in May 1994. Plant two, with 1,216 megawatts of generating capacity, was completed in 1984 and continues to operate (*NPCC Briefing Book*, 17).

155. City of Springfield v. Washington Public Power Supply System, et al., 564 F. Supp. 90 (D. Or. 1983).

156. See, for example, *DeFazio v. WPPSS (Springfield I)*, 296 Or. 550, 679 P.2d 1316 (1984); filed December 22, 1981 (Oregon municipal agencies lack authority under the Oregon constitution or enabling statutes to enter into contracts requiring long-term payments in excess of debt ceilings). Similar cases were filed in Idaho and Wyoming. *Springfield Utility Board v. WPPSS (Springfield III)*, No. 821387 (D. Or., filed November 15, 1982), sought a determination of the validity of the arrangements with respect to the net-billed plants.

157. Chemical Bank v. Washington Public Power Supply System ("Chemical Bank I"), 99 Wash. 2d 772, 666 P. 2d 329 (1983), *aff'd on rehearing*, 102 Wash. 2d 874, 691 P.2d 524 (1984), *cert. denied*, 471 U.S. 1075 (1985). WPPSS, the named defendant, agreed with Chemical Bank and raised no defenses for the participants, several of whom interposed defenses on their own behalf. The decision covered participants that accounted for 68 percent of the potential output of plants four and five. In a second decision, the Washington Supreme Court relieved all participants of their contractual obligations (ibid.).

158. Ibid., 343.

159. 99 Wash. 2d 772, 799.

160. Ibid., 809–810.

161. "Whoops Woes," *Time*, May 31, 1983; Anderson, *Illusions of Power*, 133.

162. *SEC Report*, 272.

163. Alexander, "Whoops! A $2 Billion Blunder."

164. White, *The Organic Machine*, 81.

165. Ibid.

166. In re Washington Public Power Supply Litigation, 650 F. Supp. 1346 (W. D. Wash 1986).

167. Pope, *Nuclear Implosions*, 214–215.

168. Ibid., 235–243.

169. Miller, *Energy Northwest*, 443.

170. Pope, *Nuclear Implosions*, 219.

171. White, *The Organic Machine*, 80; *NPCC Briefing Book*, 17.

172. Pope, *Nuclear Implosions*, 207–208.

173. "Hanford Site Washington, Part III," *Seattle Times*, 1995, http://seattletimes. nwresource.com/special/trinity/articles/part3.html.

174. Steve Weiss, "The Aluminum Lobby," *Oregon's Future*, Spring 2002, 68 et seq.

175. Bennett and DiLorenzo, "The Nation's Largest Municipal Bankruptcy," 1.

176. Anderson, *Illusions of Power*, 135.

177. In fairness to Hodel, it must be noted that he was acting in response to a directive issued by Rogers Morton, then secretary of the interior.

Chapter 4

1. PUHCA (49 Stat. 803, 15 U.S.C. Section 79 et seq.) was enacted at the same time as the Federal Power Act (1935). The two acts were intended to work in tandem. PUHCA addressed and sought to eliminate unfair practices and other abuses by electricity and natural gas holding companies. It imposed federal control and regulation of interstate public utility holding companies. Under PUHCA a holding company is an enterprise that directly or indirectly owns 10 percent or more of the stock in a public utility company. To simplify the structure of holding companies, PUHCA abolished all holding companies more than twice removed from their operating subsidiaries and required the remaining holding companies to register with the Securities and Exchange Commission, which regulated mergers and diversification of those holding companies whose subsidiaries engage in retail distribution. PUHCA required regulatory approval for securities issuances, loans, and intercompany financial transactions and limited the operation of nonexempt holding companies to single, integrated public utility systems and incidental business activities.

2. 16 U.S.C. Sections 824–824k.

3. 273 U.S. 83 (1927).

4. Federal Power Commission v. Southern California Edison et al., 376 U.S. 205 (1964).

5. Section 201(a), 16 U.S.C. Section 796. Wholesale transactions include utility-to-utility coordination sales and requirements sales, in which a utility sells power to a distribution company that cannot itself supply its retail customers.

6. Section 202(b), 16 U.S.C. Section 824i. Part I of the Federal Power Act deals with licensing and related aspects of hydroelectric projects. Part II governs the interstate sale of electric energy, particularly rate regulation and transmission, and authorizes the commission to require interconnections and wholesale service and regulate mergers, the disposition of property, and the purchase or issuance of securities. Part III deals with administrative matters, including accounting and reporting requirements for public utilities (16 U.S.C. Sections 791a-823, 824–824h, 824a, and 825–825u).

7. Douglas Joskow, Frank Bohi, and Peter Gallop, "Regulatory Failure, Regulatory Reform, and Structural Change in the Electrical Power Industry," *Brookings Papers on Economic Activity: Microeconomics* (1989), 134.

8. Dozier DeVane, "Highlights of Legislative History of the Federal Power Act of 1935 and the Natural Gas Act of 1938," *George Washington Law Review* 14 (1989): 35.

9. H.R. 5423, 74th Cong., 1st Sess. (1935); S. 1725, 74th Cong., 1st Sess. (1935). See J. A. Bouknight and David B. Raskin, "Planning for Wholesale Customer Loads in a Competitive Environment: The Obligation to Provide Wholesale Service under the Federal Power Act," *Energy Law Journal* 8 (1987): 239.

10. S. Rep. No. 621, 74th Cong., 1st Sess., 19 (1935).

11. Section 202a(a), 16 U.S.C. Section 824a(a).

12. S. Rep., No. 621, 74th Cong., 1st Sess. (1935), 49.

13. Section 202(b), 16 U.S.C. Section 824a(b). See *City of Paris, Kentucky v. Kentucky Utils. Co.*, 41 F.P.C. 45 (1969) (Federal Power Commission does not have authority to order wheeling under the Federal Power Act).

14. Sections 205(b) and 206(a), 16 U.S.C. Sections 824d(b) and 824e(a).

15. Matthew Cohen, "Efficiency and Competition in the Electric Power Industry," *Yale Law Journal* 88 (1979): 1526.

16. Pub. L. No. 83–703, 68 Stat. 919 (1954).

17. The 1970 Amendments to the Atomic Energy Act, Pub. L. No. 91–560, 84 Stat. 1472 (codified at 42 U.S.C. Section 2132 et seq.).

18. See, for example, Delmarva Power & Light Co., 39 Fed. Reg. 5355, 5356 (1973); James F. Fairman and John C. Scott, "Transmission, Power Pools, and Competition in the Electric Utility Industry," *Hastings Law Journal* 28, no. 1159 (1977): 1181.

19. A primary line is defined as the line transmitting power from the hydroelectric project "to the point of junction with the distributing system or with the interconnected primary transmission system" (16 U.S.C. Section 796(11)). See Montana Power Co. v. FPC, 112 F. 2d 371 (1940); cf. Western Massachusetts Electric Co., 39 F.P.C. 723 (1968), aff'd sub nom Municipal Elec. Ass'n v. FPC, 414 F.2 1206 (D.C. Cir. 1969).

20. Indiana v. Mich. Elec. Co., 33 F.P.C. 739 (1965), aff'd 365 F.2d 180 (7th Cir.), cert. denied 385 U.S. 972 (1966).

21. Federal Power Commission v. Southern California Edison Company et al. City of Colton, California v. Southern California Edison Company et al., 376 U.S. 205 (1964).

22. See Fairman and Scott, "Transmission, Power Pools, and Competition in the Electric Utility Industry," 1192–1200.

23. 16 U.S.C. Section 824a; Fairman and Scott, "Transmission, Power Pools, and Competition in the Electric Utility Industry," 1171. Pooling agreements typically established rates and charges for services interchanged by pool members. Such agreements were filed with the Federal Power Commission as rate schedules under Section 205 of the Federal Power Act and had to survive any challenge under Section 206 that they are "unjust, unreasonable, unduly discriminatory or preferential" (18 U.S.C. Section 824e). The commission's approval of a rate filing confers no antitrust exemption (ibid., 1191).

24. Joskow, Bohi, and Gollop, "Regulatory Failure, Regulatory Reform, and Structural Change," 128–136. "The problem is that the control by one firm of all generating plants and transmission lines in a region would destroy any possibility of competition at the production stage" (Cohen, "Efficiency and Competition in the Electric Power Industry," 1534).

25. T. K. McCraw, *Prophets of Regulation* (Cambridge, MA: Harvard University Press, 1984), 302.

26. Jersey Central Power & Light Co. v. FERC, 810 F.2d 1168, 1189 (D.C. Cir. 1987).

27. Thomas G. Moore, "The Effectiveness of Regulation of Electric Utility Prices," *Southern Economics Journal* 36 (1970): 374.

28. See Andrew N. Kleit and Robert J. Michaels, "Antitrust, Rent-Seeking, and Regulation: The Past and Future of Otter Tail," *Antitrust Bulletin* (Fall 1994): 697–703. Elbow Lake apparently viewed its municipal utility as a taxing device, using low-cost USBR power and tax-exempt financing to provide additional revenue for city government (ibid., 703).

29. Village of Elbow Lake, Minnesota, 40 FPC 1262 (1968); Otter Tail Power Co. v. FPC, 429 F.2d 232 (8th Cir. 1970).

30. Village of Elbow Lake, Minnesota, 46 FPC 675 (1971).

31. United States v. Otter Tail Power Co., 331 F. Supp. 54, 60 (D. Minn. 1971).

32. Ibid. Section 2 of the Sherman Act states that "every person who shall monopolize, or attempt to monopolize, or combine or conspire with any other person or persons, to monopolize any part of the trade or commerce among the several States,

or with foreign nations, shall be deemed guilty of a felony" (5 U.S.C. Section 2). Section 2 claims primarily involve unilateral action by a single entity, such as unilateral refusals to deal.

33. Otter Tail Power Co. v. United States, 410 U.S. 366 (1973).

34. Kleit and Michaels, "Antitrust, Rent-Seeking, and Regulation," 707.

35. The Supreme Court has never used the phrase "essential facility." Nonetheless, *Otter Tail, United States v. Terminal Railroad Ass'n,* 224 U.S. 383 (1912), *United States v. Associated Press,* 326 U.S. 1 (1945), and *Aspen Skiing Co. v. Aspen Highlands Skiing Corp.,* 472 U.S. 585 (1985), are often cited as foundational cases in support of the essential facilities doctrine. See Sandeep Vaheesan, "Reviving an Epithet: A New Way Forward for the Essential Facilities Doctrine," *Utah Law Review* no. 3 (2010): 911 et seq.

36. Otter Tail Power Co. v. United States, 410 U.S. 366 (1973). See John H. Shenefield, "Annual Survey of Antitrust Developments—The Year of the Regulated Industry," *Washington and Lee Law Review* 31 (Spring 1974): 1 et seq.

37. Ibid., 382.

38. Phillip Areeda, "Essential Facilities: An Epithet in Need of Limiting Principles," *Antitrust Law Journal* 58 (1989): 841.

39. Herbert Hovenkamp, *Federal Antitrust Policy: The Law of Competition and Its Practice,* 2nd ed. (St. Paul, MN: West, 1999), 305.

40. See Joseph R. Coker, "Saving Otter Tail: The Essential Facilities Doctrine and Electric Power Post-Trinko," *Florida State University Law Review* 33 (2005): 248.

41. George Stigler, "The Theory of Economic Regulation," *Bell Journal of Economics and Management Science* 2 (1971): 5.

42. Federal Power Commission v. Conway, 426 U.S. 271, 274 (1976).

43. Ibid., 278.

44. Quoted in Richard F. Hirsh, *Power Loss: The Origins of Deregulation and Restructuring in the American Utility System* (Cambridge, MA: MIT Press 1999), 61.

45. Ibid., 61–62.

46. Quoted in Julia Richardson and Robert Nordhaus, "The National Energy Act of 1978," *National Resources & Environment* 10 (Summer 1995): 62.

47. The Natural Gas Policy Act, Pub. Law No. 95–621, 92 Stat. 3350 (1978); the Public Utility Regulatory Policies Act, Pub. Law No. 95–617, 92 Stat. 3117 (1978); the Energy Tax Act, Pub. Law No. 95–618, 92 Stat. 3174 (1978); the Powerplant and Industrial Fuel Use Act, Pub. Law No. 95–620, 92 Stat. 3289 (1978); and the National Energy Conservation Policy Act, Pub. Law No. 95–619, 92 Stat. 3206 (1978).

48. Hirsh, "Power Loss," 77–78.

49. National Energy Act, House Comm. on Interstate and Foreign Commerce, H. R. Rep. No. 496, 95th Cong., 1st Sess. 13 (1977).

50. See Richardson and Nordhaus, "The National Energy Act of 1978," 66.

51. Some large industrial customers in power-intensive businesses such as pulp and paper installed their own generating systems or cogenerated to use heat from industrial processes to produce electricity. Power generated by a third-party contractor represented a logical progression.

52. Hirsh, "Power Loss," 83–86.

53. PURPA, Section 210(d). The section also applied to small power production— that is, plants of a specified size that produced electricity using biomass waste or other renewable resources.

54. Hirsh, "Power Loss," 86.

55. PURPA, Section 210, provides for interconnection and coordination services "upon application of any electric utility, Federal power marketing agency, geothermal power producer ... , qualifying cogenerator, or qualifying small power producer" (16 U.S.C. 824(i)(a)(1)). FERC's implementing regulations modified the requirement of an application and merely stated that electric utilities shall make such interconnections "as may be necessary" (18 C.F.R. Section 292.303(c)). As a practical matter, the ability of a QF to obtain an interconnection is subject to technical, operational, and reliability limitations.

56. Hirsh, "Power Loss," 87.

57. FERC v. Mississippi, 456 U.S. 742 (1982), and American Paper Institute, Inc. v. American Electric Power Service Corp., 461 U.S.742 (1983). See Hirsh, "Power Loss," 89–93; Richardson and Nordhaus, "The National Energy Act of 1978," 66.

58. Richardson and Nordhaus, "The National Energy Act of 1978," 66.

59. Quoted in Peter S. Fox-Penner, "Cogeneration after PURPA: Energy Conservation and Industry Structure," *Journal of Law and Economics* 33, no. 2 (October 1990): 520. According to Senator Percy, the new technologies included small-scale hydroelectric dams, cogeneration of industrial process steam and electricity, wind, and solar power (ibid.). Other observers were more skeptical about the intrinsic economic efficiency of cogeneration. See Paul Joskow and Donald R. Jones, "The Simple Economics of Industrial Cogeneration," *Energy Journal* 4 (January 1983): 1–22.

60. See, for example, Paul L. Joskow, "Long-Term Vertical Relationships and the Study of Industrial Organization and Government Regulation," *Journal of Institutional and Theoretical Economics* (December 1985): 587–593.

61. See, for instance, Paul L. Joskow, "Deregulation and Regulatory Reform in the U.S. Electric Power Industry," Center for Energy and Environmental Policy Research, 00–003 WP, February 2000, 14 ("The average cost-based regulatory system in the U.S. had a built in predisposition to lead to prices that are poorly aligned with the relevant marginal costs"); see also Bernard S. Black and Richard J. Pierce, "The Choice between Markets and Central Planning in Regulating the U.S. Electricity Industry," *Columbia Law Review* 93, no. 6 (October 1993): 1344–1345.

62. Harry M. Trebing, "Public Utility Regulation: A Case Study in the Debate over Effectiveness of Economic Regulation," *Journal of Economic Issues* 18 (March 1984): 228.

63. McCraw, *Prophets of Regulation* (1984), 253–255. Time-of-day rates penalized summer peak users and rewarded off-peak consumers. Long Island Lighting Company (LILCO) became the first utility to file under Kahn's marginal-cost rate plan. Its industrial customers installed meters that recorded usage by time of day, and time-of-day rates eventually applied to many other customers as well. The price spread between peak and off-peak rates reached a ratio of twelve to one. The LILCO case proved to be a landmark in the history of regulation in the United States (ibid.).

64. Quoted in Nicholas Wapshott, *Keynes Hayek* (New York: Norton, 2011), 252.

65. Richard J. Pierce, "A Proposal to Deregulate the Market for Bulk Power," *Virginia Law Review* 72 (1986): 1183–1184.

66. Paul L. Joskow and Richard L. Schmalensee, *Markets for Power: An Analysis of Electric Utility Deregulation*, The MIT Press (1983).

67. Ibid., 7.

68. Ibid., 23. Other aspects of potential competition under prevailing institutional arrangements include competition among utilities for large industrial customers considering alternative locations for new plants; competition among utilities to serve new areas not previously wired; competition between existing franchise holders and potentially competing enterprises at the time a franchise period expires; and yardstick competition enabling regulatory agencies to compare the performance of similar utilities nationwide (ibid., 20–22).

69. Ibid., 63.

70. Ibid., 23.

71. Ibid., 4, 65.

72. Scenario One contemplated the complete deregulation of all price and entry limitations, including those at the retail level, while leaving the utility industry structure intact (as had recently occurred in the airline, trucking, and railroad industries). Scenario Two proposed deregulation of wholesale transactions without any change in industry structure save for removal of transmission bottlenecks. Without monopolistic constraints on transmission access, the authors envisioned a competitive market for bulk power supplies without any forced restructuring of the industry. Under Scenario Three investor-owned utilities would divest their distribution arms but retain generation and transmission (G & T) assets. Operating as wholesale power companies, they would sell electricity to newly independent distribution companies—regulated as local franchised monopolies—on the spot market or through long-term power agreements. Independent generating companies would compete freely in selling power at wholesale. To support restructuring, FERC would encourage formation of regional power pools with central dispatch of generators.

73. See, generally, ibid., 97–105.

74. Quoted in M. Newman, "Paul Joskow: Accent on Economic Efficiency," *EPRI Journal* (October 1983): 24.

75. Ibid., 113.

76. Ibid., 114.

77. Paul L. Joskow, "Deregulation," white paper that became the *2009 Distinguished Lecture* sponsored by the AEI Center for Regulatory and Market Studies, February 10, 2009.

78. Smithsonian Institute, "Powering a Generation of Change," interview with William T. McCormick Jr., CEO of CMS Energy, June 18, 1997.

79. Paul L. Joskow, "Lessons Learned from Electricity Market Liberalization," *Energy Journal* (2008): 22. http://economics.mit.edu/files/2093.

80. Paul L. Joskow, "Deregulation and Regulatory Reform in the U.S. Electric Power Sector," in S. Peltzman and Clifford Winston, eds., *Deregulation of Network Industries: The Next Steps* (Washington, DC: Brookings Institution Press, 2000), 17.

81. Paul L. Joskow, "Challenges for Creating a Comprehensive National Electricity Policy," white paper, Technology Policy Institute, September 26, 2008, 4, http://economics.mit.edu/files/3236.

82. See, for example, Bluefield Water Works & Improvement Co. v. Public Serv. Comm'n, 262 U.S. 679 (1923); Western Union Tel. Co. v. Call Publishing Co., 181 U.S. 92 (1901); Smyth v. Ames, 169 U.S. 466 (1898); and Munn v. Illinois, 94 U.S. 113 (1876).

83. See *FPC v. Natural Gas Pipeline Co.*, 315 U.S. 575, 585–86 (1942) (construing nearly identical provisions of the Natural Gas Act); *Hope Natural Gas Co.*, 320 U.S. 591 (1944).

84. John Wyeth Griggs, "Competitive Bidding and Independent Power Producers: Is Deregulation Coming to the Electric Utility Industry?," *Energy Law Journal* 9 (1988): 429.

85. Farmers Union Central Exchange, Inc. v. FERC, 734 F.2d 1486. 1502 (D.C. Cir. 1984), cert. denied 469 U.S. 1034 (1984).

86. Notice of Inquiry, Regulation of Electricity Sales-for-Resale and Transmission Service (Phase I), IV F.E.R.C. Stats & Regs Para. 35,518, 50 Fed. Reg. 23,445 (1985).

87. Ibid., 23, 449. Coordination transactions encompass short-term purchases and sales of electricity by interconnected integrated utilities to make possible the economical use of generating plants owned by proximate utilities and to ensure reliability. Utilities traditionally owned sufficient generating capacity to meet their loads and relied on short-term coordination transactions to ensure economical and reliable joint operation of these facilities. (See Paul L. Joskow, "Regulatory Failure, Regulatory Reform, and Structural Change in the Electric Power Industry," white paper, *Brookings Papers: Microeconomics*, 1989, 131; Office of Economic Policy, "Regulating Independent Power Producers: A Policy Analysis," Federal Energy Regulatory Commission, October 13, 1987, 4–5; Wilbur C. Earley, "FERC Regulation of Bulk

Power Coordination Transactions," working paper, Federal Energy Regulatory Commission, July 1984; Federal Energy Regulatory Commission, Notice of Inquiry Re Regulation of Electricity Sales-for-Resale and Transmission Service, 31 FERC 61,376 (1985).)

88. Notice of Inquiry, Regulation of Electricity Sales-for-Resale and Transmission Service (Phase I, IV F.E.R.C. Stats & Regs Para. 35,519, 50 Fed. Reg. 27,604 (1985). FERC sets wholesale rates using embedded cost-of-service ratemaking principles similar to those the states use to set retail rates. An allocation of accounting costs between FERC and retail jurisdictions is made based on the characteristics of their respective loads on the system, including peak load, voltage at which power is taken, and load factor. A depreciated original-cost rate base, nominal cost of capital, and straight-line depreciation are used to determine capital costs. Fuel and nonfuel operation and maintenance costs, taxes, and so forth are added in much the same way as they are at the retail level (Joskow, "Regulatory Failure, Regulatory Reform, and Structural Change in the Electric Power Industry," 138–139).

89. Ibid., 132.

90. It was not clear whether PURPA and FERC's rules established avoided cost as a ceiling, a floor, or the exact amount utilities must pay. FERC's initial rules were challenged because they appeared to require that utilities pay prices equal to their avoided costs. In *American Paper Institute v. AEP*, 461 U.S. 402 (1983), the Supreme Court held that FERC had the authority to require payments up to the buying utility's avoided cost. However, the original rules anticipated that QFs and utilities would negotiate individual contracts with avoided cost available as regulatory leverage if a mutually satisfactory contract could not be negotiated.

91. Griggs, "Competitive Bidding and Independent Power Producers," 430–431.

92. Opinion No. 203, Public Serv. Co. of N.M., 25 F.E.R.C. Para. 61,469 (1983).

93. Notice of Proposed Rulemaking, *Administrative Determination of Full Avoided Costs, Sales of Power to Qualifying Facilities*, IV F.E.R.C. Stats. & Regs. Para. 32,457, 53 Fed. Reg. 9331 (1988); Notice of Proposed Rulemaking, *Regulating Government Bidding Programs*, IV F.E.R.C. Stats. & Regs. Para. 32,455, 53 Fed. Reg. 9324 (1988); Notice of Proposed Rulemaking, *Regulations Governing Independent Power Producers*, IV F.E.R.C. Stats. & Regs. Para. 34,456, 53 Fed. Reg. 9327 (1988).

94. Griggs, "Competitive Bidding and Independent Power Producers," 451–457.

95. Opinion of Commissioner Charles A. Trabandt, Concurring in Part and Dissenting in Part, IV F.E.R.C. Stats. & Regs. Para. 32,455 (1988), 32,084.

96. Joskow, "Regulatory Failure, Regulatory Reform, and Structural Change in the Electric Power Industry," 190.

97. Ibid.

98. Ibid.

99. Ibid., 195.

100. Ibid., 194. See also Paul L. Joskow and Richard Schmalensee, *Markets for Power* (Cambridge, MA: MIT Press, 1983), 114.

101. Fred C. Schweppe, Michael C. Caramanis, Richard D. Tabors, and Roger E. Bohn, *Spot Pricing of Electricity* (Boston: Kluwer, 1988).

102. See, for example, William W. Hogan, "Contract Networks for Electric Power Transmission: Technical Reference," *Journal of Regulatory Economics* 4, no. 3 (September 1, 1992): 211–242; William W. Hogan, "A Competitive Electricity Market Model," white paper prepared for the Harvard Electricity Policy Group, October 9, 1993; William W. Hogan, "Coordination for Competition in an Electricity Market," *Response to an Inquiry Concerning Alternative Power Pooling Institutions under the Federal Power Act*, Federal Energy Regulatory Commission, Docket No. RM94–20–000, March 2, 1995.

103. Schweppe et al., *Spot Pricing of Electricity*, 274.

104. Hogan, "Contract Networks for Electric Power Transmission: Technical Reference."

105. Ibid. A second major source of congestion in a power network arises from voltage magnitude constraints at buses that define operating limitations on the amount of power flowing on transmission lines.

106. Ibid., 240.

107. Ibid., 242.

108. Public Law 102–486, 106 Stat. 2776, 2905–21 (1992); 42 U.S.C.A. Sections 13,201–556 (1993).

109. Section 723 of the act requires that, in order to request transmission service, a wholesale electric generator must make a good-faith request to a transmitting utility to provide wholesale transmission service at a specific rate, subject to specific terms

and conditions. The transmitting utility must then either provide the requested transmission service at rates, terms, and conditions acceptable to the applicant or provide the applicant, within sixty days of receipt of the transmission request (or other mutually agreed-on period), with a detailed explanation of why such transmission service cannot take place. The detailed written explanation must contain specific reference to the facts and circumstances of the request, specifying (1) the transmitting utility's basis for the proposed rates, terms, and conditions for the proposed service, and (2) the utility's analysis of any physical or other constraints affecting the requested transmission service. The applicant may then use this information to seek an order from FERC mandating transmission access and service. Section 721 of the act eliminated a major impediment to FERC's authority to mandate wheeling by abolishing Section 211(c)(1) of the Federal Power Act, which prohibited FERC from issuing a transmission order unless it determined that the order would reasonably preserve existing competitive relationships between wholesale suppliers and their customers. FERC interpreted this provision narrowly.

110. Joskow distinguishes the portfolio manager model from the customer choice model. In the portfolio manager model the local distribution utility retains its traditional obligation to supply customers within its de facto exclusive franchise areas with bundled retail electricity service. But it relies on competitive procurement mechanisms to buy electricity from the lowest-cost suppliers in the competitive wholesale markets, rather than building new generating facilities to serve growing demand in its franchise area. The price for the electricity received by retail consumers continues to be regulated since they must buy their electricity from the local monopoly distributor, but regulation of the generation cost component of the retail price is based on market prices. The customer choice model allows retail customers to access the wholesale market directly by purchasing unbundled distribution and transmission access from their local utility. Individual consumers assume the obligation to arrange for their own generation service supplies with independent competing energy suppliers (Paul L. Joskow, "Restructuring, Competition, and Regulatory Reform in the U.S. Electricity Sector," *Journal of Economic Perspectives* 11 (Summer 1997): 127–128).

111. Henson Moore, quoted in Hirsh, "Power Loss," 241.

112. Joseph Paquette, quoted in Hirsh, 245.

113. Ibid., 245–246.

114. Richard Cudahy, "Retail Wheeling: Is This Revolution Necessary?," *Energy Law Journal* 15 (1994): 358. See also Robert J. Michaels, "Vertical Integration and the Restructuring of the U.S. Electricity Industry," white paper, Department of Economics, California State University, September 2004.

115. Ibid., 357.

116. Joskow and Schmalensee, *Markets for Power*, 213–214.

117. Joskow, "Deregulation and Regulatory Reform in the U.S. Electric Power Sector," 24.

118. Ibid., 25–26.

119. *Policy Statement,* RM93–3-000, July 30, 1993.

120. Joskow and Schmalensee, *Markets for Power*, 67. The New York Power Pool and Pennsylvania–New Jersey–Maryland Pool are tight pools.

121. Ibid., 200.

122. Joskow, "Deregulation and Regulatory Reform in the U.S. Electric Power Sector," 41.

123. Carl Blumstein, Lee S. Friedman, and Richard Green, "The History of Electricity Restructuring in California," Center for Study of Energy Markets Working Paper, University of California Energy Institute, August 2002, 4–5.

124. Hirsh, "Power Loss," 249–252.

125. Quoted in ibid., 252.

126. The Central Electricity Generation Board (CEGB) was the cornerstone of the British electricity industry from 1957 to privatization in the 1990s. Under the nationalized regime, the CEGB was responsible for electricity generation in England and Wales. Its purpose was to develop and maintain an efficient, coordinated, and economical system of bulk electricity supply. At the center of the CEGB's infrastructure was the National Control Room of the National Grid located in London, where engineers would cost, schedule, and dispatch generation to the main interconnected system based on information about the running costs and availability of every power-producing plant in England and Wales. The National Control Room would constantly anticipate demand, monitor and instruct the power stations to produce or reduce electricity production, or to stop producing electricity altogether using merit-order dispatch that ranked each generator based on its cost to produce electricity with a view to ensuring that electricity production was always achieved at the lowest possible cost. The present electricity market in Great Britain emerged from reorganization of the CEGB into four separate companies in the 1990s. Its generation activities were transferred to three generating companies—PowerGen, National

Power, and Nuclear Electric (later British Energy, eventually EDF Energy)—and its transmission activities to the National Grid Company. Twelve Area Boards, which controlled the state-owned distribution systems in England and Wales, were also privatized as part of industry restructuring and, together with the National Grid, made subject to regulation by the new Office of Electricity Regulation, subsequently folded into the Office of Gas and Electricity Markets. On privatization, distribution services were unbundled from generation supplied to retail customers, who were served by independent separate retail suppliers or "ring-fenced" affiliates of the distribution companies.

127. Hirsh, *Power Loss*, 252–256; Blumstein et al., "The History of Electricity Restructuring in California," 7.

128. Blumstein et al., ibid., 7–9; Hirsh, *Power Loss*, 257–258. The independent system operator would determine marginal cost pricing, differentiated by location and time, for all uses of the transmission system. It would take no position in the market or have any economic interest in any load or generation. Its coordination function would be short-term including day-ahead scheduling and hourly redispatch to make sure the system is in balance. It would also administer a system of tradable transmission contracts (Blumstein et al.,ibid., 10).

129. Blumstein et al., ibid., 10.

130. Notes from Paul Joskow to the author.

131. Quoted in Hirsh, *Power Loss*, 259.

132. Joskow and Schmalensee, *Markets for Power*, 133; also interview with Paul L. Joskow (transcript), February 1, 2013, 14–15.

133. Joskow, "Deregulation and Regulatory Reform in the U.S. Electric Power Sector," 27.

134. An applicant for a FERC order under Section 211 of the Federal Power Act had to make a good-faith request for transmission services at least sixty days prior to its application to the FERC; and transmitting utilities had to provide a good-faith reply within sixty days of receipt of the request. To determine compliance, FERC considered whether the parties had met, exchanged points of view, and provided the information requested. FERC then determined the required amount and detail of exchanged information by examining how much information a utility needed and whether a utility had used the information already provided. Mere disagreement with the other party's position was not reason to find a bad-faith request or reply. By 1995 FERC had not uncovered a single bad-faith reply

("Committee Report—Electric Utility Regulation," *Energy Law Journal* 16 (Spring 1995): 529).

135. Peter Fox-Penner, *Electric Utility Restructuring* (Vienna, VA: Electric Utility Reports, 1998), 168. See also *Promoting Wholesale Generation through Open-Access Non-Discriminatory Transmission Services by Public Utilities,* Final Rule, Order No. 888 (Ferc Stats. & Regs., Regs. Preambles, 1991–1996), para. 31,036 at 31,634 (1996), *Order on reh'g,* Order No. 888-A [Regs. Preambles], III FERC Stats. & Regs. Para. 31,048 at 30,226 (1997). Final Rule issued April 24, 1999; 75 FERC para. 61,080.

136. Peter Fox-Penner, ibid., 168.

137. Order 888 specifies the types of transmission services that must be made available, the maximum cost-based prices that can be charged for those services, the definition of available transmission capacity and how it should be allocated when there is excess demand, and the specification of ancillary services that transmission owners must provide and associated prices. The tariff was required to offer at a minimum traditional point-to-point and network transmission service. FERC ordered access pursuant to its authority over public utilities under Sections 205 and 206 of the Federal Power Act, not its authority to order case-by-case transmission under Sections 211 and 212. As a result, the open-access requirement did not directly apply to nonpublic utilities such as municipalities, most cooperatives, and federal power marketing agencies such as Bonneville Power Administration. The tariff was nonetheless accessible by any person eligible to seek a Section 211 transmission order, including any investor-owned utility, municipality, cooperative, independent power producer, affiliated power producer, qualifying facility, or power marketer. See Jeremiah D. Lambert, *Creating Competitive Power Markets: The PJM Model* (Tulsa, OK: PennWell, 2001), 7.

138. Quoted in Fox-Penner, *Electric Utility Restructuring*, 168.

139. Joskow, "Deregulation and Regulatory Reform in the U.S. Electric Power Sector," 32.

140. Order No. 888, 75 FERC para. 61,080; mimeo, 268.

141. Ibid.; Lambert, *Creating Competitive Power Markets*, 10.

142. Joskow and Schmalensee, *Markets for Power*, 200.

143. Order No. 888, 75 FERC para. 61,080; mimeo, 279–288.

144. Ibid., 283–284.

145. Joskow and Schmalensee, *Market for Power*, 114.

146. Lambert, op. cit., 21–36. The constituent utilities of PJM were BG&E, four GPU operating subsidiaries, PSE&G, PECO, and PP&L.

147. Ibid., 37–45.

148. Federal Energy Regulatory Commission, Inquiry Concerning Alternative Power Pooling Institutions under the Federal Power Act, Docket No. RM94–20–000 (October 4, 1994), 5–7.

149. The day-ahead market is a forward market in which hourly locational marginal pricing values are calculated for each hour of the next operating day based on generation offers, demand bids, and bilateral transaction schedules submitted by participants. The day-ahead market provides financial incentives for generators, retailers, and transmission customers to submit day-ahead schedules that match their actual expectations for the operating day. The day-ahead schedule uses least-cost, security-constrained unit commitment and security-constrained economic dispatch programs. Day-ahead scheduling incorporates PJM reliability requirements and reserve obligations. The resulting hourly schedules and locational marginal prices represent binding financial commitments of market participants. Day-ahead settlement is based on day-ahead hourly locational marginal pricing values. For each hour of the day-ahead schedule, (1) each scheduled demand participant pays its locational market price for the hour, (2) each scheduled generator is paid its locational marginal price for the hour, (3) scheduled transmission customers pay congestion charges based on locational marginal price differences between source and sink, and (4) fixed transmission rights holders receive congestion credits based on hourly day-ahead locational marginal pricing values (Lambert, *Creating Competitive Power Markets*, 131).

150. Atlantic City Electric Company et al., 77 FERC para. 61,148 (1996).

151. In *Atlantic City Electric Co. v. FERC*, 295 F. 3d 1 (D.C. Cir. 2002) (*"Atlantic City"*), the D.C. Circuit Court of Appeals vacated and remanded certain aspects of FERC's orders issued in connection with PJM's formation as an ISO in 1997. The court found that FERC had exceeded its jurisdiction by requiring PJM's transmission owners to relinquish their Section 205 [FPA] filing rights to PJM and obtain FERC approval under Section 203 prior to withdrawing as PJM members. On remand, in its Order Granting in Part and Denying in Part Rehearing and Accepting Compliance Filing ("Order on Rehearing") issued May 14, 2003, in Docket Nos. OA 97–261–004 et al., 103 FERC ¶ 61,170, FERC nonetheless reaffirmed PJM's right to make its own Section 205 filings in addition to a veto right proposed by the transmission owners, "thus insuring continued independent operation of the PJM grid

and avoiding undue discrimination or preference." In support, FERC cited its regulations that an RTO must have "independent authority under Section 205 of the [FPA] to propose rates, terms and conditions of transmission service provided over the facilities it operates" (18 C.F. R. § 35.34(j)(1)(iii)). On May 20, 2003, the court granted a petition to enforce its mandate, rejected FERC's assertion of authority "to revisit the prospective balance of § 205 rights and responsibilities," and directed FERC to vacate relevant portions of its Order on Rehearing (*Atlantic City II*, 2003 WL 21145942, at *2). See also Petition for Rehearing filed at FERC by PJM's transmission owners on June 13, 2003 (transmission owners have "unfettered right" to initiate Section 205 rate filings with respect to their jurisdictional facilities, and PJM has "no independent right" to do so, "except to the extent that the TOs have ceded that right to PJM") and PECO Energy Company's Request for Rehearing, also filed on June 13, 2003 (PECO has not acquiesced in PJM's veto rights with respect to PECO's Section 205 filings; nor may FERC "compromise and diminish PECO's Section 205 rights ... by granting competing rights to a third party [PJM] ... for service over PECO's facilities"). Although the D.C. Circuit Court in *Atlantic City II* acknowledged that an RTO may have certain Section 205 rights, the scope of PJM's independent right to file transmission tariffs pursuant to Section 205 remained uncertain. PJM and the transmission owners ultimately entered into a settlement agreement allocating their respective Section 205 rights and confirming the transmission owners' unilateral rights to withdraw from PJM without FERC approval (Pennsylvania–New Jersey–Maryland Interconnection, 105 FERC ¶ 61,294 (2003)).

152. When the transmission system is constrained, PJM collects more money from buyers of energy and transmission than it pays to energy sellers. This congestion rent arises because, during a period of constraint, all loads in transmission-constrained areas pay the higher market-clearing price, but generators supplying part of the flows into the transmission-constrained area are paid the lower market-clearing prices prevailing there. As a result, PJM takes in more money than it pays out. Each unit of energy transferred to the constrained area causes PJM to collect, in the form of congestion payments, the difference between the locational marginal price where energy is consumed and where it is injected. Transmission service customers acquiring network or firm point-to-point service pay the embedded cost of the system, including congestion costs for their actual use. In return, such customers acquire FTRs corresponding to the points of delivery and receipt for which firm transmission has been obtained. Each FTR entitles the holder to payment of congestion credits associated with FTR receipt and delivery points. FTRs are therefore a financial mechanism for distributing (or assigning ownership to) the congestion credits that PJM collects— that is, a contract that entitles the holder to a stream of revenues (or charges) based on the reservation level and hourly energy prices across a specified transmission path (Lambert, *Creating Competitive Power Markets*, 113–119).

153. Pennsylvania–New Jersey–Maryland Interconnection et al., 81 FERC para. 61,257 (1997).

154. PJM Interconnection L.L.C., 96 FERC para. 61,061 (July 12, 2001), received official approval as a regional transmission organization in December 2002.

155. Hunt Allcott, "Real-Time Pricing and Electricity Market Design," white paper, New York University, August 26, 2012, 6.

156. Other regional transmission organizations include the New York ISO, ISO New England, the Midwest ISO, and the Southwest Power Pool (Seth Blumsack, "Measuring the Benefits and Costs of Regional Electric Grid Integration," *Electricity Law Journal* 28, no. 1 (2007): 155).

157. Paul Joskow, "Markets for Power in the United States: An Interim Assessment," *Energy Law Journal* 27 (2006): 32–33.

158. Paul Joskow and Roger Noll, "Alfred E. Kahn, 1917–2010," white paper, MIT, 2010, 2, http://economics.mit.edu/files/8546.

159. Joskow, "Challenges for Creating a Comprehensive National Electricity Policy," 8.

160. Joskow and Schmalensee, *Markets for Power*, 216.

161. Joskow and Schmalensee, *Markets for Power*, 194.

162. Joskow, "Lessons Learned from Electricity Market Liberalization.

163. Ibid.

164. Joskow, "Markets for Power in the United States," 3.

165. Ibid., 33.

166. Joskow, "Challenges for Creating a Comprehensive National Electricity Policy," 17.

167. Ibid., 22.

Chapter 5

1. Quoted in Thomas Frank, "The Age of Enron," http://tcfrank.com/essays/The__Age__of Enron.

2. Sean Wilentz, "A Scandal for Our Time," January 31, 2002, http://prospect.org//article/scandal-our-time.

3. Jeffrey A. Sonnenfeld, Yale School of Management, quoted in Anthony Bianco, "Commentary: Ken Lay's Audacious Ignorance," *Bloomberg Business Week*, February 5, 2006.

4. Marie Brenner, "The Enron Wars," *Vanity Fair*, April 2002.

5. Bethany McLean and Peter Elkind, *The Smartest Guys in the Room* (New York: Portfolio, 2004), 4; Gary McWilliams, "The Quiet Man Who's Jolting Utilities," *Business Week*, June 9, 1997.

6. McLean and Elkind, ibid., 5.

7. In the Natural Gas Act of 1938 (NGA), Congress instructed the Federal Power Commission (FPC) to regulate interstate pipelines as if they were utilities. Congress prohibited the FPC from requiring any pipeline to transport gas for a third party. This policy decision enabled interstate pipelines to use their monopoly power over gas transportation to create and maintain monopsony power in the market for the purchase of gas at the wellhead and monopoly power in the market for the sale of gas to local distribution companies (LDCs).

In the landmark case of Phillips Petroleum Co. v. Wisconsin, 347 U.S. 672 (1954), the Supreme Court required the FPC to regulate the price of natural gas sold by independent gas producers in interstate commerce. Between 1954 and 1960, the FPC attempted to set a maximum rate applicable to sales made by each producer and later established rates applicable to all gas produced in each producing area based on average historic cost. Price controls reduced the rate of exploration and the inventory of gas supplies available to the interstate market. Eventually, supplies could not meet demand, and interstate pipelines began to reduce their deliveries to LDCs. Phillips created a bifurcated natural gas market. The federal government regulated the price of natural gas destined for the interstate market, while the states left the intrastate market unregulated. In the late 1960s, when natural gas first became less abundant and demand increased, its price rose. In the interstate market, however, regulation kept the price of natural gas artificially low. As a result, the intrastate market experienced a surplus, the interstate market a shortage.

In response Congress enacted the Natural Gas Policy Act of 1978 (NGPA) and instructed the Federal Energy Regulatory Commission (FERC), the FPC's successor, to implement a new regulatory regime applicable to the gas industry. The NGPA divided gas supplies into different categories, each subject to different rules and statutory price ceilings. The NGPA assumed that market forces were relatively weak and that the quantity of gas demanded and supplied would change slowly in response to changes in the price of gas. It contemplated that deregulation would take place gradually over a period of many years, with most gas subject to constantly increasing statutory price ceilings for a decade or more. Congress expected the statutory ceiling prices to remain below the market price of gas for the entire period in which the NGPA authorized gradual replacement of ceiling prices with prices determined by market forces. Congress also expected the shortage to persist for many years.

Instead, as the ceiling prices of gas increased, the quantity of gas demanded fell, the quantity of gas supplied rose, and the market price of gas declined well below statutory ceiling prices. Pipelines meanwhile had entered into thousands of long-term contracts to purchase large volumes of gas at high ceiling prices established by the NGPA. Because the NGA insulated pipelines from competition for the sale of gas, they were at first indifferent to the risk of contracting to buy gas at prices above those that would prevail in a competitive market. The flawed assumptions on which the NGPA was based soon became apparent. The NGA and the NGPA combined to create a gas surplus priced far in excess of unregulated market prices. Pipelines could not sell high-priced gas they had agreed to purchase. The market imbalance remained for years. (See Richard J. Pierce, "The Evolution of Natural Gas Policy," Natural Resources and Environment 10, no. 1 (Summer 1995): 53–55.)

8. Robert L. Bradley, *Edison to Enron* (Hoboken, NJ: Wiley, 2011), 291–294; McLean and Elkind, *The Smartest Guys in the Room*, 5–6; Mimi Swartz and Sherrin Watkins, *Power Failure: The Inside Story of the Collapse of Enron* (New York: Doubleday, 2003), 24.

9. Bradley, ibid., 295; McLean and Elkind, ibid., 6–7.

10. Quoted in Bradley, ibid, 304.

11. Quoted in ibid., 303.

12. Ibid., 306–312; Swartz and Watkins, *Power Failure*, 25–26; McLean and Elkind, *The Smartest Guys in the Room*, 7–8.

13. Bradley, *Edison to Enron*, 335.

14. Loren Fox, *Enron: The Rise and Fall* (Hoboken, NJ: Wiley, 2003), 10.

15. As restructured by the NGPA, pipelines no longer owned all the gas transported. Instead, customers could deal directly with gas producers, bargain for the best price, and ship the gas through open-access pipelines to destinations where it was most in demand. Pipeline rates remained regulated, reflecting the natural monopoly power of the transportation and distribution system (Jacqueline Lang Weaver, "Can Energy Markets Be Trusted?," *Houston Business and Tax Law Journal* 4 (2004): 8–9).

16. Bradley, *Edison to Enron*, 332.

17. Transcontinental Gas Pipe Line Corporation, Docket No. RP83–11–000, 23 FERC Para. 61,199 (April 28, 1983).

18. On November 10, 1983, FERC approved an amendment to the rate settlement in Transco's Docket No. RP83–11, extending the ISP program through March 11, 1984.

19. Quoted in McLean and Elkind, *The Smartest Guys in the Room*, 9. See Bradley, *Edison to Enron*, 338–340, 348.

20. Bradley, ibid., 349.

21. Bradley, ibid., 464–478; McLean and Elkind, *The Smartest Guys in the Room*, 9–10; Swartz and Watkins, *Power Failure*, 28.

22. Kenneth N. Gilpin, "Business People; HNG/Internorth Loses Top Official," *New York Times*, November 13, 1985.

23. McLean and Elkind, *The Smartest Guys in the Room*, 11–12; Swartz and Watkins, *Power Failure*, 29.

24. Christopher Bartlett and Meg Wozny, "Enron's Transformation: From Gas Pipeline to New Economy Powerhouse," *Harvard Business School Case N9–301–064*, January 5, 2001, 2.

25. John Crudele, "Enron Buys Back Its Stock," *New York Times*, October 21, 1986, D1.

26. Julian E. Barnes, Megan Barnett, and Christopher Schmitt, "How a Titan Came Undone," *U.S. News and World Report*, March 10, 2002; McLean and Elkind, *The Smartest Guys in the Room*, 13–14; Swartz and Watkins, *Power Failure*, 30–31.

27. Order No. 436, FERC Stats. & Regs. (CCH) Para. 30,665 (1985); Order No. 436-A, FERC Stats. & Regs. (CCH) Para. 30,685 (1986). While FERC Order No. 436 made the unbundling of pipeline services possible, transportation-only services by pipelines remained only voluntary. FERC Order No. 636 made pipeline unbundling a requirement (FERC Stats. & Regs (CCH) Para. 30,939 (1992); Order No. 636-A, FERC Stats. & Regs. (CCH) Para. 30950 (1992)). The order required pipelines to separate their transportation and sales services, enabling all pipeline customers to select gas sales, transportation, and storage services from any provider in any quantity. Under Order No. 636 pipelines could no longer engage in merchant gas sales or sell any product as a bundled service. The order mandated restructuring of the interstate pipeline industry. The production and marketing arms of interstate pipeline companies became

independent affiliates that could no longer maintain an advantage (in terms of price, volume, or timing of gas transportation) over any other potential user of the pipeline.

28. Weaver, "Can Energy Markets Be Trusted?," 8–11; Michael Doane and Daniel Spulber, "Open Access and the Evolution of the U.S. Spot Market for Natural Gas," *Journal of Law and Economics* 37 (October 1994): 484.

29. Natural Gas Wellhead Decontrol Act of 1989, Pub. Law No. 101–60, 103 Stat. 157 (1989).

30. Christopher Culp and Steve Hanke, "Empire of the Sun: An Economic Interpretation of Enron's Energy Business," *Policy Analysis* 470 (February 20, 2003): 5.

31. McLean and Elkind, *The Smartest Guys in the Room*, 32.

32. Culp and Hanke, "Empire of the Sun," 5.

33. Bartlett and Wozny, "Enron's Transformation," 2–3; Culp and Hanke, ibid., 5; Malcolm Salter, *Innovation Corrupted: The Origins and Legacy of Enron's Collapse* (Cambridge, MA: Harvard University Press, 2008), 21; McLean and Elkind, *The Smartest Guys in the Room*, 34–35.

34. Bartlett and Wozny, "Enron's Transformation," 3; McLean and Elkind, ibid., 35.

35. Culp and Hanke, "Empire of the Sun," 6; Salter, *Innovation Corrupted*, 21–23; McLean and Elkind, ibid., 36; Bartlett and Wozny, ibid., 5.

36. Quoted in McLean and Elkind, ibid., 38. See also Culp and Hanke, "Empire of the Sun," 6–7.

37. "Financial Oversight of Enron: The SEC and Private-Sector Watchdogs," *Report of the Committee on Governmental Affairs of the United States Senate,* U.S. Government Printing Office (82–147), October 7, 2002, nn. 152–155 (hereafter *Senate Report*).

38. The SEC staff appeared to anticipate mark-to-market accounting problems. In the SEC's nonobjection letter its chief accountant expressly conditioned acceptance of Enron's change in accounting methods on its representation that it would value long-term contracts objectively, but the SEC had no procedures to ensure that the company would comply with this requirement (ibid., nn. 156–157).

39. Milton C. Regan, "Teaching Enron," *Fordham Law Review* 74 (December 2005): 1139 et seq.; McLean and Elkind, *The Smartest Guys in the Room*, 39–43. Enron's

balance sheet also included current and noncurrent accounts captioned "price risk management assets" (PRMA). These were Enron's fair-value accounting assets. The SEC handed Enron the tools to abandon traditional principles and introduce the bookkeeping analog of financial engineering into nonfinancial companies. Enron discounted to present value as much as twenty-nine years of income from customer contracts. The result, after considerable manipulation, involved instantaneous increases in assets and offsetting equity and income. By 2000, Enron's PRMA amounted to $21 billion (31 percent of reported assets), quadruple their 1999 carrying value ($5 billion, or 15 percent of reported assets). But mark-to-market accounting did not provide cash flow. Enron had to obtain cash for its operations and projects without having to sell stock or report debt through use of off-balance-sheet debt schemes (Robert G. Haldeman, "Fact, Fiction, and Fair Value Accounting," *CPA Journal*, November 2006, 1).

40. Marie Brenner, "The Enron Wars," *Vanity Fair*, April 2001.See also D. M. Boje, Carolyn L. Gardner, and William L. Smith, "(Mis)Using Numbers in the Enron Story," *Organizational Research Methods* 9, no. 4 (October 2006): 460; Krishna Palepu and Paul M. Healy, "The Fall of Enron," *Journal of Economic Perspectives* 17, no. 2 (Spring 2003): 6; McLean and Elkind, *The Smartest Guys in the Room*, 60.

41. Quoted in Peter Behr and April Witt, "Visionary's Dream Led to Risky Business," *Washington Post*, July 28, 2002, A01; Fox, *Enron*, 39.

42. Jeffrey D. Van Niel and Nancy B. Rapoport, "Dr. Jekyll & Mr. Skilling: How Enron's Public Image Morphed from the Most Innovative Company in the Fortune 500 to the Most Notorious Company Ever," in Nancy B. Rapoport and Bala G. Dharan, eds., *Enron: Corporate Fiascos and Their Implications* (St. Paul, MN: Foundation Press 2003), 79.

43. Bartlett and Wozny, "Enron's Transformation," 7. See also Jeffrey D. Van Niel and Nancy B. Rapoport, ibid, 80; C. William Thomas, "The Rise and Fall of Enron," *Today's CPA*, March/April 2002, 1; Vince Kaminski and John Martin, "Transforming Enron: The Value of Active Management," *Journal of Applied Corporate Finance* 13, no. 4 (Winter 2001): 17 et seq.; Fox, *Enron*, 39.

44. McLean and Elkind, "Enron's Transformation," 88.

45. Quoted in Bartlett and Wozny, "Enron's Transformation," 9.

46. Salter, *Innovation Corrupted*, 33. See also Palepu and Healy, "The Fall of Enron," 9–10; Culp and Hanke, "Empire of the Sun," 8; Thayer Watkins, "The Rise and Fall of Enron," http://www.sjsu.edu/faculty/watkins/enron.htm, 9–13; Robert M. Hayes,

"Internet and Enron" (2002), http://ppt.internationalx.net/i/internet-and-enron---ucla-department-of-information-studies-w34167-ppt.ppt.

47. Watkins, "The Rise and Fall of Enron," 12.

48. Jim Yardley, "Enron's Many Strands: The Former Chairman; His Influence Lost, Lay Prepares to Answer Questions in Washington," *New York Times*, February 3, 2002.

49. Long before Enron began trading electricity and electricity derivatives, however, it controlled and operated power plants in Virginia and Massachusetts. By 1990 it was building a major plant in Teesside, England. It continued to invest in power plants during the mid-1990s as a supply base for its trading operations. By the end of the decade it had built twenty-six power plants with local partners (Salter, *Innovation Corrupted*, 30–31).

50. Quoted in "Electric Avenues" *The Economist*, February 26, 1998.

51. Ibid., 34.

52. Palepu and Healy, "The Fall of Enron," 8; Alexia Brunet and Meredith Shafe, "Beyond Enron: Regulation in Derivatives Trading," *Northwestern Journal of International Law and Business* 27, no. 3 (2007): n. 95.

53. Ibid.; Weaver, "Can Energy Markets Be Trusted?," 17; "Blind Faith: How Deregulation and Enron's Influence over Government Looted Billions from Americans," *Public Citizen*, December 2001, 1.

54. Jeremiah D. Lambert, *Energy Companies and Market Reform: How Deregulation Went Wrong* (Tulsa, OK: PennWell, 2006), 97. Power marketers selling electricity at market-based rates were not required to file their accounting records or individual contracts with FERC, and their requests for blanket approval of all future issuances of securities and assumptions of liability were routinely granted.

55. See, for example, *Entergy Servs., Inc.*, 58 FERC Para. 61,234, 61,753 (1992).

56. McLean and Elkind, *The Smartest Guys in the Room*, 87; "Blind Faith: How Deregulation and Enron's Influence over Government Looted Billions from Americans," 6–7.

57. See *Chicago Mercantile Exchange, et al. v. Securities and Exchange Commission, et al.*, 883 F. 2d 537 (7th Cir. 1989), which found that the CFTC, not the SEC, had jurisdiction over futures contracts.

58. Brunet and Shafe, "Beyond Enron: Regulation in Derivatives Trading," 669.

59. In a swap transaction, two parties agree to exchange cash flows with respect to an underlying economic variable. In an interest-rate swap a borrower with a variable-rate loan agrees to pay a dealer fixed amounts if the dealer agrees to make fluctuating payments on the loan. The borrower is thus able to convert an unpredictable, variable-rate loan into a predictable, fixed-rate loan by transferring risk to the dealer. The borrower can then hedge against fluctuations in interest rates. By the time Enron collapsed, it was a major player in swaps markets. (See "How Lax Regulation and Inadequate Oversight Contributed to the Enron Collapse," *Minority Staff, Committee on Government Reform, U.S. House of Representatives,* February 7, 2002, 3 (hereafter *House Report.*)

60. Ibid., 2–3. See also Brunnermeier and Pederson, "Predatory Trading," *Journal of Finance* 60, no. 1 (2005): 1825 et seq.

61. 15 U.S.C. Sec. 79a et seq.

62. *Senate Report,* nn. 175–180; Schroeder, "Accounting for Enron: SEC Feels Heat over Exemptions to Enron," *Wall Street Journal,* January 21, 2002.

63. *House Report,* n. 40.

64. Quoted in Miller, "Vision Vanquisher," *Industry Week,* December 21, 2004, 1.

65. Bartlett and Wozny, "Enron's Transformation," 8; Brunet and Shafe, "Beyond Enron," 16; "The Quite Man Who's Jolting Utilities," *Business Week,* June 9, 1997; "Enron," *The Economist,* February 26, 1998.

66. Salter, *Innovation Corrupted,* 34–35.

67. Quoted in McLean and Elkind, *The Smartest Guys in the Room,* 107.

68. Ibid., 108. See also Salter, *Innovation Corrupted,* 35, and Weaver, "Can Energy Markets Be Trusted?," 19.

69. Bethany McLean, "Is Enron Overpriced?," *Fortune,* March 2001. See also Lambert, *Energy Companies and Market Reform,* 8, 28–29; Bala Dharan and William R. Bufkins, "Red Flags in Enron's Reporting of Revenues and Key Financial Measures" in *Enron: Corporate Fiascos And Their Implications,* 99–100; Weaver, "Can Energy Markets Be Trusted?," 21.

70. Dharan and Bufkins, ibid., 101–103, 107.

71. Anthony H. Catanach Jr. and Shelley Rhoades-Catanach, "Enron: A Financial Reporting Failure," *Villanova Law Review* 48 (2003): 1057, 1074; "Financial Oversight of Enron: The SEC and Private-Sector Watchdogs," *Report of the Committee on Governmental Affairs, United States Senate*, Senate Print 107-75, October 7, 2002, 23.

72. *Report of Special Investigation Committee of the Board of Directors of Enron Corporation* (the "*Powers Report*"), February 1, 2002, 27–28.

73. Quoted in William H. Miller, "Vision Vanquisher," *Industry Week*, December 21, 2004, 1.

74. Phillip J. Ardoin and Dennis Grady, "The Politics of Electricity Restructuring across the American States: Power Failure and Policy Failure," *State & Local Government Review* 38, no. 3 (2006): 167; McWilliams, "The Quiet Man Who's Jolting Utilities."

75. Salter, *Innovation Corrupted*, 36–37; Weaver, "Can Energy Markets Be Trusted?," 20; "Enron," *The Economist, February* 26, 1998; McLean and Elkind, *The Smartest Guys in the Room*, 175–176, 180.

76. Karen Tumulty and Michael Weisskopf, "What $6 Million Can Buy," *Time*, January 28, 2002.

77. M. Asif Ismail, "A Most Favored Corporation: Enron Prevailed in Federal, State, Lobbying Efforts 49 Times," *Public Integrity*, January 6, 2003.

78. McLean and Elkind, *The Smartest Guys in the Room*, 175–176.

79. Quoted in statement of Joseph Dunn, California state senator, "Examining Enron: Electricity Market Manipulation and the Effect on the Western States," *Hearing before the Subcommittee on Consumer Affairs, Foreign Commerce and Tourism of the Committee on Commerce, Science, and Transportation, United States Senate*, 107th Congress, Second Session, April 11, 2002, 42 (hereafter *California Hearings*).

80. *California Hearings*, 36–37.

81. Richard Peet and Michael Watts, "Liberation Ecology, Development, Sustainability, and Environment in an Age of Market Triumphalism," in Richard Peet and Michael Watts, eds., *Liberation Ecologies: Environment, Development, and Social Movements* (New York: Routledge, 1996), 1.

82. Richard D. Cudahy, "Electric Deregulation After California: Down But Not Out," *Administrative Law Review* 54, no. 1 (Winter 2002): 338–339.

83. Chi-Keung Woo, "What Went Wrong in California's Electricity Market," *International Journal* 26 (2001): 747 et seq.

84. Act of September 24, 1996, 1996 Cal. Stats. 854; Cal. Pub. Util. Code Secs. 330–398.5 (Deering 2001).

85. Prepared statement of Hon. Richard Boucher, in "Electricity Markets: Lessons Learned from California," *Hearing Before the Subcommittee on Energy and Air Quality of the Committee on Energy and Commerce,* House of Representatives, 107th Cong., 1st Sess. (February 15, 2001), 6.

86. Paul L. Joskow, *California's Energy Crisis* (Cambridge, MA: Harvard Electricity Policy Group, 2001), 12. See also Timothy P. Duane, "Regulation's Rationale: Learning from the Energy Crisis," *Yale Journal on Regulation* 19, no. 2 (Summer 2002): 497

87. Duane, "Regulation's Rationale," 498; Weaver, "Can Energy Markets Be Trusted?," 31–32. The generating units divested by the utilities, representing almost 40 percent of power capacity in California, were sold to merchant affiliates of five out-of-state utilities: Duke, Mirant, Dynegy/NRG, AES/Williams, and Reliant. Although FERC reviewed each purchaser to determine if it could exercise market power, it did not account for the ability of generators to increase prices during periods of peak demand. Once FERC had certified that a purchaser could not exercise market power, it was free to charge whatever price it could extract. (See "Attorney General's Energy White Paper," State of California, April 2004, 15.)

88. Severin Borenstein, James Bushnell, Christopher Knittel, and Catherine Wolfram, "Inefficiencies and Market Power in Financial Arbitrage: A Study of California's Electricity Markets," white paper, September 24, 2006, 5, 17; Jerry Taylor and Peter Van Doren, "Did Enron Pillage California?," *Cato Institute Briefing Papers* 72 (August 22, 2002): 2; *California Hearings,* 38n5.

89. Suppliers could sell power in the imbalance energy market in three ways: by actively bidding into an imbalance energy market, by passively supplying more than was scheduled, or in conjunction with the supply of ancillary services or reserve capacity. Producers that simply generated more than they were committed to provide were implicitly agreeing to take whatever price obtained in the imbalance energy market. Producers that bid into the imbalance energy market could choose to offer supply at a given price for up to forty-five minutes before the hour of production. Most suppliers of reserve capacity were also eligible to earn imbalance energy revenues. These energy revenues were in addition to capacity payments earned by suppliers that committed to being available with varying response times. Suppliers to the ancillary services markets submitted two-part bids: a standby capacity price for a given reserve service and an energy price paid in the event the unit was actually

called on to generate. (See Severin Borenstein, James Bushnell, Christopher Knittel, and Catherine Wolfram, "Trading Inefficiencies in California's Electricity Markets," National Bureau of Economic Research, Working Paper 8620, December 2001, 9; http://www.nber.org/papers/w8620.pdf.

90. Borenstein et al., ibid., 7; Taylor and Van Doren, "Did Enron Pillage California?," 2; Duane, "Regulation's Rationale," 498–502.

91. *California Hearings*, 39–41.

92. James L. Sweeney, *The California Electricity Crisis*, mimeo, April 9, 2002, 41–42; Duane, "Regulation's Rationale," 501–502; Cudahy, "Electric Deregulation After California," 341–342; "Attorney General's Energy White Paper," 14–15. The CPUC's Division of Ratepayer Advocates warned that prices would go up as soon as continuing demand growth eliminated the excess capacity of the early 1990s, but these claims were dismissed by ideologically driven commissioners (Duane, ibid., n.110).

93. See, for example, Pacific Gas and Elec. Co., 81 F.E.R.C. ¶ 61,122 (1997); Pacific Gas and Elec. Co., 80 F.E.R.C. ¶ 61,128 (1997); Pacific Gas and Elec. Co., 77 F.E.R.C. ¶ 61,265 (1996); Pacific Gas and Elec. Co., 77 F.E.R.C. ¶ 61,204 (1996); and Pacific Gas and Elec. Co., 77 F.E.R.C. 61,196 (1996).

94. As FERC noted in its December 15, 2000 Order, *Directing Remedies for California Wholesale Electric Markets*, in Docket Nos. EL00–95–000: "Beginning in 1996, this Commission issued a series of orders which, at the urging of California State regulators, deferred to the State on all significant aspects of State restructuring of California electric power market and market rules."

95. Nicholas W. Fels and Frank R. Lindh, "Lessons from the California 'Apocalypse': Jurisdiction over Electric Utilities," *Energy Law Journal* 22, no. 1 (2001): 10–11.

96. Mark N. Cooper, "The Failure of Federal Authorities to Protect American Energy Consumers from Market Power and Other Abusive Practices," *Loyola Consumer Law Review* 19, no.4 (2007): 393–394. In *California v. FERC*, Slip Opinion No. 02–73093, September 9, 2004, the Ninth Circuit Court of Appeals stated that market-based tariffs "virtually deregulate an industry and remove it from statutorily required oversight" and noted that FERC's "power to order retroactive refunds when a company's non-compliance ... eviscerates the tariff is inherent in [its] authority to approve a market-based tariff in the first instance" (ibid., 5, 19).

97. Quoted in Gary McWilliams, "The Quiet Man Who's Jolting Utilities." *Business Week* (June 9, 1997), available at http://www.businessweek.com/archives/1997/b3530143.arc.htm.

98. McLean and Elkind, *The Smartest Guys in the Room*, 267–268; see also Bartlett and Wozny, "Enron's Transformation," 14.

99. Severin Borenstein, "The Trouble with Electricity Markets: Understanding California's Restructuring Disaster," *Journal of Economic Perspectives* 16, no. 1 (Winter 2002): 196.

100. McLean and Elkind, *The Smartest Guys in the Room*, 267; Duane, "Regulation's Rationale," 508; Borenstein et al., *Trading Inefficiencies in California's Electricity Markets*, 195; Fels and Lindh, "Lessons from the California 'Apocalypse,'" 10–11.

101. McLean and Elkind, ibid., 268–269; "Attorney General's Energy White Paper," 16.

102. Salter, *Innovation Corrupted*, 1, 91–93; Bartlett and Wozny, "Enron's Transformation," 1; Weaver, "Can Energy Markets Be Trusted?," 20, 23.

103. Weaver, ibid., 20–23; Jeff Madrick, review of the *Powers Report*, *Challenge* 45, no. 3 (May–June 2002): 121; Fox, *Enron*, 185; Salter, *Innovation Corrupted*, 45–46; Frank Partnoy, "A Revisionist View of Enron and the Sudden Death of 'May,'" *Villanova Law Review* 48 (2003): 1248; statement of Loretta Lynch, *California Hearings*, 51; Testimony of Frank Partnoy, *Hearings Before the United States Committee on Governmental Affairs*, mimeo, January 24, 2002, 5. "Specifically, Enron used derivatives and special purpose vehicles to manipulate its financial statements in three ways. First, it hid speculator losses it suffered on technology stocks. Second, it hid huge debts incurred to finance unprofitable new businesses, including retail energy services for new customers. Third, it inflated the value of other troubled businesses, including its new ventures in fiber-optic bandwidth. Although Enron was founded as an energy company, many of the derivatives transactions did not involve energy at all." Partnoy, *Hearings*,

104. Duane, "Regulation's Rationale," 508–509; McLean and Elkind, *The Smartest Guys in the Room*, 271–272; statement of Senator Ron Wyden in *California Hearings*, 3; Weaver, "Can Energy Markets Be Trusted?," 26–27.

105. Taylor and Van Doren, "Did Enron Pillage California?," 3–4; McLean and Elkind, ibid., 269–270.

106. Jason Leopold, "Lay, Skilling, and Enron's Washington Lobbyist Knew about the Company's Trading Schemes in California," *Counterpunch*, June 7, 2004; Weaver, "Can Energy Markets Be Trusted?," 46, http://www.counterpunch.org/200406/07/lay-skilling-andenron-s-washington-lobbyist-knew-about-company.

107. Testimony of Loretta Lynch at a hearing ("Examining Enron: Electricity Market Manipulation and the Effect on the Western States") before the Subcommittee on Consumer Affairs, Foreign Commerce and Tourism of the Committee on Commerce, Science and Transportation, United States Senate, 107th Cong., 2nd Sess. (April 11, 2002), 44.

108. Statement of Loretta Lynch, *California Hearings*, 46–47.

109. Weaver, "Can Energy Markets Be Trusted?," 60–61. Dynegy, AEP, CMS, El Paso, and Williams admitted having done round-trip trades (ibid.).

110. *Final Report on Price Manipulation in Western Markets,* FERC Docket No. PA02-2-000 (March 2003), VII-14 (hereafter, *FERC Final Report*); Lambert, *Energy Companies and Market Reform*, 129–130; "Attorney General's Energy White Paper," 18.

111. Ibid., ES-2; Lambert, ibid., 133.

112. *FERC Final Report,* IX-9 to IX-11; Weaver, "Can Energy Markets Be Trusted?," 77.

113. Cooper, "The Failure of Federal Authorities to Protect American Energy Consumers": 395–396.

114. Tyson Slocum, "Blind Faith: How Deregulation and Enron's Influence over Government Looted Billions from Americans," *Public Citizen*, December 2001, 17–20; Minority Staff, Committee on Government Reform, U.S. House of Representatives, "How Lax Regulation and Inadequate Oversight Contributed to the Enron Collapse," February 7, 2002, revised June 4, 2002, 4.

115. Sweeney, *The California Electricity Crisis*, 178–179.

116. Fels and Lindh, "Lessons from the California 'Apocalypse,'" 10–11; Duane, "Regulation's Rationale," 512–513; Sweeney, *The California Electricity Crisis*, 177–178; McLean and Elkind, *The Smartest Guys in the Room*, 277; Lambert, *Energy Companies and Market Reform*, 155–157. In 2001 the ISO accepted a real-time energy bid from Duke Energy at $3,380 per megawatt-hour. The bid generated revenues of $11 million for a single trade and was later described as an "abuse of market power" Lambert, ibid., 156).

117. Fels and Lindh, ibid., 14; Duane, "Regulation's Rationale," 517–518; Cudahy, "Electric Deregulation After California: Down but Not Out," 344–345. It is estimated that the DWR spent about $13 billion to keep the lights on through November 2001 (Duane, ibid., 520).

118. Christian Berthelsen and Scott Winokur, "Enron's Secret Bid to Save Deregulation, Private Meeting with Prominent Californians, *San Francisco Chronicle,* May 26, 2001. See f.n. 145. Also see Lambert, *Energy Companies and Market Reform,* 157–158; Fox, *Enron,* 218; Duane, ibid., 520; Sweeney, *The California Electricity Crisis,* Stanford Hoover Institution (2002), 228.

119. Laura M. Holson, "California's Largest Utility Files for Bankruptcy," *New York Times,* April 7, 2001.

120. PG&E news release April 6, 2001, available at www.pgecorp.com/news/press_releases/news_press_releases2001.shtml.

121. Holson, "California's Largest Utility Files for Bankruptcy."

122. See generally Sweeney, The California Electricity Crisis, Stanford Hoover Institution (2002); Lambert, Energy Companies and Market Reform, 157–158; Ahmad Faruqui, Hung-po Chao, Vic Niemeyer, Jeremy Platt, and Karl Stahlkopf, "Analyzing California's Power Crisis," Energy Journal 22, no. 4 (2001): 47.

123. David Barboza, "Former Officials Say Enron Hid Gains during Crisis in California," *New York Times,* June 23, 2002.

124. Public Citizen, December 2001, available at http://www.citizen.org/cmep/article_redirect.cfm?ID.

125. Slocum, *Blind Faith,* 20–21; McLean and Elkind, *The Smartest Guys in the Room,* 282; Weaver, "Can Energy Markets Be Trusted?," 39; David Barboza, "Former Officials Say Enron Hid Gains during Crisis in California," *New York Times,* June 23, 2002, A1. Profits also soared for the merchant generators that had acquired power plants from California utilities and now owned 40 percent of California's electric power capacity. For the third quarter of 2000 alone, the following increases were reported: Dynegy (up 83 percent), Reliant (wholesale energy division, up 642 percent), Duke (up 74 percent), AES (up 131 percent), NRG (up 221 percent), Southern Energy (up 59 percent) (Lambert, *Energy Companies and Market Reform,* 156).

126. McLean and Elkind, ibid., 281; see also Weaver, "Can Energy Markets Be Trusted?," 39–40.

127. San Diego Gas & Elec. Co., 93 F.E.R.C. ¶ 61,121, at 61,349–50 (2000).

128. Lambert, *Energy Companies and Market Reform,* 159.

129. Order Proposing Remedies for California Wholesale Electric Markets, 93 FERC para. 61,121 (2000).

130. Ibid.

131. Ibid. The conditions proposed for bids exceeding $150 were that (1) such bids, if accepted, would not set the market-clearing price in what were otherwise single-price auctions conducted by the ISO and the PX, and (2) the bidder, if successful, would have to submit certain information related to its actual costs and opportunity costs.

132. "Attorney General's Energy White Paper," 33.

133. Senate Committee on Governmental Affairs, *Staff Investigation of FERC's Oversight of Enron Corp.*, November 12, 2002, 19–26. A Senate Governmental Affairs Committee report found that Enron successfully exploited regulatory voids among FERC, the SEC, and the CFTC because none of the agencies communicated with the others about developments in the deregulated power markets (John Fialka, "Jurisdiction Issues Put Off Regulatory Action on Enron," *Wall Street Journal*, November 12, 2002; see also Weaver, "Can Energy Markets Be Trusted?," n. 170).

134. Carolyn Lochhead, "Energy Regulator Says Agency's Inept," *New York Times*, May 8, 2002, A1, A10.

135. Ibid.

136. PX transactions soon came to an end. The PX had no way of funding its costs and within a few months declared bankruptcy.

137. San Diego Gas & Elec. Co. v. Sellers of Energy and Ancillary Services into Markets Operated by Caiso and CalPX, 93 FERC para. 61,294 (December 15, 2000). The December 15 order did approve the previously proposed conditions on bids exceeding $150 as a temporary measure, pending adoption of longer-term market monitoring measures, and adopted a benchmark (roughly, the utilities' generation costs in June 1996), by which it would measure future long-term contracts and as a recommended standard for the CPUC in judging the prudence of such contracts.

138. Quoted in Gray Davis, "Bush's Mistake in California," *New York Times*, May 31, 2001, A27.

139. Weaver, "Can Energy Markets Be Trusted?," 39.

140. Quoted in Robert A. Rosenblatt and Richard Simon, "Federal Pact Would Give Utilities More Time to Pay Power," *Los Angeles Times,* January 10, 2001.

141. Response of the Public Utility Commission of the State of California to the November 1 Order, San Diego Gas & Electric Company et al., FERC Docket No. EL00–95–000 (November 21, 2000).

142. Quoted in George Skelton, "Price Caps Don't Fit in Cheney's Head for Figures," *Los Angeles Times,* April 19, 2001. Also see Lazarus, "Memo Details Cheney-Enron Links," *San Francisco Chronicle,* January 30, 2002.

143. Michael Janofsky, "California Official Spars with U.S. on Power Policy," *New York Times,* April 10, 2001, A10 (reporting on lobbying efforts at FERC by elected officials from California and other Western states to implement price caps on wholesale electricity).

144. San Diego Gas & Elec. Co. v. Sellers of Energy and Ancillary Services into Markets Operated by CAISO and Cal PX, 95 FERC para. 61,115 (April 26, 2001).

145. "Profile: Enron Corporation," *History Commons,* http://www.historycommons .org/entity.jsp?entity=enron. In a telephone call in May 2001, Lay told Hebert that "he and Enron would like to support [him] as chairman, but we would have to agree on principles." Hebert, a Republican appointed by President Clinton, opposed Enron's demand for FERC backing of regional transmission organizations and threatened to investigate Enron's gas trading and derivative financing schemes. At the same time, Vice President Cheney began to question Hebert's fitness and wanted to install Pat Wood as Chairman. Also in May 2001 Lay convened a meeting with Arnold Schwarzenegger (then a Republican gubernatorial candidate) and Richard Riordan, mayor of Los Angeles, to deliver a memo calling for an end to federal and state investigations into Enron's activities and suggesting consumers bear massive rate increases caused by California's disastrous experiment with deregulation (Jason Leopold, "Ahnuld, Ken Lay, George Bush, Dick Cheney, and Gray Davis," *Common Dreams,* August 17, 2003).

146. Tumulty and Weisskopf, "Has Bush Seen the Light?," *Time,* June 25, 2001.

147. San Diego Gas & Electric Company, et al., 95 FERC para. 61,418 (2001).

148. Statement of Robert McCullough, *California Hearings,* 83. In July 2000 Tim Belden had predicted that prices would remain high for another two to four years (ibid., n. 22).

149. Interview with *Frontline,* March 27, 2001, http://www.pbs.org/wgbh/pages/ frontline/shows/blackout/interviews/lay.html.

150. Paul Joskow and Edward Kahn, "A Quantitative Analysis of Pricing Behavior in California's Wholesale Electricity Market during Summer 2000," *Energy Journal* 23, no. 4 (2002): 29. See also Borenstein, "The Trouble with Electricity Markets" (inelastic supply and extremely inelastic demand); Borenstein, Bushnell, Knittel, and Wolfram, "Trading Inefficiencies in California's Electricity Markets" (risky arbitrage opportunities between the ISO and the PX).

151. Faruqui et al., "Analyzing California's Power Crisis," 40–41, citing Frank Wolak and Robert Nordhaus.

152. Robert R. Nordhaus, "Electric Power Regulation: Making Partially Regulated Markets Work," *Administrative Law Review* 54, no. 1 (Winter 2002): 373.

153. Statement of Joseph Dunn, *California Hearings*, 39, 41.

154. Senate Governmental Affairs Committee, Majority Staff Memorandum, November 12, 2002.

155. Salter, *Innovation Corrupted*, 46, 55, 57; William W. Bratton, "The Dark Side of Shareholder Value," *Tulane Law Review* 76 (2002): 1288; Francis Grabowski, *Enron* (Barcelona, Spain: Universitat Pompeu Fabra, 2002), 5; McLean and Elkind, *The Smartest Guys in the Room*, 313.

156. McLean and Elkind, ibid., 314, 318–323, 339–340, 343–344, 349; William Thomas, "The Rise and Fall of Enron," *Journal of Accountancy*, April 2002, 4; Madrick, review of the *Powers Report*, 118–119; Grabowski, ibid., 8. Between 1998 and 2000 Lay sold $201.6 million in stock, netting a profit of $119 million (ibid.).

157. "Skilling Steps Down Citing Personal Reasons; Lay Takes Duties," The Wall Street Journal, August 15, 2001.

158. Fox, *Enron*, 247–251; Swartz and Watkins, *Power Failure*, 273–292; Thomas, ibid., 4; McLean and Elkind, 342–351. Watkins later discussed her concerns with James Hecker, an audit partner of Arthur Andersen, Enron's outside auditor, who contacted the Enron audit team (Healy and Palepu, "The Fall of Enron," 4; "Text of Letter to Enron's Chairman After Departure of Chief Executive," New York Times, January 16, 2002, C6).

159. Bratton, "The Dark Side of Shareholder Value," 1317.

160. *The Powers Report*, February 1, 2002, 19.

161. See Bratton, "The Dark Side of Shareholder Value," 1318–1319. Also see Healy and Palepu, "The Fall of Enron," 4, 12; Michael Frontain, "Enron Corporation," in

Texas State Historical Association, *Handbook of Texas Online,* https://www.tshaonline
.org/handbook/online/articles/doe08; John Emswhiller and Rebecca Smith, "Enron
Jolt: Investments, Assets Generate Big Loss," *Wall Street Journal,* October 17, 2001,
C1; "Chronology of a Collapse," *Time,* June 24, 2002; Ronald Sims and Johannes
Brinkmann, "Enron Ethics (Or: Culture Matters More than Codes)," *Journal of Busi-
ness Ethics* 45, no. 3 (July 2003), 248.

162. Cathy Booth Thomas and Frank Pellegrini, "Why Dynegy Backed Out," *Time,*
December 5, 2001.

163. In re Enron Corp., 302 B.R. 455 (Bankr. S.D. N.Y. 2003) (No. 01–16034); Swartz
and Watkins, *Power Failure,* 338; Bratton, "The Dark Side of Shareholder Value,"
1319–1325; Healy and Palepu, "The Fall of Enron," 4; Texas State Historical Association, *Handbook of Texas Online;* McLean and Elkind, *The Smartest Guys in the Room,*
308–403; Bratton, ibid., 1277; Thomas and Pellegrini, "Why Dynegy Backed Out,"
December 3, 2001.

164. Bratton, ibid., 1293, 1323; Oppel, "Former Head of Enron Denies Wrongdo-
ing," *The New York Times,* December 22, 2001, C1; McLean and Elkind, ibid., 415–
416; *Powers Report,* 19; Frontain, "Enron Corporation," 4.

165. For a partial list of Enron legal commentary, see Gregory Mitchell, "Case Studies, Counterfactuals, and Causal Explanations," *University of Pennsylvania Law Review*
152, no. 5 (May 2004): n. 4.

166. Salter, *Innovation Corrupted,* 47–48.

167. Robert Bradley, "Who Was Ken Lay?," *Master Resource,* July 7, 2009, https://
www.masterresource.org/climate-policy/who-was-ken-lay-the-senate-should-know-
the-industry-father-of-us-side-cap-and-trade.

168. See, for example, Bartlett and Wozny, "Enron's Transformation,"
seriatim.

169. McLean and Elkind, *The Smartest Guys in the Room,* 416–421; Michael Frontain,
"Enron Corporation"; Julie Rawe, "The Case against Ken Lay," *Time,* July 19,
2004.

170. Wendy Grossman, "Shaking Ken Lay's Cool," *Time,* April 28, 2006; Rawe, ibid.;
McLean and Elkind, ibid., 421.

171. Vikas Bajaj and Kurt Eichenwald, "Kenneth L. Lay, 64, Enron Founder and
Symbol of Corporate Excess, Dies," *New York Times,* July 6, 2006.

Chapter 6

1. Amory Lovins, "Energy Strategy: The Road Not Taken," *Foreign Affairs* 55 (1976): 65–96.

2. Ibid., 92.

3. Ibid., 77.

4. Benjamin K. Sovacool, "The Problem with the 'Portfolio Approach' in American Energy Policy," *Policy Science* 11, no. 3 (September 2008): 258.

5. Lovins, "Energy Strategy," 67. Lovins was not the first to express concern. In 1967 Syukuro Manabe and Richard Weatherald, members of Princeton's Geophysical Fluid Dynamics Laboratory, issued a famous paper predicting that a doubling of atmospheric CO_2 would increase global temperatures by three or four degrees. In 1979 the Charney Committee, under the auspices of the National Academy of Sciences, prepared a report declaring the risk of global warming from burning coal to be very real. The JASON committee, a panel of leading physicists advising the Department of Defense, concluded there was "incontrovertible evidence that the atmosphere is indeed changing and that we ourselves contribute to that change" (Daniel Yergin, *The Quest: Energy, Security, and the Remaking of the Modern World* (New York: Penguin, 2011), 448–450).

6. Anthony J. Parisi, "'Soft' Energy, Hard Choices," *New York Times,* October 16, 1977.

7. Amory B. Lovins, *The Essential Amory Lovins* (Oxford: Earthscan, 2011), vii.

8. Parisi, "'Soft' Energy, Hard Choices."

9. Ibid.; Lovins, *The Essential Amory Lovins*, vii–ix.

10. Amory B. Lovins, *Soft Energy Paths* (New York: Harper, 1971), 150–151.

11. Eric Schatzburg, review of *Natural Capitalism: Creating the Next Industrial Revolution, Technology and Culture* 43, no. 1 (January 2002): 2

12. Franklin Tugwell, "Energy and Political Economy," *Comparative Politics* 13, no. 1 (October 1980): 109.

13. Vaclav Smil, "Rocky Mountain Visions: A Review Essay," *Population and Development Review* 26, no. 1 (March 2000): 171.

14. See A. C. Pigou, *The Economics of Welfare* (London: Macmillan, 1920), 134; David B. Spence and Paula Murray, "The Law, Economics and Politics of Federal Preemption Jurisprudence: A Quantitative Analysis," *California Law Review* 87, no. 5 (October 1999): 1154.

15. The Price-Anderson Act, Pub. L. No. 85–256, 71 Stat. 576; 42 U.S.C. Secs. 2012 et seq. As originally enacted, Price-Anderson required the owners of commercial nuclear power facilities with rated capacities of 100 megawatts or more to carry the maximum liability insurance "available at reasonable cost ... from private sources" and to contribute to a secondary risk pool when a major accident caused damages greater than primary insurance coverage. If damages exceeded the total primary plus secondary coverage, the statute required the Nuclear Regulatory Commission to indemnify for the excess liability, subject to an aggregate dollar cap on liability. The Supreme Court upheld the constitutionality and validity of Price-Anderson in *Duke Power Co. v. Carolina Environmental Study Group*, 438 U.S. 59 (1978).

16. John Levandis, Walter Block, and Joseph Morrel, "Nuclear Power," *Journal of Business Ethics* 67, no. 1 (August 2006): 38.

17. Joel Yellin, "High Technology and the Courts: Nuclear Power and the Need for Institutional Reform," *Harvard Law Review* 94, no. 3 (January 1981): 498.

18. Quoted in Susan R. Schrepfer, "The Nuclear Crucible: Diablo Canyon and the Transformation of the Sierra Club, 1965–1985," *California History* 71, no. 2 (Summer 1992): 230–231.

19. Lucas W. Davis, "Prospects for Nuclear Power," *Journal of Economic Perspectives* 26, no. 1 (Winter 2012): 50.

20. Paul L. Joskow and John E. Parsons, "The Economic Future of Nuclear Power," *Daedelus* 138, no. 4 (March 30, 2009): 45–59.

21. Amory Lovins, "Out of the Frying Pan and into the PWR," *Nature* 271 (January 5, 1978), 2; Lovins, *The Essential Amory Lovins*, 147.

22. Lovins, *The Essential Amory Lovins*, 145.

23. Yellin, "High Technology and the Courts," n. 235.

24. Lovins, *The Essential Amory Lovins*, 164; Lovins, "Nuclear Socialism," *The Weekly Standard* 16, no. 6 (October 25, 2010): 15; Levandis, Block, and Morrel, "Nuclear Power," 40.

25. 43 U.S.C. Secs. 601–609 (renewing the Price-Anderson Act insurance provisions), 621 (providing that the forty-year life of a combined construction permit begins to run on the date the NRC authorizes the facility's operation), 638 (creating a government-backed risk insurance program for up to six entities that apply for, or have been granted, an operating license for a new nuclear power plant), 1306 (creating a tax credit for advanced nuclear reactors placed in service prior to 2021), and 1310 (granting utilities tax deductions for amounts contributed to qualified decommissioning funds) (2006). (See Roland M. Frye, "The Current 'Nuclear Renaissance' in the United States, Its Underlying Reasons, and Its Potential Pitfalls," *Energy Law Journal* 29, no. 2 (2008): 335.)

26. Three changes in U.S. nuclear plant licensing procedures reduced regulatory burdens. The NRC now certifies specific reactor designs, which can then be used at multiple sites without further review. It also issues early site permits for new reactors in connection with which it approves one or more sites for a nuclear power facility independent of an application for a construction license. Finally, the NRC has consolidated two formerly separate licensing processes—one to construct a plant and the second to operate it—into a single, combined construction and operating license. (See generally Joskow and Parsons, "The Economic Future of Nuclear Power," *Daedalus* 138, no. 4 (2009), 45–59.

27. Davis, "Prospects for Nuclear Power," 49; Joskow and Parsons, ibid.

28. Quoted in Frye, "The Current 'Nuclear Renaissance' in the United States," 1–2.

29. Fukushima was not the only nuclear damage caused by weather. In December 1999 in Blayais, France, dikes that protected a nuclear power facility—designed to exceed 1,000-year storm surge projections—were breached by exceptional flooding, winds, and waves. Two of the plant's four units were severely affected by incoming water. A July 1993 flood on the Missouri River collapsed a levee upstream of the Cooper nuclear power station in Nebraska, causing below-grade rooms in the reactor and turbine buildings to suffer leakage (Frye, "The Current 'Nuclear Renaissance' in the United States," 373).

30. Davis, "Prospects for Nuclear Power," 49–50. A 2002 MIT study concluded, less optimistically, that only by implementing a carbon tax of $200 per ton on conventional power plants could nuclear reactors be cost competitive with existing technologies (Benjamin Sovacool, "Coal and Nuclear Technologies: Creating a False Dichotomy for American Energy Policy," *Policy Sciences* 40, no. 2 (June 2007): 141).

31. Lovins, "Nuclear Follies," *The Essential Amory Lovins,* 150.

32. Lovins, "Nuclear Socialism," ibid., 165–166; Lovins, *The Weekly Standard* 16, no. 6 (October 25, 2010), 15.

33. The Bush administration's proposed solution to the spent fuel storage problem— the Yucca Mountain High-Level Waste Repository—was strongly opposed by the former majority leader, Senator Harry Reid of Nevada. The president and the secretary of energy stated that Yucca Mountain "is not a workable option for a nuclear waste repository." Other possible solutions have not gained traction. (See Frye, "The Current 'Nuclear Renaissance' in the United States," 356; Alex Funk and Benjamin Sovacool, "Wasted Opportunities: Resolving the Impasse in United States Nuclear Waste Policy," *Energy Law Journal* 33 (2013): 113 et seq.

34. Joskow and Parson, "The Economic Future of Nuclear Power."

35. William Nordhaus, *The Climate Casino: Risk, Uncertainty, and Economics for a Warming World* (New Haven, CT: Yale University Press, 2013), 280–281. Forward estimates have been modeled by the Joint Global Change Research Institute and National Renewable Energy Laboratories.

36. Lovins, *The Essential Amory Lovins*, 310–311

37. Quoted in Amory Lovins, "The Fragility of Domestic Energy," *Atlantic Monthly*, November 1983; ibid., 262.

38. Lovins, "Long-Term Constraints on Human Activity," *The Essential Amory Lovins*, 31; see also Lovins, *Environmental Conservation* 3, no. 1 (Spring 1976), 3–14.

39. Frye, "The Current 'Nuclear Renaissance' in the United States," 375–376.

40. Lovins, *Soft Energy Paths*, 38.

41. Ibid., 40–41.

42. Ibid., 45.

43. Lovins, "Energy Strategy," 83.

44. Quoted in Fen Montaigne, "Amory Lovins Lays Out His Clean Energy Plan," *Yale Environment* 360 (February 20, 2012).

45. Quoted in Sovacool, "The Problem with the 'Portfolio Approach,'" 258.

46. Severin Borenstein, "The Private and Public Economics of Renewable Electricity Generation," *Journal of Economic Perspectives* 26, no. 1 (Winter 2012): 67.

47. Ibid., 68–69.

48. Electricity demand also varies during the day in ways that the supply from wind and solar generation may not match. Thus, even if renewable forms of energy have the same levelized cost as conventional ones, the value of the power they produce may be lower. According to Charles Frank of the Brookings Institution, solar power is the most expensive way to reduce carbon emissions; wind is the next most expensive; hydropower provides a modest net benefit; and nuclear power is the most cost-effective zero-emission technology ("Free Exchange: Sun, Wind and Drain," *The Economist,* July 26, 2014, 63).

49. Ibid., 73–77.

50. Ibid., 78.

51. Ibid., 86–87.

52. Ibid., 69.

53. Jerry Taylor and Peter Van Doren, "The Soft Case for Soft Energy," *Journal of International Affairs,* Fall 1999, 209–235.

54. Amory Lovins, *Reinventing Fire* (White River Junction, VT: Chelsea Green, 2011), 189.

55. Ibid., 191. GE prediction made in May 2011.

56. *Bloomberg Businessweek,* November 18, 2013, 52. The largest PV plant worldwide, with 5.2 million solar panels, is the Agua Caliente station in Yuma County, Arizona, which will sell power to Pacific Gas & Electric and 250 megawatts of capacity to the grid (ibid.).

57. Ibid., 199.

58. Ibid., 200. Achieving high levels of wind and solar power in the U.S. electricity system is estimated to require new transmission spending of $3 to $4 billion per year, roughly 50 percent more than is currently spent. Inclusion of additional transmission costs would increase the cost of wind-generated power by about 15 percent. Integration of large-scale variable power sources would add additional cost of

between 4 and 6 percent, making windpower more expensive than natural gas–fired power but less expensive than nuclear power or coal-fired power (with carbon capture and storage) (Paul Komor, *Wind and Solar Electricity: Opportunities and Challenges*, Pew Center on Global Climate Change, 2009, 36, http://www.c2es.org/docUploads/wind-solar-electricity-report.pdf).

59. Amory Lovins, "Three Major Energy Trends to Watch," *District Energy*, August 23, 2013, http://www.districtenergy.org/blog/2013/08/23/amory-lovins-three-major-energy-trends-to-watch. If the California percentage included only nonhydro renewables, the figure shown would be much lower.

60. The Renewable Energy and Energy Efficiency Technology Competitiveness Act of 1989, P.L. 101–218, set specific goals for the United States with respect to wind, photovoltaics, and solar thermal energy programs. The Solar, Wind, Waste, and Geothermal Production Incentives Act of 1990, an amendment to the Public Utility Regulatory Policies Act of 1978 and the Federal Power Act, removed size limitations placed on renewable energy facilities, including solar and windpower, to be eligible for PURPA benefits. The Energy Policy Act of 1992, P.L. 102–486, enacted the renewable electricity production tax credit and established a federal performance-based incentive for renewable energy. The production tax credit has been expanded and extended by the Job Creation Worker Assistance Act of 2002 (P.L. 107–47), American Jobs Creation Act of 2004 (P.L. 108–357), Energy Policy Act of 2005 (P.L. 109–58), and American Recovery and Reinvestment Act of 2009 (P.L. 111–5), among other legislation.

61. Michael K. Heiman and Barry D. Solomon, "Power to the People: Electric Utility Restructuring and the Commitment to Renewable Energy," *Annals of the Association of American Geographers* 94, no. 1 (March 2004): 95–96, 101.

62. Quoted in Lovins, *Reinventing Fire*, 218.

63. Mary Ann Ralls, "Congress Got It Right: There's No Need to Mandate Renewable Portfolio Standards," *Energy Law Journal* 27, no. 451 (2006), 451 However, the Energy Policy Act of 2005 did require state regulatory authorities, on behalf of their rate-regulated electric utilities and all nonregulated utilities with sales above a certain threshold, to consider implementing fuel diversity plans and distributed generation interconnection. Fuel diversity plans would ensure that energy is generated using a diverse range of fuels and technologies (Energy Policy Act of 2005, Pub. L. No. 109–58, Sec. 1251, 119 Stat. 594).

64. Robert J. Michaels, "National Renewable Portfolio Standards: Smart Policy or Misguided Gesture?," *Energy Law Journal* 29 (2008): 79. In Europe renewable power is helping to push electricity prices down and has begun to displace nuclear and

fossil-fueled electric power. Lovins notes that Germany has built a low-carbon energy business to the point where new solar power needs few subsidies, where wholesale energy prices are falling, and where threats to the reliability of the grid have not materialized. However, the rise of renewable power has also caused utilities to suffer large losses and potentially threatens grid stability. "The subsidy cost ... has been large, the environmental gains non-existent so far and the damage done to today's utilities much greater than expected" ("How to Lose Half a Trillion Euros," *The Economist*, October 12, 2013, 30).

65. Quoted in Jeremiah D. Lambert, "Tres Amigas Tie Up," *Public Utilities Fortnightly*, July 1, 2010, 48.

66. Ibid.

67. Steven Bushong, "Is FERC Rule 1000 the Key to Getting Green Power to Market?," *Windpower Engineering*, May 29, 2012; Erica Gies, "New Federal Rules Boost Grid Access for Wind, Solar, Storage," *Forbes*, June 29, 2012.

68. Lovins, *Reinventing Fire*, 199–200.

69. Order No. 1000, *Transmission Planning and Cost Allocation by Transmission-Owning and Operating Public Utilities*, FERC Stats. and Regs. Para. 31,323, 76 Fed. Reg. 49,482 (2011) (18 C.F.R. pt. 35) (FERC Docket No. RM1–23). The referenced consultant, the Brattle Group, filed comments with FERC in connection with Order No. 1000, FERC Docket No. RM1–23, 32.

70. Ibid.; "Report of the Electricity Regulation Committee," *Energy Law Journal* 33 (2012): 229–230; Illinois Commerce Commission v. FERC, 576 F.3d 470 (7th Cir. 2009).

71. Illinois Commerce Commission v. FERC, No. 11–3421 et seq. (7th Cir. 2013).

72. Ibid.

73. Ibid. The relevant provision of the Michigan statute, MCLS Sec. 460.1029, requires eligible facilities to be located within the state or outside the state if within the territory of a utility that is not an alternate electric supplier.

74. http://www.ccnr.org/amory.html.

75. Ibid.

76. Ibid.

77. Ibid.

78. Cited in Paul L. Joskow and Donald B. Marron, "What Does a Negawatt Really Cost? Evidence from Utility Conservation Programs," *Energy Journal* 13, no. 4 (1992): 42.

79. Ibid., 70.

80. Ibid., 44, 49. Under many state utility programs, conservation investments are treated on a level playing field with supply investments and are allowed to enter the rate base. The utility is then allowed to retain a share of the hypothetical reduction of consumers' electricity bills as a profit, labeled shared savings. Because demand-side management inflates the rate base, the utility has considerable discretion to manipulate the programs so that little actual conservation results (Franz Wirl and Wolfgang Orasch, "Analysis of United States' Utility Conservation Programs," *Review of Industrial Organization* 13 (1998): 478).

81. Amory B. Lovins, Carl Blumstein, Jeffrey Harris, and Peter M. Miller, "The Cost of Energy Efficiency," *Science* 261, no. 5124 (August 20, 1993): 969.

82. Paul L. Joskow and Donald B. Marron, "What Does a Negawatt Really Cost? Further Thoughts and Evidence," white paper, MIT (MIT-CEEPR 93–007WPO), May 1993, 2.

83. Ibid., 5.

84. Paul L. Joskow and Donald B. Marron, "The Cost of Energy Efficiency," *Science* 262, no. 5132 (October 1993): 319–321.

85. Jerry Taylor, "Energy Conservation and Efficiency: The Case against Coercion," Cato Policy Analysis No. 109, March 9, 1993, 16 (quoting Benjamin Zycher, "The Theoretical and Empirical Fantasies of Amory Lovins," paper presented at the annual meeting of the Western Economic Association, Seattle, June 29–July 3, 1993, 39). Franz Wirl, another critic, refers to the "myth" of conservation programs and notes that consumers will engage in strategic behavior to manipulate incentives, including the rebound effect (overuse of energy at reduced prices), free ridership, and so-called moral hazard (deterring conservation initiatives by third parties) (Franz Wirl, "Lessons from Utility Conservation Programs," *Energy Journal* 21, no. 1 (2000): 89–90).

86. Evan van Hook, "Conservation through Cooperation: The Collaborative Planning Process for Utility Conservation and Load Management," *Yale Law Journal* 102, no. 5 (March 1993): 1237–1238.

87. Taylor, "Energy Conservation and Efficiency," 1.

88. "The Elusive Negawatt," *The Economist,* May 8, 2008.

89. Neil Peretz, "Growing the Energy Efficiency Market through Third-Party Financing," *Energy Law Journal* 30, no. 377 (2009): 381.

90. Lovins, *Reinventing Fire,* 79.

91. "The Elusive Negawatt."

92. Lovins, *Reinventing Fire,* 80.

93. Lee Schipper, "Energy Efficiency: Lessons from the Past and Strategies for the Future," *Proceedings of the World Bank Annual Conference on Development Economics* (Washington, DC, The International Bank for Reconstruction and Development, 1993); Peretz, "Growing the Energy Efficiency Market," 385.

94. "The Elusive Negawatt," available at http://www.economist.com/displaystory .cfm?story_id=11326549.

95. Prices regulated below avoided costs are necessary (but not sufficient) to induce profitable demand-side conservation programs. Costs for a negawatt, it is said, must not exceed the difference between avoided costs and the regulated price (Wirl and Orasch, "Analysis of United States' Utility Conservation Programs," 477).

96. Lovins, *Reinventing Fire,* 103.

97. Paul L. Joskow, "Creating a Smarter U.S. Electricity Grid," *Journal of Economic Perspectives* 26, no. 1 (Winter 2012): 33.

98. Under locational marginal pricing (LMP), "Prices are designed to reflect the least-cost of meeting an incremental megawatt-hour of demand at each location on the grid, and thus prices based on location and time" (Sacramento Mun. Util. Dist. v. FERC, 616 F.3d 520 524 (D.C. Cir. 2010)). LMP "communicates[s] the true market value of electricity at each location"; "create[s] financial incentives to dispatch the lowest cost energy"; and "encourage[s] transmission and generation investment at appropriate locations" (ibid.).

99. Dynamic rates also include critical peak price, in which customers pay higher peak [period] prices during a few days of the year but a discounted off-peak price during the balance of the year, peak-time rebates, and real-time pricing where participants pay for energy at a rate linked to the hourly market price of electricity

(Ahmad Faruqui and Jenny Palmer, *The Discovery of Price Responsiveness—a Survey of Experiments Involving Dynamic Pricing of Electricity*, white paper (n.d.), 3).

100. Demand response is defined as a "reduction in the consumption of electric energy by customers from their expected consumption in response to an increase in the price of electric energy or to incentive payments designed to induce lower consumption of electric energy" (FERC 18 C.F.R. Sec. 35.28(b)(4)). Section 1252 of the Energy Policy Act of 2005 speaks of "time-based pricing and other forms of demand response … whereby electricity customers are provided with electricity price signals." PJM defines demand response as "voluntary, temporary reduction in the use of electricity" and "a resource with a demonstrated capability to provide a reduction in demand or otherwise control load" (John Shelk, "Demand Response: What Is It?," white paper, Harvard Electricity Policy Group, Calgary, Alberta, June 13, 2013, 7).

101. William W. Hogan, *Implications for Consumers of the NOPR's Proposal to Pay the LMP for All Demand Response*, quoted in *Brief of Robert L. Borlick et al. as Amici Curiae in Support of Petitioners*, in *Electric Power Supply Association, et al. v. Federal Energy Regulatory Commission, et al.*, No. 11–1486, June 13, 2012.

102. Michael Milligan and Brendan Kirby, "Utilizing Load Response for Wind and Solar Integration and Power System Reliability," white paper, 2010, 2, http://www.nrel.gov/docs/fy10osti/48247.pdf.

103. Order No. 745, 76 Fed. Reg. 16,658 (March 24, 2011), FERC Stats. & Regs. Para. 31,322 (2011), *reh'g denied*, Order No. 745-A, 137 FERC Para. 61,215 (December 15, 2011).

104. Jon Wellinghoff and David Morenoff, "Recognizing the Importance of Demand Response: The Second Half of the Wholesale Electricity Market Equation," *Energy Law Journal* 28, no. 2 (2007): 395–396; *A National Assessment of Demand Response Potential*, staff report, FERC, June 2009.

105. Amory Lovins, "Energy Strategy," 72.

106. Electric Power Research Institute definition quoted in Joskow, "Creating a Smarter U.S. Electricity Grid," 30.

107. Nordhaus, *The Climate Casino*, 37, 39.

108. Lovins, *Reinventing Fire*.

109. Ibid., 167.

110. Ibid., 171–176.

111. Ibid., 186.

112. Ibid., 200.

113. Ibid., 206.

114. Ibid., 222.

115. Ibid., 238–239.

116. Nordhaus, *The Climate Casino*, 17–19.

117. Ibid, 230.

118. Ibid., 223–233.

119. Quoted in Elizabeth Kolbert, "Mr. Green—Environmentalism's Optimistic Guru Amory Lovins," *New Yorker*, January 22, 2007.

120. Ibid., 246–252.

121. Coral Davenport, "Large Companies Prepared to Pay Price on Carbon," *New York Times*, December 5, 2013, A1.

122. Nordhaus, *The Climate Casino*, 280.

123. Ibid., 286.

124. Lovins, *Reinventing Fire*, xvi.

125. "Reforming the Energy Vision," New York State Department of Public Service Staff Report and Proposal, Case 14-M-0101, April 24, 2014. See Matthew Wald, "State Energy Plan Would Alter New York Utilities," *New York Times*, May 5, 2014.

126. Ibid., 239.

Chapter 7

1. Eric Pooley, *The Climate War: True Believers, Power Brokers, and the Fight to Save the Earth* (New York: Hachette, 2010), 74–76; Gabriel Chan, Robert Stavins, Robert Stowe, and Richard Sweeney, "The SO$_2$ Allowance Trading System and the Clean

Air Act Amendments of 1990," Harvard Environmental Economics Program (2012), 25–26, http://www.nber.org/papers/w17845.pdf; Richard Schmalensee and Robert Stavins, "The SO$_2$ Allowance Trading System: The Ironic History of a Grand Policy Experiment," *Journal of Economic Perspectives* 27, no. 1 (Winter 2012): 103.

2. Richard Conniff, "The Political History of Cap and Trade," *Smithsonian Magazine,* April 2009.

3. Pooley, *The Climate War,* 76–78; Schmalensee and Stavins, "The SO$_2$ Allowance Trading System," 105; Paul Joskow and Richard Schmalensee, "The Political Economy of Market-Based Environmental Policy: The U.S. Acid Rain Program," *Journal of Law and Economics* 41, no.1 (April 1999): n. 10. Separate sources of pollution have different marginal costs for abatement. Facilities with the highest costs of reducing emissions will find it advantageous to reduce their costs by buying additional allowances from other facilities rather than trying to meet the pollution limits established by their initial allocation of allowances. Facilities for which it is relatively inexpensive to reduce emissions will find it profitable to sell some of their allowances because the sale of allowances will exceed additional abatement costs. Trading will lead to more abatement by those facilities that can reduce emissions most cheaply and drive abatement costs toward equality, a condition for cost minimization. Regulators therefore do not need to know the marginal abatement costs of individual facilities. (See Lawrence H. Goulder, "Markets for Pollution Allowances: What Are the (New) Lessons?," *Journal of Economic Perspectives* 27, no.1 (Winter 2013): 88–89.)

4. Conniff, "The Political History of Cap and Trade."

5. Joskow and Schmalensee, "The Political Economy of Market-Based Environmental Policy," 40–42; Schmalensee and Stavins, "The SO$_2$ Allowance Trading System," 105–106.

6. Pooley, "The Smooth-Talking King of Coal—and Climate Change," *Businessweek,* June 3, 2010.

7. Clive Thompson, "A Green Coal Baron?," *New York Times,* June 22, 2008.

8. James Rogers, "How I Did It: On Learning to Work with Green Activists," *Harvard Business Review,* May 2011.

9. Julie Schlosser, "How Duke Energy's CEO Got Started," *CNN Money,* August 11, 2009.

10. Thompson, "A Green Coal Baron?"

11. Rogers, "How I Did It."

12. Ibid.

13. Schmalensee and Stavins, "The SO_2 Allowance Trading System," 106–107.

14. Ibid., 109–110; Conniff, "The Political History of Cap and Trade"; Pooley, *The Climate War*, 60.

15. Ibid., 118.

16. Amy Cortese, "Private Sector—From Green Knight to Utility King," *New York Times*, April 6, 2003.

17. Rogers, "How I Did It."

18. Cortese, "Private Sector."

19. Mike Boyer, "Cinergy Settles Pollution Suit," *Cincinnati Enquirer*, December 22, 2000; Pooley, *The Climate War*, 150. Power plants existing at the time the Clean Air Act was amended in the late 1970s were "grandfathered." Utilities were not required to retrofit existing plants with new air pollution control equipment unless they undertook major modifications of older plants. The defendants each made major modifications to their plants in order to extend their lives and avoid the cost of building new plants. Under the Clean Air Act, modifications of this kind require installation of the "best available control technology," which the defendants did not do, resulting in emission of millions of tons of sulfur dioxide, nitrogen oxides, and other pollutants.

20. *Public Citizen*, "America's Dirtiest Power Plants: Plugged in to the Bush Administration," May 2004. Under new-source review, a utility could operate an old plant as long as it was not substantially modified. Eventually, it was assumed, the utility would have to update its equipment, at which point new-source rules required the utility to install the best available pollution-control technology. Utilities could therefore phase in the switch to cleaner plants over time instead of all at once. New-source review sought to encourage utilities to replace old, heavily polluting coal-fired plants with cleaner new ones. Some power companies did replace coal plants with cleaner ones that burned natural gas; many others retooled plants to keep them running long past their expected life spans. Few were fitted with the scrubbers and other equipment required under new-source review.

21. Quoted in Andy Hoffman, University of Michigan, Case Studies, "Managing 'Stroke of the Pen' Risk," *Pew Center for Global Climate Change*, 2006, 64. See also Bruce Barcott, "Changing All the Rules," *New York Times*, April 4, 2004.

22. "Duke, Cinergy Merger May Aid Retirement of Coal-Fired Power Plants," *Inside EPA.com*, May 11, 2005; Jad Mouawod, "Duke Energy Will Acquire Cinergy for $9 Billion in Stock," *New York Times*, May 10, 2005.

23. Pooley, *The Climate War*, 150–151.

24. 549 U.S. 497, 504–05 (2007).

25. Pooley, *The Climate War*, 142.

26. Ibid., 141.

27. Ibid., 144, 157, 159–160.

28. Quoted in Thompson, "A Green Coal Baron?"

29. *Testimony of James E. Rogers, Chairman, President and CEO of Duke Energy Corporation, before the Senate Environment and Public Works Committee*, June 28, 2007.

30. Ibid.

31. Lawrence Goulder, "Markets for Pollution Allowances: What Are the (New) Lessons?," *Journal of Economic Perspectives* 27, no.1 (Winter 2013): 96–97.

32. Jürgen Weiss and Mark Sarro, "Freely-Allocating GHG Allowances: Reducing Carbon Market Efficiency and Creating Windfall Profits," Brattle Group, April 2009.

33. S. 2191, 110th Cong. (2007). S. 2191 was later modified by the Senate Committee on Environment and Public Works and debated under a new name, the Lieberman-Warner Climate Security Act of 2008, S. 3036, 110th Cong. (2008). See generally Jonas Meckling, *Carbon Coalitions* (Cambridge, MA: MIT Press, 2011), 158–161.

34. Ibid. Matthew Schuman, "Can Global Warming Laws Redistribute Wealth?," *Review of Law and Social Justice* 18, no. 2 (2009): 469; Thompson, "A Green Coal Baron?"

35. Pooley, *The Climate War*, 187.

36. "The Economics of America's Climate Security Act of 2007:(S. 2191, Lieberman-Warner Climate Bill)," Senator James M. Inhofe, Ranking Member, United States Senate Committee on Environment and Public Works, May 2008, 9.

37. William Beach, David Kreutzer, Ben Lieberman, and Nicolas Loris, "The Economic Costs of the Lieberman-Warner Climate Change Legislation," *Heritage Foundation, Center for Data Analysis Report #08–02 on Energy and Environment,* May 12, 2008.

38. "Analysis of the Lieberman-Warner Climate Security Act (S. 2191) Using the National Energy Modeling System," March 12, 2008, http://accf.org/analysis-of-the-lieberman-warner-climate-security-act-s-2191-using-the-national-energy-modeling-system-nemsaccfnam.

39. Pooley, *The Climate War,* 191–192.

40. http://www.duke-energy.com/news/releases/2014111301.asp; http://www.duke-energy.com/news/releases/2007111501.asp.

41. Thompson, "A Green Coal Baron?"; Pooley, *The Climate War,* 192.

42. Thompson, ibid; Pooley, ibid., 226–227.

43. Executive Office of the President, Office of Management and Budget, "Statement of Administration Policy," June 2, 2008.

44. Pooley, *The Climate War,* 241.

45. Eric Pooley, "Why the Climate Bill Failed," *Time,* June 9, 2008.

46. Kate Sheppard, "Climate Security Act Dies, Failing to Muster Enough Votes to Move Forward," June 6, 2008, http://grist.org/article/an-inhospitable-climate; Bill Moyers, "Contemplating 'Climate Security,'" June 27, 2008, http://www.pbs.org/moyers/journal/06272008/profile2.html.

47. Weiss and Sarro, "Freely-Allocating GHG Allowances"; Adele Morris, "Equity and Efficiency in Cap-and-Trade: Effectively Managing the Emissions Allowance Supply," Energy Security Initiative, Brookings Institution, Policy Brief 09–05, October 2009, http://www.brookings.edu/research/papers/2009/10/cap-and-trade-emissions-allowance-morris.

48. Ibid. "Distributing valuable commodities to businesses free of charge puts the government in the position of picking winners in the market ... distort[ing] competition both domestically and internationally"; David A. Super, "From the Greenhouse to the Poorhouse: Carbon Emissions Control and the Rules of Legislative Joinder," *University of Pennsylvania Law Review* 158, no. 4 (March 2010): 1116.

49. Remarks of President Obama as Prepared for Delivery, Address to Joint Session of Congress, February 24, 2009, available at http://www.whitehouse.gov//the_press _office/Remar.

50. Quoted in "The Obama Budget: the Effect on Energy and Green Advice," *Think Advisor*, February 27, 2009, available at http://www.thinkadvisor.com/2009/02/27/ the-obama-1.

51. Quoted in Rick Piltz, "Climate Change and Sustainable Energy in President Obama's Proposed FY 2010 Budget. *Climate Science Watch*, February 26, 2009, available at http://www.climatesciencewatch.org/2009/02/26/cli.

52. "Conrad Remarks at Hearing on Budget with OMB Director Orszag," transcript of remarks by Senator and Committee Chairman Kent Conrd (D-ND) at hearing on President Obama's FY 2010 budget with OMB Director Peter Orszag on March 10, 2009, available at http://www.budget.senate.gov/democraticpublic/ii. Also see Chris Holly, "Obama Answers Critics of Allowances Auction," *Power*, March 31, 2009, http://www.powermag.com/obama-answers-critics-of-climate-allowance-auction; Pooley, *The Climate War*, 326, 345; Jim Efstathiou and Kim Chipman, "Carbon-Market Backers Split over Obama Climate Plan (Update 1)," http://www.bloomberg. com/apps/news?pid=newsarchive&sid=aVzbV8Sc35PY.

53. *Testimony of James E. Rogers, Chairman, President and CEO of Duke Energy Corporation, before the Energy and Commerce Committee of the United States House of Representatives*, January 15, 2009.

54. Efstathiou and Chipman, "Carbon-Market Backers Split over Obama Climate Plan."

55. Quoted in Pooley, *The Climate War*, 329. See generally Meckling, *Carbon Coalitions*, 161–162.

56. Pooley, ibid, 327–331.

57. H.R. 2454, 11th Cong., tit. III, subtit. E, Section 312 et seq. (2009). For a detailed summary of the bill, see *Pew Center Summary of H.R. 2454: American Clean Energy and Security Act of 2009*, http://www.c2es.org/docUploads/Waxman-Markey%20 summary_FINAL_7.31.pdf; Robert N. Stavins, "A Meaningful U.S. Cap-and-Trade System to Address Climate Change," *Harvard Environmental Law Review* 32 (2008): 317–319.

58. Steven Hayward and Kenneth Green, "Waxman-Markey: An Exercise in Unreality," *AEI Online*, July 10, 2009, http://www.aei.org/publication/waxman-markey-an -exercise-in-unreality.

59. Pooley, *The Climate War*, 348.

60. Tom Mounteer, "Comprehensive Federal Legislation to Regulate Greenhouse Gas Emissions," *Environmental Law Reporter* 39 (November 2009): 1068 et seq.

61. Pooley, *The Climate War*, 345–347.

62. *Testimony of James E. Rogers before the Committee on Energy and Commerce, U.S. House of Representatives*, April 22, 2009.

63. H.R. 2454, Section 700(13).

64. Tina Peng, "Tweak Climate Bill or Endanger Economy: Experts," *Law360.com*, April 23, 2009, http://energylaw360.com/articles/98366.

65. Barack Obama and Joe Biden, *New Energy for America*, September 23, 2008, http://my.barackobama.com/page/content/newenergy_more.

66. Pooley, *The Climate War*, 351, 370; Mounteer, "Comprehensive Federal Legislation to Regulate Greenhouse Gas Emissions," 11077; Robert Stavins, "The Wonderful Politics of Cap and Trade: A Closer Look at Waxman-Markey," Belfer Center for Science and International Affairs, Harvard Kennedy School, May 28, 2009.

67. Stavins, ibid. "By giving carbon allowances to electric distribution companies and requiring them to pass the value on to customers, it used the cap and trade mechanism to address genuine cost imbalances between regions of the U.S.—making the system fairer and helping the heartland people who most wanted to see the whole thing wither and die" (Pooley, *The Climate War*, 386).

68. Pooley, ibid., 399.

69. Ibid., 362.

70. National Center Blog, "Outrage of the Day: The Costly Waxman-Markey Global Warming Tax," April 6, 2009, http://www.nationalcenter.org/2009/04/outrage-of-day-costly-waxman-markey.html.

71. David Fahrenthold and Steven Mufson, "Deconstructing the Climate Bill," *Washington Post*, July 6, 2009, A6.

72. Hayward and Green, "Waxman-Markey."

73. Quoted in Pooley, *The Climate War*, 402.

74. Stephen L. Kass, "The Waxman-Markey Climate Change Bill," *New York Law Journal,* June 15, 2009.

75. Paul Kane, "Push and Pull in Senate May Recast Climate Bill," *Washington Post,* July 7, 2009, A3.

76. Pooley, *The Climate War,* 414.

77. During the administration of President George W. Bush the initiative for environmental legislation remained with the Senate, which failed to pass the Climate Stewardship Act of 2003, a bill introduced by Senators McCain and Lieberman that included an emissions trading system. The sponsors revisited the proposal in 2005, but it again failed to pass. In 2007 Senators Lieberman and Warner made a third attempt at climate change legislation, but the bill lost on a filibuster in June 2008. (See Matto Mildenberger, "The Politics of Strategic Accommodations: Explaining Business Support for US Climate Policy," white paper, School of Forestry and Environmental Studies, Yale University, June 2013, 18–19.)

78. Ryan Lizza, "As the World Burns," *New Yorker,* October 11, 2010.

79. John Kerry and Lindsay Graham, "Yes We Can (Pass Climate Change Legislation)," *New York Times,* October 11, 2009.

80. Quoted in Steve Benen, "Political Animal," Washington Monthly, December 10, 2009.

81. Joe Romm, "Graham, Kerry, Lieberman Embrace Market-Based System," *Climate Progress,* December 10, 2009.

82. Pooley, *The Climate War,* 437–438.

83. Jeanne Cummings, "Coming Together on Climate Bill," *Politico,* February 8, 2010.

84. Lizza, ibid.

85. Quoted in Paul Chesser, "What a Bunch of Krupp-ola," *The American Spectator,* March 26, 2010.

86. Lizza, "As the World Burns". See also Dustin R. Turin, "The Challenges of Climate Change Policy: Explaining the Failure of Cap and Trade in the United States with a Multiple-Streams Framework, *Student Pulse* 4, no. 6 (2012), 1.; John M. Broder, "'Cap and Trade' Loses Its Standing as Energy Policy of Choice," *New York Times,*

March 25, 2010; Eric Pooley, "The Smooth-Talking King of Coal," *Businessweek,* June 3, 2010.

87. Bryan Walsh, "Senate Climate Bill: Last Chance for Cap and Trade," *Time,* May 13, 2010; Andrew Chamberlain and Feliz Venture, *Chamberlain Economic Policy Study no. 2010–06,* June 2010, http://instituteforenergyresearch.org/wp-content/uploads/2010/06/KL-APA-Final-Study.pdf. The bill mandated a shrinking cap on total GHG emissions from major industrial sources, starting with a 17 percent cut in emissions (below 2005 levels) by 2020 and achieving reductions of 42 percent by 2030 and 83 percent by 2050; allowed regulated entities to purchase a limited number of "carbon offsets" in lieu of emissions allowances by funding reforestation and other GHG-reducing projects in the domestic and foreign agricultural sector; imposed a tariff on imports from countries that have not established mandatory limits on GHG emissions to protect "trade-sensitive" U.S. industries and deter businesses from outsourcing their operations to avoid GHG regulations; preempted EPA's ability to limit GHG emissions under existing Clean Air Act mechanisms while phasing in Clean Air Act new-source performance standards for coal-fired power plants by 2020 and retaining EPA authority to continue to regulate GHG vehicle emissions; permitted expansion of offshore drilling; provided financial incentives for construction of new nuclear power plants; and funded development of renewable energy sources and carbon capture and sequestration technology. The bill was considered more industry-friendly than its House counterpart, Waxman-Markey, which lacked provisions for nuclear power, offshore drilling, and protective tariffs.

88. Quoted in John Downey, "Duke: Climate Bill Eases Customer Impact," Charlotte Business Journal, May 13, 2010.

89. "Industry Reactions on Kerry Lieberman American Power Act," *Electric Power & Light,* May 12, 2010; Walsh, "Senate Climate Bill"; Darren Samuelsohn, "Kerry, Lieberman to End the Suspense with Climate Bill Rollout Today," *New York Times,* May 12, 2010.

90. Lizza, "As the World Burns."

91. Schmalensee and Stavins, "The SO_2 Allowance Trading System," 113.

92. Thompson, "A Green Coal Baron?"

93. Duke Energy Annual Report 2009, Form 10-K , available at www.sec.gov/...d10k.htm.

94. Pooley, *The Climate War,* 80. See also Mildenberger, "The Politics of Strategic Accommodations," 16, 19, 35.

95. Schmalensee and Stavins, "The SO_2 Allowance Trading System," 117; Super, "From the Greenhouse to the Poorhouse," 1102; Pooley, *The Climate War*, 397. Cap and trade is nonetheless alive and well in regional, national, and subnational markets worldwide. The European Union established an Emission Trading System in 2005; other systems operate in New Zealand, California, the Northeastern United States, Quebec, Australia, and South Korea. "Carbon markets are now the largest class of environmental or emissions trading markets in the world, in terms of both volume and market value" (Richard G. Newell, William A. Pizer, and Daniel Raimi, "Carbon Markets 15 Years After Kyoto: Lessons Learned," *Journal of Economic Perspectives* 27, no.1 (Winter 2013): 123–124). On June 2, 2014, EPA issued a rule prospectively imposing a national limit on carbon pollution from coal-fired power generation; reducing CO_2 emissions 30 percent below the 2005 level by 2030; and allowing each state to develop its own plan to cut CO_2 emissions based on a menu of options including wind and solar power, energy-efficiency technology, and creating or joining cap-and-trade programs, such as those operated by California and Massachusetts (EPA Docket no. EPA-HQ-OAR-2013–0602; Carol Davenport, "Obama Said to Be Planning to Use Executive Authority on Carbon Rule," *New York Times*, May 29, 2014, A20).

96. Steve Dorst, "Jim Rogers' Boardroom Coup and the New Carbon Rules," *Bloomberg*, August 16, 2012, http://www.bloomberg.com/news/print/2012-08-16/jim -rogers-boardroom-coup-and-the-new-carbon-rules.html.

97. Felicity Carus, "Technology Is Reinventing the Utility Industry at Duke Energy: Jim Rogers," *Breaking Energy*, June 18, 2012, http://breakingenergy.com/2012/06/18/ technology-is-reinventing-the-utility-industry-at-duke-energy-j.

98. Scott DiSavino, "Duke to Retire Older U.S. Coal Power Plants as New Units Start," *Chicago Tribune*, February 13, 2013. See, however, *EPA v. EME Homer City Generation, LP*, no. 12–1182, April 29, 2014, where the Supreme Court upheld EPA's authority to regulate cross-state air pollution from coal-fired plants.

99. Mark Muro, "New EPA Carbon Rule Tackles CO_2 from the 'Bottom Up,'" *Brookings*, June 2, 2014.

100. Paul Barrett, "Jim Rogers, the CEO Who Wouldn't Leave," *Businessweek*, September 20, 2012.

101. Ibid.

102. DiSavino, "Duke to Retire Older U.S. Coal Power Plants."

103. Meckling, *Carbon Coalitions*, 174.

Chapter 8

1. Walter Guzzardi, "Putting the Cuffs on Capitalism," *Fortune*, April 1975, 194.

2. Donald P. Berk, "Approaches to the History of Regulation," in Thomas McCraw, ed., *Regulation in Perspective* (Cambridge, MA: Harvard University Press, 1981), 196–199.

3. David M. Hart, "Corporate Technological Capabilities and the State: A Dynamic Historical Interaction," in Kenneth Lipartito and David B. Scilia, eds., *Crossing Corporate Boundaries: History, Politics, Culture* (New York: Oxford University Press, 2004). Professor Bonbright, a utility sage, also attributed to regulation capital-attraction, efficiency-incentive, demand-control, and income-distribution functions.

4. Samuel Insull, *Central Station Electric Service* (Chicago: n.p., 1915), 116.

5. Stephen N. Neuse, *David E. Lilienthal* (Knoxville: University of Tennessee Press, 1996), 71.

6. The Schumpeter Blog, "The Entrepreneurial State," *The Economist*, August 31, 2013 (review of Mazzucato, *The Entrepreneurial State*).

7. Mariana Mazzucato, *The Entrepreneurial State* (New York: Anthem, 2013), 136.

8. Ibid., 119.

9. "The End of Laissez Faire," Sydney Ball Foundation Lecture, Cambridge University, November 1924; quoted in Mark Buchanan, "Who Created the iPhone, Apple or the Government?," *Bloomberg View*, June 19, 2013, http://www.bloombergview.com/articles/2013-06-19/who-created-the-iphone-apple-or-the-government-.

Index

Printed in the United States
by Baker & Taylor Publisher Services